Houses of the Holy

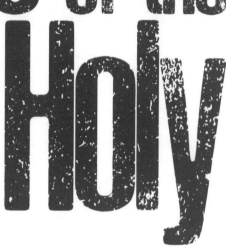

A Nightmare Web of Hate, Crime, Corruption and Child Abuse

A Memoir by
Mark Harris

Afterword by
Dr. Richard Spence

Published by:
Trine Day LLC
PO Box 577
Walterville, OR 97489
1-800-556-2012
www.TrineDay.com
trineday@icloud.com

Library of Congress Control Number: 9781634244565

Harris, Mark. HOUSES OF THE HOLY—1st ed.
p. cm.

Epub (ISBN-13) 978-1-63424-457-2
Trade Paper (ISBN-13) 978-1-63424-456-5

1. Mark Harris 1963- . 2. Memoir. I. Harris, Mark. II. Title
.

FIRST EDITION
10 9 8 7 6 5 4 3 2 1

For more information: housesoftheholy.net

Distribution to the Trade by:
Independent Publishers Group (IPG)
814 North Franklin Street
Chicago, Illinois 60610
312.337.0747
www.ipgbook.com

PUBLISHER'S FOREWORD

If happy little bluebirds fly
Beyond the rainbow
Why, oh why can't I?
— Harold Arlen/E.y. Harburg, 1939
© Emi Feist Catalog Inc.

Double, double toil and trouble;
Fire burn and cauldron bubble.
—William Shakespeare,
Macbeth: IV. 10-19; 35-38

Enter ye in at the strait gate: for wide is the gate, and broad is the way,
that leadeth to destruction, and many there be which go in thereat: Be-
cause strait is the gate, and narrow is the way, which leadeth unto life,
and few there be that find it.
— Matthew 7:13-14 (KJV)

I love those who can smile in trouble, who can gather strength from dis-
tress, and grow brave by reflection. Tis the business of little minds to
shrink, but they whose heart is firm, and whose conscience approves
their conduct, will pursue their principles unto death.
— Leonardo da Vinci (1452-1519)

The only thing necessary for the triumph of evil is for good men to do nothing
— Edmund Burke (1729-1797)

I began by saying that our history will be what we make it. If we go on as
we are, then history will take its revenge, and retribution will not limp
in catching up with us.
— Edward R. Murrow, (1908-1965)

There have been many attempts by poets, playwrights, prophets, painters, politicians, and, yes even, pundits to inform us that there *is* a way to walk, to act, to move forward, *to be* on this planet.

Why do people care? What makes some kind and others cruel? Whence does evil come? Will I survive?

Mark Harris asked those questions and many more. His book, *Houses of the Holy* gives voice to a horrendous experience. Mark was working as a pilot, he was lonely, met a pretty girl, fell in love and got married. His life soon got very … interesting.

Mark was born and bred in the deep south. He saw extreme racism, the wide economic divides and evangelical religiosity. A child of seeking and striving boomers, Mark began working in his teens, became enamored with flying and soon joined the U.S. Air Force to accomplish his dream.

I had heard about Mark's story before we met. Professor David Denton of The JFK Historical Group mentioned Mark and his experience at a conference. We talked over the phone and then through hours of Zoom discussions with him, some witnesses, the ghostwriters, Dr. Richard Spence (Professor Emeritus, University of Idaho) and a multitude of documents Mark's tale was extracted. *And what a tale!*

So, please strap in, and prepare for a sojourn to "hell" with Mark. As a pilot he was gone on a regular basis. He began to see troublesome signs pointing to sexual abuse occurring to his boys. He first attempted to get help, from his church and then through local, state and federal officials. He gets nowhere. His main antagonist, his father-in-law, uses the children as a cudgel to control events.

Over and over again, Mark tries to get people to help him protect his children. Some folks do, only to be stopped later by higher-ups. Mark was taken aside by his lawyer and told, "You're dealing with a cult. If you keep going with this, your life is in danger." I was incredulous. She repeated, "This is a cult. You should stop now."

What would you do?

> *Be content with what you have;*
> *rejoice in the way things are.*
> *When you realize there is nothing lacking,*
> *the whole world belongs to you.*
>
> – Lao-Tzu

Onward to the Utmost of Futures,
Peace,
R.A. "Kris" Millegan
Publisher
TrineDay
November 4, 2024

FOR TOBY AND GABE

All for one and one for all. We were the Three Musketeers.
This was all for you, and you are the real heroes of the story.
Despite everything that was thrown at us, we made it.
May your bravery and honesty eclipse the cowardice and lies of those who tried to intimidate,
silence and discredit you and inspire other victims to stand up for themselves.

Never, never be afraid to do what's right – especially if the well-being
of a person or animal is at stake. Society's punishments are small com-
pared to the ones we inflict on our soul when we look the other way.
-Martin Luther King Jr.

Courage is an inner resolution to go forward despite obstacles. Coward-
ice is submissive surrender to circumstances. Courage breeds creativity;
Cowardice represses fear and is mastered by it. Cowardice asks the ques-
tion, is it safe? Expediency asks the question, is it politic? Vanity asks the
question, is it popular? But conscience asks the question, is it right?
– Martin Luther King Jr.

Acknowledgements

Kris Millegan, a publisher with the courage to tackle subjects that others fear. He saved this project when I was over my head because he believes the truth matters.

My mother, Lonnelle Harris, and my father James Harris. Both stood by me and my kids when almost no one else did. My mother also spent countless hours of research helping me untangle this complex web of connections as these events were occurring.

My wife Kat, who put up with my endless hours of work and stress over the last two years of working on this book.

Mary Smith, a real hero for children, who courageously permitted an interview, despite fear of retaliation, which in fact came swiftly.

Carolyn, who had the courage to be interviewed and tell her story of abuse and the abuse of her children.

Therapists Karleen Shuster, Kelly Beck, and Pamela Powers, who left a record of testimony invaluable to this book and were among the many professionals who advocated for my sons.

Travis Heerman, a talented writer who took on this massive project with me and was tragically killed before it's completion.

Dr. Richard Spence, who spent many hours with me, my publisher, and others involved in this project, contributing his knowledge and expertise.

Patrick Lowry, whose investigative research was invaluable in connecting the dots and finishing this project where Travis left off.

Camille Cole, who spent many hours under pressure to meet a deadline, working one-on-one with me editing the book.

> *Each time a man stands up for an ideal, or acts to improve the lot of others, or strikes out against injustice, he sends forth a tiny ripple of hope, and crossing each other from a million different centers of energy and daring those ripples build a current which can sweep down the mightiest walls of oppression and resistance.*
>
> – Robert F. Kennedy

CONTENTS

Names in Order of Appearance

CHRISTY HARRIS: My ex-wife, daughter of Mike and Wanda Nobles

WANDA NOBLES: Mike Nobles' wife

MICHELLE "SHELLY" RIGGS: Mike and Wanda Nobles daughter

BRIAN RIGGS: Michelle Riggs' husband; Mike and Wanda Nobles son-in-law

MICHAEL STEPHEN NOBLES: My ex-father-in-law: Church of Christ leader, convicted Patriot Network antigovernment activist

WILLIAM "BILLY" NOBLES: Mike and Wanda Nobles' son

ROWENA NOBLES: Billy Nobles wife; Mike and Wanda Nobles daughter-in-law

FAITH NOBLES: Mike and Wanda Nobles' daughter

EMILY NOBLES: Mike and Wanda Nobles' daughter

GABRIEL HARRIS: My son

JOE PALMER: Pastor, Niceville Church of Christ

ALAN AMAVANTO: One of Mike Nobles' business partners

MATT: Toby's presumed biological father

TOBY HARRIS: My son

LESLIE MICHAEL OSMAN: Jerry McCormick's brother-in-law, real estate attorney and developer, Church of Christ leader, Hialeah Church of Christ

RON LONG: Christian Counselor for multiple Churches of Christ

JERRY MCCORMICK: Church of Christ Elder, Mike Nobles business partner, brother-in-law to Leslie Michael Osman

MARIANNE MCAULIFFE: Gabe's first therapist

ED FERRELL: Deacon, Destin Church of Christ, developer from Birmingham Alabama

CAROLYN PALMER: Joe Palmer's ex-wife

DAWN GRIFFIN: Emerald Coast Child Advocacy Center (ECCAC) therapist

DON SUBLETT: Elder, Destin Church of Christ, Air Force veteran

DR. FREDERICK DESHON: Psychologist and therapist

DANNY G. NOBLES: Mike Nobles brother, retired US Army Col, political activist, and minister

TOM DUNN: Case Advocate for child abuse cases in Okaloosa, Walton, and Santa Rosa Counties at the Emerald Coast Child Advocacy Center; part time Niceville, Florida police officer

JOSEPH "JOEY" FORGIONE: Niceville, Florida police officer

JERRY WILLIAMS: Home Inspector from Birmingham Alabama

ED FLEMING: Real estate attorney

JOHN SPENCER: Pastor Coastline Calvary Chapel; Gulf Breeze, Florida

JOANNA MORRIS: Founder, owner, and principal of Lighthouse Private Christian Academy

MARILYN REED: First nanny for Toby and Gabe

KARLEEN SHUSTER: Therapist

SARAH JOHNSON: Florida Department of Children and Families (DCF), Child Protection Investigator (CPI), Santa Rosa, County, Florida

KEITH SOARES: Okaloosa County Sheriff's Department deputy

ROBERT NORRIS: Okaloosa County Sheriff's Department Deputy; former Air Force Office of Special Investigations (OSI) agent

JOSEPH KEARNES: Niceville, Florida police officer

LIBBY LEONPACHER: Florida Department of Children and Families (DCF) Child Protection Investigator (CPI), Okaloosa County Florida

BONNIE EMMONS: Toby's teacher at Lighthouse Private Christian Academy (LPCA)

JEANNA OLSON: Florida Department of Children and Families (DCF) Child Protection Investigator (CPI), Okaloosa County, Florida

PETER GALLAS: Florida Department of Children and Families (DCF) Supervisor, Santa Rosa County, Florida

DANIEL FORGIONE: Mob-tied union boss connected to Santo Trafficante Jr, the Gambino Crime Family, and Tony Accardo and the Chicago Outfit

SANTO TRAFFICANTE: JR: Boss, Trafficante Crime Family

ANTHONY FORGIONE: Okaloosa County Sheriff's Department Deputy (killed on duty)

DOUG HELMS: Atlantic Southeast Airlines (ASA), Chief Pilot

SHERRY TAYLOR: Decatur, Alabama nanny

MARY SMITH: Former foster parent; former member of the Niceville Church of Christ and Destin Church of Christ

DOUG BRINGSMAN: Santa Rosa County Sheriff's Deputy

BRYAN WAYNE LONDON: Santa Rosa County Sheriff's Deputy

BRAD BYNUM: Destin Church of Christ Pastor, Okaloosa County Chaplain (former Boston Church of Christ Elder)

CHARLIE MORRIS: Okaloosa County Sheriff

LARRY ASHLEY: Okaloosa County Sheriff's Department (OCSO) Chief Deputy, then Sheriff

CONNIE EDGAR: Florida Department of Children and Families Child Protection Investigator and supervisor, Santa Rosa County

KIMBERLY UBERROTH: Florida Department of Children and Families Child Protection supervisor, Santa Rosa County

JENNIFER CLARK: Florida Department of Children and Families (DCF) Child Protection Investigator (CPI), Okaloosa County Florida, Emerald Coast Child Advocacy Center

DONNA PARISH: Supervisor, Florida Department of Children and Families, Emerald Coast Child Advocacy Center

NANCY LOCKE: Cadaver dog trainer, Southwest Panhandle Search and Rescue

PHILLIP DIXON: Calvary Chapel

BETTY THOMAS: Attorney (domestic violence case)

JOE PRESTRIDGE: Coastline Calvary Chapel, Assistant Pastor

TIMOTHY KYLES: Santa Rosa County Sheriff's Deputy

NICOLE FRYBACK: Therapist, Emerald Coast Child Advocacy Center

THOMAS SANTURRI: Judge, Santa Rosa County, Florida

CHARLES MERKEL: Vietnam Army Veteran: former military contractor

JEFF MILLER: Florida congressman, and Freemason

MICHEL RAPHAEL BARTHELEMY: Rob-Roy McGregor and Church of Christ minister, Bob Lewis, (partner)

ROB ROY MCGREGOR: Partner in Worldwide Internet Access Corporation; top civilian Pentagon procurement officer for weapons research

BOB LEWIS: Church of Christ Minister and publisher; Rob-Roy McGregor and Michel Raphael Barthelemy (partner)

TY OSMAN: brother of Leslie Michael Osman; Solomon Builders, founder

CHARLES WALTER RUCKEL II: Executive Committee member, John Birch Society; Cofounder, Freedom First Society. Emerald Coast Child Advocacy Center. Board of Trustees; owner, 1118 Rhonda drive while under construction

JAMES E. PLEW: Founder, Valparaiso, and Niceville Florida

ROBERT LEE FULTON SIKES: U.S. congressman; developer, Eglin Air Force Base

STEPHEN RUCKEL: Former president, Vanguard Bank; founder, Vanguard Ministries

CONSTANCE WAYNE JONES: Freemason Knight of Kadosh leader; builder, 1118 Rhonda Drive, Noble' home; developer, Sandpiper Cove condominiums; board of trustees, Emerald Coast Child Advocacy Center (ECCAC)

MICHAEL GIBSON: Attorney for Mike Nobles

JUDGE GARY BERGOSH: Santa Rosa County Florida judge; former Military Judge Advocate General Corp officer (JAG)

TIGER: Nickname of a Nobles' associate

HEATHER PAGANO: Florida Department of Children and Families (DCF) Child Protection Investigator (CPI) based at the Emerald Coast Child Advocacy Center

RICK KARSHNA: Florida Department of Children and Families Child Protection Investigator, Santa Rosa County

MICHAEL L. SCHNIEDER: Florida Judicial Qualifications Commission General Counsel

EDWARD NELSON: Niceville, Florida police officer

JOSEPH T. (TIM) KINARD: FBI Special Agent, Joint Terrorism Task Force; former Air Force Intelligence Officer

RANDY SALLEE: Niceville Police Department Lieutenant

MARY LOU COLLINS: Okaloosa County Evidence Custodian

GEORGE HENRY SHELDON: Florida Department of Children and Families, Secretary

ED SPOONER: Okaloosa County Sheriff

CHARLIE MORRIS: Once Sheriff, Okaloosa County

MARILYN REED: Nanny

CHARLIE CHRIST: Florida Governor, 2009

WILLIAM EDDINS: State Attorney, First Judicial Circuit of Florida

WILLIAM STONE: Okaloosa County Judge

ROGER NOBLES: Mike Nobles brother

CRAIG ROEGNER: ATF Agent

RANDY BEACH: Resident in Charge, ATF Pensacola office

JOE PRESTRIDGE: Assistant Pastor Coastline Calvary Chapel

DALE WALTMAN: Children's Minister, Coastline Calvary Chapel; Pastor, Life Church Gulf Breeze

LASHAWN RIGGANS: Okaloosa County Assistant District Attorney (ADA)

MARK PEREZ: Florida Department of Law Enforcement (FDLE) Chief Inspector, Office of Executive Investigations

JACK STEPHENS: Murder victim

MARY LOU COLLINS: Okaloosa County Sheriff's Evidence Custodian

BRAD DENNIS: KlassKids President; Search and Rescue leader; dog trainer; preacher

ELAINE WOODS: Psychologist, Cleveland, Georgia

LEILANI MASON: Therapist, Santa Rosa County Kids House

TRACI RITCHEY: Director, Santa Rosa County Kids House

STEVE GAISER: Niceville, Florida Police Lt.

WILLIAM SCHNEIDER: General Council, Florida Judicial Qualifications Commission

JIM BRIMBERRY: General Manager of Human Resources, ExpressJet Airlines

BRAD SHEEHAN: Chief Pilot, Atlanta Southeast Airlines (ASA); and later Director of Safety, ExpressJet Airlines

RICHARD SMALL: Former Auburn Maine Police Chief; Freemason and Shriner

ERIC GOLDBERG: Psychiatrist

JAMES LORENZ: Captain, Walton County Sheriff's Department

MARK WOLLMAN: Airline Pilots Association Attorney

CHARLES RICHARD HARPER: Aviation Medical Examiner (AME); Founder, Aeromedical Inc.; former US Navy Flight Surgeon; Former Medical Director, United Airlines

MICHAEL HABERMAN: Atlanta Psychiatrist

JOE FIGUROA: Former Air Force OSI agent; nanny

STEVE D. HURM: Okaloosa County Sheriff Captain and Legal Advisor: previously Regional Legal Advisor Florida Department of Law Enforcement (FDLE); Son-in-law, Senator, and former Governor Bob Graham

FIONA HILL: Psychologist

DR. MICHAEL BERRY: Manager, Medical Specialties Division, Office of Aerospace Medicine, Federal Aviation Administration (FAA); former Flight Surgeon, USAF; former Chief, Flight Medicine Clinic, Johnson Space Center, NASA

GLEN SWIATEK: Attorney

DR. WILLIAM MILLS: Military researcher, Civil Aerospace Medical Institute

WARREN SILBERMAN: Manager, Aerospace Medical Certification Division, Civil Aerospace Medical Institute; former Oklahoma Air Guard Air Surgeon

SANDY CLYMER: Officer of Dr. Warren Silberman, Federal Aviation Administration (FAA), position unknown

CHARLES CHESENAW: Chief Psychiatrist, Federal Aviation Administration (FAA)

ALAN SAGER: Psychiatric Consultant, Federal Aviation Administration (FAA)

STEPHEN GOODMAN: Senior Flight Surgeon, Western Pacific Regional Medical Office

CHARLES ALDEN BERRY: Director of Life Sciences, NASA, Apollo program

MARIANNE MCCAIN, PHD: Psychologist

KELLY BECK: Therapist

CHRIS SMITH: Assistant State Attorney, Okaloosa County

DIANE GASTON: Real estate agent

DURELL PEADEN: Florida Senator who oversaw the Florida Department of Children; responsible for the stand your ground law

RICK SCOTT: Florida Governor

TAMMY BROWN: Aviation Safety Specialist, Federal Aviation Administration (FAA)

BRAD SECKER: Airline Pilots Association officer

GARY BERGOSH: Santa Rosa County Judge; former Judge Advocate General officer

JANINE WILLIAMS: Special Agent Supervisor, Florida Department of Law Enforcement (FDLE)

BRIAN PEREZ: Our family doctor

PAMELA POWERS: Program therapist, sexual and physical abuse treatment program, Lutheran Services

TIMOTHY YARBROUGH: "Patriot Network" leader

TONY DEMURRAY: "Patriot Network" leader, NASA engineer

ROBERT CLARKSON: Founder, "Patriot Network"

SYLVIO CARDOSO: Former University of Miami running back: Hialeah zoning board member

RAUL MARTINEZ: Hialeah Florida, Mayor

ANTHONY MIJARES: Business partner, Sylvio Cardoso

CARLOS CARDOEN: International weapons trafficker, tied to Anthony Mijares

BOB GRAHAM: Senator and former Florida governor

ALBERTO SAN PEDRO: Lane developer

ERNIE YARBROUGH, Son of Timothy Yarbrough, Alabama State Senator

BURL MCCORMICK: Politician, developer; activist, Church of Christ

GEORGE POLANSKY: my Florida neighbor

MARK POTOK: Senior fellow, Southern Poverty Law Center (SPLC)

AL DENNIS: Florida Department of Law Enforcement Inspector General

DR. JOHN DOYLE: Talbot Recovery Psychiatrist, Air Force Veteran

HENRY DOENLEN: Gabe's psychiatrist, Pensacola, Florida

MARSHA WEAVER: Okaloosa County Sheriff General Council

ERIN ROMEISER: Investigations Manager, Office of the Governor of Florida, Office of the Inspector General

KATIE GEORGE: Florida Department of Children and Families (DCF), Assistant Regional Council

TOMMY TUCKER: Investigator, Office of State Attorney, First Judicial Circuit

JENNNIFER GREEN: Mossy Creek Elementary School Principal, White County Georgia

CHRIS HIRST: Inspector General, Florida Department of Children and Families (DCF), Office of Inspector General

MIKE THOMAS: Assistant Pastor, The Torch Habersham County Georgia

JOHN LANCE: Biker Preacher, White County Georgia

MIKE JOHNS: Director, Mustard Seed Counseling; head of drug court

MICHAEL VAUGHN: Director of Addiction Services, Peachford Hospital; Medical Director, Metro Atlanta Recovery Residence (MARR)

DAVID WYLIE: Supervisory Agent, FBI, Gainesville, Georgia

CLIFFORD HARDWICK: Attorney for Dr. Charles Harper

JOE JOHNSON: Harvest Assembly of God, member; Vietnam Veteran from Birmingham Alabama

JIMMY SARGENT: Pastor, Harvest Assembly of God Cleveland, Georgia; White County Sheriff Chaplain

JOHN DORAN: Circuit Judge, Gwinnett County Georgia

TERRY SATURDAY: Attorney Airline Pilots Association (ALPA)

CALVIN A SHIVERS: Assistant Director Criminal Investigations Division, FBI Headquarters

LEON RODRIGUEZ: Director, U.S. Department of Health and Human Services, Office for Civil Rights

BARBARA DIANE PYE-TUCKER: Attorney, Georgia Legal Services

ROY L. AUSTIN JR.: Deputy Assistant Attorney General

SALLY QUILLIAN YATES: U.S. Attorney

STUART F DELERY: Acting Assistant Attorney General

LISA D. COOPER: Assistant United States Attorney

DIANE KELLEHER: Assistant Branch Director

PETER J. LYNCH: Assistant Chief Council for Enforcement FAA

MARCIA K SOWLES: Senior Counsel, US Department of Justice

KATHY HARRIS: Vice President, People Resources, ExpressJet Airlines

ELMA BROOKS, U.S.: Equal Employment Opportunity Commission Investigator Support Assistant, Atlanta Office

LASHARN HUGHES: Georgia Composite Board of Medical Examiners, Executive Director

WILLIAM P. SMITH III: Ethics Council, State Bar of Georgia

TINORAH FRETT: Assistant Director/Investigator, Veterans Employment and Training Service, US Department of Labor

RICHARD STORY: Federal Judge, Gainesville, Georgia

I have letters from the following individuals not mentioned in the book:

DAVID S. MCLAUGHLIN: Georgia Department of Law, Senior Assistant Attorney General

WALT COOK: Florida Abuse Hotline Director

HEATHER ROBINSON: Operations and Management Consulting Manager, Florida Department of Children and Families (DCF) Office of Inspector General

EVANGELINE RENTZ: Operations and Management Consulting Manager, Florida Department of Children and Families (DCF) Office of Inspector General

RANDAL FLEMMING: Community Relations Consultant, Florida Department of Children and Families (DCF)

For more information: housesoftheholy.net

PREFACE

He told me Paw Paw was a Secret Agent for the government, that he had, "...killed people for the president."

My son drew a picture of a display case. He sketched an enshrined rifle with a scope, bullet cartridge, and a single pistol. Several newspaper articles, tucked in with the guns, had been sketched in surprising detail.

"Paw Paw says that's the gun that killed the president." He glanced at me, intent on sharing what he had heard and seen.

"He said it is a hero's gun."

"What president?" I asked.

He kept drawing.

Since only one president has ever been murdered with a rifle, I understood then that Paw Paw possessed a rifle he believed to be the one that killed John F. Kennedy.

Then came the weird stuff.

Chapter One

Learning to Fly

When I was growing up in White County in the northeast of Georgia, I had no idea what kind of real-life horrors existed in the world. Evil was an abstract concept, something that mostly existed in movies – which I wasn't allowed to watch as a child – and the fire-and-brimstone sermons I was forced to sit through once or twice a week. I spent my whole upbringing, it seemed, hearing about sin. But the thing is, true real-life evil is tough to recognize in the moment. It's only when that sick feeling settles in your gut you realize you have just encountered something terrible like looking a serial killer in the eye from across a crowded bar. Sometimes it's as banal as a corrupt bureaucrat or a philandering preacher, sometimes; it's as sharp and deadly as a sociopath's hidden blade. It's only with thought and retrospect you begin to realize the fullness of it, the insidiousness of it, the depth of it. Because it thrives in the shadows, no one expects it to show up front-and-center, in your face. If you're lucky, you may never have to find out how far it will go.

I was an all-American kid from the South – steeped in God and Country ideals – with dreams of settling down one day with a beautiful wife and a family.

My dad came from a family of upholsterers, but he lost his inheritance when he married my mother and moved out of Atlanta into the mountains. Back then, you could see smoke rising from backwoods moonshine stills all over those hills. After moving to the country, my parents had sixteen acres of beautiful forest and a small creek. We had three acres of garden that allowed us to grow nearly all our own food. We cooked on a vintage wood stove and heated the place with a homemade wood-fired heater. Pretty rustic and isolated. My dad built the house himself. He did everything himself. I learned a lot from him, including stubborn determination.

I was home-schooled until third grade, then until eighth grade, went to a tiny church school with about twenty students. Yes, it was a very sheltered secluded life out there in the Georgia woods. We marinated in strict Old-Time Southern Religion. Once or twice a week, my parents took us to church where we heard fire-and-brimstone sermons about the evils of smoking, drinking, dancing, masturbation, extra-marital sex, caffeine, Catholicism, the Illuminati, movie theaters, and Saturday morning cartoons. We were told about how we were entering the "time of trouble" from the Book of Revelations, that that government would soon try to force us to wear the Mark of the Beast. We were told that if we didn't comply, we would have to go hide in the woods or the government would kill us. That stuff gave me nightmares, but also made religion a big part of my life.

* * *

I held a fascination with paper airplanes. I wanted to fly like a bird, to be free of all those hidebound ideas that felt like a leaden blanket, even if I couldn't put it to words at the time. Flying sounded like the coolest thing a human could possibly do. I tried to build hang-gliders out of sticks and plastic. I experimented with homemade "parachutes" – a.k.a. umbrellas and plastic bags – by jumping off the roof of my dad's van. Lucky for me, I didn't break any bones.

My parents' rustic hippie lifestyle couldn't pay the mortgage, so the seven of us moved to Cleveland, Georgia, a small town of just over three thousand people. For a while we made numerous trips deep into Mexico in an old beat-up van and once in a school bus. We went there to buy pottery and leather goods to sell. Those were great adventures.

I went from an eighth-grade class of two boys to a high school freshman class of over a hundred. It was sink or swim. What I discovered – to my pleasant surprise – was that I swam pretty well. I made straight As. I was the MVP on the cross-country running team and first chair trumpet in marching band. I was number two in my graduating class and made the second highest SAT score.

My family's financial situation always hung by a thread. If I wanted anything, I had to get it for myself. So, I started mowing lawns at twelve-years-old, then bagging groceries and washing dishes at fifteen. I washed dishes at a legendary local restaurant, famous for its chicken and named after the white owner. However, an old black lady, Alma, did most of the cooking and work in the kitchen. Alma never used the front door of the restaurant. To her, it wasn't her place to do so. She always came in the back door directly into the kitchen. That's how things were in White County. By the time I graduated high school, I was on my third car. While most of my classmates had pickup trucks with gun racks in the back window, my passion was foreign sports cars. By my second year in college, I had owned a Volkswagen Rabbit, a Volkswagen GTI, a Fiat Spyder convertible, a Toyota Celica, a Nissan 300ZX with a T-top, and a vintage Porsche 911 Targa. I paid for them all by working two jobs at times.

I didn't quite fit in in White County that bordered two sunset counties, where African Americans were not allowed to live or even visit after dark. Such places still existed, and the county name was no joke.

While most of my classmates were listening to Hank Williams Junior singing "A Country Boy Can Survive," my first two concerts were Genesis and Yes at the Omni in Atlanta. I was the only one in my circle of friends with a car and a license, so I drove us all there. My small circle comprised the other smart kids. An Asian, a Jewish kid, and a Black kid who was gay and had to hide it. None of us fit in there in White County. I had dreams of fast cars and fast women. Adventure and travel. And most important, getting the hell out of White County, Georgia.

* * *

I learned of injustice at a young age. My parents were poor, and there was a time we had to use food stamps. We qualified for free lunches at school. If you haven't experienced that, imagine having to produce a little blue coupon for your lunch while the other kids looked at you funny. Now they knew for sure you were poor.

My freshman year I was bullied by some muscle-bound biker punk who was far too old to be in ninth grade. He and his girlfriend developed what could be called a sick game. She would flirt with me to provoke him, and then he would harass, bully, and threaten me. I didn't know either one of them nor had any interest in the girl. One time in homeroom, he walked up and knocked my books off my desk and kicked my desk while screaming in my face. He was so close. I could feel his spittle. I stared him down and stood my ground, infuriating him. The homeroom teacher did nothing. Finally, this escalated, and he and one of his redneck friends attacked me in the hallway. Instead of expelling the creeps, the principal called me to his office and beat me with a wooden paddle. I didn't know until I was a much older adult that my dad went to the school and threatened to sue the principal and the school to stop the bullying.

During the summer between my junior year and senior year, I spent time at the Truett McConnell College pool. You could pay a small fee and go there to sun and swim. And oh yeah, there were college girls in bikinis. Driving to the pool one beautiful sunny day, I crested a hill on a small side street and found a vehicle blocking the entire road on the other side. I had nowhere to go but the ditch. My car flipped. I wasn't wearing a seatbelt, and the sunroof was open. My head bounced on the ground through the sunroof. By rights, I should have been killed or horribly injured. After the car came to rest upside down, disoriented and dirt in my hair, I reached up to turn off the engine and instead cranked the car to start. I was lucky it didn't explode, as gas was spilling everywhere.

I extricated myself from the wreck in time to see the driver of the other vehicle speed away.

I was given a ticket for "driving too fast for conditions." The police report said it was overcast and raining. It was sunny, and I was on my way to the pool. It turns out the driver of the other vehicle was sloppy drunk, and he happened to be the brother-in-law to a local city policeman.

That's how things work in the South.

* * *

My high school achievements garnered me a scholarship to North Georgia College, now known as North Georgia University. I applied to the Air Force Academy but wasn't accepted. I didn't know then that those appointments aren't based on achievement but on political connections. I was accepted to Princeton and MIT, but the tuition costs made those schools a pipe dream. I was the son of a poor upholsterer. I really wanted to go to Georgia Tech, but the scholarship sealed the deal. The scholarship wasn't a full ride, so I still had to work two jobs to get through, but I did it. In 1989, I graduated magna cum laude in just over three years with a bachelor's degree in physics, the top of my class in my major and dual minors in French and Math.

But I still dreamed of flying.

And not just any kind of flying. I wanted to fly jets. And there was only one place to do that: the U.S. military.

After I got my bachelor's degree, I applied for U.S. Air Force Pilot Training and Officer Training School (OTS) and then watched the mailbox like an anxious hawk every day until the response finally came. Getting my acceptance letter was one of the happiest days of my life. I had never flown in anything before. But the end of the Cold War put my training on hold. The U.S. military was drawing down, and there were no open training slots. Now I had to wait a year for my number to come up.

Prior to Officer Training School, I had to go through the USAF Flight Screening Program in Hondo, Texas. I still remember the smell of crop-dusting chemical there. The program consisted of ten flights in a

USAF T41 (an old beat-up Cessna 172 painted in USAF colors), a solo flight, and a flight evaluation (check ride). My only experience in an airplane was a short ride in a small Cessna, which my mom had bought for me after I had signed up for the USAF. Sink or swim once again. I didn't think I would make it. Struggling prior to solo, a change of instructors solved the problem. An old timer who smoked cigars, he was practically a stereotype of the old hard-bitten, cigar-chewing pilot who's seen everything. He took me out for a few flights around the runway pattern. Then without warning, he said, "Pull over onto the apron."

Then he added, "This is my favorite airplane. I am going to go over there and smoke this cigar. Bring it back in one piece." Then he got out.

My jaw dropped to meet the pit in my stomach.

Wondering if this was going to be my last day on earth, I taxied away from him, lined up onto the runway, and took off. That was the easy part, but those early landings were a festival of flop sweat. On my first attempted solo landing, I hadn't lined it up properly, feeling a rattled intuition that "something ain't right," so I went around again. This time, I nailed it. The grizzled cigar-chewing instructor shook my hand and graduated me. I moved on to OTS.

In OTS I was selected as the Upper Flight Captain to lead my flight. I will never forget our flight commander, Captain Davis, telling my parents at my graduation that I was "the best damn Upper Flight Captain" he had ever had. I graduated with honors as the flight leader for my OTS flight and with a top academic award as well.

I got my wings in March 1992 at Columbus AFB Mississippi.

But then my dream ran smack into the reality of the military draw down. There weren't enough cockpits available. I had to wait three years. I took that as an opportunity to go back to school and get my master's degree in Aeronautical Engineering Technology which I received in 1994 through an Air Force program from Arizona State University.

Then finally I got the cockpit seat I had been waiting for flying C130 cargo planes out of Moody Air Force Base in Valdosta, Georgia. I served ninety days in a Saudi Arabian combat zone, received several air medals, and was selected to upgrade to Aircraft Commander and be transferred to Air Force Special Operations Command at Eglin Air Force Base in Florida. For the rest of my Air Force career, I flew the MC130P Combat Shadow, a special operations support aircraft designed for night-time airdrops and low-level refueling operations at night, mostly for helicopters.

I spent many hours wearing night vision goggles and flying in close trail formation.

As a young pilot, I did what so many young pilots did: I worked hard, and occasionally I played hard. For me, it was always about the job. Sometimes I blew off a little steam with friends and fellow pilots, but I was never much of a partier on my own. I took my career seriously. Military life wasn't always fun, but it felt like what I was doing mattered. It was life on steroids.

Eglin AFB is situated on the Gulf Coast of the Florida panhandle on Choctawhatchee Bay and is home to Air Force Materiel Command with a host of functions including fighter squadrons and a strong Special Operations component. It's also the host to Army Ranger training and a base for covert operations around Latin America.

I spent the last year of my Air Force career attached to Hurlburt Field about ten miles to the west and home of Air Force Special Operations Command. This is where the Air Force trains its commandos and supports covert operations throughout Latin America. Of note, Eglin AFB is the main jumping off point for those missions. Most people don't think of the Air Force as having commandos, but they very much do.

These two Air Force installations dominate the culture and economy of that area. The nearby small towns of Niceville, Fort Walton Beach, Ocean City, and Shalimar are full of current and ex-military, including old-guard war dogs all the way up to include former Pentagon officials and top brass plus their civilian counterparts such as defense contractors.

In 1998, a minor off-duty incident that mushroomed into a nightmare abruptly ended my military career. This was via a military board of inquiry in 1999 that ended up a bizarre side-show reminiscent of *A Few Good Men* (where officers ordered a code red on someone who had simply been following orders). Due to the sleazy allegations made over the years regarding this in a "kill the messenger" strategy, a summary of the actual incident is included in the appendix, "Military Madness."

* * *

I used my G.I. Bill to pay for civilian flight training and certifications at the Eglin AFB Aero Club and off base at Pensacola Airport. I hadn't flown a Cessna since my first days of Air Force training, so a little brush up was in order. I finished my civilian aviator training at the top of my class, a point of professional pride. I took a one-year contract with a company called Flight Express, Inc. They flew courier jobs mostly ferrying lab specimens and payroll checks around Florida and Georgia in single-engine, single-pilot Cessna airplanes that were a couple decades older than I was. I could say these were "duct tape and baling wire" airplanes, but that would be an insult to duct tape and baling wire.

I was the only pilot in my training class to stick it out for the full year. I guess I'm just that kind of determined and loyal even in the face of the dangers and difficulties forced upon me. But I had made a commitment for a year and was determined to finish. I flew long hours of some seriously scary and dangerous stuff.

Flight Express had a minimal training and onboarding program. They simply threw their pilots into the deep end and hoped they didn't crash in a swamp, which one pilot did. My first flight was out of Miami-Opa-locka Airport, a joint civil-military airport used mostly for civil aviation and private jets. I had to show up at a closed airport in the middle of the night, find a hidden key to unlock the gate, find an unfamiliar airplane on a dark ramp, and take off for the first of my nightly runs. With no air traffic control on duty at that hour, I was so nervous for my first professional flight, I forgot to click the mic to turn the runway lights on, so I took off in the dark.

Their planes were mostly Cessna 210s, single-engine aircraft converted for cargo with no autopilot and no weather radar, a far cry from the planes I'd been flying in the Air Force. And now I had no crew. I was on my own. It was like going from a brand-new, full-featured SUV with more horsepower than the Almighty to a forty-year-old Ford Pinto with a limp.

Thanks to Florida weather, I spent most flights dodging thunderstorms and tropical storms. It was the most consistently scary flying I've ever done, including combat zone missions after the first Gulf War. But at least I survived. One of my runs involved eight hours of flying and sixteen hours of total duty, five days a week, the maximum allowed by FAA regulations. I didn't have time for a social life, or for much of anything except work and sleep.

My runs migrated around Miami, Panama City, and Atlanta-Hartsfield, the busiest airport in the world, which has its own special kind of nerve-wracking. I spent this period living in cheap or extended stay hotels, too busy to think about how lonely I felt. Over Florida – in this new civilian position – I once found myself face-to-face, while flying, with a private pilot who appeared out of nowhere with no flight plan. I could almost see the whites of his eyes, and maybe he could hear my jaw clench as I performed emergency evasive action.

Over Georgia, I ran into a wall of weather that forced me to land at an uncontrolled field in Dublin, Georgia. When I thought the weather had broken, I went back up and headed for Florida, only to be caught in severe turbulence over Tallahassee. If you can imagine finding yourself on the world's biggest invisible rollercoaster without a safety belt, you're in the ballpark. Without warning, in seconds my plane was thrown upward 500 feet, then flung downward 1000 feet. I came out of it pointing in the opposite direction. I learned afterward that I had met my very first tornado.

I had a route circulating around Panama City, Crestview, Pensacola, Tallahassee, and Tampa. That many hours alone in an airplane at night feels isolating. It gets to you, but that's the job.

The company's airplanes were fraught with mechanical problems. I repeatedly experienced electrical failures. I could tell when such a failure was imminent by the buzz growing in my headset. Alternator malfunctions, dead batteries.

One night I had a flickering light on the instrument panel. I tried to brighten it, and sparks flew. All the cockpit lights went out, leaving me with only moonlight to see. I fished out a flashlight from my flight bag and finished the flight. The company pressured me into flying the next leg, so I flew from Pensacola to Tallahassee by flashlight. When I got to Tallahassee, I swapped airplanes, but as soon as I started the engine, flames poured out from the engine. I shut it down, grabbed my logbook, and ran. The company tried not only to pressure me into finishing the run using the malfunctioning aircraft that had no instrument lights but tried to send me into an area of severe weather, turbulence, and icing. I agreed to fly one leg back the other direction where my car was.

Did I mention duct tape and baling wire? Maybe there was a shortage.

* * *

As I developed a reliable reputation and seniority at Flight Express, I was able to angle for the routes I wanted to fly and to stop living in cheap hotels. I moved into my grandparents' old house in Destin, Florida. With more stable living conditions under my feet, I had more moments to lament my utter lack of a social life. I hadn't had a date in years. I had walked away from all my military friends, perhaps in part because of the bitterness of my experience there. I was alone, and when I had a few moments to sit still, the loneliness piled on. In what little spare time I had, I dialed up AOL.

In aviation, there's sometimes a distinction between what's the most frightening in the moment and what's the most dangerous. You're often too caught up in the emergency to be scared. Training kicks in and you become hyper-focused. Other times, you get too much time to think about things, letting worry turn to alarm, then to near-terror.

My most frightening civilian aviation story would be the time I took a short cut out over the Gulf of Mexico, between Panama City and Tampa. Normally, this would be strongly discouraged – and in the planes I was flying, it was seriously ill-advised – but the pilot who had flown the run before me had set the precedent to do this, and the air traffic controller offered me the option. So, there I was at 6,000 feet in my decrepit Cessna, fifty miles out over the Gulf, far beyond gliding distance, when I ran into a line of severe thunderstorms that kept pushing me farther and farther out to sea. Every time I tried to avoid one of the storms, it closed in around me. I remember looking around the cockpit for anything that would float in case I went down. I had no life raft or life preservers. This is the kind of experience –you're stonewalled at every decision you make – with every choice, the stakes go up. The fuel gauge clocks ever downward, I couldn't help but think about the engine that had caught fire and all the electrical problems I'd already experienced. Fortunately, I was able to land in Tampa with all my limbs intact. It would take a while before my hair lay back down.

My most dangerous experience featured my engine quitting on a night flight over Tampa. A single-engine aircraft means you don't have a spare. But after suppressing that stomach-dropping oh-shit! moment, I managed to restart the engine. But the darn thing sputtered and then quit again. I restarted. It quit. I restarted, it quit. This is why pilots must always be cognizant of gliding distance. It's the kind of situation that pushes your nerves to the limit. Pilots simulate this kind of occurrence in training, but having it happen for real is so much more nerve-wracking, and it's exacerbated by the knowledge that your aircraft is a piece of junk. You keep your cool or you're dead. Those are the only options.

So, I declared an emergency with air traffic control and made an emergency landing at Tampa International. As pilots say, any landing you can walk away from is a good one. It's only after an experience like this is over that the torrent of cold sweats cuts loose.

* * *

In my slivers of time off, I would log into AOL and look for local people to chat with. I was never a barfly sort of person, and since leaving the military, I had little interest in it anymore, and I certainly didn't have the time. So, the Internet was my only social outlet. As a lonely single male who didn't get out much anymore, I looked for women to chat with.

I struck up a conversation with a woman named Christy. I found her enjoyable to talk to. She was smart, funny, charming. But we were both busy, and I doubted I had time for a girlfriend, so I generally tried to steer myself away from romantic or sexual chat. After a few weeks of sporadic chatting, I still didn't know much about her except that she lived somewhere in the area and worked at her father's Subway, but she intrigued me. Then she began to open up to me in surprising ways, telling me about ex-boyfriend drama and some of her romantic hopes and dreams. She came across as an open, big-hearted person, a good church-going person, if a little wounded. The big reveal came when she told me she was pregnant by a man who was no longer around. I felt for her, imagining all the shame she must be feeling, how desperate her situation might be, especially if her family was as religious as she made them sound, but there wasn't anything I could do except listen.

Amid the difficulties, dangers, and frustrations of my job, there were moments of wonder. One night I was stuck in Crestview waiting for a break between bands of an incoming tropical storm. I was carrying lab specimens on ice. If I waited much longer, they would be ruined, so I went for it. Once I was in the air, I felt the sense that it was almost creepy smooth, serene, and a welcome respite of sheer peace between swaths of meteorological tumult. Out there in the dark beneath a starry sky and bolts of lightning in the distance in every direction, ethereal golf balls of blue-green static electricity crawled up my windscreen. A feather-light, glowing nimbus of color formed in my field of view along the windscreen and fuselage. St. Elmo's fire.

Christy clearly loved it when I told her about that. As the spring of 2000 became summer, she started flirting with me in our chats. I'm one of those guys who needs a whack between the eyes with a rubber mallet to realize when someone is flirting, but I finally thought it would be a good idea to reciprocate. I had no idea what she looked like, but our conversations had become a much-needed safe harbor from the stresses of being a low-level commercial pilot. I sought her out more and more often, began communicating with her regularly.

After a year of being soaked with sweat every time I walked away from one of Flight Express' aircraft, in January 2001 I finished my contract with a sigh of relief. They begged me to re-up, but I was pretty sure I had spent seven or eight of my nine lives. I was the only one whom they had hired from my training class to finish the one-year contract. But I guess I'm just stubbornly loyal, often to the detriment of my own self-interest and well-being.

* * *

In June 2001 I started work with Atlantic Southeast Airlines (ASA) – a Delta Airlines sub-carrier – which felt like a serious upgrade from my earlier travails. It proved to be another shoestring operation where management pressured employees to fly broken airplanes and to violate rest requirements. The company had an unwritten policy that it was cheaper to pay FAA fines than to comply with FAA regulations. I stayed with my aunt in Atlanta and occasionally visited Florida.

About that time, Christy and I started talking on the telephone. She had a sweet voice full of life and charisma, but she sounded a little young. She told me she was nineteen. I was thirty-four. Her son Gabriel had just been born, and she was living with her parents in Niceville, Florida, a small, one-Walmart town adjoining Eglin AFB. The attraction between us built. I felt it in my gut and heard it in her voice. I looked forward to talking with her, and I thought about her a lot. My upbringing had limited my skills or desire to be a womanizer, but our conversation reached a point where it felt like a meeting simply had to happen soon.

But then, September 11, 2001. All bets were off. The United States had been attacked. Were we going to war? What was going to happen? Amid all this chaos and uncertainty, there was no flying happening at all, and I found myself with a pocketful of downtime.

I called Christy and said, "I would love to meet you in person. How would that be?"

"That would be great," she said.

With an enormous, shit-eating grin on my face, I said, "Great!" An updraft hit my stomach.

That was the beginning.

Chapter Two

Meet the Parents

I walked into the Subway restaurant in Fort Walton Beach, Florida, in late September 2001, and our eyes met instantly. She was working behind the counter but took a break straight away. The two of us sat together in a booth. Christy was still wearing her Subway uniform. She was as cute and charming in person as I had imagined during our online, and then phone, chats. I was relieved. I didn't know what to expect having never seen her picture, and I hoped I wasn't being catfished.

Her big, brown eyes sparkled with enthusiasm. She was a small girl – and I say "girl" because she looked more like seventeen than nineteen. She had the curves to go with the face despite her petite frame.

"It's so great to finally meet you in person!" she said. "You're so handsome. More than I was expecting."

"Thanks," I said. Not exactly the silky-smooth womanizer, I was unsure if I should return the compliment.

We'd had months of conversations online where we talked about deep, personal things. But now, in person, everything felt new and awkward as if we had just met for the first time. Even so, there was something about her, a sense of maturity far beyond her years, an "old soul," and that drew me to her. We sat there in the booth for about an hour, and by the end of that time, our conversation had returned to the comfort I enjoyed during our chats from afar. She'd been working here for a few years. Her son Gabriel had been born a few months earlier. Her mother babysat Gabriel while Christy was working. Gabe's father had fled for the horizon, and she had no idea how to or any desire to reach him. Her eyes flashed with hurt and anger. That was her story, but I would discover that there was more to it.

"After what I went through for him," she said with controlled anger.

Snippets of what I would call over-sharing – I keep my cards much closer to the chest, by nature – had sometimes come up during our online chats, but her hurt was real, so I asked to hear the story if she was willing to tell it.

She shrugged. "When I couldn't hide the belly anymore, I had to go up in front of my whole church, get up in the pulpit, and read a letter begging for everyone's forgiveness. Reverend Palmer made it sound like I was the whore of Babylon herself. I was so embarrassed. My sister had to do the same thing with her son Jake." She tried to smile it away as if it were no big deal, but her face had paled, and I had no doubt – thanks to my own ultra-religious childhood – that this had been the modern-day equivalent of putting her in the village stocks or painting "Adulteress" on her forehead. "It didn't matter that he told me he wanted to marry me, or that we had moved in together. I was eighteen. It wasn't any of their business. But my father is a church elder, so…" She shrugged again.

We talked about churches, compared notes. Her family's church was the Niceville Church of Christ. I had grown up as a Seventh Day Adventist, but my parents stopped attending those services when I got to high school. I never knew why, but it may have had something to do with "bad things" that happened to children at the Adventist summer camp, their legalistic doctrine, or perhaps the fact that it was based on a false prophet. As an adult, I know what that means. Back then I was too naive to figure it out, but already I had come to feel like it was more of a cult than a church. I didn't want any part of it. I had gone to some nondenominational services in the Air Force which, compared to the Adventists' apocalyptic fire-and-brimstone, barely felt like church at all. It was so … *friendly and nice,* and a welcome break with free donuts. I still considered myself a Christian, but I hadn't found a better fit or anything that really spoke to me. I was too busy flying.

When it became time for me to go, Christy and I got up and went out to the parking lot where she threw her arms around me and hugged me as tight as she could, as though clinging to a life-preserver or a rescuer.

* * *

The next thing that happened was that Christy wanted me to meet her family. I thought this a bit odd, but maybe she wanted to do things by their rules now that she'd had a child out of wedlock. Maybe she was trying to make amends with them. Maybe she wanted her family's approval of a possible new boyfriend.

I was nervous when I pulled up outside 1118 Rhonda Drive in Niceville, Florida. Less than a mile from Boggy Bayou and Rocky Bayou, their house was a modest, single-story ranch-style on a quiet, small-town street. The house was a dark slate-blue with white trim and a driveway wide enough for two cars. The garage had been converted into living quarters. Niceville was a town of strip malls, fast-food chains, and churches.

I approached the house with all the confidence I could muster. The impression that Christy had given me of her family was of a staunchly religious and secretive clan. And I was expecting a chilly reception, given our age difference.

When I rang the doorbell, Christy opened the door looking beside herself with nervous excitement. She ushered me inside, where I was met with a short, scrawny, older man who introduced himself as Michael Nobles, Christy's father. Never have I ever felt such sharp scrutiny. His piercing eyes seemed to look through me. When I shook his hand, it was dry, careful, but then his face beamed with a smile, and he welcomed me as if I were a long-lost relative.

I don't remember the details of the small talk on that day. A short, blonde woman came up behind Christy, Wanda Nobles, Christy's mother. She was friendly enough, but reserved, and I noticed something haunted there in her eyes. A defeated look.

Then came Christy's older sister, Shelly, who also had a child about the same age as Gabriel. Her husband, Brian Riggs, joined this welcoming committee.

Carrying five-month-old Gabe on her hip, Christy gave me a tour of the place. Her parents' bedroom was located in the back hallway, and I would learn that this door was always conspicuously locked.

"What's in there?" I asked.

"Oh, that's Dad's bedroom."

What could he be hiding in a bedroom so that it needed to be locked all the time? I shrugged off the thought and moved on. But for some reason, I stored this information away.

There was a home office with a computer on the desk in the living room. "That's where Daddy does the business stuff," Christy said.

The garage had been converted into living quarters for Christy's sister Shelly and her husband, Brian. It also served as a room for her older brother, Billy Nobles, and with his wife, Rowena.

I then spotted two little, dirty-faced girls hiding around the corner. They eyed me timidly and looked to be about three and five years old. Christy introduced them as Faith and Emily. As soon as Christy spoke their names, their faces twisted with fear, and they ran for Wanda's skirts, where they clung like baby lemurs. At the time, I didn't register the difference between shyness and terror.

There were various small cages around the house containing guinea pigs and rabbits, pets for the children, so I tried to break the ice with the little girls by asking about their animals.

Eyes drooped, Faith said, "They die all the time." There was a callous weariness in her voice I thought odd for a three-year-old.

Out in the back yard I noticed a couple of vent pipes sticking up out of the ground and wondered what was being vented as the house had no basement.

We all sat down for supper. They didn't say grace, which I thought odd in the home of a church elder. Over the course of the meal, I noted how deferential everyone was to Mike Nobles. He made several provocative statements – racist, misogynist, and antisemitic statements – but no one challenged him. I could tell he was measuring my reaction. I gave non-committal responses, not wishing to alienate the father of my would-be girlfriend. He sounded like tons of other Good Ol' Boys, but he said those things with the kind of conviction that made me wonder if he had a white hood in his closet behind that locked door. I knew enough about Christy to be certain she didn't share those views, and that was what mattered. Such views were hardly unusual in the South, but those kinds of discussions were not for polite conversation. And "crazy in-laws" were practically a cliche. Was I already thinking along those lines? Throughout dinner, Christy touched me often and gave me every come-hither glance she thought she could get away with.

Billy Nobles' wife, Rowena, was from Guyana, South America. She was a pretty brown-skinned woman with the kind of eyes that indicated fear to speak as though she'd accepted a life of misery. They had two kids who looked at their grandfather as though Mike wielded the power to smite them into non-existence. Billy had convinced the church to sponsor him on a "mission trip" to Guyana, and lo and behold he had come home with a wife. Rowena did all the cleanup after supper, and the whole family treated her like she was almost a slave. Billy laughed about how, because he never bothered to pursue the paperwork on her immigrant status, she couldn't legally work or drive in the United States. She was a prisoner in the Nobles' home. I felt for her. She spent the rest of the evening doing housekeeping chores.

Despite Mike Nobles' coarse beliefs, I found him to be a charming, charismatic man who knew how to hide his secrets. I sensed he had many. What I didn't realize until much later was how awful they were. He treated me exceptionally well, like I was the most important guest the family had ever had. The entire family did. I came away feeling like they were trying a little too hard to welcome me into their fold, but at the time it all simply registered as a vague uneasiness. Despite some of what I had seen that evening, I found myself liking Mike Nobles. Christy's brother Billy and brother-in-law Brian rubbed me somewhat the wrong way. But being in the military taught a person how to tolerate the occasional abrasive asshole.

A high point of the evening was meeting Christy's son, Gabriel, a sweet little boy who seemed to take to me. Christy noted this affinity early on when he let me hold him for a few minutes. "He never lets anyone else hold him!" she said, wildly pleased. There was something odd about Gabriel, but I didn't know enough about kids to put my finger on it. When he got fussy, I gave him back to his mom.

When it came time for me to leave, Christy followed me out to the car and gave me a lovely kiss good night. I could feel the eyes on me from the house, but smitten, I didn't care.

She called me later and said, "I thought that went well."

I agreed.

"My dad certainly took to you. *Nobody* who isn't family gets in our house. I mean, *nobody.* So, it's like you're family already." And over the next six plus years, I never saw anyone outside the family enter that house.

* * *

Our first real date was in a pizza shop in Niceville. We took her car with Gabe riding in the back seat. This was the first time I saw her all dolled-up, tight jeans and a low-cut blouse. If I wasn't gobsmacked before, this time I felt like I'd won the lottery, regardless of the possibility of an insta-family.

To show her I was first-rate father material, I offered to extract Gabe from his car seat. As I did, however, I managed to bump his little head on the car door making him cry. I was mortified, horrified, but she calmed him down and said, "Don't worry, he does worse than that to himself all the time."

So, we went inside the restaurant and enjoyed a lovely date having fun and delighting in each other's company. Before our time together was over, we were holding hands. After the meal, she needed to take Gabe home and put him to bed. But before we parted, there was a passionate kiss beside her car.

I went home feeling like a million bucks.

* * *

A couple of weeks later, I invited her over to my place. I had arranged a modest feast of take-out food. Christy arrived as beautiful as ever.

As soon as she walked in, she laid the hottest kiss on me yet, the kind of kiss that sets your body on fire and makes it easy to miss a forest of red flags.

At one point, she plopped down on my sofa and picked up a copy of *Maxim* magazine that was sitting on my coffee table. She flipped through the pages, amused, eyes sparkling. "Oh, aren't you naughty," she said to me with a wink as I brought in the takeout.

I hemmed and hawed, embarrassed, but then she stood up and threw her arms around my neck and kissed me again. This girl knew how to kiss, and the next thing I knew, we were on the sofa, and she was peeling both our clothes off. She showed me the kind of enthusiasm I wasn't aware existed.

* * *

I discovered several things in my conversations with Christy in the following weeks, usually after sex, when she opened up and talked about her family. She was at once deeply entrenched in their dramas and at the same time derisive of them. But there was an undercurrent of fear, something armored deep within her. I sensed a shell buried under the veneer of her beauty and charm, especially when she talked about her father. Faith and Emily were Mike Nobles' two youngest daughters. Emily was still being potty trained, and both girls still wet the bed often. It didn't dawn on me at the time, but they lived in total social isolation.

Mike Nobles had threatened to kill himself over his shame at his daughters' wanton promiscuity. His reputation had been ruined in church over his two daughters bearing children out of wedlock. He had resigned from being a church elder and apologized to the congregation. A bizarre tradition of apologies by church leaders followed by Nobles being reinstated soon after.

Christy told me a story about her father. When she was little, she had a dog that she loved very much, but one day it disappeared. He told her it had gone off to live on a happy farm. Years later, he told her he had shot it, and then laughed as he told the story. I would learn later of many other pets he had killed..

I asked her how she coped with all this, imagining how difficult it must have been for her. She told me about all the journals she'd been writing for years, expressing her deepest and most private thoughts. "They're a little dark, but it's good to get stuff off your chest, right? Nobody can judge you except the Lord."

I started going to church with Christy and her family at the Niceville Church of Christ, a congregation of about two hundred. I hadn't been to church regularly since I was at home, but I felt it was important to ingratiate myself with the Nobles if I was going to date Christy. I had to prove I wasn't looking for just a piece of ass, that my intentions were serious, that I was different from Gabe's father who had allegedly run for the hills, never to be heard from again. Christy was so sweet, and clearly in love with me. She loved me so much it was like a pressure. I wanted to be worthy in her eyes and those of her family.

* * *

I became more and more aware that Mike Nobles was a mover-and-shaker in the Niceville area. As an elder in the church, people were unfailingly deferential to him.

Christy told me all sorts of salacious, eyebrow-raising gossip about various members of the Niceville Church of Christ. They were a tight-knit bunch, and I could sense, but not fully grasp, the web of associations, loyalties, and betrayals lurking below the surface of every handshake and amiable smile.

The pastor, Joe Palmer, was a squat, beady-eyed man who I would learn later was steeped in allegations of beating and raping his wife and sexually abusing his children. Seeing that family during services, their haunted sullen faces led me to believe the allegations. For some, it was "just the way things are." He and Mike Nobles appeared to be close friends, and after services would occasionally go off and speak privately.

This was not the kind of church where black and white mingled. The entire congregation was as white as bedlinen.

Time and again, Pastor Joe Palmer went down the list of other denominations, expounding point by point on how their theology was wrong, how they were all going to hell. "*We* are the One True Church."

I'd heard that song and dance before while growing up in Georgia.

* * *

It was at my first Thanksgiving with the family when Mike Nobles decided to show off his guns. He brought them out like they were religious relics. Pistols, shotguns, rifles. Each gun came with a story, and the whole family listened quietly or chimed in with familiar bits.

One long rifle in particular was treated with such reverence it could have been the Ark of the Covenant. "It belonged to my dad, who passed it to me."

What I did not learn until much later was that Mike Nobles was already a convicted felon prohibited from possessing any firearms at all.

* * *

I was there for Gabe's first Christmas. I bought him one of those battery-operated toys with removable, interlocking gears. It fascinated him, which pleased both me and Christy.

It was around this holiday that on a visit to the Nobles' home I met Roger Nobles, Mike's brother. He was a thin, sharp-eyed man with a sharp-boned face. He lacked Mike's glib, superficial charm and never spoke much to me during the visit, which was fine because I disliked him at once. He had the soulless eyes of a lizard. We exchanged a few words about both of us being Air Force veterans, but that was all. Roger had an interest in the occult, *something I would learn years later.*

This whole sordid stew was significantly off-putting. I wasn't blind to it. But all I cared about was that I had a sweet, smart, witty, beautiful woman in my arms who thought I was her knight in shining armor. The sex was incredible. Her son was adorable, and he and I were getting well attached. Her family seemed to love me to death.

So, I bought a ring.

Everybody's family had drama, right? Everybody's closet had skeletons.

What I didn't realize was that Mike Nobles' skeletons were real.

As I look back on my first meetings with Christy's family, it is with no small amount of chagrin at my naiveté. The signs that things were not right were literally everywhere. There was no way I could have known about the dark secrets of the house of horrors on 1118 Rhonda Drive.

In January 2002, I asked Christy to marry me.

All hell broke loose.

Chapter Three

Sleeping With the Enemy

Sitting there on her front porch, I opened the little black box and said, "Christy, will you marry me?"

She stared at me for a long moment, a freight train of emotions whipping across her face so quickly I couldn't catch them until the last two pulled into the station. Sadness and anger.

"I can't," she said, her voice choking.

I stared at her for a long moment, feeling the world crash down on my head, a knife twisting in my heart. I'd been so sure she would be kissing me joyfully right now. Finally, I managed, "Uh, can you tell me why not?"

"I don't love you!" she said.

"That's not what you said yesterday."

"This always happens!" She got up and grabbed her purse. "I have to go."

I got up, too, wishing I could stop her. "Wait! Is this it then?"

She gave a look that was half-heartbreak and half-viciousness. "I guess it must be. You couldn't leave well enough alone." She turned toward the door again.

"Can I say goodbye to Gabe?"

"Fine. You can do it when I'm not there." Then she left.

I was too stunned and heartbroken to move.

* * *

Not knowing what else to do, I called my parents in Georgia. They were outraged for me, worried about me. I'd told them all about Christy and they wanted to come down and support me. They said they would be down in a few days.

Meanwhile, I jumped into the coping mechanism for heartbreak that goes back centuries – a bottle of tequila – and I swam around in there for a couple of days.

But then my phone rang. It was Christy.

"I'm so sorry, Mark. I love you. I was wrong. I want to marry you."

My heart must have sung an old country song, one of hopeful ones. I dashed across town to meet her, and we made up. She couldn't keep her hands off me. The sexual energy just poured out of her. I was as happy as I'd ever been.

* * *

My family arrived later that night and found a vastly different situation to the one they were expecting. In the space of the drive, their son had gone from bereft to engaged.

They were puzzled when I told them what had happened, and no less worried. They saw the red flags that I was blissfully ignoring and raised concerns. I, however, would have none of it. I was going to marry Christy come hell or high water.

They acquiesced and, since they were in the neighborhood, decided to meet their son's future in-laws. We had a big get-together at the Nobles' house the next day. It was the only time I ever saw anyone outside their immediate family at their home.

The whole affair was far less cordial than when they'd met me. Everyone seemed to be walking on eggshells. My dad happened to sit in a particular chair, and everyone panicked. *That was Mike's chair.* No one else was allowed to sit in it, and the level of protest – and fear – they showed when my father did was beyond reasonable. My dad tried to laugh it off, but I could tell he was seriously creeped out by this strange overreaction.

After the awkward get-together ended, my parents told me they were skeptical about the whole thing. She was too young, and she already had a child. But love clouds all judgment and sense of reason. Neither of those things mattered to me. But what about her flaking out when I proposed? It all turned out all right. She just got cold feet. I brushed off my parents' concerns. They went back to Georgia worried about the whole situation. Mike Nobles must have sensed their uneasiness because he wrote a letter to my mother trying to reassure her that the Nobles were a fine upstanding family. Mom didn't buy it.

* * *

During the three months Christy and I were engaged, she switched from making sandwiches at Subway to working in her father's office, which was collocated with one of his Subway restaurants. Occasionally I would visit her there. To assuage my boredom while she was busy working, she let me use her father's desktop computer. While surfing around for this and that, I saw some things in the browser that gave me alarm, so I decided to look at his search history.

There I found child pornography. Searches for pre-teen, pre-puberty, and father-daughter incest, among other things. I immediately brought this to her attention, but she uncomfortably assured me that it couldn't have been her father. It must have been her brother Billy or Mike's business partner, Allen. *But I didn't believe her, and she knew it.* I could tell she didn't believe it either. I suggested she talk to him about it, she turned ghostly white.

I discovered more such things on his home computers on at least two other occasions when he wasn't there, stuff that I was certain would get him sent to jail if I told law enforcement about it.

Another time I was allowed to enter Mike's master bedroom and use the master bathroom for a shower. As he opened the lock, he acted like he was doing me the biggest favor in the world by letting me into his bedroom. None of his kids were allowed in there. It felt weird being allowed into the locked room, but there was nothing overtly odd about the room itself. It was all innocuous. The master bathroom was situated through the master bedroom along the back of the house. In that bathroom above the sink was a skylight, about two feet by two feet, that admitted nice natural light.

On April 24, 2002, we were married in Niagara Falls, just the two of us. It was a package deal that came with a pastor and a honeymoon suite in a nice hotel. We had a great time, in and out of bed. But her typical enthusiasm for romance was subdued or even absent, which seemed odd for a honeymoon. She was, it felt, a little blasé about the whole thing.

When we returned to Florida, she and Gabe moved in with me. And everything changed with a sound like a record scratch.

* * *

Almost from the minute we returned to Florida, my sweet, funny, witty sexual dynamo turned jealous, manipulative, controlling. I can't begin to describe all the crazy arguments that erupted over nothing, and it was all I could do to keep the peace.

The *Maxim* magazines that had amused her not so long before became "the work of the Devil." She demanded that I throw them out.

Not one who appreciated being unequivocally dictated to, I refused.

"Throw them *out!*" she shrilled.

"I'll put them away," I finally said, so I bundled up the handful of them and stowed them away in my closet.

"I can't believe you'd keep that kind of pornography in our house!"

I couldn't believe the words I was hearing after what I had seen on her father's computer, what we had *both* seen.

Within a couple of months after our marriage, she came to me distraught and told me she had just had a miscarriage. I did my best to comfort her, set aback by the depth of her grief. She wanted to have a child with me as soon as possible. In the back of my mind, it felt like that was some sort of way of "sealing the deal." I was in less of a hurry, but I'd married her because I wanted a family. When she went to the doctor after the miscarriage, he told her to wait six months before trying again.

* * *

In those intervening six months, however, a shift happened. I was an airline pilot, so I was away from home more often than not. Wanting a place of our own (we were still living in my grandparents' old house), we bought a fixer upper across the street from the bay in Fort Walton. This was as close as I could afford to my dream of living on the water.

During this period, I hired a guy to do some work for me on our new house, a friend of Christy's sister Shelly. He was down on his luck, so I threw him a bone. I discovered later that he'd been throwing Christy a bone as well.

Six months after being pregnant, she informed me she was pregnant again. I was overjoyed, looking forward to meeting this new member of our family. Then I found a Dear John letter to Matt the tile man. In this letter she was breaking up with him and telling him she was pregnant, and the child might be his. I confronted her with it, and all hell broke loose.

Then I came home to find that she had also written me a Dear John letter, in which she said she had never loved me, and couldn't possibly believe that I loved her because "no one could ever love a cold bitch like me…. Deep down you don't really love me either. I mean, do you really believe that I am your soulmate? Do you really want to spend the rest of your life with a bitch like me? I am a mess. I can't love myself, let alone someone else."

We talked in circles for hours. Were we broken up? Were we not? Was she cheating on me? So much of my time with her was a storm of appeasement, bad judgment, guilt, shame, and capped off by a stubbornness to "do the right thing."

* * *

Christy moved out and went back to her parents for several months. Finally, she agreed to counseling at Pattison Professional Counseling, a Christian counseling service. After our intake, the counselor wanted to see her one on one. During these sessions she disclosed having been sexually abused as a child. Years later when I needed those records they had somehow disappeared.

But before I knew it, I was the best thing since sliced bread again and we reconciled. She told me how much she loved me for being willing to forgive her. It wouldn't last.

* * *

Meanwhile, Mike Nobles had embraced me and brought me into his family, so I asked if he would help me with some real-estate deals – buying, remodeling, and selling houses – something I had started on the side with thoughts of doing it full time so I could be home and try to save my wreck of a marriage. We worked together like this for several years.

Some days, Christy and I were barely holding it together. As the hormones associated with her pregnancy started spurting, I had a crazy woman on my hands who bounced manically from depression to rage to a kind of frenzied sweetness. And as always, sex was the band-aid for every negative interaction. I began to get apprehensive every time I had to fly, wondering what she'd get up to while I was gone, if she'd fall off the cliff of depression and hurt herself. My absences sparked wild swings of jealousy, and she was sure I was shacked up with every stewardess from Tallahassee to Seattle.

She would leave me notes as I was preparing to leave for my next flights.

You have heard that it is said to those of old, "you shall not commit adultery." *But I say to you that whoever looks at a woman to lust for her has already committed adultery with her in his heart.* Matthew 5:23-29.

Despite everything she put me through, I was never unfaithful to her.

Then Toby was born. Those boys became the centers of joy in my life. There was nothing I wouldn't do for them.

* * *

I knew it was possible that Toby wasn't my biological son, but when I agreed to reconcile with his mom, I made the decision that I would be his father regardless. It was a choice for which I paid a heavy price, but I have no regrets. When I first saw him in the hospital, I was nervous. Would he look like me? When I did see him, it no longer mattered. He was just an innocent baby, and how he came into the world was not his fault. It wasn't until he was twelve that I had a DNA test done and learned that I was not his biological father.

Christy became like a tropical storm on the horizon, something I had to keep a wary eye on. Things between us slipped into that gray, sleep-deprived abyss of taking care of a newborn. Buried in the necessities of taking care of Toby every minute that I was home, I could ignore the feeling of our marriage crashing against the rocks over and over again. But Toby was my boy, and I was so proud of him and his brother.

As the boys grew, bleak black months spiraled into years. Toby became a toddler as Gabe grew from toddler to preschool.

* * *

Over time, I recognized a pattern with Christy's behavior. She would exhibit periods where she was a reasonably attentive mother – if emotionally distant – even as she expressed to me time and again how she had never wanted kids, how she couldn't wait for them to grow up so that she could be free of them. She had her good moments with them, but then seemed to "fall off the wagon," periodically trying to be a good mother for a while and then seemingly giving up.

Christy became such a toxic disruption, so neglectful of the boys, that I was afraid aviation might no longer be a viable career for me because I had to spend so much time away. This was the height of the real estate bubble of the mid-2000s, so the real estate ventures were somewhat becoming more lucrative than a pilot's salary. I focused more of my attention on the real estate side of things, working with her father on several projects and properties.

While we were busy renovating (we did all the work ourselves) and flipping houses, among other activities, Nobles told me all sorts of things that painted a dark picture. He described how he had run a black-market operation while he was in the military in Germany. That he greatly admired Olympic bomber Eric Rudolph as a man of courage and patriotism, and gloated for the five years that Rudolph evaded capture. Nobles had been a member of the extreme-right-wing neo-Confederate Patriot Network for years. During this time, according to his stories, he and his cohorts had been collecting gold bars as currency for the coming civil war. He bragged about how he'd hidden his guns in the chimney when the Feds had raided his house, how he'd seen the plates his Posse Comitatus friends had used to counterfeit money, and how he'd stolen the notebook of an IRS investigator so that he could blackmail him. He spoke fondly of his friends in the Posse Comitatus, a hate group militia. He also lavished praise on his lawyer, Leslie Michael Osman, who could "fix anything."

At the time, right-wing extremism and anti-government rhetoric weren't the imminent dangers they have shown themselves to be in recent years. Nobles was just some crazy Good Ol' Boy, a small-town business-man doing his thing and trying to stick it to the Feds at every turn. It's part of the cultural underpinnings of Florida to "stick it to the Feds." I didn't give it much thought until years later when it became glaringly relevant. The guy was a respected church elder and businessman. People deferred to him. People respected him. And the relationship between Christy and me was so stormy that I was chronically distracted. Her dad treated me like a friend and often served as a sympathetic ear when Christy was acting out.

There were some things I realized at the time, and some things I didn't discover until later, *things* that fit like puzzle pieces into Christy's behavior.

* * *

One time, I came home and found a used condom in the bedroom.

Another time, I found that she had installed spyware on my home computer.

I found an unfamiliar cell phone in the house. When I asked her about it, she said a man had given it to her; but of course, that relationship was all over.

There were at least a dozen affairs that I knew about, sometimes with multiple men at a time. I have no doubt there were more.

It's amazing, the rationalizations people are capable of. I hated the affairs, but I needed somebody to take care of the boys while I was gone. Being a pilot, I didn't always come home at night. Also, I had come to believe she was mentally ill and was acting out because of it. I wanted to get her into treatment and thought I could get her help. *I wanted to "rescue her."*

* * *

Christy would write disturbing things in journals and notepads – poems, diary-like essays – and leave them lying around for me to find. What she wrote about were shockingly dark musings that represented self-hatred, extreme shame, paranoia, fear her "secret" would be discovered, and repeated fantasies of suicide. She wrote that she was "Damaged" – the name of one of her poems. So riddled with shame, Christy said she didn't want mirrors in her house because she hated the sight of herself. She kept a whole stack of journals from previous years in her closet which I did not read because I wanted to respect the privacy of her past.

When I was away, she grossly neglected the boys. I would come home, and the house would be a squalid nightmare. All the dishes and clothes would be dirty. Toby was locked in his room smearing feces from his diaper on the wall.

I went to her family, begging for help. Mike said he'd talk to her. I hired a maid, but she became overwhelmed and quit.

I went to our church, hoping to get some kind of counseling. On Mike Nobles' recommendation, I went first by myself. These were with Ron Long, a local Church of Christ counselor.

Elders of our church included Mike Nobles' long-time business partner, Jerry McCormick, and Mike's father-in-law as well, a WWII veteran of the Army Air Corps. Mike had resigned his position as Elder over the "shame of his daughters' immorality," but in no time reclaimed that position. I had been told that the church had forced Wanda Nobles into an arranged marriage to Mike Nobles.

The church soon referred both of us to counseling. Throughout all of this, I clung to hope that Christy could get better, that I could find the woman I'd fallen in love with. It took me a long time, years, to realize she had never really existed.

* * *

Christy had been deeply religious since I'd known her, but she abruptly declared herself an atheist – at least to me. Whether she had the courage to say this to her father, I don't know, although for nearly three years she cut off ties with him and her mother for the most part.

When I would get home from a trip, she would take this as her license to party. I had barely put down my suitcase before she was headed out the door to hit the town with her friends. The boys would scream and cry and beg her not to leave. In a cold callous manner she would yell, "I deserve to have fun!" The door would slam in their little faces behind her.

Sometimes she would be gone for days, and I couldn't reach her. I worried about her, but without her there, I could enjoy my time with the boys without the chaos.

Our new marriage counselor, Ron Long, wanted to see her individually. After a few sessions, she related, he began to peel back the layers. So, she quit, not wanting to face the truth. After the few sessions with her alone, he contacted me for a private meeting.

Ron didn't normally discuss individual meetings with family members, but he thought I deserved to know. He believed she had borderline personality disorder, stemming from severe childhood sexual abuse. In his opinion, she had no business raising children and belonged in a group home. I continued to see him. He told me that he believed it was her father who had abused her, something I had refused to believe for years.

29

* * *

In 2006, Christy began to disappear for longer stretches of time. Days at a time. She would tell me she wanted a divorce, then would change her mind.

During one of her periods of absence in 2007, hammered by the responsibilities of job and special needs childcare, I dug those journals out of her closet and read – hoping for answers or clues about what to do – looking for what made her tick. What had happened to her? The answers were shocking.

Many of these entries below predate our relationship, but they show a clear pattern of severely troubled behavior that went back years.

> 8/23/99
> *I don't know what's wrong with me, It's like I opened a dark door within and now I can't be happy. If I'm happy for a few seconds the darkness comes and washes away all smiles.*

> 9/9/99
> *I don't miss Steve, and I don't miss Ben … don't miss Chad or Peter or Adam or any of those countless, meaningless guys. I miss being liked. I miss having arms to fall into. I miss having well known lips that are used to kissing mine. I'm so alone.*

> 11/1/99
> *Matt is an asshole he was dating me on the side … I wonder if the fact that I am under 18 could get him in trouble with the military. I want to screw up his life so bad. I could tell someone that he felt me up (true) and tried to get me to sleep with him (not true) well I don't want to lie to someone in power because I could get myself in trouble.*

> 11/8/99
> *I had Travis Wednesday night and I had Brad Thursday night. Travis means nothing to me but Brad does.*

> 2/22/00
> *Justin has been cheating on me…. My brother is pissed. He and his friend Rob are going to go after Justin … Billy and Rob are going to do their best to ruin his life. He should have known better than to try to fuck with me. If it comes down to physical violence, I will ask them to put a letter from me (typed) in his pocket and bring me a souvenir, his glasses. That would be perfect. He should never have fucked with me. When I get mad, I get even and he's about to get fucked UP.*

7/19/00

I am home on the couch. I met many two days ago. Yesterday morning Rob came over and we had sex. I gave him the shot glass I bought for him in San Pedro. Last night I went to Manny's house and had sex with him. I don't know what I am doing. I try to be so casual and blow it off, but someone is eventually going to get hurt and I never wanted that.

9/1/00

<u>OVER</u>
Frightened, I wrestle with these
Possibilities.
My life has become a mess
But to come clean is too
Painful, too intense
I want to take it all back
To wake up from this nightmare
Or if it's real
To fall asleep and never wake up again
I hate the things I do
But I do these things I hate
I want to be at peace
I want to go home
I just want this torment
To be over

10/00

I don't know why it seems necessary to hurt him but it does. I can't help it. I don't want to be here with this thing, this parasite growing inside me. It would be so easy to dig another hole, to kill the child, to claim it was just a miscarriage, but I am not capable of such atrocities. It is my burden to bear, no one else's and I just don't know what to do anymore. I've fallen out of love, and I have nothing left to cling to. He loves me, and my not returning that love is destroying him, but hatred is breeding and boiling in me, and I am so afraid of the explosion.

10/21/00

I struggle with impure thoughts. It's hard but I am daily making progress.

10/6/2002

I have no notice of other men anyway because I am so happy with my husband. Finally, things have come together and I have my kind, dependable, caring, strong rock to give my heart, body, mind and soul to. Finally, someone loves and takes care of me and I am not facing this world alone ever again.

31

THE HARD WAY

Hey there baby, I was wondering
How you been?
I got me a little boy
He's four months old
He's got his daddy's goofy grin
You only wanted what you can't have
And baby, you can't have me now
I gave my heart to another
Yeah I'm a mother and he's a father
And we're a family and we got each other
And I found out the hard way

Here is a poem she wrote while pregnant with Toby, just a few months after referring to me as her "rock."

MY DOWNFALL

I long for the honest repose of death
Only then I could forget
This shame, this recrimination
But the fear in me of what lies ahead
Keeps me firmly rooted in this world
Where I sin now to repent later
All the time convinced that I am going to burn
So burn I do, and crucify myself
But it' not enough suffering for my crime
I know you'd like to take a shot at me
You'll get your turn, just wait in line
Please, punish me, I am too weak
Naked and chained, I wait for the blows
I'm tired of sneaking and hiding the truth
But what will they think of me when they know?
Another bastard child is mine to love
How many times until I learn?
Sex is my downfall and men are a curse!
Slutty behavior for one so stern

There are nearly 100 more pages of similar writings which Christy wrote between the ages of 17 and 26 about her experiences growing up in Mike Nobles' house. It was painful to see her referring to Gabe as a "parasite," and to read about her fantasies about killing him. She referred to Toby as "another bastard child to love." Bastard child? Even if Toby wasn't my biological child, that mattered little to me by then because Toby was 110% my son, and Christy's endless string of infidelities was old news.

* * *

To me, knowing Christy so well by then, it seemed to me this darkness stemmed from the shame imposed by her family and church.

This discovery was horrific, so disturbing that I showed it to a psychologist. Like the counselor, he said Christy showed symptoms of bipolar disorder, borderline personality disorder, and complex PTSD.

Her journals also contained disturbing religious references. She said she was "preyed on by Satan," tormented by demons, and that she deserved to be crucified and burned. She made references to being "trapped in a hole and locked in a cage," to being "naked, chained, and burned."

There were repeated references of the most gruesome stories in the Bible, repeated ideation of suicide and even one of infanticide. She wrote about her inability to trust, toxic guilt and shame, self-hatred, fear that her "Secret" would be exposed, and paranoia that everyone was watching her. Her journal also included examples of extreme unfounded jealousy. Those cycles repeated like a broken record.

* * *

Christy had spent her adult life continuously looking for a rescuer, a savior. Could that be me?

Christy's journals graphically described her sex addiction. She was repeatedly involved sexually with multiple men at once, one-time documenting multiple sexual encounters with different men in one day. She wrote, "I can't open my heart, so I open my legs."

When those "relationships" ended, she would lash out – perceiving that she had been abandoned – and seek revenge. One time she plotted to have her brother Billy and a friend assault one of the men and bring back his glasses as a souvenir. Another time she plotted to make false allegations of a sexual nature against a military airman to get him in trouble out of revenge.

She referred to her father as "the Antichrist."

I did everything I could to hold things together and get her help – walking on eggshells for years – but she kept quitting doctors and any other form of support and aid. The chaos kept spiraling wider and wider. She was eventually diagnosed with bipolar disorder. *I wasn't ready to give up on her.* I occasionally caught glimpses of the sweet, charming girl I'd fallen in love with, and that was enough to drive me to try to fix things, fix *her.* I was The Supportive Husband, *the Rock.*

* * *

In March 2007, I cosigned a loan for her tuition to massage therapy school. While she was there, she had an affair with the instructor and another student, plus an overlapping affair with two other men and a female classmate.

I don't relate any of this to harm or embarrass her. She was a victim of heinous crimes as a child, deeply troubled, and she acted out in ways such victims do. That was the simple reality of the situation, the unbearable chaos of our family's world. Trauma begets trauma.

Over and over, I remember thinking, "This is the worst it could possibly be." *But I was always wrong.*

CHAPTER FOUR

LET US PREY

As the boys grew, their mother was present in their lives less and less, leaving the responsibilities of parenting to fall completely onto me. I was determined, despite all the drama and trauma that their mother and her family subjected them to, that those boys would have the best life I could give them. I wanted them to have something akin to normalcy. I wanted them to have hope for their future rather than letting them slide inexorably into all the hopeless, toxic stereotypes of White Southern Rednecks that surrounded us. Our family struggled more and more as time went on. As their mother abandoned them by degrees, I wanted to provide the boys, my boys, the best role model I could because I loved them both with everything I had.

I taught the boys to fish, swim, and ride a bike. I took them to the circus. I signed them up for soccer and karate at the YMCA, which they loved. Their mother never saw them play a game or practice. I tried to involve her, she wasn't interested, lost in her own world of men, her friends, and partying. I attended all the parent and teacher conferences alone. In many ways I felt like a single parent even before she left.

* * *

Toby loved Superman, even at three years old, so on his third birthday in October 2007, I made him a Superman cake (decorated it myself) and we had a little party. Christy staggered in an hour late, hungover, having been out all-night partying. The kids had lots of friends. *Sadly, that would change.*

One night, Christy was out partying with her cousin and friends. Her cousin dumped her kids on me while they were out partying. The boys got the bright idea to take a ride down the stairs in a laundry basket, and Gabe was the first guinea pig. So, when one of his cousins pushed him, Gabe went tumbling and broke his collar bone.

Gabe's therapist, a mandatory reporter, filed a report that Gabe had been injured.

> The home the family lives in is a pig sty. There is laundry all over the home. The dishes are all over the place. The mother is bipolar

and takes her medication inconsistently. The mother drinks every day. She goes out drinking in the evenings. The father is with the children.

I was really hoping that the Florida Department of Children and Families (DCF) would give us some kind of help. They were going to do an inspection. Tipped off, Wanda Nobles spent the next two days cleaning our house, removing all evidence of the squalor and neglect. So, when the DCF investigator showed up to find a nice, well-kept house. I was livid.

The DCF's report stated:

> The family is working with [DCF program] Families Count in the home. According to Families Count, the parents are being very cooperative and are actively involved. The home was discovered to be clean and appropriate.

All attempts at getting Christy to stick with counseling failed. I begged the DCF investigator to help. She callously said, "You just need to get a divorce." DCF referred us to a class. Christy refused to attend, so I went alone.

* * *

It was during this time I shared with Christy's parents my belief that she was sexually abused as a child. They bristled and told me I needed to "quit diagnosing her." I talked them into meeting with the church counselor, Ron Long, who repeated what he had told me, that she was a danger to herself and the kids. Nobles said that no one could have done anything to her except maybe Wanda's father or Mike McCormick, son of his partner, Jerry McCormick, whom he now hated because McCormick had accused Nobles of embezzling. Nobles pressured me to get a divorce and promised to help me get custody.

When I told him about the journals, he grew visibly agitated, claimed she was crazy and that everything in the journals was a "fantasy." Nobles freaked out and wanted me to give them to him "for safe keeping." He said it was impossible that she could have kept them secret because he would have found them, a creepy statement by itself. *I've never let him touch them.*

He asked me to make a video tape of the house showing how awful Christy let the mess get while I was gone as evidence that she was an unfit mother. I let him hold onto that tape. I would later take the tape.

When I expressed concerns about the effects of divorce on the kids, Nobles said, "The most horrific things can happen to a child when they're young, and when they're older they won't even remember it."

* * *

In those days, I embraced the church for Christy's benefit. I rationalized that I wanted to do things the Christian way, so in February 2008, Christy finally agreed to enter the Meier Clinic, a two-week intensive, "Christian-based," rehabilitation and treatment program. I drove her to Chicago and left her in their care. I had entered her in that program with the expectation that they would help Christy with her mental illness, find a way to help her deal with her lifetime of trauma, and God help us, start to heal. She very much understood how broken

The Meier Clinic

The Meier Clinic had gone through a series of mergers and name changes, likely to shed the PR fallout of a long succession of scandals. It originally went by the name New Life Treatment Centers, which practiced "gay conversion therapy," among other things, and was the target of numerous lawsuits and accusations of sexual misconduct[1] and abuse,[2] including therapists having homosexual sex with their "gay conversion" patients.[3]

1   Whitley, Glenna, "UPDATE Abuse of Trust." *D Magazine*, January 1, 1992, https://www.dmagazine.com/publications/d-magazine/1992/january/update-abuse-of-trust/
2   Whitley, Glenna, "The Seduction of Gloria Grady." *D Magazine*, October 1, 1992, https://www.dmagazine.com/publications/d-magazine/1991/october/the-seduction-of-gloria-grady/
3   Marquis, Julie, "New Life Centers Named in Suits by Ex-Patients: Litigation: Laguna-based Christian therapy program denies responsibility – or liability – in the sex-related cases," *Los Angeles Times,* November 13, 1994, https://www.latimes.com/archives/la-xpm-1994-11-13-mn-62259-story.html

she was, and there were moments when she wanted to fix it. My quiet hope was that after this program, maybe she would come back to Florida and choose to continue mental health treatment. *Maybe someday we could be a functional family.*

* * *

At one point, I journeyed back to Chicago in a version of Planes Trains and Automobiles during a winter storm for a "family therapy session" that proved to be *not* what I was expecting.

The therapist opened the meeting, "Your marriage is over. It's time for you to grieve. Let's pray about it."

I immediately objected. Christy wasn't there so that we could "fix our marriage." She was there because she was suicidal, spiraling out of control, and endangering the kids.

They tried to make it all about religion, God and Satan, sin and shame, instead of mental health treatment or anything with a basis in science or medicine. I felt completely misled. We had wasted a pile of money on a program that came across as a hypocritical religion-based scam.

* * *

Christy quit the program halfway through and called to tell me she was coming home. It was a Sunday. The boys and I attended church that morning, as we had done for the last two years without Christy. I had chosen this very day to open up to some church members about what we had been going through. This was her community, the only one she had known her whole life. Everyone said they "would be praying for her."

In the midst of this disclosure, church deacon Ed Ferrell approached me under the guise of "wanting to help." Ed Ferrell was an old Southern gentleman from Birmingham, Alabama, about eighty years old, tall and thin with a stately head of gray hair. He had recently moved to the area, and in no time at all he became one of the church deacons. He was involved with real estate speculation, like many other people in this story. They were all surfing the wave of real estate boom.

We were now attending the Destin Church of Christ after the Nobles left Niceville due to a nasty falling out with Mike's fellow elder and business partner Jerry McCormick.

* * *

My grandmother's funeral was on the day Christy was supposed to return to Florida. We tried to make the best of the situation, planning a little coming-home party for her. *I missed my grandmother's funeral that day.*

When she did finally arrive, she was worse than ever, completely shut down. I don't know what they did to her, what they told her, but they had made things worse. She just lay on the couch, and ignoring the kids. She was completely dysfunctional. She told me to give up, that she was never going to change, that I could throw her out if I wanted to. In retrospect, maybe I should have had her hospitalized. At the very least, I didn't dare leave the boys with her.

I was worried that something terrible would happen when I went on my next trip for work, so I asked her if it might be a good idea for her to stay with her parents while I was gone. She agreed that it probably was. She and the boys went to stay with her parents.

* * *

Christy never came back. Not only that, but she also left everything behind. All her childhood mementos, pictures, mementos of the kids, even what Gabe called his Baby Box including the outfit and wristband from when he was born. She just walked away and left it all.

When I finally reached her on the phone, her voice sounded like she had one foot in the grave. She told me that she had some of the boys' things in her car, and she wanted me to take them. She said the boys were better off with me. Bleak depression was sadly old hat by this time, but this was a new, darker level. I feared she planned to kill herself. She was right back living among her abusers.

* * *

Another concurrent series of stressors and catastrophes, just to add some extra texture to the landscape of what was happening to us, was the bursting of the real estate bubble in 2008. Mike Nobles had enlisted Christy and me to serve as middlemen in various real estate deals. We had made enough money to buy what we called our "Dream Home," a beautiful little place on a canal, as well as two other investment properties. By this point, I was willing to do almost anything to keep her mental state between the ditches. But then, in part because of the real estate crash, in part because of her chaotic mental state, we lost the investment properties to foreclosure. Ultimately, we lost the Dream Home, too, as our finances came crashing down.

A rational, thinking person might, at numerous points in this story, raise questions about the wisdom of various actions or the lack thereof, and that person would be reasonable to do so. So much of what I know now was only beginning to emerge then.

There's a saying in aviation: you don't crash an airplane by making a single mistake, you crash an airplane by making an unbroken chain of mistakes. Breaking any link in that chain would have averted the crash.

But it's impossible to fully understand, from the outside, someone's unique situation with all its scores of conflicting pressures – financial, parental, marital, societal, even biological, when it comes to things like sleep deprivation, hunger, and mental resilience to trauma. The phrase, "walking a mile in that person's shoes" comes to mind. The miles I walked were so clouded and murky from the horrors only beginning to come to light that my judgment was questionable.

There's another saying, this one attributed to Winston Churchill: *When you're going through hell, keep going.*

I've been second-guessing many of those decisions ever since, trying to forgive myself for all the glaring signs and red flags I overlooked, and wondering what I could have done differently to prevent what was coming.

* * *

So, I found myself a full-time single parent. I'd been getting a lot of practice in increasing degrees, but it still came as a shock.

Around this time, before my relationship with Mike deteriorated completely, he insisted on giving me a cellular phone. I didn't realize until later that the phone may have been tampered with.

Nevertheless, Christy and I saw each other occasionally. We never "got back together," but we did meet for dinner or lunch a few times. Maybe we were both trying to decide if our marriage was really over. I thought she would hit rock bottom and want real help, but her family was propping her up and hiding her problems.

She lived for months like a child in the Nobles' home while I took care of the boys and sent her financial support. During this period, Christy filed for child support, even though I was the primary parent. Nevertheless, she offered to start taking the kids while I was flying. I had reservations about her mental state and what they might be exposed to in the Nobles' home, but I was desperate. I couldn't afford daycare.

* * *

I need to make one thing perfectly clear: Christy and I squabbled over many things, but never over custody of the boys. She had made it clear in word and deed for years that I was the one who should take care of them because she had never wanted to be a mother. But I was grateful, despite my misgivings, for the help with childcare, however meager it was.

Many times, during these few months, Gabe would call me at work, utterly distraught, screaming and crying.

"Dad, it's bad here! I want to come home!"

"What's wrong? What happened?"

"Come and get us right now! It's bad here!"

It broke my heart because there was nothing I could do. I was off doing my job, not even in town. We were at the end of our financial rope, and I had nowhere to turn.

And then, increasingly, the boys' behavior took a sharp and alarming turn. They began having nightmares and unusual emotional outbursts.

* * *

One time, after picking up Gabe and Toby and from the Nobles' house, Gabe had a total meltdown. He cried and kicked the back of the seat, screaming, "I need to make Mom come home!"

I tried to explain to him that mom wasn't coming home, but then he appeared to go into shock and lose consciousness. He was unresponsive. I took him to the emergency room, but they couldn't find anything wrong with him. I had to take him home with a feeling of dread like I'd never experienced before.

Joe and Carolyn Palmer -
Niceville Church of Christ

I had heard rumors for years that Joe Palmer had raped and beaten his wife and physically and sexually abused their children. Pornography was discovered on the church computer.

Carolyn Palmer describes him as "very sexually abusive."[1] His style of abuse was one of complete control. "If I went to the grocery store, I had to defend every purchase I made," down to the cost of what brands of tampons to buy and isolating her from friends. "He left bullets out for me to find," on the pillow or in the medicine cabinet. After one particular incident of rape, she gave him a final warning to "never do that to me again," a warning he ignored, so in 2005, she decided to divorce him.

"I told the [church] elders that, and he told them that that was his cry for help, because I didn't make him feel loved."

The church elders bought everything Joe Palmer said, and turned on Carolyn as a deviant, a Jezebel. I must confess that in 2005, so indoctrinated was I in that hypocritical belief system, that I was one of them. That belief that divorce was wrong, a terrible sin, was part of what kept me from divorcing Christy, even though our relationship had become incredibly toxic. A few years later, as I came to see the error of those beliefs, I felt so bad that I called Carolyn and asked her forgiveness.

Even more heartbreaking, when she finally told her children about her intention to divorce Joe Palmer, her middle, thirteen-year-old daughter got down a little fairy from a shelf, and in the fairy was a secret compartment containing a note describing how she had already contacted the Child Advocacy Center. Palmer had been abusing her, too. The youngest daughter also admitted that he had "touched her."

Her caseworker, Dawn Griffin, ultimately resigned from the Child Advocacy Center over what happened with the Palmer family. She was a friend of principal Joanna Morris and said she lost a lot of sleep after hearing what Joe Palmer had done to his kids.[2]

She described a phone conversation with him, in which he demanded to know what Carolyn and the children had been saying about him. The Child Advocacy Center was *supposed* to operate under an umbrella of "secrecy and safety" for its clients, but somehow Joe Palmer not only knew that Carolyn had been there but also the date and time of an upcoming appointment. "He knew everything," she said. That he already knew about his wife's dealings with the Child Advocacy Center confirms the existence of the back-door information pipeline that I experienced.

For pastor positions, the whole family is part of the hire, so extremely conservative Southern churches like these cannot have the merest whiff of impropriety, and for them, it's *always* about protecting "their own," not justice or simple Christian decency. When Carolyn went to the elders about what Joe had done to her and the children, they told her not to say anything to anyone except a woman in the church named Paula Wilcox. So, Carolyn confided in her for a while, until she discovered that Wilcox was reporting everything Carolyn said back to the church elders, so it was getting back to Joe as well.

After it was known the Palmers were divorcing, their youngest daughter was still forced to undergo visitation with her father. On a particular evening of visitation, Carolyn and Joe had had "a big row," and the girl didn't want to go. But Joe demanded it violently. He threatened Carolyn with law enforcement intervention, forcing her to

1. Carolyn Palmer, interview with the publisher, July 17, 2023.
2. Dawn Griffin, interview with the author, 2008.

"leave my baby curled up in a ball on his front steps." According to the daughter, Joe immediately went into the house and called Paula Wilcox, saying, "Paula, we've got a problem."

After that, "he called *everybody*, telling them I was having a mental breakdown … that I was crazy basically."

I couldn't help but wonder, at first, why the congregation allowed him to keep his position, but over time, the patterns became clearer. This was the guy who had forced Christy to write a letter of apology to the congregation for her "sexual immorality."

When Carolyn Palmer filed for divorce, not only did the congregation, led by Mike Nobles and others, rally around their pastor, rather than the abused mother and children, they engaged in a whisper campaign smearing Carolyn as a homewrecker and adulteress, painting a scarlet letter on her.

The Palmers had been close friends with Mike and Wanda Nobles, often socializing, having dinner together, and so on.

"I met Mark [Harris]," Carolyn said, "when he married their daughter Christy. Wanda was so excited, because he was good to Christy and everything."

When the Palmers were going through their divorce, Mike acted as if he was still Carolyn's friend, offering to be an intermediary between them, writing the child support decree. The lawyer Carolyn engaged rolled over like an abused dog when he learned who Joe's lawyer was. Carolyn's second lawyer expressed skepticism that Joe had engaged the lawyer that he had, because his fee was astronomical. But Joe was getting that lawyer's services for free through the same internecine connections that would later try to destroy my life as well.

With no money, no credit, and no job, having been a housewife for twenty years, Carolyn Palmer needed a place to live that wasn't with her abusive husband.

Mike Nobles bought the Palmers' house to "help them out," and then offered to loan Carolyn the money in a contract to buy the Nobles' house. But they bought it for $100k less than it was worth, depriving Carolyn Palmer of a sizable chunk of her shared marital assets. He then "sold" his own house at 1118 Rhonda Drive to Carolyn Palmer on a contract so that she and her children could live there – never intending to let her keep it – at least in part to keep her quiet about the sexual abuse.

A year later, Nobles sold the Palmers' house for $100k more than he paid for it on an inside deal to a real estate developer.[1] Did he share those profits with righteous ol' Pastor Joe?

Joe Palmer was forced to pay the staggering sum of $25.00 per month in child support for each of their five children. And even that he refused to pay. A local television station ran a series of public service announcements called *Deadbeat Dads,* aiming to publicly shame deadbeat dads into paying their child support. Joe Palmer appeared briefly in these segments, until he flexed his contacts and got himself removed from it.

At the Palmer's divorce ground through its various stages, their teenage son got in trouble with the law. Carolyn took him to the Niceville Police Station to have him turn himself in, but officers *refused to book him* without Joe Palmer's permission. They would do nothing until he arrived. What kind of civilian has that kind of power over an entire police department? Later, a female officer informed Carolyn that Joe wanted to speak to her privately. Carolyn adamantly refused, wanting a neutral third party to be present. The officer tried to coerce her, but she still refused. The officer offered to set up a camera to record the entire meeting, in case things got out of hand. This Carolyn

---

1. This was a prominent developer, the president of Dooley Mac Construction. He was a member of the Okaloosa County Economic Development Council and was involved with an organization called Children in Crisis. His father, like Wanda's was a veteran of the Army Air Corp and background checks indicate the families were connected in some way.

agreed to. So Carolyn and Joe met in a room at the police department with a camera recording the interaction. As she had expected, he launched into a vitriolic tirade, calling her crazy, delusional, claiming she heard voices that convinced her he wanted to hurt her.

When it was over, she asked the female officer, "Did you get all that?"

The officer said, "We sure did."

"Can I have a tape of it?"

"Not until after your son's case is over."

Carolyn went to the police department every week to ask for that video tape, because Joe was tirelessly slandering her throughout the community. She wanted people to hear how he talked to her. The day after her son's court case, she went to the police department and asked for the tape, but she was told that someone had cleaned the evidence room and the tape had been thrown away.

I also started hearing disturbing things through the grapevine from friends – Mike Nobles was spreading rumors that I was mentally ill. He even had claimed he called the Meier Clinic and Christy's therapist had said I was the crazy one. I was livid and called the therapist who had never spoken to Nobles and acknowledged Christy had symptoms of borderline personality disorder.

When I confronted Mike Nobles about this, he denied it of course, but I was well acquainted by now with how smooth a liar he could be. He tried to persuade me to file for divorce, saying he knew what an unfit mother Christy was, that he would do everything he could to help me get custody of my sons. One of the last things he had done before cutting off ties was to give me a cell phone, and the name of a divorce attorney – the same one Joe Palmer had used – who would "destroy Christy like Joe Palmer destroyed Carolyn."

During this period, I discovered my house had been robbed. Mike Nobles had sent his son-in-law, Brian Riggs, to break in and take whatever he wanted – tools, fishing equipment, and a couple thousand dollars' worth of other stuff, including my utility trailer. A small, single-axle wooden flatbed I kept in the back yard was gone. The situation was already so ugly that I chose not to file a police report. We later arbitrated this through the church, and it was all chalked up to "a misunderstanding." Brian Riggs claimed he was "just following Mike's orders."

This utility trailer would later become evidence.

* * *

In May 2008, Nobles called to declare that Christy was well. Everything was fine. I scoffed that this could not possibly be true given the depth of her mental illness. I was told that she wouldn't be undergoing any therapy, counseling, or mental health treatment, as all of that was unnecessary. I was already well-versed in the cycles of abuse and strategies of abusers. One of those strategies is isolating the victim, cutting them off from any contact with other people who might help the wounded or challenge the abuser. I recognized it then, but there was nothing I could do.

Despite any illusions we had that we were keeping everything under wraps, our family's dirty laundry was hanging out for all the congregation to see for months. Destin Church of Christ deacon Ed Ferrell asked me to come to weekly counseling sessions with him alone. At first, I welcomed the help. Mike Nobles had resumed his position as one of the church deacons at the Destin Church of Christ, and I needed to tell *someone* about the things he was up to – sexually abusing his children and maybe others, the child pornography I'd found on his home computer – but to my shock, Ferrell pressured me not to report anything. Making these kinds of waves was simply not done. He told me to divorce Christy and move on with my life, to find "alternatives" to reporting Mike. It soon became apparent that Ferrell was more interested in sweeping this under the rug than helping my family in any meaningful way.

* * *

The boys and I did a lot that summer. I wanted, was determined you could say, to give my sons good memories, hoping to outweigh the awful ones. Maybe we could have enough adventures to help them get past whatever had happened to them. They were sad about their mother leaving, but they were also aware enough to be relieved. I felt grateful for the respite from perpetual crises and the parade of men hanging around waiting for their chance with Christy.

The boys and I went to the beach often. They accumulated a huge collection of seashells. One particular day was jam-packed with adventures, a day I treasure. We watched a hurricane-damaged condo as it was demolished by explosives. It was quite a sight, and I'll never forget the looks of wonder on their faces. After that, we visited the Navy Museum in Pensacola, then a historic lighthouse, and then took a tour of a historic fort where Toby fell asleep. I carried him to the car and later carried him from the car upstairs to bed. We all had so much fun. They told me it was "the best day ever." This still chokes me up to remember it. And as they both have told me often, said "You're the best dad in the whole world."

Other adventures that summer included dirt-track stock car and sprint races. We explored the public areas of Eglin Reservation and found some fishing holes just right for little boys to throw a line in the water. I sometimes had overnight trips to Key West for work, and I would bring back seashells or coral for them. The kids called it the Island Far, Far Away. Money was incredibly tight, but I splurged and bought Gabe a butterfly collection in a glass case. He loved to draw fish and butterflies, so we frequented the Butterfly House and the Shark Museum. Toby loved to play the claw machines. When I thought I could spare the change, I would let him play, holding him up so he could reach the controls.

Because money was so tight, the clerks at the local Dollar Tree got to know us well. I sometimes would stop there and let the boys buy a trinket. Toby's great loves were Pokémon cards, Bakugan toys, and of course, to play the claw machines.

One day, out of the blue, one of the clerks said to me, "You're such a good dad. They're lucky to have you."

I almost broke down right in front of her. In that instant, for the first time, I felt *seen*, acknowledged. Someone outside of our immediate circle saw something terrible happening and recognized that I needed to hear that. When you're nostril-deep in constant, churning crisis, it's easy to fail to notice that other people have perceptions, minds, and hearts. Some are good people. You might think you have everything bottled up, tied down, under control, that people can't tell. Sometimes you tell yourself that every moment of every day. But you're not the closed book you might believe. I will never forget people like that who recognized our struggle.

* * *

June 2008 was an eventful month. I didn't know it at the time, but I was at the cusp of an entire universe I didn't know existed.

I had wanted to avoid the cost-prohibitive process of adopting Gabe, so Christy and I signed an affidavit of paternity, claiming Gabe as my child. I had never met his biological father, and his name didn't appear on the birth certificate. The Nobles had cut him out of Christy's life.

I had initially thought that Gabe's biological father had wanted no part of Gabe's life, but I pieced together later that he had made several attempts to get in contact with Christy, to confirm that he wanted to be part of Gabe's life. But she sent him a "my love has turned to hate" message and cut off all contact. Mike Nobles blocked the guy from Christy's life, and subsequently she constructed a scenario that he had abandoned her. Was this because of his dark skin? Maybe. But by now he was truly long gone.

When Christy told me the legal process of changing Gabe's birth certificate to include my name was finished, she said I was to go to the Nobles' home and pick it up. She said that no one would be home, and they had left the door open for me to pick up the birth certificate.

* * *

By this time, everything about Mike Nobles I had seen and heard led me to believe that he was hiding some serious crimes. I felt like a fool. I had let myself overlook it for the sake of family harmony. He treated me as a friend for all that time. The child pornography I had seen on his home computer was an enormous red flag I had hitherto ignored. I was certain sexual abuse was going on in his home, and someone needed to call him out on it. I took a small, disposable camera with me to document anything I might encounter.

While I was there I decided to check the computer. I opened his computer to look for the child pornography I had seen earlier. I found dozens of password-protected files. I couldn't open them, but the filenames alone would turn one's stomach. Names related to incest.

I took a few photos of this list of filenames.

In the kitchen, I noticed some medication prescribed to Faith, Christy's younger sister. When I researched it later, it proved to be a treatment for bed-wetting. At this time, Faith was an adolescent, twelve-years old, and she was what one might call "an early bloomer," sized like a grown woman. I knew from the reading I'd been doing that bed-wetting was a common symptom in children of anxiety and PTSD. *I couldn't deny the obvious any longer.*

* * *

As I was leaving the house, I spotted the videotape on a shelf I'd taken of the state of our house, the result of Christy's neglect. I took it with me.

Poor Faith and Emily were two children imprisoned in complete isolation from the rest of the world, completely under Nobles' control. The only times those little girls were allowed to leave the house were to attend school at Agape Christian Academy where Mike Nobles was president of the school board. Gabe had just finished kindergarten at Agape Christian Academy. His attendance there had seemed natural given our family connections.

This organization went defunct soon after, for reasons unknown.

I had to confront Nobles about what I thought was going on. I had to know. He should at least let Christy get some counseling and mental health treatment.

* * *

In a meeting with Nobles and his friend, Don Sublett, an elder for the church, I laid out my summation of allegations, and he exploded. I did my best to keep my composure while he ranted and railed, waving his arms and shouting as he denied everything. He was proud that he'd disowned Christy when she moved in with her boyfriend at eighteen years old, proud that he had her humiliated in front of the whole congregation.

I left the meeting determined to protect my boys.

* * *

By this time, the boys' mental state worried me tremendously. I was sure something had happened to them at the Nobles' house. So, I consulted psychologist Dr. Fred Deshon about the whole situation. Dr. Deshon was a tall and stately-looking professional with a New Age vibe. His office was decorated with crystals and objects of Eastern religious art and philosophy. He listened thoughtfully as I described the shattered landscape of our lives, my marriage, and Christy's history as best as I knew at the time. Christy agreed to meet with him for an evaluation.

Dr. Deshon and I had many interesting conversations over the years, but the one that still sticks with me was one about religion.

He stated that he was not a religious man, but that he believed in God. The reason he believed in God was that he also believed in the Devil. He believed in the Devil because he had seen the Devil's work, the horrible things people do to each other and to children.

He concurred with me about all the warning signs with Faith and Emily and with Gabe. He cautioned me that Faith and Emily, if they had been

Agape Christian Academy

The name "Agape" has no linguistic or cultural connection to education. It is pronounced "ah-GAH-pay." This seemingly innocuous name was the opening of rabbit hole into another universe.

It appears also in the name of the Agape Lodge,[1] also known as Agape Sex Magick Lodge, a chapter of Ordo Templi Orientis,[2] or "Order of Oriental Templars."

Agape Lodge was founded by Jack Parsons, founder of the Jet Propulsion Laboratory. Yes, *that* JPL, the one later absorbed into NASA.

Ordo Templi Orientis was an occult secret society headed at one point by the infamous occultist and self-purported black magician Aleister Crowley.

When I discovered this connection, I felt like my brain had just taken the off-ramp to Never-never Land. But it was just a name, right?

The logo for Agape Christian Academy was an alchemical symbol featuring three crosses inscribed with "body, mind, spirit," which are the Masonic elements of alchemy.

1. https://en.wikipedia.org/wiki/Agape_Lodge
2. https://en.wikipedia.org/wiki/Ordo_Templi_Orientis

molested, might be acting out sexually themselves and possibly victimizing my boys.

After evaluating Christy, he told me, "Something truly horrific happened to your wife as a very young child, and you need to protect your sons."

Of Mike Nobles, he said, "Unfortunately, people like him always get away with it."

* * *

At times throughout this process of getting help for my wife, I could hardly believe the implications roiling around in the revelations. But now, given Nobles' prominence in his church and the community, I knew I needed support and corroboration if I was going to go to the law. I sought advice from several others, some knew the Nobles. One urged me to file a report with law enforcement and the Florida Department of Children and Families (DCF). The church counselor Ron Long had told me in private that he had suspected for a long time that Christy had been molested by her father.

With all this information in hand, I did my best to brace myself for whatever fight was coming. It was time to do something about it. I started asking questions in earnest.

I talked to Carolyn Palmer about her situation, as well as her caseworker at Emerald Coast Children's Advocacy Center (ECCAC), Dawn Griffin. The horrible things they told me led me to check for law enforcement records on Joe Palmer. I discovered that none existed, even though reports had been filed. An officer found a DCF report that claimed the allegations were "false allegations of a bitter ex-wife."

I went to Agape Christian Academy and talked to the principal and Gabe's teachers who had some damning information. They said they were so glad that the kids were with me. They told me that when I was out of town, the boys would be brought to school looking "unkempt." The Nobles girls, Faith and Emily, were severely withdrawn, that Faith had thrown up in the classroom, and one time, passed out. They reported that her behavior was by turns clingy and isolated. They were clearly living in a house of horrors. The principal told me about the pornography found on Joe Palmer's church computer and that the computer had been destroyed to keep this under wraps.

I called Mike McCormick, son of Nobles' partner and fellow church elder, whom Nobles had insinuated might have been Christy's childhood abuser. I told him was I was going to report Nobles for sexual abuse, and he said, "Good!" Days later, he called me back backpedaling, telling me it would be a bad idea. He clearly didn't want anyone digging.

I also called Mike Nobles' brother, Danny. The only sibling of Mike Nobles I had met before was Roger, that one time when Christy and I first gotten together. Danny Nobles was a colonel in the U.S. Army, and a base commander for Fort McCoy. He worked at the Pentagon. It was an odd, disjointed conversation. I told him about what Mike had done to Christy and probably several others, and he simply told me he had no knowledge of that. He then prayed for me over the phone, praying to "bind demons." During his military career, he got in trouble for bringing his troops, in uniform, to a George W. Bush rally. Troops are forbidden from supporting any political candidate while in uniform. Dan Nobles went on to establish his own ministries, was active in multiple denominations, and was a professor at Pat Robertson's Regent University. He was practically a stereotype of the Christian Crusaders, as I call them.

These people are no strangers to me.

Hell is empty and all the devils are here."
– William Shakespeare, *The Tempest*

CHAPTER FIVE

THE CALM BEFORE THE STORM

My concern that something terrible had happened to my sons, and my certainty that Faith and Emily had been horribly abused, led me to suspect that all these children were molested by the same perpetrator. This knowledge, strengthened by a comment or two by others, spurred me to get the authorities involved. My priority was to protect the boys and have them receive some care and counseling from professionals. I called the Emerald Coast Children's Advocacy Center (ECCAC) in Niceville, a non-profit organization with the stated purpose of providing services for victims of abuse and their families. I was referred to case Advocate Tom Dunn, a man of about fifty with a graying walrus mustache and a stubble haircut, with the gruff directness of an ex-military policeman. Dunn was the case advocate for child abuse in three counties – Walton, Santa Rosa, and Okaloosa – and in that role had the ability and responsibility to assign investigators, arrange forensic interviews, etc. He was also a part-time Niceville police officer.

I was by turns nervous and desperate. I didn't know how Nobles would react when law enforcement came sniffing around. Despite everything, I feared for Christy's safety, and that of Faith and Emily. I needed to keep my boys away from him. He'd blown up in my face once already. This was the first time I'd talked to anyone with the power to do anything about the situation. Theoretically, ECCAC had connections with law enforcement and could help with any investigation. I nurtured hopes that Nobles would soon be called to account for the things I suspected he had done.

I sat down with Tom Dunn and laid it all out for him: the absolute certainty that my wife had been horribly abused by her father; I was certain that abuse had broken her; my near certitude that he had abused Faith and Emily as well; and my fear, based on the sudden shifts in their behavior, that Gabe and Toby had been abused in the Nobles' home.

I gave him the Internet Protocol (IP) address for Mike Nobles' computer, hoping there was a way to investigate the child pornography or his downloads of it.

As I spoke, his face was like a dark, stone mask that I interpreted as a look of concentration. He took a moment to respond, but when he did, I could hardly contain my shock and disappointment. He advised me *not* to report the abuse, and then went on to say that my sons would probably face retaliation from Mike Nobles if I did.

I was incredulous. "Are you saying that he would go after his own grandsons?"

"That's what I'm saying, and probably you, too. He'd take your kids away from you, and you'd never see them again."

"How can you be so sure?"

But he just chewed on his mustache. "Are you one hundred percent determined to go to the police?"

"Something must be done. The law needs to know about what he's doing."

He leaned back in his chair, crossed his arms, and wouldn't look me in the eye. "If you're going to go to the police – and I wouldn't advise it – you need to talk to Sergeant Joey Forgione of the Niceville Police Department. He's the guy you want. Don't talk to anybody else."

When I thanked him somewhat tepidly for his help, he gave me his direct number and card. My cloak and dagger world had begun.

I told him I'd be helping with any investigation in every way I could.

* * *

On July 3, 2008, Dr. Fred DeShon diagnosed Toby and Gabe with anxiety disorder.

A few times that month, the boys went to visit their mom, a couple of hours here and there.

But then I heard that Mike and Christy had gone to Mexico with a church "mission trip" as youth chaperones. Thinking this might be a chance to prove what Nobles was doing, I went over to his house with a portable hard drive and the intention of obtaining incriminating evidence.

When I arrived there, however, the house was in a state I'd never seen before. Nobody home. All the windows and doors locked; the blinds closed. Even the gate to the back yard was locked. I called Wanda Nobles and asked her if I could borrow the computer for something. When she got home, she let me in. I plugged in the portable hard drive when she wasn't looking, but as soon as I opened it up, I knew it was a different computer entirely. The desktop and all the files were different. This one was loaded with pirated video games, which meant that it more than likely Billy Nobles' computer, not Mike's. There was nothing here.

I hurriedly got out of there, my mind spinning through the possibilities.

Had someone tipped them off?

* * *

In mid-July, Christy filed for child support, even though the boys were living with me full time and they could count on their fingers the number of hours they'd seen their mother since she left. I felt she filed for child support at her father's coercion. The request was ultimately withdrawn.

I emailed Tom Dunn about Mike Nobles' computer and the child pornography. A week later, he responded, telling me that Nobles' IP address was "clean." He reiterated his advice that I bury any investigation, that Nobles would come after me and

Wanda Nobles

When she was very young, Wanda Nobles had fallen in love with a youth minister who turned out to be a man of whom Wanda's parents adamantly disapproved. When they found out about the relationship, they forced her to end it. Suffering this loss threw Wanda into a deep depression. Her father then decided that Mike Nobles was the man she should marry, even though Nobles was much older than Wanda.

She went through with the marriage, but spent her married life using various forms of self-medication to survive the things she had to endure.

She confided all this to Carolyn Palmer at lunch one day while Carolyn was in the midst of divorcing Joe Palmer. Wanda no doubt knew about the abuse Carolyn and her children had suffered. It was all over the church, all over the community, and she also no doubt had heard all the horrible lies that Joe was spreading about Carolyn.

Wanda said to Carolyn, "You know, I think we have lived very similar lives.[1]"

1. Carolyn Palmer, interview with the publisher, July 17, 2023.

my boys if I reported him. I told him, "I will have to report him eventually." There was no way in good conscience that I could sit on it.

With a war brewing between me and the Nobles, I couldn't take the boys to Destin Church of Christ anymore. I happened to be in a McDonald's and heard a group of men talking about Calvary Chapel Gulf Breeze. I struck up a conversation with them. By the end of it, they had invited me to join their congregation. This church has since changed its name to Coastline Calvary Chapel.

On the day I visited, one of the congregation's prominent members, Jerry Williams, approached me. An Alabama transplant with a history in the construction industry, he was over-the-top friendly – a real schmoozer – offering to take me and the boys to lunch after church. Jerry was the owner of Beacon Inspection Group LLC. He was a home inspector. Beacon is a word associated with Freemasonry and the Niceville newspaper.. He is also a Vietnam veteran and former member of the 82nd Airborne.

I was grateful for the friendship. He poured on the charm and seemed genuinely interested in hearing about what we were going through and lent a sympathetic ear.

I was baptized by the pastor, John Spencer, that fall in a mass beach baptism. When he baptized me, he said, "God has a plan for your life, and so does the Enemy." Back then, I didn't yet know who the enemy truly was, that I may have had enemies lurking in this very church.

* * *

Meanwhile, I enrolled the kids in Lighthouse Private Christian Academy, a network of non-denominational Christian parochial schools with several locations around Florida. Gabe was going into first grade and Toby into pre-kindergarten.

At an initial interview, I met the principal, Joanna Morris. She's one of those people who simply exudes warmth and compassion. I hadn't intended to air our family's secrets to a stranger, but she's a perceptive, charismatic woman who deeply loves children. So, I opened up a little about what we'd been going through, in part because I needed to warn her about the Nobles family, and in part because I could tell she truly wanted to help.

After hearing the kids' story, she did want to help. I felt like I had been smothered by "Christian" hypocrites for years, and she was a rare gem – a person who walked the walk, not just talked the talk. She was critical later in preventing an even worse fate for the boys.. If not for her help, and that of therapist Karleen Shuster, I could have lost them forever. My kids lives would have become a nightmare, and they might not have survived.

I'll never forget the boys' first day at Lighthouse. They were so cute in their little uniforms. They fit in and immediately began to thrive and make friends. We went to birthday parties and school events. I was an oddball as the only male single parent, but the other parents embraced me. As best I could, I deflected questions about where the boys' mother was and why she was not participating in their lives.

After drawing my conclusions on the Nobles family, I hired a nanny and told Christy I didn't want my kids staying in that house. She agreed and said she planned to move out and the kids could stay with me full time until she had her own place, and then we would resume shared custody.

One night in August, I came home to a disturbing story from Marilyn Reed, the nanny I had hired to take care of the boys while I was away for work. She was a kind, conscientious woman who did a great job with them. She told me she had found the boys engaged in "inappropriate sexual conduct." I listened as calmly as I could. The boys were asleep, so as gently as I could, I asked them about it the next day, where they'd learned it. They said Faith and Emily had shown them.

"How did Faith touch you?" I asked him.

"With her fingers," he said.

"Where did this happen?"

"On the couch in Faith and Emily's room. It was just Faith. Emily left. She said messing with her cousin was disgusting."

* * *

My hopes that this behavior would be kept private evaporated when Principal Morris called me to say that there were serious signs of abuse and that the boys were terrified of the Nobles' home. I was afraid she would kick us out, but instead she offered to help and referred us to therapist Karleen Shuster. Ms. Shuster was the therapist counterpart to Principal Morris, kind and compassionate with a strong code of ethics around protecting children.

After one interview with the boys, Shuster pointedly told me that all the signs of sexual abuse were there. She instructed me to report the abuse to the authorities. If I didn't do it, she would have to and to report me for failing to protect them.

But Tom Dunn's warning had done a job on me. I was afraid that the Nobles family would come after me somehow. They had already broken into my house and stolen items including my utility trailer. They were playing manipulative games trying to label me crazy. Things would get much much worse.

* * *

Christy called me one night to chat, asking after the boys and whether they'd started school. It had been two weeks since she had spoken with them. After we hung up, Gabe gave me a frightened look, "Don't tell Faith I told you!" He held firm to the story of what happened to him.

About a week later, Toby told me, "Emily played with Gabe's weenie," and that she held him down, pulled on and slapped his penis, calling him "daddy." He said, "Paw Paw was watching through the crack in the door."

Gabe crawled in bed with me in the middle of the night, crying. He'd just had a nightmare. He said, "I really love you, Daddy. I thought you were gone." I consoled him as best I could and let him stay with me the rest of the night.

A few days later, I found both boys upset and crying. When I asked them what was wrong, they said they were sad because they hadn't seen Mom in a long time. Gabe said he was afraid.

"What are you afraid of?" I asked.

"The *Devil!*" he wailed. "He's going to get us!"

"Who told you that?"

"Emily!"

Again, I tried to console him as best I could. The Devil only comes after bad people, I told him, and that he and Toby were good boys. This quieted him some, but I could tell he was still chewing on it.

* * *

In late August, I sent Dunn a draft of the complaint I was preparing to file. This email is in the Department of Children and Families case file, along with a thumbnail of the report I filed, but the full text of my complaint is not, only the line "Documents Omitted." I should point out that Tom Dunn was a mandatory reporter. He was legally obligated to report cases of child abuse.

On September 4, 2008, he responded that I should wait a week to file the report, reiterating his warning that Nobles would come after me and the kids.

So, following his advice, I filed a report with the Florida Department of Children and Families Abuse Hotline.

The very next day, investigator Sarah Johnson came to my house to interview the boys. Gabe refused to talk to her, but Toby disclosed enough to corroborate what had been in my report.

When the interview was over, she told me, "You need to file another report, but in Okaloosa County. Go directly to law enforcement."

We were living in Santa Rosa County. Sarah claimed to have no jurisdiction, and I came away from that meeting frustrated because she seemed to be washing her hands of the whole thing.

* * *

On the afternoon of September 7, 2008, I filed a lengthy report with the Okaloosa County Sheriff's Department, speaking to a Deputy Soares. Soares took my statement, asked meaningful questions, and seemed appropriately concerned. I came away from that conversation certain I had done the right thing, hopeful that something meaningful would come of it. I anticipated that the wheels of justice were in motion.

What happened next was that Deputy Soares filed a report with the Abuse Hotline. The investigator assigned was a man named Douglas Dandridge, an abuse hotline counselor in Tallahassee. He was never really an investigator, nor was he local. No investigation was ever performed. The report record is now blank.

This law enforcement report was forwarded to the Niceville PD by Okaloosa Deputy Robert Norris, whose name repeatedly appears in police reports related to me and Mike Nobles. Like Tom Dunn, and the Sheriff himself, Norris is a former military policeman, ex-Office of Special Investigation (OSI), and his name would come up again and again on reports regarding me, my kids, and Nobles. He was later responsible for the resignation of a deputy who complained about religious fanaticism of then Sheriff Ashley and the department leadership.

The next day, a report of sexual abuse was filed against Mike Nobles by the Niceville PD. According to his report, on September 8, Sergeant Joey Forgione went to the Nobles' home and interviewed Mike Nobles. His investigation consisted of asking Mike Nobles if he molested his daughters. Nobles denied it, and apparently that was sufficient for Forgione whose report, dated September 9, closes the case as "unfounded" and adds "there is no further investigation required." So, in effect, he closed the so-called investigation before any investigation occurred.

However, he did not file this paperwork until February 2009. None of it has any mention of my children, child-on-child abuse, or child pornography. The report states that Forgione was both the reporting office and the approving supervisor. Over a year later, Officer Joseph Kearnes was added to the record as the investigator, but he never once took part in a single investigation in this matter that I am aware of. I have both versions of the same report, one that lists Joey Forgione as the investigator, the approving officer, and the supervisor, all three. A subsequent report was edited to list Joseph Kearnes as the investigator. There was another edit made to this report, the nature of which is unknown, on February 5, 2009, the same day that I was at the Nobles' home with the FBI. Coincidence seems unlikely, especially considering Forgione declined Mike Nobles' request to be present for that visit.

* * *

On September 10, 2008, Emily Nobles, ten years old at the time, was interviewed by Sergeant Joey Forgione and DCF investigator Libby Leonpacher (after Forgione had closed his "investigation"). Soon after questioning began, Emily curled up into a fetal position. To every question, her answer became, "I don't know."

Victims of trauma sometimes assume the fetal position under extreme stress, an instinctive response from the body and mind trying to protect itself from further trauma.[1]

The DCF case file states: "Once this CPI [Child Protection Investigator] and LE [Law Enforcement] began to ask questions, she began to draw her legs to her chest. She denied ever being touched in any area that made her uncomfortable. However ... LE asked her how she got disciplined if she didn't listen to what happened, and she stated she didn't know. Every question after just a few minutes from the beginning of the interview, she stated she didn't know."

Libby Leonpacher's notes state that, "... she and Joey Forgione, Niceville PD investigator, went to the Nobles' home. Everyone denied any inappropriate sexual contact. She and Detective Forgione did not have a good feeling about it and felt that there was some dishonesty."

* * *

Soon after this, Libby Leonpacher was removed from the case and none of this would be in any report. Only in the DCF case file notes.

Much of the information presented here I discovered somewhat after the fact, digging through public records and police reports, but I want to present it here as sequentially as is possible. My state of mind was that of relief that something was being done, and I believed that the authorities had the matter under control. Despite several annoying glitches, I still had faith that justice would prevail.

* * *

An astute reader will notice, however, that the dates don't match up. Forgione closed the case on September 9 as unfounded, either on that day or after the fact, but before anyone was ever interviewed. And yet Faith and Emily were interviewed on September 10. This is one of numerous such inconsistencies because records were deleted and altered ex post facto to cover whose tracks over and over.

What was happening behind the scenes was a bizarre Jurisdiction shell game. On September 11, 2008, Okaloosa Sheriff's Department investigator, Monty Easterday, officially referred the case to Sgt. Forgione at the Niceville PD. He then closed the case, despite being directed to investigate by the DCF (Department of Children and Families), a state agency. Forgione claimed he was already investigating.[2] According to the police report, which Forgione filed in February 2009, he had closed the investigation on September 8. There is no documentation that the investigator of record, Joseph Kearnes, conducted any investigation or contacted any witnesses.

But I did not know any of this yet. I had so much else to deal with on my emotional plate.

* * *

Principal Morris at Lighthouse contacted me to inform me that Gabe begged her not to have to go back to the Nobles' home ever again: "I wish my daddy wasn't even a pilot. I don't ever want to go to Grandma's again. I wish my daddy had a different job so he could stay with me."[3]

During this time, Toby's teacher, Bonnie Emmons, reported to the DCF that he was acting out sexually "on a daily basis." She was concerned about "glaring signs of sexual abuse." DCF investigators refused to interview the school, the kid's therapist, or any relevant witnesses.

* * *

I discovered later that the abuse report, forwarded to the Florida DCF, found its way back to investigator Sarah Johnson. On September 16, she closed her reports stating that the Okaloosa Sheriff's Department and the DCF in Okaloosa County were investigating, and the children were no longer around their grandfather. In her previous report about child-on-child abuse, she had made a finding of "some indicators of child-on-child sexual abuse." Because she filed it in a separate document, it didn't appear in any future reports.

In her report on adult-on-child abuse, her finding was "no indicators." There's no indication she ever asked my boys about it, nor did she meet with Mike Nobles or anyone in his household. In fact, she did not even know where the Nobles lived. Her report indicates the household was in Crestview, but the Nobles lived in Niceville. She was given the names, phone numbers, and addresses of everyone involved, including our nanny, our therapist, and Lighthouse Academy. She contacted none of them. Her reports reflect that everything, including the household of the offenders, the feelings of the children living in the household, and the children's exposure to pornography were "unknown" to her. The only school she contacted was Holley Navarre Primary School who told her they had nothing to be concerned about. The truth is: neither Gabe nor Toby attended Holley Navarre.

Her ineptitude and negligence staggered me. Worse, her unprofessional and incorrect "report" was later cited by Mike Nobles and federal, state, and local law enforcement as "proof" of his innocence. And later as an excuse to not investigate acts of further abuse.

*　*　*

By this time, Christy had moved out of her parents' house and gotten an apartment by herself. For their first visit with their mom in a month, the boys spent the night with her. When she brought them back to the nanny's house, Marilyn called me at work to tell me they were "clearly traumatized." Her whole family was worried about them. Toby was badly scratched up. Gabe turned violent and tried to run away.

On September 24, Marilyn took the kids to Karleen Shuster, the therapist associated with Lighthouse, who then contacted me to tell me that Toby disclosed another instance of sexual abuse that happened at the Nobles' home three days previously. What she could tell me was that it had a specific time and place, that it was forced, that Toby objected but the abuse continued. His account even included what room they were in and what was on television at the time. She had already filed a report with DCF. I learned two years later that Shuster's dated report in DCF records was a copy/paste of the first report. It stated that the incident was at an "unknown time," which directly contradicts what she told me, both in person and in writing. This "unknown" was used to justify closing the investigation as a "duplicate, "and she reiterated her concern that I wasn't doing enough to protect the boys. She also expressed the opinion that, from behavior that she had been observing, Gabe might have attention deficit disorder.

When I got home from my trip, I did my best to comfort my boys. I asked Toby about the scratches.

"It was a squirrel," he told me, "I tried to hold it."

"Where did you get a squirrel?"

"Grandma and Paw Paw's house."

Against my express wishes and our agreement, Christy had taken the boys to the Nobles' home.

*　*　*

Fearing rabies from the squirrel scratches, I took Toby to the doctor. Fortunately, there was no infection, but he was still traumatized and didn't want to talk about anything.

I called DCF *again* and spoke to Jeanna Olson who worked in Okaloosa County. By this time, I had gotten a lot of practice giving these reports and accompanying details. She referred me to Sgt. Joey Forgione, giving me his number. She assured me a criminal investigation was underway. (It clearly wasn't. Police reports and public records show there were no such investigations underway at all. They had been closed or shuffled around to other jurisdictions.) This was the second encounter with Forgione.

Sergeant Joe Forgione

Joey Forgione, sergeant in the Niceville Police Department, is the son of a mobster. When I first met him in person, I saw a big, beefy man with beady eyes, broad features with a ruddy, rugged complexion, and receding stubble of hair. Everything about him was thick, including the midsection. He looked like a poster-child for myocardial infarction.

His father, Daniel Forgione was a mobster and union boss who was directly tied to Santo Trafficante Jr and also had ties to the Gambino crime family and Chicago outfit. Joey Forgione was also an Air Force veteran. One of the many military ties.

The Trafficante Crime Family was the Southern leg of the American Mafia, with criminal operations across Florida – primarily Miami and Tampa – alongside New York's Five Families.[1] They also owned and operated casinos and resorts in Havana before the Cuban Revolution.

Conspiracy theories surrounding the mob abound, but Santo Trafficante, Jr., is documented to have been hired by the CIA to assassinate Fidel Castro after the Cuban Revolution. There are also known connections with Jack Ruby. Some believe Ruby visited the Mafia boss in Cuban prison – Trafficante had been captured during the Cuban Revolution and imprisoned – and secured his release. He may have later been part of a Castro-Mafia plot to assassinate John F. Kennedy.[2]

Danny Forgione was murdered in 1984, shot six times in the head and chest, possibly to silence him over other murders he may have been ordered to commit.[3] Before his death, he was also involved in pornography and drug trafficking.

After his father's death, Joey Forgione worked for Nick's Restaurant, a seafood establishment in Walton County, Florida, owned by Constance Wayne Jones, a prominent businessman and real estate builder in the Florida panhandle.

1. https://en.wikipedia.org/wiki/Five_Families
2. Hunt, Thomas, "Jack Ruby's curious Havana holiday," The American Mafia, https://mafiahistory.us/a001/f_ruby.html
3. Lednovich, M. Anthony and Staff Writer, "Dead Man 'Snitches' on Drug Suspects," South Florida Sun-Sentinel, May 31, 1986.

---

* * *

An email, which I obtained later from Jeanna Olson to Pete Gallas, the DCF investigator for Santa Rosa County, states the following, with sinister implications about "stuff":

> Mike [sic] Harris wants a copy of his reports – 08-467823 and 08-468534 … he was a little upset the collaterals [witnesses] he gave were not contacted, but appeared ok. There was stuff going on in Okaloosa County that I could not tell him. Please call him when [the reports] are ready.

The next day, Pete Gallas called to inform me my reports were ready. He assured me again that a serious investigation was underway in Okaloosa County and involving both DCF and law enforcement. He gave me Sgt. Forgione's number.

So, I finally called the Niceville Police Department and asked to speak to Sergeant Joey Forgione. When he came on the phone, his voice was gruff, disinterested. I laid it all out there again. Christy's past, the child porn I had seen on Nobles' computer, the abused little girls, the boys' terror of going to the Nobles' home. After I ran out of steam, he said, "There's already an ongoing investigation. I can't discuss it."

I waited for him to say anything substantive, or at least ask some pertinent questions, but instead, he said, "In my experience, if a woman don't want to be with you anymore, you should just find another one." Then he hung up on me.

I sat there in stunned silence.

* * *

Without any clear results from Sarah Johnson, I called her for an update, but of course there was nothing. I discovered later that Johnson had closed Shuster report as a duplicate. There were no investigations at all, and they never contacted the Nobles.

I asked her, "What do I need to do to protect my kids?"

She told me to file a Domestic Violence Injunction (DVI), a restraining order against Mike, Faith, and Emily Nobles for sexual abuse. I did so.

* * *

On September 30, a DCF report was generated, likely resulting from the restraining order. The report states, "The grandfather is under investigation for child pornography." This report is then closed as a "duplicate," claiming "the allegations of child porn have been investigated." The report references Sarah Johnson's (non-)investigation as evidence for this decision. It is under the purview of law enforcement, not DCF, to investigate child pornography.

Throughout this account, there are glimpses of the system trying to work as it was intended. Good cops and well-meaning people found this case in their hands, and they attempted to do their jobs. However, through a combination of incompetence and nefarious intent, the system not only failed, but it was also used as a weapon against me and my boys.

Amid all this chaos and emotional turmoil, I took the boys to a few fall festivals in an attempt to find some sanity and fun for my family of three. At one of these, Gabe was riding a little tractor, got going too fast, and tipped over. It scared him, but he was physically fine. He clung to me like a little monkey. Sometimes I feel stuck in that time and the subsequent months of hell. The best times of their childhoods one day, and the next, indescribable hell.

* * *

On October 1, 2008, Mike Nobles was served with the restraining order. He was forced to surrender four guns and 643 rounds of ammunition, all strategically located around the Nobles' house. He was the only one home at the time. These were weapons, he later told my sons that they were there to "shoot the bad guys." And by "bad guys," he meant cops. This single event would dirty the hands of a staggering number of people – including federal agents. Corruption begat corruption.

* * *

Right after I filed the restraining order, I found myself in conversation with another guy, an attorney named Ed Fleming.[4] Years later, I would discover that he was George W. Bush's personal attorney during *Bush v. Gore*, the 2000 presidential election case. Many believe that Bush's father, George H. W. Bush, was involved in planning the Kennedy assassination He was eager to commiserate about awful ex-wives. He wasn't a member of the church and just showed up right after I filed, and joined several of the groups I was in, where I would sometimes discuss my ongoing travails, and seemed unusually interested in my story. He later even offered to be guardian ad litem. He is also a prominent real estate and construction attorney and served on the Judicial Qualifications Committee.

Later he would disappear as soon as he had appeared. In retrospect, it was apparent that he was keeping tabs on me.

* * *

A Rash of Violence

At around the time all of this was happening to me and my family, there was a spate of murders in that area of Florida, including three cops. One of those police officers was Deputy Anthony Forgione of the Okaloosa County Sheriff's Department.[1]

Anthony Forgione was Sergeant Joe Forgione's brother. Rumors abounded how much he hated his brother Joey, thought he was a "scumbag."

Anthony Forgione was killed by an escaped mental patient. The mental patient, Mark Rohlman, had just escaped from a mental hospital. Rohlman was a man who was terrified of the government, so much so his family had him locked up. He escaped and found himself surrounded by the SWAT team. Anthony Forgione, for reasons unknown, went in after Rohlman alone and was killed by a shotgun blast.

Newspaper stories conflict about whether Rohlman took his own life or was subsequently shot by other officers[2]

1. https://www.heraldtribune.com/story/news/2008/07/22/shootout-kills-okaloosa-county-deputy/28650638007/
2. https://www.nwfdailynews.com/story/news/2017/07/22/honoring-deputys-sacrifice-on-9-year-anniversary-of-death/20098523007/

All of this was taking a toll on my ability to do my job. Former Atlantic Southest Airlines Chief Pilot, Doug Helms, saw my plight. Unbeknown to me, he emailed ASA Vice-President, Charlie Tutt, describing me as a good man and a dedicated employee. He asked Tutt if there were non-flying duties for me so I could be home with my kids every night. His request was ignored.

* * *

On October 4, Christy was supposed to pick up the boys for a visit, but she was a no-show. The excuse she gave was that the "cat was sick."

In mid-October, we had Toby's fourth birthday party. Christy called and said she couldn't come because she was sick.

Since I was still paying for her cell phone, I was able to review her call records. The records showed calls to her father and to a woman named Sherry Taylor, a nanny who lived in Decatur, Alabama, the same area where I would later understand Nobles and his white-supremacist cronies, the Patriot Network, were active in the 1980s. Christy had placed an ad on Nanniesforhire.com for my kids.

Christy picked up the boys for a visit on October 17. The next day she insisted I come to pick them up at her apartment. I had to ask her for directions because I didn't know where she lived.

When I got there, we had what I thought was a frank and open talk. She lectured me for not knowing anything that was going on in her life and said that she had no intention of getting involved in the restraining order. "That's between you and him," she said.

I believe she meant it at the time.

I asked if I could use her bathroom, but she refused, saying there was a huge mess in there because of a "hole" in her cat's neck. Gabe would later tell me a story about Mike Nobles shooting his cat. Based on Mike's general attitude toward animals and the sheer number of pets large and small that had mysteriously died in that household over the years, I believe Mike Nobles shot it as a warning to her.

Before I left, she told me, "I want to warn you. He's planning to Baker Act (involuntary commitment) you." I laughed darkly. A serial sexual predator and sociopath was planning to have *me* committed.

Christy and Sherry Taylor, the nanny from Alabama, exchanged phone calls over a few days. Again, it appeared Nobles was looking for a place to hide my children in another state. There was no other possible reason for this.

Meanwhile, Gabe (I was informed by the school) was acting out in school nearly every day. My worries that he would be expelled grew with every incident.

October 28, someone filed a motion to dismiss my DVI (Domestic Violence Injunction) against the Nobles, the day before the first hearing on the matter, but I was not aware of this until the following day when I appeared at the hearing. I was about to get blindsided once again.

Endnotes

1   https://navacenter.com/vocabulary/fetal-position/

2   Public records, September 11, 2008. Niceville PD police report, filed in February 2009, indicates that Forgione closed his investigation on September 8

3   Report from Principal Joanna Morris, September 11, 2008.

4   https://www.pensacolalaw.com/edward-p-fleming

Chapter Six

Silencing the Lambs

On the morning of October 29, 2008, I had no idea that I was about to fall into a rabbit hole of nightmares, a hole I had no idea even existed, or even *could* exist in a country that claims to uphold the rule of law. On its face, it's about a serial sexual predator and sociopath and some of the crimes he committed and continues to commit. Encountering such a creature, having him as part of one's family, is traumatic. But the truly astonishing part is what forces – local, state, and ultimately national – rose up to protect him. The even bigger question is: *Why?*

That day was the court hearing for the restraining order I'd filed against Mike Nobles. I showed up expecting to tell the judge my story, offer my evidence, and go on with Mike Nobles excised from my sons' lives.

When I arrived, however, he and Christy were waiting. I was not aware that a motion to dismiss the Domestic Violence Injunctions (DVIs) for Gabe had already been filed the day before.

Christy wouldn't look at me while she stared blankly into the abyss of her own internal hell.

The presiding judge for the hearing was Judge Thomas Santurri, someone I would encounter over and over again.

When Nobles was given the opportunity to speak, he immediately attacked my paternity. I wasn't Gabe's father. Christy then chimed in. She swore that Gabe wasn't mine.

I informed the court that I was, in fact, Gabe's legal father, and that I was prepared to produce documentation, including an affidavit of paternity – an affidavit that both Christy and I had signed – and a birth certificate.

Without preamble or emotion, Santurri dismissed the DVI associated with Gabe on the grounds that, because I wasn't Gabe's father, I had no standing to file the injunction.

Case closed. It took less than fifteen minutes.

* * *

To have a sworn officer of the court so blithely and blatantly ignore the law stunned me in ways I still cannot grasp. Gabe was my legal child.

Christy had willingly signed those papers. Judge Santurri would certainly have been aware of Florida law around affidavits of paternity. This judge had knowingly and willfully placed my sons back in harm's way. But *why?*

That was the question that began to ring in my head, louder and louder: *WHY?*

Out in the parking lot, feeling like I'd just taken a roundhouse to the face, my ringing cell phone brought me back to the moment. It was Mary Smith who had been babysitting the boys for some time. Mary is a kind, pleasantly quirky woman with a heart the size of football stadium. Having taken care of dozens of foster children in addition to her own kids, she has a great many people who call her "Mom." She made it her life's work to care for children.

She described numerous harassing phone calls over the last few days, calls with silence on the other end or immediate hang-ups. My mother and I received the same. But then she launched into a shaky recount of a "meeting" she'd had with Mike Nobles two days before in the parking lot of Food World in Niceville. Nobles had called her and wanted to meet at her house, but she didn't want him anywhere near her place of residence.

"Tell Mark to back off," Nobles said to her. "Tell him to drop the whole thing. If he doesn't, we'll take his kids, and he'll never see them again. You tell him that."

Mary was not only scared for the boys, but she was also frightened for her own safety, and she wanted to warn me. I thanked her, and we hung up. The warnings I had gotten from Tom Dunn might have been justified. But how had Tom Dunn known before I had even made the decision to report Nobles' abuse to the authorities?

With rising alarm, I called Lighthouse Academy to warn them of an imminent kidnapping threat. Principal Joanna Morris took my story seriously.

That afternoon, stewing in a cauldron of anger and incredulity, I called Ed Ferrell, the friend from church who had brought me into the discipleship program. I vented to him for almost half an hour, and he responded with platitudes.

* * *

The next day, Mary called me again to tell me that Christy had just been at her house, distraught and crying. She told Mary that she was happy with the arrangement between us. She didn't want the children, but her father was forcing her to take them.

That night, according to phone records, Christy called Sherri Taylor in Decatur, Alabama, whom the Nobles were trying to hire to hide the boys. Taylor would later offer to testify to that fact, but then retracted her offer because she feared for her life.

* * *

On Oct 30, 2008, in an unrelated case, Florida Congressman Matt Gaetz, an attorney at that time, was arrested in Okaloosa County for DUI after leaving the Swamp nightclub. He was staggering drunk and refused a breathalyzer. State Attorney Bill Eddins refused to bring it to trial and dropped the charges. The Okaloosa County Sheriff Department destroyed the video of the drunken Gaetz's in custody and forced the arresting officer to resign.

* * *

The Attempted Destruction of Mary Smith

Mary Smith paid a high price for trying to protect Gabe and Toby.

On one of the occasions when she testified in court, she moved herself and her family into a hotel room for their safety.

A string of false complaints against her to the DCF began, as part of a concerted effort to destroy her, each of which spawned an investigation. The worst any of the investigations ever found was a dirty towel on the bathroom floor.

Sergeant Joey Forgione of the Niceville PD tried to coerce her into shutting up about my case and general corruption in Niceville and in the DCF, threatening to arrest her African-American foster child.

Mike Nobles called her house and threatened her children. Nobles and his son Billy would ride their motorcycles back and forth in front of her house. He called her employer and slandered her, like he would later to do me. Nobles was working as the head of security at a condominium complex built by Constance Wayne Jones, the developer who built Nobles' house. He was Mary Smith's husband's direct boss. Nobles terrorized her husband to the point he resigned.

Because her husband was a veteran, she received her medical care at the VA. She discovered at one point that a diagnosis of borderline personality disorder had been falsely inserted into her medical records. She had never been diagnosed with any such thing. *She fears for her family's safety to this day.*

Halloween came on the heels of the hearing. I took the boys to school, nervous about what might happen, but I trusted that the school would protect them. I had the day off and I felt the need for some spiritual and social bolstering, so I went to a bible study meeting.

Thanks to phone records, I can lay out the sequence of that day's events. A lot of what occurred can be deduced by reading between the lines.

9:08 A.M. Christy leaves me a strange voicemail asking how I am doing.

9:27 A.M. Christy calls her father.

9:47 A.M. I listen to Christy's voicemail. After the way she had thrown me under the bus two days before, I am immediately suspicious, believing her purpose is to determine my whereabouts.

10:06 A.M. I call the bible study organizer to let him know I am running late.

10:13 A.M. I call Lighthouse Academy to check on the kids. They are reported to be present and fine.

10:14 A.M. Christy, enroute to Lighthouse, attempts to call her father with no answer.

10:15 A.M. She calls her mother, no answer.

10:16 A.M. She calls her sister, Shelly Riggs. No answer.

10:23 A.M. She calls nanny Marilyn Reed. No answer.

10:34 A.M. She tries to call her father again. No answer.

10:34 A.M. She calls her sister again, no answer.

10:36 A.M. Mike Nobles calls Christy back. They talk for nine minutes.

10:45 A.M. She tries again to call Marilyn Reed who is out of town, but Marilyn answers this time. Christy asks where I am and where the boys are.

10:57 A.M. Christy calls her father again, a fifteen-minute call.

11:15 A.M. Christy arrives at Lighthouse and demands to take the boys with her, citing a "family emergency." No one at the school knows who she is, because she has never been there nor ever spoken with or met anyone at the school.

11:23 A.M. Principal Morris calls to inform me Christy is there, acting crazy, claiming there was a family emergency and wanting to take the kids. I immediately drop what I'm doing and head for school. Christy is observably pale and shaking. When asked about getting Gabe's backpack, she says she doesn't need it. She is in a hurry.

11:31 A.M. Principal Morris calls again. She doesn't want to let the kids go, but she fears the legal implications if she refuses.

11:35 A.M. I call the school back and ask to talk to Christy. They put me on the phone with her. Extremely agitated, on the verge of incoherence, she refuses to say why she is taking the kids. I then talk with Principal Morris, who agrees we need to call law enforcement. She calls Officer Doug Bringsman of the Santa Rosa County

Sheriff's Department, an officer she knows because his daughter attends Lighthouse. Bringsman would later pressure Joanna Morris to stay out of the situation and be quiet about it. She didn't. She and the school would soon face retaliation from local officials, blocking her expansion plans, claiming the fire extinguishing system was not to code.

11:36 A.M. I call Officer Bringsman – I also knew him through Lighthouse – and explain the situation to him, that I fear the boys are being abducted.

11:41 A.M. I attempt to call Mary Smith to apprise her of the developing situation, but no answer. I leave a voicemail.

11:47 A.M. I arrive at school. Officer Bringsman and a female officer are already on the scene. Gabe and Toby are in Christy's car, with Christy standing outside of it. Across the parking lot, away from Christy, I show Bringsman my ID. He checks the status of the restraining order against Mike Nobles to determine if he can prevent her from taking the kids. Christy and I do not speak to each other.

It should be noted that the restraining order against Mike Nobles regarding Toby was still in place. Toby's teacher, Bonnie Emmons, would later go on the record saying that Toby didn't want to go with his mother that day. But she grabbed him and took him by force.

11:48 A.M. Nobles calls Christy to check the status of the kidnapping. They remain on the phone for the entirety of the abduction.

12:01 P.M. Female officer is on the phone looking for direction for how to proceed.

12:14 P.M. Mike Nobles calls Christy again, who is still being detained.

12:25 P.M. I ask Bringsman if I can talk to the kids. They look distraught. He speaks to Christy, who agrees. I go to the car and try to reassure them that everything will be okay, that I will pray with them, that I will get them back.

12:26 P.M. Because the injunctions don't include Christy, Bringsman gives Christy the go-ahead to leave, which she does.

Phone records of the next few hours show a flurry of calls between Christy, her sister Shelly Riggs, their father, Shelly's husband Brian, one of their cousins, and Sherri Taylor in Decatur, Alabama. Meanwhile, I was also calling everyone I could think of.

12:41 P.M. I call my sons' therapist, Karleen Shuster, to tell her what was going on. They had an appointment scheduled that day.

1:40 P.M. I call the Okaloosa County Sheriff's department to report the kidnapping. No one responds.

1:51 P.M. Christy calls me asking to meet and discuss the situation. She says she'll meet me at 5:00 P.M. at the Chick-Fil-A in Destin.

3:40 P.M. Christy calls me. Again, she refuses to say why she took the kids or where they are. She says they are not with her. She confirms our meeting at Chick-Fil-A at 5:00 P.M.

I smell a rat, but I have no alternative. What I need is a witness. So, I called my *friend* Ed Ferrell, Deacon of the Destin Church of Christ, but he is unwilling to help me. I settle on another of the church elders, Tommy Carter, who agrees to accompany me to the meeting with Christy. Carter was not part of Mike Nobles/Brad Bynum crowd, and he was unhappy about what he saw going on in the church.

5:00 P.M. Tommy Carter and I arrive at Chick-Fil-A. There's no sign of Christy.

5:06 P.M. A man I've never seen before approaches the car and serves me with a subpoena. The subpoena is for a deposition for court appearance for the restraining order against Nobles, still in effect for Toby.

They could have served me at any time. They knew where I lived. But they timed it for hours after the kids were kidnapped, used them as bait to harass and intimidate me.

The rest of that day is a stunning and mindless blur. I had done everything I could think of doing. I had reached out for help from law enforcement, DCF, Emerald Coast Child Advocacy Center, and my church. Now my boys were back in the hands of a serial sexual predator.

It was one hell of a Halloween, and I don't believe it was a coincidence that this day was chosen for my sons to be kidnapped.

* * *

Upon later investigation, I discovered that the police report of the incident was a complete fabrication. It alleges a simple domestic disturbance regarding custody. It claimed Christy and I had a "…verbal confrontation about parental rights." I stayed away from her until given permission to speak to the boys for the simple fact I didn't want to start a confrontation and never spoke a word to her. She already looked like she'd been through an emotional wringer. In fact, the report references that my conversation was with Officer Brian Wayne London, whose name is listed as preparing the report. He was not even present. I have never met him. The report contains none of the facts presented to the officers by either me, Principal Morris, or anyone from the school. Brian Wayne London has since been convicted of aggravated stalking, grand larceny, and grand theft auto.

The report also claimed that Christy was just picking up the kids at school and that we had an agreement that the kids would live with her. The author of the report claimed I confirmed all of this. I never made any such statement, and this claim would reemerge in Nobles' deposition. In other words, London was repeating another fabrication by Nobles. Words were being put in my mouth. It happened so often I started calling it the Ventriloquist Effect. The truth was, she had long since abandoned the kids and had never been to the school. Yes, it was all a complete fabrication. But by whom and for what purpose?

Furthermore, because it was now an official record in a police report, this false account would be repeated over and over by Mike Nobles in his later testimony, and by local, state, and even federal officials. This story was repeated even after Nobles changed this version. On down the line, it constituted a kind of parrot effect. Whatever Nobles said, authorities would repeat as true, even when he changed his story.

It was the beginning of a disgraceful and disheartening pattern.

* * *

I spent a sleepless night at a complete loss. I felt heartsick and had been failed by every institution I had trusted to protect my children. I didn't know where they were or what was happening to them. I couldn't expunge from my memory the tortured looks on their faces as they sat in Christy's car. After months and years of increasingly sporadic contact, they barely knew her, and she had put them back in the hands of people who abused them. She didn't want them herself; she never had.

November first was a Saturday. I called Ed Ferrell and others from Mike Nobles' church to see if they might help me determine whether the boys were all right. No one called me back.

* * *

This was the first day of what I came to call the Investigation. In conjunction with my banging on every door I could think of to get the boys back, I began to dig into public records, police reports, and newspaper articles, hoping to explain what had happened, hoping to create a documentation trail of the blatant, mind-boggling corruption peppered with a significant amount of institutional incompetence that I was *only beginning* to encounter. It makes sense to assume incompetence first, or else one can fall into paranoid rabbit hole of imagining malevolence and conspiracy everywhere.

My expectations of, and trust in, law enforcement and child protective services, everything I had believed about justice and decency had been thrown into a trash barrel. The things I discovered over the next days, weeks, and months set it all on fire. There were glimmers of hope here and there, like maybe the church could help. Maybe Principal Morris could help. Maybe I could still find some sort of support from a good cop somewhere. What mystified and plagued me was how the authorities could ignore every single report I had filed, every sliver of evidence, in favor of a con man and serial sexual predator. *And as it would turn out, maybe even a cold-blooded killer.* I began to dig.

I was also done with these churches – Destin Church of Christ and Niceville Church of Christ – who swept sexual abuse under the rug. On Sunday, I called Pastor Brad Bynum of the Destin Church of Christ and left a simple message with Claire Hatcher, Mary Smith's mother.

"Ephesians 5:11-12. And have no fellowship with the unfruitful works of darkness, but rather expose them. For it is shameful even to speak of those things which are done by them in secret."

I intended to expose them.

* * *

Brad Bynum called me immediately after he met with Nobles, as verified by a church member. "You should have kept all this in the church. You should never have made these accusations publicly."

I argued with him. How could Nobles possibly be held to account if I hadn't reported him? Evil thrives in the shadows.

"Mark, you are warped, twisted, and unstable," he said. "If you don't stop this, I will publicly rebuke you and disfellowship you. God is against you. He repeatedly cited Mathew 18:15, a scripture that has historically been used by churches to cover up sexual abuse. *'Now if your brother sins, go and show him his fault in private; if he listens to you, you have gained your brother.'* Matthew 18:15."

* * *

I had no doubt he would follow through with trying to destroy my reputation in any way he could. Mike Nobles was the deacon in charge of elementary education at the Destin Church of Christ, and his daughters were routinely put in charge of small children. During our conversation, I got the strong implication that Bynum *knew* what was happening, and that he was on board with whatever Mike Nobles had planned and executed.

What Bynum attempted to do to me was a form of spiritual abuse, a technique in which he was well-practiced. Prior to his installment at the Destin Church of Christ, Brad Bynum was an elder in the Boston Church of Christ, a documented cult that targeted and abused college students. And this threat was also a felony under Florida law.

I should point out that Bynum was the Chaplain for the Okaloosa County Sheriff's Department under Sheriff Charlie Morris, a post he inherited after a rancorous coup in the Destin Church of Christ ousting the former pastor. The former pastor urged me early on to report Nobles. Bynum was also from a military family – his father served in the USAF.

* * *

The next day, I got a phone call from Ed Ferrell, the elderly genteel Alabamian, proposing a meeting with himself and two church elders, Dub Stearn and Al Jordan. He said that they had already met with Mike Nobles, and that the "biggie bottom issues" were Nobles' reputation and my getting my kids back.

Ferrell said, "I think it's a given he would like to see his name cleared, and I think it's a given you would like to save the kids. I realize we are operating under time constraints. We are looking for a solution where everyone comes out whole or not too badly damaged. We are looking for a win-win situation." I recorded the conversations.

What time constraints was he talking about? Obviously, the boys were in immediate danger of more abuse, but it sounded as though he was talking about something else. A deadline.

I agreed to meet them on Wednesday, November 5, at Destin Church of Christ. I wanted to wear a wire and record the meeting, fully intending to have them all prosecuted for conspiracy to kidnapping and extortion, but unfortunately Florida is a two-party state. Nothing I recorded would be admissible in court.

* * *

On November 4, I went to the Okaloosa County Sheriff's Office to try to meet with Sheriff Charlie Morris, still desperate to find any help from law enforcement. If I had to, I was going to talk to every cop in three counties.

Chief Deputy Larry Ashley, a square-jawed, flat-topped man dripping with self-righteous arrogance, intercepted me. I explained the situation and told him I wanted to wear a wire to any meetings. He not only refused to sanction this, but he also refused to take my statement or file a report. Larry Ashley routinely got up before congregations and gatherings of law enforcement officers, wearing his badge and gun, to preach about "God's Law." His speeches were steeped in homophobia and thinly veiled Christian nationalism. After Charlie Morris' conviction, Ashley became sheriff. A department whistleblower described Ashley as a religious fanatic. After consulting with trusted friends and the refusal of the Okaloosa Sheriff's Department to investigate, I decided it was too risky to go to the meeting at the church. It reeked of a setup and a trap. In retrospect, it was wise to heed those alarm bells.

* * *

On November 5, Shelly Riggs, Christy's older sister, brought Toby to ABC Pediatrics in Niceville for a serious eye injury. He had a swollen, infected black eye with green drainage. His aunt claimed to be Toby's guardian and told the attending physician the injury had occurred at school, but he had been removed from school five days previously and hadn't returned. When I last saw him in Christy's car, he had had no injury, and the school attested to this. He still has a small scar.

According to Gabe's later account, what really happened was that Brian Riggs, Shelly's husband, had punched Toby in the eye for stealing something. Toby had a stealing problem that began when he was about three years old. According to his therapists, this and other problems stemmed from an attachment disorder caused by his mother's neglect.

On one unknown date during the abduction, Gabe says he escaped one night from the Nobles' house and ran through the streets of Niceville crying out for help, crying out for me, for anyone who would protect him. He was hunted down like an animal and returned to the Nobles.

* * *

On November 6, Billy Nobles called me and offered to be a "mediary" between me and Mike Nobles. He offered me supervised visits with my children. All I had to do would be to recant everything, say I had lied about everything.

During our conversation, Billy went off on a bizarre rant: "They've always thought this, they've always thought this, that if anything ever hap-

Therapist Karleen Shuster's Second Report

On November 5, 2008, Karleen Shuster made her second report to the abuse hotline expressing concern for the physical safety of the children.

"At an unknown time, Emily/Faith has been fondling Toby and Gabriel. The girls pulled down and yanked on Toby's 'weenie.' Toby did not like the girls pulling on his 'weenie,' and he asked them to stop. The girls told Toby to 'let us do it.' As a result Toby is very aggressive.

"At an unknown time, Emily/Faith fondled Gabriel. It is unknown how Gabriel was fondled. As a result, Gabriel is all over the place and very 'withdrawn.' The grandfather has walked into the room and peaked [sic] at the girls as they fondled Gabriel and Toby. The grandfather did not do anything to prevent this incident from occurring. The mother is also aware of this incident, however she continued to allow the children to go to the grandfather's house.

"There is concern for the children's welfare. On 10/31/08 the mother took the children from school and their whereabouts are unknown. It is believed that the children are with the maternal family. The children's aunts, Emily and Faith, had been molesting the children. It was stated that Faith pulled on Gabriel's penis and squeezed it. Emily also pulled on and slapped Toby's 'weenie.' The children did not like when this happened. The grandfather observed through the door the incidents and would watch all the time. This incident happened '100's of times' as long as no one was around. Their last visit [with me] was on 10/24/08 and the children were a wreck. The mother refuses to tell the father where the children are. As a result of this, Toby was sexually acting out in school and tried to inappropriately touch another boy. Gabriel stated that he did not want to go back to the grandfather's house. The mother has a history of emotional abuse and neglect towards the children. No other detail is known."

This report was filed with the DCF Child Protection Investigator Connie Edgar, with supervisor Kimberly Uberroth. Edgar cut-and-pasted the original child-on-child allegation and closed the report two and half hours later as a "duplicate."

Donna Parish ordered Edgar on November 6 to cease any investigation. Parish claimed that the family had moved to Okaloosa County and the kids were now attending Calvary Christian Academy. All of these were lies.

At this point, Jennifer Clark of the DCF "took over" the case.[1]

---

1. From Mike Nobles' deposition, January 21, 2009.

pened, they were going to keep this stuff from me because they think I might go psycho and like, start to do something."

I had no idea what he was talking about at the time, except that the "they" he was referring to were his parents.

The "stuff" he was referring to was, I believe, what Mike Nobles had buried in his back yard, accessed through a rat hole hidden under a storage shed.

Billy later denied everything to law enforcement and claimed he called me "more or less about my mental capacity." Gaslighting. Since then, I have passed five psychological evaluations and a polygraph.

* * *

That same day, I received a voicemail from Ed Ferrell expressing regret that Mike Nobles and I had not come to "some positive resolution," confirming the motive for taking my sons and his own part in negotiating.

I called him back and unloaded on him for using my children as pawns. I told him I recorded the previous conversations.

He accused me of betraying him and hung up. He later lied to the police and denied this had ever happened, claiming that he had only called to ask about my health. More gaslighting.

* * *

Throughout all of this, several people, including the kids' therapist and school principal, urged me to go find the kids and get them. There was nothing legally preventing me from doing that, but my gut told me it would end very badly. I wouldn't find out until later just how right my gut was. I have no doubt I would have been killed or imprisoned.

Records reflect that on November 6, the new Child Protective Investigator from DCF, Jennifer Clark, spoke with Christy and the kids, whom she instructed to file a restraining order against me and continue hiding the children from me. At this meeting, she had to have clearly seen Toby's awful, infected black eye, but disregarded it as a "bump." She claimed this injury occurred when Toby fell and hit a table at school. *This incident, which I confirmed with the school, never happened.* Clark never contacted the school or the nanny. *She refused to.*

During this meeting, the boys asked to see me, but their request was denied. They were told their father was "sick and needs time to get better."

* * *

The number of people involved kept increasing and multiplying in disturbing profusion. Some of Florida DCF's multitude of failures can be chalked up to incompetence, but at a certain point, a distinct malevolence begins to come into focus. That focus began to sharpen with the involvement of CPI Jennifer Clark, wife of a military special operations soldier.

Christy took this advice and filed a Domestic Violence Injunction against me in Okaloosa County, most likely written by her father and CPI Clark. The restraining order alleged that I was stalking Christy, that I was a "deadbeat dad," and that I was abusive and mentally ill. The report mentions CPI Clark by name as having instructed Christy to file the injunction. The report claims I showed Mike Nobles a list of places Christy had been, and that constituted stalking. The truth is that I had almost no knowledge of Christy's life by this point. There was no such list. For the day of the abduction, she claimed she was just picking up the boys from school when I showed up. The police were called, and I was detained. Christy had claimed to be "afraid" I was planning to kidnap the boys and "flee the state or flee the country."

I smelled Mike Nobles all over that report. The entire basis for calling me mentally ill was that I had reported Nobles and sought a restraining order.

The narrative of the injunction mirrors Clark's report almost verbatim and was approved with only Clark's and Mike Nobles' phone numbers as supporting evidence.

* * *

The case was later transferred to Santa Rosa County in a convoluted scheme of judge shopping. The case subsequently landed on the bench of Judge Thomas Santurri.

It was starting to feel like there was a large corrupt funnel constructed to swat away cases such as mine like gnats on an elephant's backside. I have no paranoid delusions that this was all about me – although Mike Nobles and his cronies were most definitely out to get me – but it was much bigger than that, and I had just found myself in a giant invisible web.

As I mentioned earlier, Jennifer Clark's supervisor at DCF was Donna Parish. DCF records confirm that Donna Parish instructed Clark to advise Christy to file the restraining order. Clark had claimed I was "erratic and unstable" for believing that my children were being sexually abused, even though there was proof. Her report specifically states that all this was already investigated and proved unfounded.

Both Jennifer Clark and Donna Parish worked out of the Emerald Coast Child Advocacy Center (ECCAC) under Tom Dunn.

* * *

On November 7, Karleen Shuster gave me a letter of professional opinion describing me as a loving, caring father. Her letter documented disclosures of sexual abuse, and that in her professional opinion, sexual abuse was occurring in the Nobles' home. Her report to the DCF should have resulted in an Amber Alert, but instead it became an "All Agencies Assist" report by Clark in order to frame me.

Caught in a web of lies, with extortion demands caught on tape, following written instructions from Church of Christ member and DCF Supervisor at the ECCAC, Donna Parish, Clark filed police reports with three different agencies – the Okaloosa County Sheriff's Department, Santa Rosa County Sheriff's Department, and the DCF. She claimed I was "continually making reports to the hotline alleging sexual abuse," reports that were "already found to be unsubstantiated." She knew the report was made by Karleen Shuster, who had expressed "grave concern" for the physical safety of the children. She knew I had only made one report, and in that report, there was a finding. She also knew that there was a long history of abuse in the Nobles' home, including findings by previous investigators.

This was all an attempt to falsify records and frame me. Why? To discredit me and pressure me into shutting up. A Church of Christ deacon had kidnapped my kids. The other deacons were engaged in an extortion scheme. I had been threatened by the Church of Christ pastor who served as the Sheriff's Chaplain, and now another Church of Christ DCF official was trying to put me in prison after a therapist made a report.

It is a textbook tactic used by gaslighting abusers to accuse the victim of the crimes perpetrated, in fact, by the abuser. I was asking too many questions and trying to collect actual proof. I was backing them into a corner. This began a pattern of culpability and cover-up.

Every time "Mickey" Nobles was backed into a corner, forces would crawl out of the woodwork to try to discredit and frame me.

Like clockwork...

CHAPTER SEVEN

VANISHED IN THE NIGHT: PANDORA'S BOX

E very day brought a new series of events, outrages, and escalation; some I was aware of at the time, some didn't emerge until later. It was an exhausting, never-ending whirlwind of phone calls, emails, meetings, and encounters.

Throughout it all, I kept one of Toby's Bakugan toys in my pocket as a sort of talisman, reminding me of what I was fighting for.

It should be noted that at this time, after being instructed to do so by the boys' therapist, I filed only a single report of child sexual abuse, and there was a legitimate finding, though no real investigation.

By this point, Donna Parish had all the information from the boys' therapist. She had the initial report with its finding of "indicators of sexual abuse." She had access to accounts of Christy's lack of contact with her children. There were at least two prior reports with findings of abuse, one that found "some indicators" and another that determined "inadequate supervision." In other words, child-on-child abuse occurred due to inadequate supervision. And she knew of prior reports regarding foster children in Nobles' home. Records that would disappear.

All child protection parties had been apprised of the history of the abuse in the Nobles' home. And yet, the report Parish later stated in a response to an Inspector General complaint: "There is no basis for this allegation." Even worse, Parish's account of the abduction was a complete falsehood, to which Principal Morris and Kathleen Shuster later testified.

The mother picked up the children from school on October 31, 2008. The school contacted the father, and the father came to the school. Law enforcement responded and advised the father that there was no custody arrangement in place and that the mother had the right to take the children; there was nothing they could do. The CPI obtained a copy of the [law enforcement] report concerning this incident and had no reason to believe that the mother had kidnapped the children, as the LE report stated otherwise. Furthermore, there is no evidence that the CPI instructed or assisted the mother in obtaining the injunction against the father. Documentation in the Notes indicates that this was the mother's idea and plan.[1]

But why would they create this elaborate web of lies? The answer to that would come later.

Donna Parish's father not only founded the Boggy Bayou Church of Christ, but he was also an Army Air Corps veteran, as was her mother, Walter Ruckel, Wanda Nobles' father, and others associated with this web. Old military families all. Boggy Bayou is effectively part of Niceville.

Note that Clark, Parish, and Dunn, all the way up the chain of command, all denied in writing having anything to do with Christy's restraining order against me, even though Christy stated in the injunction that it was Clark who instructed her to do it, and the case files prove it.

* * *

In my desperate quest to find someone in law enforcement who would listen and do something, a member of Calvary Chapel connected me with Nancy Locke, a woman who trained cadaver dogs and worked with various local law enforcement entities. She had tremendous law enforcement connections going all the way to the federal level, including then FBI Director, and later the Special Counsel who investigated Donald Trump, Robert Mueller. At the time all this happened, Mueller was Director of the FBI. In Locke I found someone who gave credence to my story and wanted to help. She advised me to make a report to the Florida Abuse Hotline and told me to use specific language: "I fear for the lives and safety of my sons." This would require an immediate amber alert and response by law enforcement. When she tried to help me herself, she was stonewalled the same as I was.

The Nobles' Foster Children

When I first started dating Christy, I became aware of some of the Nobles family history. Christy spoke occasionally of how the Nobles household had taken in a number of foster children when she was younger. She had two photos of them with their names and showed me a letter she had received from one of them, which was signed, "Your foster sister."

In his deposition on December 12, 2008, Mike Nobles testified under oath that he had in fact had foster children in his house in the early 1990s, that he and Wanda had gone through the mandated classes and paperwork for being foster parents. According to Nobles, the DCF *asked* him to be a foster parent.

Around the time of my children's abduction, Mary Smith told me about reports, shown to her by an ECCAC employee, that those children had been removed from the Nobles' home and the Nobles' status as a foster family was revoked for abuse.

Today, the State of Florida "has no record" that Mike Nobles was ever a foster parent.

So, I made that call at 9:24 A.M. on November 8. I explained in detail the sexual abuse allegations, the Domestic Violence Injunctions and violations, the kidnapping, the extortion demands, and the fact that my sons had been concealed from their primary guardian for eight days. I specifically used the language, "I fear for their lives and safety," because Nancy Locke had advised me that this specific language would trigger an investigation. I called back at 2:22 P.M. and confirmed the report was received and accepted. Note that this was after Parish and Clark tried to have me framed for filing multiple spurious police reports. Until this point, there had been *eight* reports filed, but only one of them by me.

And the response was ... nonexistent.

Nothing happened.

* * *

It was around this time I took roughly a month of personal leave from work. I was in no state to fly an airplane. Over the next interminable weeks, I could not sleep or eat. I lost thirty pounds. It was a state of emotional misery I wouldn't wish on anyone. The frustration, outrage, and helplessness took an enormous toll. It was a series of betrayals by a system I had been taught to trust that traumatizes me to this day. When I returned to work, I had to make several trips to Canada where I was routinely detained at customs because of this phony restraining order. It was humiliating.

On November 9, after services at Calvary Chapel, a bible study group leader took pity on my plight and offered to help me raise money through the church to hire an attorney to get the kids back. His kindness was blocked by Joe Prestridge, who later demanded that I shut up about the abuse my sons suffered and demanded that I "submit to his spiritual authority." I would later learn that Nobles had mailed Clark's report to the church and called the pastor who had concealed this from me. When I found out and confronted him, he refused to give it to me.

This forced me to start asking the question more and more: what were all these churches wanting so desperately to cover up? It felt like Joe Palmer and Brad Bynum all over again.

* * *

I knew now that I desperately needed a powerful attorney. I went to the office of Ed Fleming, the high-powered lawyer who had approached me at Calvary Chapel. George Bush's former attorney who had offered to be guardian ad litem for my kids.

When I entered his office, however, he was visibly nervous, seemingly uncomfortable that I would be seen there. Instead of taking my case himself, he quickly referred me to another attorney by the name of Betty Thomas. Still hoping desperately that I might find someone to help me, I retained her with every penny I could scrape together, including asking for help from friends and family, $3,500.

* * *

November 10 was an eventful day on several fronts.

Toby was taken to the doctor to check up on his eye, which was improved but still very much black and blue.

Faith and Emily Nobles were interviewed by the Child Protection Team at the Niceville Child Advocacy Center. Toby and Gabe were also supposed to be interviewed, but their session was rescheduled. I suspect this happened because Toby still had a black eye, and somebody didn't want that on camera.

In a mind-boggling breach of confidentiality, Mike Nobles, who had been reported to have abused both his children and mine, was invited into the Emerald Coast Child Advocacy Center where the therapist provided him with details of the interviews with Faith and Emily. Play therapy had suggested to the therapist that terrible things had happened to Faith and Emily. Mike Nobles, the accused perpetrator, later confirmed in a deposition that he had direct knowledge of the details of these interview sessions.

A professional I asked about this, who wished to remain anonymous, called it a "gross violation of ethics and rules to allow Nobles into the Child Advocacy Center and to provide him with details of his children's play therapy. He shouldn't have been allowed in the building.[2]"

* * *

That same day was the first time Betty Thomas appeared in court on my behalf before Judge Stone in Okaloosa County where Christy had filed a DVI against me. Betty informed me, *after the fact,* that she had made a deal with Christy to transfer the case to Santa Rosa County, where my case and Christy's case would be heard together. Judge Thomas Santurri would hear the case, the same judge who had dismissed my injunction against Mike Nobles for Gabe's safety. She tells me that we'll have an advantage because she used to serve as a clerk for him.

It was all another set up. I had not only just set $3,500 on fire, but it had also caused my case tremendous harm. She had made this deal without consulting me.

The case was transferred to Santa Rosa County, but not initially to Judge Santurri. But then, for unknown reasons, the case was transferred to Judge Santurri's court. That she knew in advance it would be assigned to him suggests "the fix was in." I felt like I was in a funnel facing the same corrupt authorities over and over again.

* * *.

I spent several days making phone calls and visiting the courthouse to report DVI violations. Mike Nobles was still under a restraining order to stay away from Toby, but the boys were in the Nobles' residence. Judge Santurri somehow "lost" all my filings. They wouldn't be recorded for months and there would be no hearing for over a year.

A few days later, I called Theresa Gomez of DCF, laying everything out for her as I had already done so many times. She already was quite familiar with who I was. I pressed her on the DCF's failure to investigate the Nobles' family's crimes in any meaningful way, but she got nervous and refused to comment. Instead of making any attempt to address the questions, she told me repeatedly to simply file for divorce.

Telling me to file for divorce when they should have been protecting my kids became a bizarre mantra. *Over and Over.* Why would "they" continue to pressure me to file for divorce when that was never the issue? The relationship between Christy and I had *nothing* to do with the fact that my children were in danger from a serial sexual abuser, and *I* had been painted as the bad guy. The reason was: if I filed for divorce, then all my allegations would be painted as stemming from a custody dispute. The same claim was used in the Palmer case.

* * *

I sent a desperate email to Tom Dunn, blasting the DCF's failure to respond. He did not reply. Later he asked me not to email or call him at work. I was told only to call him on his cell phone. Up until this point, I had assumed that he was on my side, that he was dealing with me in good faith. But now I began to question what was going on with him too.

The pattern that was emerging was that certain people with things to hide had successfully begun to paint me as some kind of crackpot making spurious, unfounded police reports against a prominent member of the community. This characterization plagued every interaction I had with law enforcement and child protection officials throughout this ordeal, even those who might have been well-meaning, earnest professionals. *Word was getting around that I was a crazy deadbeat dad.*

* * *

I tried to report Nobles' restraining order violations to the Santa Rosa County Sheriff's Office where Deputy Kyle and his supervisor attempted to intimidate me, refused to take my report, and called it a "tit for tat" between me and Nobles. My attorney intervened. As soon as they called Betty Thomas, they became willing to take my report. The report stated that an arrest warrant would be issued for Mike Nobles, but this request was blocked, and no arrest warrant was ever issued.[3] Betty did nothing about this.

On November 25, Gabe and Toby were interviewed by the Child Protection Team at the Niceville Child Advocacy Center. The stated purpose of this interview, from Donna Parish's notes, dated November 8, 2008, at 9:40 P.M., was "to make sure nothing happened." Not "to find out what happened." I was unaware of this interview until maybe a year later. During that interview, both boys disclosed sexual abuse and sexual assault, nearly identical disclosures to what I had reported in September. They described twelve-year-old Faith, victim turned perpetrator, sexually abusing four-year-old Toby while Gabe watched. They had told their grandmother who, as always, covered for her husband and family.

This disclosure was buried by Jennifer Clark.

* * *

That same day, I requested a meeting with Tom Dunn of ECCAC, Sergeant Joey Forgione of the Niceville PD, and Jennifer Clark, the investigator from DCF. The patterns that had emerged were beyond disturbing, and I wanted to confront some of the people involved and demand answers. Jennifer Clark was the only one who showed up. This was my first face-to-face encounter with her, and found her to be cold, calculating, and utterly callous toward the welfare of my children.

Clark later called therapist Karleen Shuster, who affirmed the boys' disclosures,[4] but Clark pretended the call failed. Shuster confirmed that was a lie.

At one point, Clark looked me in the eye and told me that therapist Nicole Fryback of the Child Advocacy Center determined during the boys' interview that "nothing happened." Nicole Fryback would later testify to the contrary, further incriminating Clark, Dunn, and others in this web of lies.

I provided Clark with Shuster's written statement as I did to other DCF investigators. That and every other incriminating document was purged from the case files.

By this time, I had lost the capacity for shock. As the lies, misrepresentations, and stonewalling mounted, I began to expect it from everyone I encountered, but Clark's bald-faced lies were among the most egregious.

I played her my recordings of Billy Nobles threatening to "go psycho" on me and one of Ed Ferrell trying to extort me. She listened without comment.

I gave her copies of Christy's journal entries fantasizing about suicide and infanticide and perpetually engaging in sexual relationships with multiple men. Repeated references to sacrifices, crucifixion, hell, Satan, and demons, being locked in a cage and imprisoned in a hole. She plotted revenge against her lovers. She acted out sexually, including having sex with multiple men in the same day. Pages filled with self-hatred, toxic shame, and belief that she was condemned to hell. There was paranoia and fear everyone was going to learn her secret. Repeated gruesome religious references. All of these were dated when Christy was aged 17-26. There were dates included. These records and every subsequent incriminating record I gave Clark were omitted from the DCF case files.

I showed her a photo album full of the names and faces of foster children that had been in the Nobles' home, one of whom had written to Christy and signed, "your foster sister." They had been removed for abuse, but these records would be destroyed.

Clark simply sat there stone-faced and silent.

I ultimately left her office beside myself with disgust.

* * *

Jennifer Clark later denied that these foster children existed. The State of Florida says it "has no record" and that Mike Nobles was never a foster parent.

In her report on this meeting, she lied about everything: the disclosures my sons made earlier that day, the evidence I showed her.

Her report states:

CPI [Clark] explained that the boys had been interviewed at the CAC this afternoon by an expert who specializes in [sexual abuse] with children and he did not believe that they indicated sexual abuse … [Harris] wanted the CPI to look at a scrapbook and read the poems that his wife and friends had written when she was twelve to show what her life was life. The scrapbook was typical of any twelve-year-old girl, no indicators of trauma to the [mother] at that age.[5]"

Other professionals – Dr. DeShon and Counselor Ron Long – had viewed Christy's journals, met with her several times, and they all concluded she had been horrifically abused as a child, and that she was a danger to herself and her children. Christy had documented symptoms of textbook borderline personality disorder and complex PTSD in her journals. But Clark characterized them as "…normal words of a twelve-year-old girl." What on earth would Clark characterize as *abnormal*?

* * *

The mountains of stonewalling I endured propelled me to pursue the question: *WHY!?* There had to be some underlying web of connections powerful enough to make people commit felonies such as fraud and obstruction of justice. There had to be one or more puppet masters pulling strings. What I hadn't noticed yet was that they all had military and religious ties. Why were so many entities going to such lengths to prevent a scrawny little swindler, serial abuser, and federal convict the likes of Mike Nobles from being called to justice for his crimes? Why were they putting their own livelihoods on the line to do so?

Throughout those horrific couple of months, I made myself an expert in acquiring public records: real estate filings, child protection reports, police reports, newspaper articles. I followed every lead I could scrape up, went down every rabbit hole that crossed my path, and discovered that some of those rabbit holes went *all* the way down. There were County Clerks and the librarians – who oversaw the microfiche – who knew me by name.

I sensed the presence of invisible – possibly nefarious – connections all around me. Those were the only reasonable explanations for what was happening. When I began to uncover them, my shock and dismay grew with each discovery.

What came to be revealed was a web so convoluted and complex it was difficult to tell where it began. Furthermore, it wasn't just one web, but several overlapping ones.

In my quest for answers, I enlisted all the help I could. Joanna Morris, the Lighthouse principal, ran a background check on Mike Nobles and gave it to me. Names like Leslie Michael Osman, Nobles' attorney, and Jerry McCormick, his business partner in the restaurant business and other ventures, appeared in the background check. It also included a real estate property in Walton County that puzzled me.

* * *

It was a shot in the dark, but I was desperate for answers, so I went to Walton County to investigate this property. It was in the Lake Sharon subdivision, a postage stamp area called Freeport along State Highway 20 East of Niceville. The property was numbered 8 Gale Court. I found the house on a narrow asphalt road buried in trees, the kind of place no one would ever go to by accident. There were neighbors on every side, but vegetation blocked any curious eyes on the adjacent property. It turned out that the house had been renumbered to 9 Gale Court for some reason. A not uncommon practice in the real estate world is that if a crime or terrible event happens at a particular address, the number of the property will be changed so that the property is no longer associated with the event. People who go looking for the site of an infamous occurrence can no longer search for it. Names associated with the house included Mike Nobles, his business Partner Jerry McCormick (who built it and had lived there), and their attorney and partner Leslie Michael Osman, also McCormick's brother-in-law. All Church of Christ leaders.

I knocked on the neighbor's door to see if they knew anything about the history of the house. While I waited for someone to come to the door, I saw a pet hedgehog through the window. A blustery, flat-topped, boar-jowled white man in his sixties or seventies came to the door, beady-eyes narrowing.

"Yeah?"

I said, "Hi, I'm wondering if you could tell me anything about that house next door, 9 Gale Court."

"What do you want?"

Through his open door, I could see stacks and stacks of papers, like one might see in an episode of *Hoarders.* "I was wondering about the history of that house— "

"There's nothing in the house!"

His vehemence pushed me back off the step.

"Look, I'm sorry to bother you, but if you don't mind, I just want to ask a couple of questions – "

His voice rose to a shout. "You can't see inside the house!"

"I never asked to see the house—"

"I said you can't see inside the house! Get the hell out of here before I call the police!"

"Look, sir, sorry, but—"

His eyes blazed. "I said get out of here before I call the cops!"

I raised my hands and backed away.

He stormed back inside and slammed the door.

* * *

As I returned to my car, which was parked on the narrow street, I spotted a neighbor who lived across the street watering her garden. She had witnessed the entire spectacle and gestured me over. I found her much friendlier. We sat down in the shade, her husband came out, and the two of them told me about their belligerent neighbor, Charles Merkel, a retired U.S. Army major, decorated Vietnam veteran turned military contractor. He owned both his own house and the one next door at 9 Gale Court.

No one had been living in it for years. Jerry McCormick, Mike No-bles' business partner, built it, owned it, and was the last to occupy it. He had sold it to another Niceville Church of Christ member, Melissa Dye, in 2005 for $350,000. However, she never moved in, never had any visible activity there, and only came to check on the property occasionally. Charles Merkel bought the property in April 2008 out of foreclosure, after which it continued to sit vacant.

The neighbors had to call the fire department for two large mysterious fires that had broken out on the property even though no one lived there.

They lamented to me that their quiet neighborhood had been "…taken over by fundamentalists and survivalists," of which Merkel was one of the more problematic. According to the neighbors, he had a virtual Confederate Museum and an arsenal of weapons in his house. I mused that this was the perfect neighborhood to hide such a thing. Merkel venerated George Armstrong Custer to the point he wrote a book about him, which he self-published in 1977. Also in his museum, there existed a number of Custer-related relics.

Merkel used to play bridge with Jerry McCormick and a Catholic priest who lived in the neighborhood and was apparently harboring an underage boy, which the neighbors found suspicious.

I later found photos on the web of Charles Merkel with Florida governor Rick Scott,[6] as well Iran-Contra figure Richard Secord and Florida Congressman Jeff Miller, an ultra-right-wing Christian conservative and Freemason who sat on the House Intel and House Armed Services Committees, and whose District Representative's husband was Judge Thomas Santurri. Merkel was close enough with the congressman that Miller read Merkel's service record into the Congressional Record. This guy was the epitome of a hard-headed hard charger, an ex-military stereotype. Merkel is the vice president of Lake Sharon Incorporated and has served as a director previously. Other directors have included Kevin Jerome, past owner of 2 Kathy Lane West, and Oscar Ferrell, another resident. Ferrell is a member of the Crestview Masonic Lodge and the District Deputy Grand Master, the highest office in the Masonic District.

How many degrees of separation are required before a connection becomes irrelevant?

All these connections were threads in a web.

* * *

This chance meeting proved to be the opening of a Pandora's Box, a flurry of names and connections that ought to require a warehouse-sized white board to keep straight if this were a television crime drama. It all made my head spin. Have you ever blithely opened an old rickety cellar door, lifted a piece of random backyard junk, or disturbed a piece of derelict machinery and were unpleasantly surprised by a seething nest of angry wasps?

That was what happened that day.

In the course of our conversation, the neighbors told me about another property about a block away at 2 West Kathy Lane, a split-level house bordered by trees on all sides. In the 1990s, the owner had housed many oddly withdrawn foster children and had frequent friendly visits by Walton County Sheriff's Deputies.

The owner and foster parent was a "Frenchman" named Michel Raphael Barthelemy, a French national married to a Panama City stripper. He threw around money like crazy, buying new sports cars and installing a new swimming pool and a large radio transmission antenna, the likes of a ham radio transmission tower. Then, one night, he and his wife and all the foster children disappeared and were never seen again. Computer equipment, cameras, and a cache of child pornography were found in the house and apparently made to disappear.

Barthelemy was a donor to National Republican Congressional Committee, which I believe was illegal as he is a foreign national. I have been able to confirm that Barthelemy is French and has since returned France. His Facebook page is full borderline pornographic posts by very young looking men, and he has an international friends list of powerful people. He also had ties to the Past Master of the Herman Masonic lodge, who was also a military veteran of Eglin AFB, through another property associated with him. Meanwhile, a recent view of the wife's Facebook reveals she is a homophobic, ultra-right conspiracy theorist. The address of one of the corporations incorporated by the couple is a vacant lot

Was this part of a human trafficking operation exploiting foster children. A honey trap?

* * *

It was so hard to believe that, just to make sure these nice folks weren't feeding me a line, I went to the house next door to 2 West Kathy Lane, and those neighbors told me the same sordid story – a sketchy French guy with a sketchy wife, frequent law enforcement visits, and a house full of sullen foster kids, all of whom disappeared in the middle of the night. *Three neighbors told me the same story.*

Public records show that Barthelemy's house was originally built by Charles Kelly, a researcher for the National Advisory Committee for Aeronautics (NACA), the predecessor of NASA. Kelly was married to a woman who had been a secretary in the Pentagon for some years, Elsie Kelly.[7] After NACA, Charles Kelly became a test engineer at Eglin AFB, and later a real estate developer.

According to public records, Michel Raphael Barthelemy had founded a corporation named Worldwide Internet Access, which had some sort of contract with the Walton County Sheriff's Department, purported to be Internet technology related. The president of the company was named as Rob-Roy McGregor. Other officers included Robert Lewis and Dennis E. Smith.

When I started following threads like this, commonalities started popping up, like notes in a dissonant chord.

* * *

After my visit to Kathy Lane and Gale Court in Walton County, I had realized something was off on the background check that had led me there, and the niggling problem was with these property transactions.

Then I remembered visiting the former home of Pastor Joe Palmer, after the Nobles had moved in. I had observed a space that didn't add up. The size of a small room. When I asked Nobles, he claimed it was a "dead space." What was up with these houses, all tied to Church of Christ leaders? This issue led me to investigate the history of Mike Nobles' house, 1118 Rhonda Drive in Niceville, so I dug into every public record I could find.

The land had been originally owned by Charles Walter Ruckel II, a billionaire land baron from the Florida panhandle and his son Stephen Ruckel, a member of the Christian Coalition. Ruckel owned huge swaths of property across that area. He sat on the board of trustees for the Emerald Coast Child Advocacy Center. He was a leader in the John Birch Society,[8] the extreme right-wing fringe political organization that was a precursor to the Republican party splinter group calling itself the Tea Party. He had been appointed by Mr. Robert Welch himself. Ruckel served on the Executive Council with none other than oil baron Nelson Bunker Hunt, who had taken out the infamous newspaper ad "Welcome Mr. Kennedy" attacking the president on the day of his assassination. Hunt and fellow Bircher Larry McDonald, also a JBS peer of Ruckel on the Executive Council, were involved in the Iran Contra scandal and created the Western Goals Foundation, a civilian front for the CIA. Today it has morphed into a cadre of extreme, right-wing activist oligarchs bent on strangling the federal government until it no longer exists in any meaningful way.

According to the Southern Poverty Law Center, the John Birch Society "advocate[s] or adhere[s] to extreme antigovernment doctrines."[9] They call it a "Patriot Group," but this designation lumps it in with the most extreme splinter militias that pepper remote areas across the U.S., one step short of calling them a hate group. General Edwin Walker, who some believe helped plan the Kennedy assassination, was also a leader in the John Birch Society, as was an apparent conspirator in a Chicago plot to kill the president, Thomas Vallee. This plot involved Cuban Nationals, and Secret Service Agent Abraham Bolden was framed by the federal government for trying to expose it, just as I would be framed.

* * *

RobRoy McGregor

Named after a Robin Hood-type character, president of Worldwide Internet Access, RobRoy McGregor was the Director of the U.S. Procurement for the Department of Defense, Department of Research and Analysis under Presidents Carter, Reagan, and George H.W. Bush. He was a West Point graduate with a master's degree in nuclear engineering.

McGregor's son, RobRoy McGregor II, wrote the following in his father's obituary: "Chautauqua Est Delenda, till we meet again, Dad, in heaven on Earth."

Chautauqua est delenda is translated as "Chautauqua must be destroyed." An obscure phrase, but it appears to have originated in *The Equinox*, the periodical published by the sex magic cult known as A∴A∴, headed by Aleister Crowley[1], who was commenting on the work of Helena Blavatsky, the nineteenth century Russian mystic and occultist who founded Theosophy.[2]

Years after his father's death, RobRoy McGregor was interviewed in *Emerald Coast Magazine*. The article states:

McGregor is currently riding across his ancestors' hometown of Glasgow, Scotland, and working on a new exhibit, "The 13 Acacia Trees of Life Art Project."

"The tree of life in art has been a mystical concept alluding to the interconnectedness of all life on our planet," McGregor says. "In Egyptian mythology, it is said that Isis and Osiris emerged from the Acacia Tree of Saosis, the Egyptian tree of life. In the Hebrew/Christian bibles, the tabernacle and the Ark of the Covenant were both made of acacia wood, and the burning bush was an acacia tree."

Occult father, occult son.

1. https://hermetic.com/crowley/libers/lib71/index
2. https://en.wikipedia.org/wiki/Helena_Blavatsky

Robert Lewis

Robert Lewis was an officer of another corporation, in partnership with another Church of Christ minister from Alabama, John Mark Hicks, who is now a professor at the Church of Christ's Lipscomb University.

This same Lipscomb University is associated with James Allen, of the Destin Church of Christ, and Ty Osman, who founded Solomon Builders, a construction company based in Tennessee. Ty Osman's brother is Leslie Michael Osman, the attorney Mike Nobles engaged to clean up his messes.

Lewis was the pastor of the Oakwood Hills Church of Christ in DeFuniak Springs and later active in the same church as Ty Osman in Nashville. Ty was one of Nobles partners.

Building on the empire started by his father and grandfather, James E. Plew,[10] Ruckel became one of the most powerful men in Florida. His father had partnered with Al Capone[11] in the founding of Niceville, Florida.[12]

In cooperation with Robert Lee Fulton Sikes,[13] the Ruckel family "donated" much of the property to Eglin AFB, a deal that no doubt funneled incredible wealth into his coffers,[14] as they developed the land. The federal government poured in money, brought in contractors and land buyers.

Named after Robert E. Lee, Sikes was the son of a Confederate soldier, a virulent segregationist, one of those old-time Southern Democrats. Like so many other bigots and neo confederates of his time, he was also a Scottish Rite Knight Templar 32nd degree Freemason, Knight Commander Court of Honor, Knights of the Red Cross of Constantine, Shriner, and member of the Crestview Lodge.

I should point out that Knights Templar degrees are the only degrees of Freemasonry that require one to be a professed Christian. You could say they are Christian Crusaders in their minds. Sikes career in Congress ended in 1976 when he was reprimanded by the House of Representatives (the vote was 361-4) for fi-

The History of Niceville

In the early 1900s, it was called Boggy. The area is called the Emerald Coast, but along with Lower Alabama it's often called the Redneck Riviera for its natural beauty, beautiful bay and coastline, and population of Good Ol' Boys. Back then it was sparsely populated.

All of this made it popular for a guy you've heard of named Al Capone. Back in the 1920s and 30s, Capone often came to golf in Florida, escaping bitter Chicago winters, and bought a house for his wife in Miami for $100,000.

The coastline was perfect for bootleggers during Prohibition, with isolated, hard-to-reach areas, smooth seas, easy landing places – and no prying eyes. Untold barrels of Cuban rum passed through Choctawhatchee Bay.

In March 1930, Florida governor Doyle E. Carlton tried to banish Capone from Florida, ordering law enforcement to detain Capone wherever they found him and escort him to the state border with orders not to return. However, "[o]nce you explore the track record of many panhandle sheriffs, it's not too difficult to understand why the Governor's wishes weren't carried out. In fact the behavior of many law enforcement agents towards Capone, almost revering him as a celebrity, meant that he was untouchable."[1]

There is little photographic evidence that Capone frequented the Florida panhandle, except for recently uncovered photos of him vacationing in Panama City, but oral histories abound. The story goes that Capone sometimes referred to the Boggy area as "Niceville," and the residents adopted the name. Family histories all through the area have Al Capone stories. Capone became somewhat of a local celebrity, a folk hero, with accounts of people cheering as his long, black limousine rolled down the streets. The people of this area nursed a deep streak of disdain and distrust of authority, especially "outside" authority, and they still do, even as nowadays they offer endless lip service to "law and order."

1. Buccellato, Robert, *Rum Runners and Moonshiners of Old Florida*, Createspace, 2019, p. 107.

nancial misconduct, using his seat for personal gain.[15] He did not seek re-election. No doubt he profited handsomely, however, from the placement of Eglin Air Force Base in his district.

Ruckel was a pro-military icon in northwest Florida. For years, he was the Master of Ceremonies for parades in Niceville, a town that still honors his family as well as Bob Sikes.

For Ruckel and others, the John Birch Society was apparently too liberal and level-headed, so they split off and founded the Freedom First Society which propagates Qanon-style nonsense and conspiracy theories.[16] He was responsible for founding the Air Force Armament Museum in 1985.[17]

When he died in 2012, he was eulogized in Congress by Congressman Jeff Miller.[18]

* * *

Charles Walter Ruckel II was a man with tremendous influence, enormous piles of money, and deep ties with the military-industrial complex, an empire built in part on early twentieth-century ties with the Mafia. He owned the land upon which 1118 Rhonda Drive was built during it's construction, although someone else obtained the permit

His son, Stephen Ruckel, is the heir to the Ruckel empire and heavily involved with evangelical endeavors. He is an officer of Vanguard Ministries.[19] He was also the president of Vanguard Bank. A vanguard is the leading part of an advancing military formation. *Onward Christian Soldiers*! He was once the president of the Military Bankers Association and a professor at Pat Robertson's Regent University. He also served as the two-time president of the United Way.

Rhonda Drive was named after Stephen Ruckel's wife, and cross streets were named after his children. Obviously, a special place for the Ruckels.

The permit to build the house was filed in 1986 by Constance Wayne Jones at the request of Mike and Wanda Nobles. 1986 was an eventful year for Mike Nobles. He was neck deep in the white supremacist anti-government organizations, Posse Comitatus and Patriot Network. These networks epitomized the extreme right-wing Patriot movement of the 1980s.[20] Nobles was married to the daughter of a Niceville Church of Christ Elder and military veteran. He worked for Jerry McCormick, a Niceville Church of Christ Elder, and a builder who owned Subway restaurants. Their attorney was Leslie Michael Osman, McCormick's brother-in law and an elder at the Hialeah Church of Christ where McCormick's father had been an elder. Osman was simultaneously involved in a major racketeering case involving mobsters and politicians (including the mayor of Hialeah) that ultimately got the attention of the White House. Nobles flipped and made a deal in 1986, as did Osman a few years later in separate unrelated cases. These racketeering activities involved extortion, bribery, and rezoning (real estate fraud). During that period, Osman had signed a power of attorney for McCormick to do real estate deals for him in the Florida Panhandle.

Directly before this, Osman and his brothers opened numerous Subway restaurants through pyramids of shell corporations. Nobles and Jerry McCormick were two of the partners. I believe this was strictly a money laundering operation. One of the other partners, Allen Amavanto, had five aliases. He told me the restaurants never made a dime.

The bottom line is that in 1986 Nobles was at the center of a tangled web of right-wing nuts, Knight Templar kooks, evangelical church leaders, corrupt business dealings, mobsters, and politicians. One of the central tenets, or rationalizations, of those Patriot move-

More Mob Connections

Briefly, James E. Plew and Al Capone were partners in the Chicago Country Club which is now the Eglin Golf Course. There are various sources citing Plew, Capone, and Chicago "investors." Capone stayed at Plew and Ruckel's Valparaiso Inn. Plew was from Chicago, was an aviation pioneer, and a member of the Cisero Flying Club. Part of the development plan included designating 10 acres of each parcel of land for farming sugar cane, a parcel just large enough to grow some sugar cane for bootleg rum. The only industry of record was "turpentine distilleries."

I interviewed one of the Niceville area's oldest living residents, a man named Salty Brunson, and he told me of his encounters with Capone, and the whiskey running out of Boggy Bayou for the Chicago Syndicate using a fast speedboat probably driven by Donna Parish's grandfather.

The town that morphed in Niceville was originally called Valparaiso, which was founded by a Chicago investor named John Perrine, who may or may not have had had ties to the Chicago mob. Salty Brunson, who attended John Perrine's funeral in 1921, believed Perrine may have faked his death to escape all the Chicago mobsters he had ripped off in shady land deals, or else he had likely been murdered.

James E. Plew and his son-in-law C.W. Ruckel purchased Perrine's development in Valparaiso for pennies on the dollar[1], and that was the foundation of their empire.

This is all a scratching of the surface to show how deeply the history of the Florida panhandle is connected to organized crime. It goes way back, and their descendants, such as Joey Forgione, are still in positions of power throughout the area.

1. "History of Valparaiso," City of Valparaiso, Florida. https://www.valp.org/community/page/history-valparaiso

ment groups was "tax protest," meaning they wanted to starve the federal government of funds until it could no longer function by refusing to pay their taxes. This echoes the sentiments of right-wing D.C. lobbyist Grover Norquist, who founded Americans for Tax Reform in 1985 at the urging of President Reagan. Norquist famously said, "I don't want to abolish government. I simply want to reduce it to the size where I can drag it into the bathroom and drown it in the bathtub.[21]"

That sounds to me like the perfect environment for people like these to do whatever they want with impunity.

When Nobles went to trial in 1986 on federal charges of conspiracy to defraud the government, aiding and abetting others to prepare fraudulent tax returns, fraud, and making false statements related to his involvement with those hate groups, he pled down to fraud and making false statements. In return, he turned state's evidence as an informant. He had taught members of the group how to file fraudulent tax returns with the stated goal of overthrowing the federal government. He taught people how to hide assets and "opt out of" the banking system, how to convert money into gold. When he flipped, he used a wire to lure his accomplice out of the Bahamas.

* * *

On the day of Nobles' conviction, Constance Wayne Jones bought the property on Rhonda Drive. He sold the property to an active-duty military person, James Rex Oliver, who later sold it to Nobles.

Constance Wayne Jones was a military veteran and a thirtieth-level master Freemason, also known as a Knight Kadosh,[22] and a member of the Knights Templar. One of Jones' major partners in construction and development was also a Freemason named Boyette. The father of Boyette's lawyer was a 33rd degree Knight Templar and a Shriner. Jones and Boyette are possibly related according to background checks and the name they share, Wayne, which literally means "craftsman."

Jones was a member of the Crestview Masonic Lodge, the same lodge that included former U.S. Congressman and Knight Templar Robert Lee Fulton Sikes.

Constance Wayne Jones also sat on the board of the Emerald Coast Child Advocacy Center, as did Walter Ruckel. Other members of the board included actor Wayne Rogers of *M*A*S*H* fame, and disgraced Florida Congressman Ray Sansom, one of Ruckel's cronies.

Connections were coming into focus.

* * *

The home was built at the highest topographical point in Niceville. It appears to be the first home built in the subdivision and there was no logical reason for it to be numbered 1118. The house numbering on the street doesn't even make sense. However, the year 1118 was the year the Knights Templar were founded.

Connections were not only coming into focus, but also getting weird.

The Knights Templar were founded as an order of religious knights to fight in the Crusades. For a number of reasons – both trumped up and legitimate, political and religious – they were declared heretics in 1312, their order was dissolved, and they were hunted down by the Catholic Church. Surviving members went into hiding and their order evolved into several secret societies over the centuries.[23] The Templars' has a complex and often mysterious history. Nowadays, any number of organizations besides Freemasonry can stake a claim to the term Knight Templar,[24] such that real connections can become murky. Today there are over 1,700 organizations using the term, including criminal organizations.[25]

This is a printout from the county planning office of the permit information for 1118 Rhonda Drive.

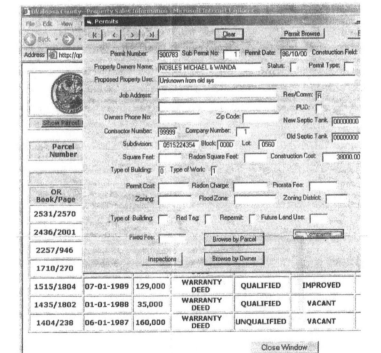

The planning office claimed the original permit had been destroyed in a "flood." A year later, I discovered that this electronic record had been deleted from their system. Fortunately, I had the foresight to print it out when I had the opportunity.

In similar fashion, records showing Michel Barthelemy as the owner of 2 West Kathy Lane have been deleted from public records. For years there was an unexplained gap in the records that was closed after I inquired about it adding to the mystery.

The common threads in all these houses created a web spun by ultra-conservative billionaires, corrupt congressmen, unscrupulous builders, Southern Freemasons, and Knight Templar occultists, ultra-conservative evangelicals of various overlapping sects like Church of Christ ministers and elders, and child sex abuse and human trafficking of foster children.

Endnotes

1   Excerpt from a response to a DCF Inspector General complaint, authored by the very people I complained against.

2   Interview with the author, November 11, 2023.

3   Santa Rosa County Sheriff report, obtained November 24, 2008.

4   Shuster testified to this under oath on January 21, 2009.

5   Jennifer Clark, CAC Report, November 25, 2008.

6   https://www.fvhofsociety.org/merkel.html

7   https://www.findagrave.com/memorial/162575251/elsie-eleanor-kelly. And https://www.legacy.com/us/obituaries/nwfdailynews/name/charles-kelly-obituary?id=21107703

8   https://en.wikipedia.org/wiki/John_Birch_Society

9   https://www.splcenter.org/fighting-hate/intelligence-report/2009/patriot-groups

10   "History of Ft. Walton Beach," Emerald Coast Magazine, November 26, 2008. https://www.emeraldcoastmagazine.com/history-of-ft-walton-beach/

11   "Chicago Golf Club of Valparaiso Photo Tour - Eglin AFB Eagle," Golf Club Atlas. https://www.golfclubatlas.com/forum/index.php?topic=54373.0;wap2

12   "History of Valparaiso," City of Valparaiso, Floridahttps://www.valp.org/community/page/history-valparaiso

13   https://en.wikipedia.org/wiki/Bob_Sikes

14   "History of Ft. Walton Beach," Emerald Coast Magazine, November 26, 2008. https://www.emeraldcoastmagazine.com/history-of-ft-walton-beach/

15   https://en.wikipedia.org/wiki/Bob_Sikes

16   https://www.freedomfirstsociety.org/

17   https://www.legacy.com/us/obituaries/sfgate/name/charles-ruckel-obituary?id=19454464

18   https://www.congress.gov/112/crec/2012/04/25/CREC-2012-04-25-pt1-PgE655-3.pdf

19   https://projects.propublica.org/nonprofits/organizations/541863719

20   https://extremismterms.adl.org/glossary/patriot-movement

21   https://theconversation.com/the-shutdown-drowning-government-in-the-bathtub-111333

22   https://en.wikipedia.org/wiki/Knight_Kadosh

23   https://en.wikipedia.org/wiki/Knights_Templar

24   https://www.knighttemplar.org/about-us

25   https://thetemplarknight.com/2020/05/16/knights-templar-today/

CHAPTER EIGHT

THE VERDICT

As the connections began to come into focus, as I dug deeper into the people involved, I felt as though I had fallen down an occult rabbit hole populated by Freemasons, Knights Templars, rabid evangelicals, white supremacists, the mafia, corruption, on and on, down and down, deeper and deeper until I feared there was no bottom. How many of them were connected, and how deeply difficult were these ties to figure out, to put together in a way that makes sense? It had become painfully clear I had stumbled into a swamp full of reptiles. In over my head, these people I was dealing with were seriously dangerous. Was I being paranoid? Nevertheless, I began checking my vehicle for bombs whenever I returned home from trips. I had not yet learned how far they would go.

Weeks passed as I flogged the law enforcement and child protection systems in vain to get my sons back. Meanwhile, schemes and plots were churning behind the scenes, none of it good.

On December 12, I had to appear for Mike Nobles' deposition regarding the DVI that was still in force for Toby. I had been ambushed by a process server in a parking lot on Halloween, the day the boys had been abducted from school.

It is difficult to convey the depth of emotion I felt at the sight of Nobles, a cauldron of rage, incredulity, and the ongoing fear for my children's safety. His testimony was a mix of perjury, inconsistency, and even self-incrimination. This was a guy who lied for a living, surrounded by people and forces that enabled him to do so.

Mike Nobles was questioned by Betty Thomas, my attorney.

During his deposition, he spoke extensively about the foster children he and Wanda took in during the mid-to-late 1990s, including having to go through training and classes to make it official, which he claims to have done.[1] The State of Florida has no record of him ever being a foster parent. Those records were erased at an unknown date. More on this later.

The next big lie came when he was asked about his criminal record. He admitted to a conviction in 1986, but "couldn't remember" many details. He said he had been a "tax protester," but it had been on behalf of his involvement with Posse Comitatus and the Patriot Network. This was only the beginning, however. By the time I knew him, he could have been described as a professional tax evader.

He served three years' probation, then got a letter from the State of Florida saying his rights had been restored.

Then Thomas asked him: "You can carry a firearm?"

"Huh? No, not a firearm. Everything except firearms."

"And you don't have any firearms?"

"No.[2]"

This was one of many bald-faced lies, and among the most egregious. I had seen the guns and heard him talk about the hallowed family treasure handed down to him by his father. So had the boys. He later claimed that the guns belonged to Wanda.

He talked about what a great father I was to the boys, stating several times that I was a very moral person. He went on to describe what a terrible unfaithful wife and neglectful mother his daughter was, but when asked if he thought she was capable now of watching her children said, "I absolutely do.[3]"

He then went on to lie about Christy and the boys living with him for months, beginning in February, launching into a series of wild contradictions from his own previous statements. He told a story about how Christy and I had agreed that she would be the custodial parent. He spent a great deal of the deposition talking in circles about what happened and when.

He denied Billy Nobles ever calling to threaten me, even though I have the recording. He claimed Billy called "out of love." He lied about ever asking anyone from any church to contact me.

In another bald-faced lie, he said that Mary Smith said – the boys told him – I was having them rehearse making videotapes of their statements about what he had done to them. This was his motive for taking the boys – he admitted – because I was forcing them to make a videotape that would incriminate him (I wasn't).

He claimed that he had no knowledge of Christy's plan to take the boys until she was on the way to Lighthouse Academy, and she called him. According to him, she said I was planning to "take the kids and skip the country.[4]" He then contradicted himself and said his daughter Shelly came up with the idea and admitted the motive that it wouldn't be in his best interest for me to have the kids if they were making statements against him.

He then went on to blame the boys for inappropriate sexual behavior. "They would run through their house, pull their pants down and show that thing off. My girls didn't like that one bit. I believe that something happened.[5]" He called whatever happened "playing doctor."

He describes Faith's and Emily's therapy sessions in such detail he was apparently allowed to be present or watch video of the sessions, a serious professional breach. A possible abuser under investigation should be no-where near a victim's play therapy, much less fed information about it.

In his testimony, he said, "During their play therapy, they were playing in the sand box, they get thousands of little figurines and stuff they get to pick and play. Anyway, Faith picked hers out and she was hiding under an umbrel-la with a machine gun. Then they got this big monster, the bull, half man half bull, I don't remember what you call that thing, but anyway, they got it down."

He inadvertently confirmed that the DCF and ECCAC had been feed-ing him information about my sons' case. He knew exactly how many re-ports had been coming in against him and "…that's when Jennifer Clark took over." These are the same institutions that fed confidential informa-tion to Joe Palmer while *he* was under investigation during his divorce.

He blamed my wife's mental instability on me.

He talked about his attorney who "came up with some crazy names" for their corporations, among them, Androgynous and Alchemy, two names with occult significance. For more information, see Appendix.

One might surmise that this is all a game of he-said/he-said, the kind of stuff that happens all the time in courtrooms everywhere. Through-out his deposition, Nobles made himself sound like the saintliest, most wrongfully accused poor fellow ever to walk the earth. Everything was somebody else's fault. He practically dripped honey. The difference be-tween what I said and what he said, however, is that I have all the receipts.[6]

What was possibly the most disturbing was that Betty Thomas *already knew* all of Mike Nobles' legal and criminal weaknesses and hid them from me. And she clearly knew his Achillies heal, his guns, and withheld it from me.

* * *

On December 14, 2008, Jennifer Clark filed a report with DCF that lied about literally everything, most egregiously saying, "Neither child disclosed any type of harm or abuse when visiting their Maternal Grandparents."

She turned the abduction into a case of me being the dangerous abus-er, that I was detained by the police so Christy could get away. Christy was just picking the boys up from school.

She described both boys as "healthy and happy," and that they had been seen around the community at school and by relatives. She added, "No services needed."

She described me as having "a criminal history that could impact child safety," which of course was a complete fabrication.

The report stated that Christy was planning to get a DVI against me, that she didn't feel safe, that she was afraid that, because I was an airline pilot, I "could easily take the boys out of the country and not come back."

Her report recommends counseling for the boys, but none was ever offered. In fact, I battled for years to get my sons counseling at the Santa Rosa Kids House, the child advocacy center in Santa Rosa County where we lived. Clark and the DCF blocked it.

The case was closed.[7]

* * *

This report represented an escalation and another brick in the wall of disinformation. They were fabricating a story where all the truths were flipped, getting it in writing, and then repeating it in enough official places that all the falsehoods took on the weight of truth. All the information I had provided, all the reports I had filed, everything the boys were saying, everything school officials reported, everything that mental health professionals had reported about Christy and the boys, all the glaring evidence of trauma and abuse, it was all being buried or had been buried. Reports were ignored, investigations quashed, records destroyed.

Repeat a lie often enough and people believe it. I call them Goebbels lies.

It took me months to acquire this report.

The DCF stonewalled at every turn.

* * *

Nobles took this report with the ink barely dry and sent it to my church, following up with phone calls asking the pastors to "get him some help." It seemed that Nobles, or parties associated with him, had turned the entire Florida panhandle into an army of flying monkeys.

I want to be exceedingly clear. Jennifer Clark knew exactly what Mike Nobles was, what he was about. Her actions were part of a clear and deliberate pattern of conduct. She knowingly put my children in harm's way and showed cold, calculating, callous disregard for their safety and the safety of the other children in the household. Her actions resulted in severe mental injuries to my sons. She knowingly falsified a child protection report, conspired to kidnap and hide my sons, conspired to commit fraud in the court system, instructed Christy to file a false restraining order, attempted through three avenues to frame me on false charges. Then she and her superiors denied any of this had happened, showing cognizance of guilt.

The purpose was obvious: to destroy any credibility I had, undermine any support I had, and make me feel unsafe anywhere, even at church.

* * *

On December 16, I filed an emergency petition for a custody hearing, citing grave danger to my sons. Judge Santurri refused to hear the petition.

I tried to go to the media, contacting a reporter from *The Destin Log,* Destin's local newspaper, regarding the cover-up of abuse and extortion by leaders in the Destin Church of Christ. Instead of reporting the story, they tipped off Nobles and the church.

The New Year came and went. I had had no contact with the boys since Halloween.

* * *

On January 8, 2009, Judge Santurri dismissed the restraining order meant to protect Toby. Santurri did so out of court, and without a hearing that would have allowed me to object. I found no record that Nobles' attorney even filed a motion to dismiss. This was a unilateral action by Santurri who was determined to prevent me from getting a hearing and would continue to do so. The reason? I had no standing to file an injunction because the boys did not live with me. How's that for a mind-twisting abandonment of reality, the law, and common sense? I didn't have standing to protect Toby because he didn't live with me. Because he had been kidnapped because I refused to drop the restraining order. The court was aware that Nobles had threatened to abduct the boys and then coerced Christy into doing it. When I found out I wanted to throw up right then and there. I was once again in utter disbelief.

* * *

On January 14, I had a court hearing regarding the DVI Christy had filed against me.

My attorney, Betty Thomas, took me aside before the hearing and said, *"You're dealing with a cult. If you keep going with this, your life is in danger."*

"What are you talking about?" I asked.

But she wouldn't say any more about that. She repeated, "This is a cult. You should stop now."

I had filed the emergency petition for a custody hearing, so I was expecting a custody hearing, but turned out to be a status hearing that went nowhere. My petition for a custody hearing was ignored. During the hearing, Thomas asked Judge Santurri if I could be allowed to give my children Christmas presents. The request was denied.

But then Thomas dropped a bombshell on me. She abruptly announced to the court that she was leaving the case, despite having promised to represent me at the next and final hearing on January 21.

After the hearing was over, she would not speak to me again until almost a year later. She wouldn't accept or return phone calls.

* * *

Before all of this blew up, I had been confiding to Mike Nobles about Christy's behavior, he urged me to document her neglectfulness with a videotape. He didn't approve of her promiscuity. So, one time when I returned from a four-day trip, I had videotaped the squalor of our home – dirty dishes, clothes and half-eaten food everywhere, two unwashed, unfed boys. The place looked awful.

I had given this camera with the tape in it to Betty Thomas, and she disappeared with it. I never got it back. Sadly, it had several happy family outings on it as well, and those recordings were lost as was the camera.

So, with no attorney, I had exactly one week before my final hearing on January 21. I needed to scramble to learn the legal system. I would have to represent myself. So, I did. I subpoenaed witnesses and acted as my own attorney.

What I didn't know, but Betty Thomas did, was that on January 15, Mike Nobles and his attorney, Michael Gibson, submitted a request for Nobles' guns to be returned to him, claiming that he was not, in fact, a convicted felon. This was accompanied by a letter requesting that this order be entered without a hearing, despite the requirements of Florida law to notify me and hold a hearing. A copy was provided to Betty Thomas, who concealed it from me. Recall that she asked Nobles about his prohibition to possess firearms during the December hearing, a move that surprised me because she hadn't spoken to me about it.

Judge Santurri would soon sign the order to give Mike Nobles his guns back, and Betty Thomas abandoned me and ran for the hills, either in fear for her safety or to avoid any whiff of complicity. Maybe both.

It is important here to point out that I had filed the case against Mike, Faith, and Emily Nobles in Santa Rosa County where it was assigned to Judge Gary Bergosh. Christy's injunction against me was filed in Okaloosa County with Judge William F. Stone. Both cases were somehow transferred to Judge Thomas Santurri. It felt like I was being railroaded by the same people time and time again. Clark, Parish, Dunn, Forgione, Santurri.

Betty Thomas had previously served as a clerk for Thomas Santurri. Had she been part of the fix all along? I believe she dropped me abruptly because she was ordered to, or she panicked because of the return of Nobles' firearms.

A few days later, in response to my contacting *The Destin Log,* the local newspaper and the Destin Church of Christ abruptly launched a true dog-and-pony show called Civic Sunday. Pastor Brad Bynum, who had called me "warped, twisted, and unstable" and had threatened to "disfellowship" me, led the circus which also featured several local politicians and civic leaders, including Circuit Judge Terrance Ketchel, City Councilman James Wood, and Mayor Craig Barker. "Civic Sunday" was an overblown sermon, or a version of kangaroo court where these officials played the part of God. Child pornography and sexual abuse were loudly decried from the pulpit in the presence of children who were too young and innocent to understand it. Mike Nobles was deacon in charge of children. Afterward, I met with Christian Counselor Ron Long, and he described this event as "offensive" and "very inappropriate." It was obvious to him that this was cover for what was occurring in that church. Those that rail the loudest are the ones throwing up chaff to cover wrongdoing. Ron once again encouraged me to involve federal authorities.

I mulled that over and over, unsure of whether I could trust *any* authorities.

* * *

On January 21, 2009, I appeared before Judge Thomas Santurri representing myself. I had subpoenaed therapist Karleen Shuster, Pastor Brad Bynum, and Mary Smith. I let Dr. DeShon bow out because his wife was ill. Christy brought her father as her only witness. I performed all my own questioning and cross-examination.

Bynum confirmed, under oath, that he had tried to coerce me into dropping the whole thing by saying that if I didn't, he would "publicly rebuke and disfellowship" me.[8]

Karleen Shuster's testimony was both vindicating for me and damning for Nobles.

She said, "Toby had actually told me about visiting with his mother and they had gone to their grandparents' house. And during this time, he stated that he was watching Star Wars and that the aunts were playing with him. And I asked him what they were doing, and he didn't respond. I said, well, were you playing with them in return? He says, no, girls don't have weenies… I said, … did you enjoy what they were doing? He said, no, I told them to stop but they said just let us do it.[9]"

She confirmed in no uncertain terms that both Gabe and Toby showed signs of sexual abuse.

She believed that I was a good father trying to protect my children, that I was not erratic and unstable, and that being separated from me had caused them emotional damage.

She said DCF had contacted her only once regarding the report she had filed as a mandatory reporter. She told the caseworker that something was definitely going on in the Nobles family. She further said that it was reasonable for me to fear future abuse in the Nobles household.

Judge Santurri asked her if there were any signs that that the children had been coached by either parent. She responded, "There wasn't."[10] Then she reiterated that it was Marilyn Reid, the nanny, who had brought them to their session.[11] I was out of town.

Mary Smith's testimony was particularly damning for Christy and Mike Nobles. Mary had been friends with the Nobles family for thirteen years. She talked extensively about her worries over Christy's mental health, that she wasn't taking care of the kids. I had asked Mary and several other women from the church to look in on the boys while I was away because I didn't trust Christy to take care of them, and Mary confirmed my fears were justified.

She described conversations she'd had with Christy, who "… admitted to me that it was very tough for her at times to take care of the boys. She said she did not feel comfortable being the only caregiver of the children."[12]

According to Smith, Christy "… never wanted to take them away from Mark because that was the only dad they knew.[13]"

> Q. (By Mark Harris) Did my wife approach you the night before she took the kids?
>
> A. Yes.
>
> Q. Did she indicate why she was taking the kids?
>
> A. She felt as though you were going to flee with the children or that the children would be harmed by you.
>
> Q. She did not indicate that her father pressured her?
>
> A. She did not directly say that, but her father had called me earlier that day and that was the first time he had called me in months. So I

did know that every – because everything she came to me and said was from the conversation that I had had with her father.

…

Q. Do you recall informing me … Mr. Nobles had requested to meet with you and had threatened to take my children away?

A. Yes, yes.

Q. And what were the reasons he threatened to take my children?

A. *To shut you up. That was his exact words, to shut you up. If he had to use the children to shut you up, he would.*

Q. Okay. And did he say he would deny me access to the children?

A. Yes. Yes, he did.[14]

Then I asked her if anyone had attempted to influence her testimony, and she declared that Nobles had.

Q. How did he do that?

A. Just when all this started he was my husband's supervisor, and he made it very difficult. My husband actually left the job because Mike made it to the point where my husband just didn't feel comfortable with him being his boss anymore because I, still at that time, wanted to still help Christy and still want to help Christy, and he made it very uncomfortable. Wouldn't speak to my husband anymore although we had been friends, and the year before he bought my children Christmas for the two years prior to that. So yeah.

At the end of her testimony, I asked her a couple more questions.

Q. Knowing all parties, would you allow your children in Michael Nobles' home?

A. Absolutely not. Not without me.

Q. And are you aware that there are others in the children's program who would never allow their children in that home, as well?

A. Yes, I am.[15]

When Christy called her father to the stand, he was nothing if not consistent.

He accused me of stalking Christy, said he had a list of places she had been like I was following her around. He was, essentially, declaring me to be erratic and unstable.

He claimed that my erratic behavior was proven further by the fact that I had accused him of sexual abuse. He claimed that the reason the boys were with their mother now was because she and I had agreed to it. He said that Jennifer Clark had told him to "be careful" and that he should keep his kids and pets inside. A particular irony as he had kidnapped my kids and killed pets left and right to control his victims. Throughout his testimony he downplayed Christy's mental illness, in one breath implying that it was all something I had made up, and in the next, he told how she was getting treatment for it, even though he had no idea who had diagnosed her or where she was getting treatment. He accused me of coaching the boys to make accusations against him on videotape, and that he'd been tipped off on this by Mary Smith. He admitted that it "might have crossed his mind" to have me Baker Acted, in other words, involuntarily committed. He admitted that the Destin Church of Christ immediately tipped him off about me contacting *The Destin Log*.[16] He admitted to showing church members the confidential reports from DCF, of which he should never have had possession.

He came across like a double-talking clown for a hearing that was a sideshow. I had come prepared. My witnesses were spot on. Christy and her father had nothing. Christy even testified that I was a good man and a good father. She had no evidence of "stalking" beyond her father's ridiculous story.

It felt good, I must admit. Even though the game was rigged, I scored some points. Backed into a corner, Judge Santurri dismissed the restraining order against me.

His ruling left those two with their jaws hanging open. They had been sure the fix was in. The Nobles family took off out of the courtroom, barely able to conceal their panic, ran across the "Do Not Walk on the Grass" sign outside the courthouse, jumped into their vehicle, and took off.

According to what they both told me later, Joanna Morris and Karleen Shuster thought this reaction was fishy, so they followed the Nobles' vehicle. Nobles was speeding, looking over his shoulder, weaving in and out of traffic. Christy snatched Gabe out of school, citing a "family emergency," and they all took off to hide him again.

* * *

With the injunction lifted, I went to visit Gabe at school, Calvary Christian Academy in Ft. Walton Beach, the very next day. I found him to be absent, however, with no notice from the Nobles family about why, so I filed a report to the abuse hotline, all but panicking over what might have happened to them. I hadn't seen or spoken to them since Halloween. I later discovered this report was also quashed. Meanwhile, I went home dejected and nearly desperate.

The next day, however, January 23, I tried again and found Gabe at school.

At the sight of me, he came running, threw his arms around me, and said, "I love you, Dad. I want to go home."

I was so relieved. I just wanted to spend time with him. I didn't want to talk about any of the nastiness. We had lunch together, and it was one of the nicest moments of that whole awful period. My son was alive. He had all his limbs and organs. I asked after Toby, and Gabe responded, "He's okay."

Toby had never been put back in school. As I understood it from the court hearings, the boys were bouncing back and forth between the Nobles' home and the Riggs' home, Christy's sister and her husband Brian. He had been in preschool, but now, nothing.

It was with great reluctance I let Gabe go back to class, but he was okay for now. At least I had that.

And then, two days later, Christy called and left me a terse message. *"We need to talk…"*

Endnotes

1   Michael S. Nobles Deposition, 6:3-8:24 (December 12, 2008).

2   Nobles Dep., 13:17-21 (December 12, 2008).

3   Nobles Dep., 23:7 (December 12, 2008).

4   Nobles Dep., 42:21-22 (December 12, 2008).

5   Nobles Dep., 52:18-21 (December 12, 2008).

6   Nobles Dep., 42-16-17 (December 12, 2008).

7   Clark, Jennifer, DCF report, December 14, 2008.

8   Christy Harris v. Mark Harris, Whittle, Bynum Testimony 5:9-17 (First Circuit Court Santa Rosa County, Florida 2009)

9   Christy Harris v. Mark Harris, Whittle, Shuster Testimony 5:16-6:6 (First Circuit Court Santa Rosa County, Florida 2009)

10   Christy Harris v. Mark Harris, Whittle, Shuster Testimony 13:20 (First Circuit Court Santa Rosa County, Florida 2009)

11   Christy Harris v. Mark Harris, Whittle, Shuster Testimony (First Circuit Court Santa Rosa County, Florida 2009)

12   Christy Harris v. Mark Harris, Whittle, Smith Testimony 5:23-6:6 (First Circuit Court Santa Rosa County, Florida 2009)

13   Christy Harris v. Mark Harris, Whittle, Smith Testimony 6:13-14 (First Circuit Court Santa Rosa County, Florida 2009)

14   Christy Harris v. Mark Harris, Whittle, Smith Testimony 7:6-8:10 (First Circuit Court Santa Rosa County, Florida 2009)

15   Christy Harris v. Mark Harris, Whittle, Smith Testimony 18:22-19:3 (First Circuit Court Santa Rosa County, Florida 2009)

16   Christy Harris v. Mark Harris, Whittle, Nobles Testimony (First Circuit Court Santa Rosa County, Florida 2009)

CHAPTER NINE

SYMPATHY FOR THE DEVIL

I had no idea, when I finally got her on the phone, what Christy intended. She wouldn't tell me what it was about, though I asked several times. She said she was coming over to the house, our dream home by the bay, the next day. My emotions were nauseating cycles of fury, suspicion, and fear. The last time she'd requested a meeting, I'd been ambushed with a subpoena.

When the time came, Monday afternoon, January 26, 2009, I waited warily, half-expecting some sort of ambush and fingering the voice recorder in my pocket.

When I spotted Christy's car coming, my heart leaped at the sight of two little heads in the car with her. She parked, wouldn't look at me, and shut the engine off.

The boys piled out of the car and ran toward me yelling, "Dad! Daddy!"

I fought back tears and hugged them, looking them over to see if they were injured. Toby's eye had healed. Joy filled their faces, but it was mixed with something else – profound relief. It was one of the happiest moments of my life.

Christy just stood leaning against her car, arms crossed, looking anywhere except the happy reunion right in front of her.

"We get to stay home with you, Dad!" Gabe told me excitedly.

I looked at Christy. She still wouldn't meet my gaze.

I told the boys how much I loved them, how much I missed them, how happy I was they were home. Then I told them to wait in the house. I had to talk to their mother.

When the door shut, I said to Christy, "Is this some kind of trick?"

She lit a cigarette and blew out a big puff of smoke. "No trick."

"I'm not sure what to say here."

"It was all just a big misunderstanding," she said.

I scoffed. "A *misunderstanding!*"

"None of it had to happen this way. It was all because of Mary talking shit."

"This is all Mary's fault?" This weird twist had me confused. "You took the kids, took me to court, your father started spreading lies about me across three counties, and it was all *Mary's* fault."

"You got 'em back."

"Does your father know?"

She shook her head. "Not yet."

I glanced in at the boys, who were standing at the front window. The joy on their faces had vanished. They stared at me now, hollow-eyed and fear stricken.

"There's something I want to know," I said, "something that's been bothering me since that day in court. Can I ask you?"

She shrugged.

"Can I record our conversation?" I knew by now that Florida was a two-party state. I needed her permission for the recording to be admissible in court.

"Go ahead," she said with a cold sigh. "What do you want to know?"

I hit RECORD on the recorder in my pocket.

"This has been eating at me. My attorney started asking your dad about his guns. The guns he showed me way back when I first met him."

She shrugged again. "He always had guns. Can't remember him not having any. He offered one to me, once upon a time. I didn't want it. He gave one to Shelly."

"Convicted felons aren't supposed to have guns."

"Tell that to the law."

"But ... how did *my* attorney know to ask him about that? She never discussed it with me."

For the first time, she looked squarely at me. "How the hell should I know? You think he tells me a goddamn thing except what to do?"

"Does he still have them in the house? The guns. Did he ever let the boys have them?"

"Dunno. Not while I was there. I didn't think it would be safe."

"Why?" I asked.

"Why any of it! Why take them! Why bring them back!"

She just shrugged and got in her car. Without another word, she drove off.

* * *

But what she left me were two little boys who were traumatized beyond their capacity to understand or express.

When I went inside, Gabe volunteered, "Paw Paw's got tons of guns, Dad."
Beside him, Toby nodded fervently.
"He showed 'em to me. A whole gun room."
"Really?" I said. "Where?"
"In the gun room."
I had been to the Nobles house many times, but I'd never seen a gun room. Gabe just shrugged.
"You don't know?" I asked.
He just looked out the window and neither of them would say anything more.

I knew something was dreadfully, terribly wrong with them from that moment forward. They moved with a slow, shambling gait as if every step might land them in trouble or danger. As a military veteran, I knew the thousand-yard-stare of PTSD when I saw it.

As happy as I was to have my boys home with me, safe, I had the sick sense of dread that this was only the beginning. As I looked at them, I hid the burgeoning anger at what happened to them. Bad things had happened, no question, and I wanted to get to the bottom of what. I wanted to hold those who were responsible accountable for what they had done..

That first night was the beginning of endless nights of screaming nightmares.

* * *

Any parent knows how nerve-wracking it is to have a screaming child at 3:00 A.M., when they can't be comforted, when they scream and cry in your arms and you don't know how to help them, every minute is an eternity.

What I discovered over the coming days and weeks was they had been traumatized beyond description. I don't remember now the exact sequence of how their trauma manifested or all the terrible revelations. Now, years later, it's all a blur of escalating horrors. But I took them to professionals as soon as I could. They were diagnosed with severe PTSD.

There would be no more soccer games, no more karate, because as soon as we got to the class, to the practice, they would begin screaming and crying, and then take off running like rabbits in terror-stricken flight.

Gabe did this all the way into middle school. He ran away from two schools, from church. He was terrified of everything.

I couldn't leave the room without telling them, and they would follow me. If I didn't, they would panic and start screaming and crying to the point of hyperventilating.

* * *

Over the coming years, both Gabe and Toby would require a number of inpatient stays in mental hospitals, incurring hundreds of thousands of dollars in mental health expenses.

They were terrified of talking about what happened to them. Many of these bits and pieces came out only after years of treatment and therapy.

Gabe was terrified of zombies. He was sure they were going to come and get him. His grandfather had made him play *Resident Evil,* a super-violent horror video game with chainsaw-wielding zombies and blood spattering on the screen. His grandfather kept telling him zombies were real, and he needed to learn how to fight them. He was also encouraged to play another game called *Crackdown,* made by the same game designer as *Grand Theft Auto.* In mid-February 2009, Nobles kept the boys up all night playing *Crackdown,* showing them how he "recorded" his guns into the game, so they were "all gone now."

"It's all a lie now," he had said. He attached the weapons to a wire attached to the video game and brought up images of the guns on the screen to show how guns can be "recorded" into the game. This idea became an obsession with Gabe, alongside his fixation on guns and violence which he drew obsessively for years. He went on and on about it.

* * *

Their grandfather had terrorized both children wearing a Satan mask, convincing them the Devil was coming to get them. He also scared them with some kind of puppet.

He locked Gabe in a closet with a Halloween toy, a screaming skull with glowing eyes.

One night, Gabe woke up to a witch flying in circles around the ceiling, another Halloween toy. Gabe knew it wasn't real, but it terrified him. Another time he found a fake skull hanging in his room.

Halloween "fun?" Sure, except that he also threatened to crucify Gabe if he "talked about Paw Paw's guns or messing with this wiener." Nobles demonstrated crucifixion by nailing a rag doll to the wall in the bathroom and left it there as a reminder.

He threatened to slit Gabe's throat if he told anyone about shooting the cat. He had killed and mutilated pets in front of Gabe.

* * *

Why Gabe and not Toby? It appears Nobles was attempting to groom Gabe. And he showed him and told him everything, not believing I would ever get him back and not knowing of Gabe's photographic memory. Gabe was older and better able to understand what was happening. At seven years old, he understood that his grandfather was trying to scramble his brain through terror and abuse. Anything Gabe said would be discredited as all just video games and toys. But Gabe understood what was real and what wasn't.

One of the ways that Gabe dealt with what had happened to him was through art. Prior to this, his drawings were all about nature, mostly fish, turtles, and flowers. He began drawing incessantly, obsessively, and it was these drawings that opened his cabinet of horrors. Having lived a relatively sheltered life with me, after I got him home, he became obsessed with guns and violence. His drawings reflected guns, weapons, and murder. He also kept drawing a particular kind of red and white cross. The Templar cross.

I asked him where he had seen it.

"Paw Paw's house."

But he grew agitated when I pressed him about it, so I backed off. It was like that every time I asked the boys questions. They would either clam up or get upset. When the boys did talk to me, the things they said were consistent. Anyone who works with traumatized children knows how malleable their memories can be. So, I was very careful not to ask them leading questions, just letting them talk when they chose to.

* * *

"Toby shot one of Paw Paw's guns," Gabe told me one day.

In what was probably the tenth stab of alarm that day, I asked Toby, "You did?"

Toby nodded fervently.

"Where did this happen?" I asked.

"In Paw Paw's closet," Toby said.

"Did Paw Paw give you the gun?"

When it looked like he was going to cry, I did my best to assure him he wasn't in trouble, nor would he ever be for talking about any of this stuff.

Finally, he admitted. "I just found it. I was looking at it."

"Was it scary?"

He nodded fervently. "And loud!"

"Do you mean Paw Paw's closet in his bathroom?"

He nodded again, eyes full of tears.

* * *

The master bathroom had a linen closet with a stepladder for climbing up to the skylight access to the attic. Gabe joked about playing a trick on his grandfather and moving the ladder when his grandfather was up there. Gabe also drew a detailed drawing of the attic and a map to a place near the chimney where there were guns. Toby had used the ladder to get one of his grandfather's guns from the top shelf of the linen closet, a pistol.

The pistol had gone off and put a hole through one of the pictures hanging in the master bedroom.

* * *

On one occasion, Gabe told me his grandfather and "bad guy officers" and "army men" took him to a "rocky cave." What he drew looked very much like a military-style bunker, complete with abandoned military vehicles, a gate, and a No Trespassing sign. Obviously on the Eglin AFB range.

Gabe talked about a biker named "Tiger" and drew pictures of his tattoos and his jacket which had a skull in a top hat with an ace of spades, a common motif on biker jackets, symbols that were also used during the Vietnam War to signify death. Then he described how he was forced to watch his grandfather "blow him up."

Gabe drew rooms with automatic weapons hanging on the walls, shelves full of ammunition, grenades, and rocket launchers. Gas masks were hanging on the wall. "Explode cans" which I later was able to determine were gas cylinders. And "Paw Paw's science lab," which appeared to be a drug lab. Gabe even drew the drug making process step by step and numbered. There were also bars of gold and a safe full of cash. Gabe even knew the combination, digits from Nobles' phone number. All guarded with "robot guns," which were automated sentry guns with tracking cameras (which are military and classified). A four plex of screens monitoring the property with a surveillance system. This surveillance system creeped Gabe out so much he told me about hiding under the table so he wouldn't be watched.

* * *

Then came the really weird stuff. He drew what was in effect a Knight Templar temple filled with Knight Templar swords, an altar with bones and skulls, burning candles, robes, statues of Anubis holding spears, pyramids, round columns with the Eye of Horus, grail cups, and a Papal Tiara. Also, Templar swords and a mace. He also said that there was a miniature Ark of the Covenant. He repeatedly drew a dragon like image. He said his grandfather had a spell book (Nobles' brother collects spell books) and described rituals with people wearing robes.

He talked about what sounded like a torture chamber, with an electric chair, complete with five legs to keep it stable and a chord plugged into the wall, a machine that stretches people (a medieval rack which he drew), a saw for sawing people, and a guillotine, complete with a bucket to catch blood. It would be a decade and a half later with a lot of research and the help of others to figure out the meaning of all of this. One of the odd things he drew that fascinated me was a set of ornate skeleton keys. What were they for? What did they unlock? I will never forget Gabe getting upset one day and putting an x across the picture of keys and saying, "They aren't real anymore." In similar fashion he said that the gun room was not real anymore. When I pressed him, he said that Paw Paw blew it up. He drew Knight Templar crosses and swords, occult symbols including an ouroboros (a circular symbol depicting a snake swallowing its tail, an emblem said to be of wholeness or infinity), guns, and explosives. It was all coming out in a disjointed fashion, but what couldn't be denied is that my sons had experienced incredible trauma.

* * *

All of these are associated with Masonic initiation rituals. Specifically, Scottish Rite. The altar with bones, the candles, and other items, are consistent with a masonic Reflection Chamber, which throughout history, have been hidden in underground vaults, this one at a house numbered for the year the Knights Templar were founded, and built by a Knight Templar leader. This is where the candidate goes through a period of isolation surrounded by symbolic objects. Placing the Papal Tiara on a skull and putting a dagger in it then trampling it are part of a 30th degree Knight Kadosh ceremony. But what about the torture/execution devices? These devices described and drawn by my son, have historically been used by Freemasons for near death rituals. The guillotine stops just short of cutting off the head, as the saw stops just short of its victim. The electric chair is real but not intended to kill. These rituals, combined with the reflection chamber, are intended as a rebirth of the candidate. A "tabula rasa" (also the name of one of Osman's companies) which means a "clean slate" followed by a symbolic death and rebirth into Freemasonry. Part of a Secret Alchemical Ritual (alchemy was another corporate name). Immortality, and rebirth, are symbolized with an Ouroboros, one of the symbols that Gabe drew when he was only 7 years old. And it turns out that skeleton keys are one of the most important symbols in Scottish Rite Freemasonry.

* * *

Toby described "mean guys with guns under their jackets" yelling at Paw Paw telling him to "get out of our of their house." At Mike Nobles house. So, whose house was it really? Nobles had told Gabe he was a "secret agent" for the government and "killed people for the president." He talked about "good guy" policemen" and "bad guy." He also showed him "blueprints" to blow up an IRS building, seemingly a contradiction.

* * *

Then, amid the overwhelming legal and law enforcement chaos that I was embroiled in, Gabe drew a picture that I couldn't spare the mental energy to focus on at the time but might contain a key to what all this was about. At some point, though, I did focus on it. It was a drawing of a display case. The case enshrined a rifle with a scope, bullet cartridge, a single pistol, and several newspaper articles.

* * *

The true treasure of southern Freemasons, who believe they are the modern-day Knights Templar, and their military, religious and mob allies. Housed here at a true X marks the spot site, numbered 1118. Not the cup of Christ, or the Ark of the Covenant. Not the bloodline of Christ. But the holy grail of these delusional knights, the club of Confederate general Albert Pike, Grand Wizard Bedford Forrest, Governor George Wallace, Senator Strom Thurmond, Senator Jesse Helms, Governor Lester Maddox, Senator Trent Lott, Congressman Bob Sikes, Senator Robert Byrd, and so many other hate mongers, whose membership overlaps that of the Ku Klux Klan, is a symbol of treason.

* * *

"Paw Paw says that's the gun that killed the president," Gabe said.
"He said it is a hero's gun"
It took me a moment to register what my son had said.
"What president?" I asked.
He just shrugged and kept drawing.
It could only mean one thing.
Since only one president had ever been murdered with a rifle, Mike Nobles possessed a rifle that he believed to be the one that killed John F. Kennedy.

* * *

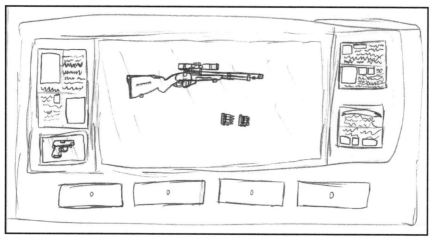

Gabe said his grandfather called this "a hero's gun" and said it was "the gun that killed the president." The newspapers are articles about the Kennedy assassination. Notice also the ammo clips, and a pistol were included. I can only speculate that the pistol was the gun that allegedly killed Dallas police officer JD Tippit. Gabe was only 7 when he told me about this and had never been taught about the Kennedy assassination.

Gabe called this a "robot gun" and said the camera tracked motion and the gun fired automatically. ATF Intelligence agent Greg Moore in Tennessee looked at this and other drawings and said they were credible, and that this was called a sentry gun. I can only speculate that this is a classified military weapon.

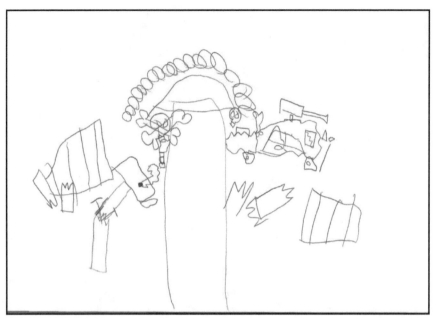

Gabe called this a "rocky cave" and said his grandfather, "army men" and "bad guy officers" took him there. I asked him to draw it and what he drew was a military bunker, through a gate, and past a no trespassing sign, with old disabled military vehicles along the road. All of these features are consistent with the Eglin Air Force Base reservation.

Another depiction of a military bunker Gabe was taken to which he called "the rocky cave."

Gabe said this was in the "gun room," a bunker or underground vault, if you will, on Nobles' property. Neither he nor I knew the significance. It appears to be a pyramid, and statues of Anubis, god of the dead, holding spears.

An apparent rocket launcher, one of many military weapons Gabe was exposed to.

An explosives timer Gabe drew.

A crate marked TNT. Gabe said his grandfather had grenades and explosives.

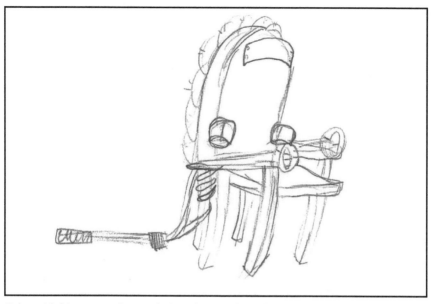

Gabe said this was an electric chair and pointed out that it had 5 legs to stabilize it as the victim convulsed. He included the power cord plugged into the wall.

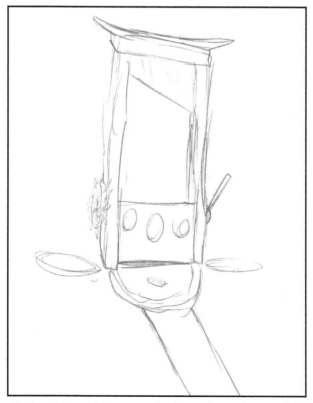

A guillotine. Gabe said there was a bucket underneath to catch blood.

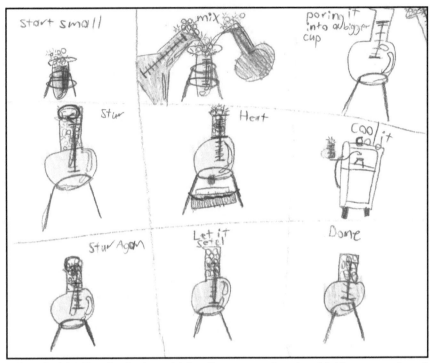

Gabe called this "Paw Paw's science lab," and it appears to be a drug lab. He even numbered every step of the process and said he accompanied his grandfather selling the drugs.

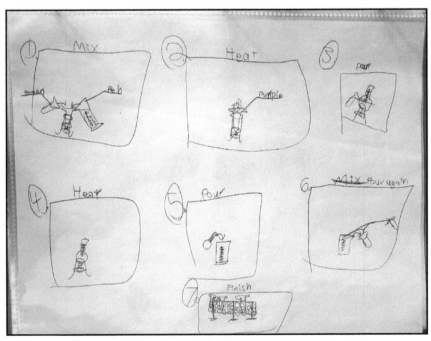

Another picture of "Paw Paw's science lab, an obvious drug lab.

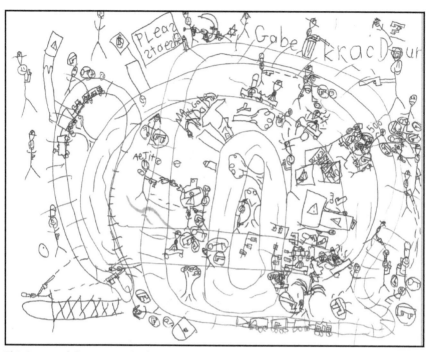

This is one of the extremely detailed pictures Gabe drew obsessively of a game called "Crack Down. This was an obscene and violent game Nobles forced Gabe to play and into which his grandfather "recorded his guns" so they "weren't real anymore." A mind game on a young autistic child.

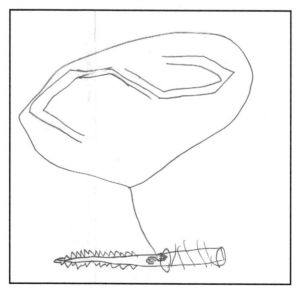

This is a picture Gabe drew of an implement his grandfather allegedlly used to rape children. Only after he and his brother disclosed this to me, his therapist, his doctor and a child protection investigator did I discover that Nobles' brother, Roger, made these implements, magic wands, and sold them on the internet.

This drawing depicts a tow truck towing what I believe was my stolen utility trailer. The trailer was used to haul off items from Nobles' bunker, and also to transport human remains

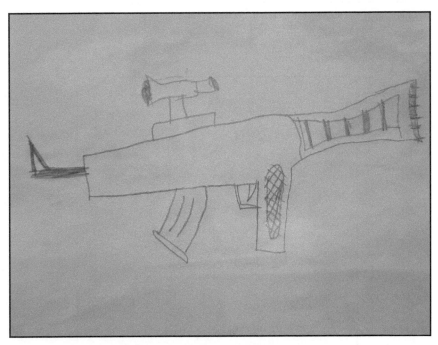

One of the many pictures of guns drawn by Gabe.

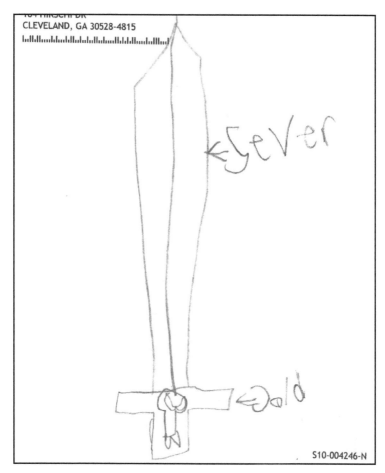

Gabe drew this in church one day. It depicts a sword with a skull on the handle and the fact that the blade was silver and the handle gold colored.

A masked robed individual holding a staff. The Ouroboros is an interesting detail as neither he nor I were familiar with this symbol when he drew this, other than what he had seen with his grandfather.

125

An apparent alter complete with bones and a skull with a demonic looking 4 horned beast above it. Guarded by what appears to be statues of Anubis holding spears.

Another apparent alter, with burning skull and bones, and what looks like possibly a serpent with legs. Guarded by a demonic goat headed creature holding a trident and a gun.

One of many iron crosses that Gabe drew.

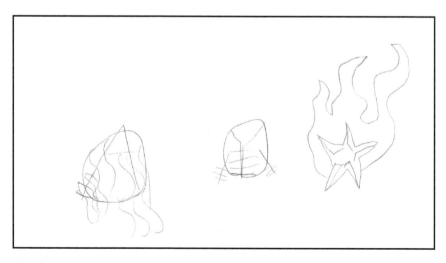

These are occult looking symbols that Gabe drew that to this day, I have been unable to identify other than the Pentacle or Pentagram.

A tattoo from one of Nobles associates who Gabe called a "bad guy." It is a burning templar cross.

This was on the jacket of a biker Gabe knew as Tiger. Gabe says he saw his grandfather kill this man.

A ceremonial looking sword with a skull on the handle and a candle holder with 3 candles. The candles are likely "tri-luminaries" representing the Sun, the Moon, and the Master of the Lodge.

129

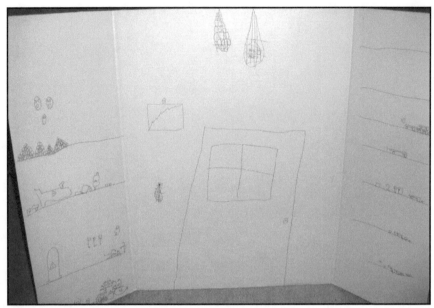

This was a 3D cardboard cut out that Gabe used to draw what he called "the gun room." This drawing depicts masks, guns, grenades, skeleton keys, along with a door.

Gabe said his grandfather wore this and made fun of Jesus. Is this a papal tiara possibly, which is associated with Knights of Kadosh rituals?

Another tattoo from the man Gabe knew as Tiger.

I believe this drawing was of a mask Nobles used to terrorize the kids.

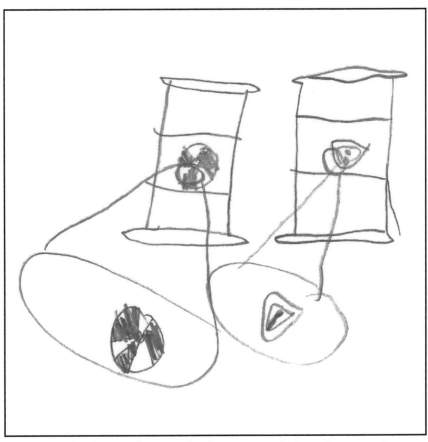

55 Gallon drums Gabe saw on Nobles' property with hazardous symbols

Another picture of a pyramid guarded by statues of Anubis.

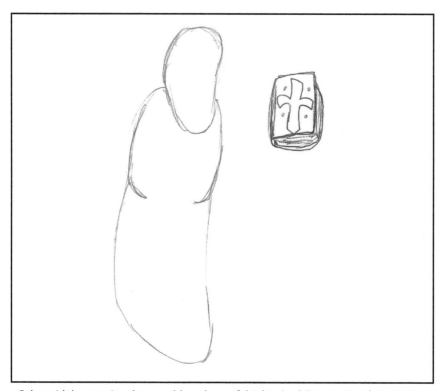

Gabe said the men in robes would read out of this book while torturing their victims.

Gabe was not familiar with medieval racks. He called this a machine that stretches people. The robes are very similar to a type of Ku Klux Klan robe.

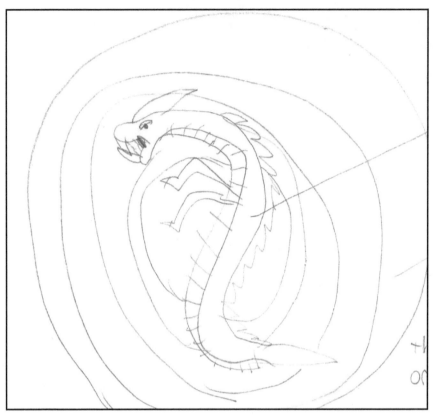

Another depiction of what looks like a 2-legged serpent or a dragon. This one was a tattoo Gabe said.

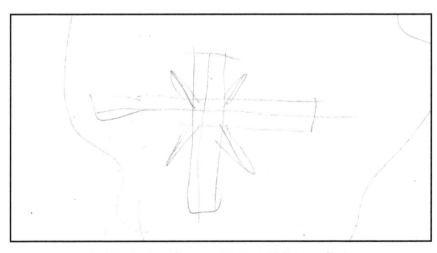

Another version of a cross, this one with beams of light.

While all these revelations were starting to come out, I was trying to figure out what to do. Meanwhile, other forces were moving.

The same day I got the boys back, Judge Thomas Santurri signed a judicial order that all court correspondence to me be sent to a non-existent address nowhere near where I lived. The address he assigned was basically an intersection with no buildings. It amounted to all my court-related communications being delivered to a culvert.

* * *

The day after that, on January 27, Judge Santurri ordered that Mike Nobles' guns and ammunition be returned to him despite being a felon prohibited from possessing firearms of any sort. There was no waiting period, and no further hearing. Regardless of the DVI against him, I was never notified of course as my notification was going to a nonexistent address.

The fact that Toby had found and fired a loaded firearm constituted child endangerment. There was no way I could allow Mike Nobles to have legal access to my boys ever again. Over the next few days, I contacted an attorney, a law enforcement officer in Okaloosa County, and the Santa Rosa Kids House to determine how and with whom to file a report.

My request that Santa Rosa Kids House interview my children was denied, claiming lack of jurisdiction. The old Jurisdiction Shell Game, Florida's most convenient excuse.

I took the boys to see their therapist, Karleen Shuster, who said the boys' account was credible and that I had to report it. She documented that the boys said the guns were there to "kill the bad guys," *and the bad guys were the police.*

* * *

I didn't relish the idea of throwing myself back into the corrupt meat grinder of the local judicial system, but I had no choice. On January 30, I submitted a request in Santa Rosa County to reinstate the DVIs protecting my sons from Mike Nobles. Up until that point, I had wanted to keep Christy out of it, seeing her in large part as a victim in this whole sordid tale. If she couldn't or wouldn't protect her children from her abusive father, I needed an injunction against her as well. I requested that she be given supervised visits and counseling.

Inexplicably, after all the sworn testimony, all the damning accounts of sexual abuse of the previous hearing, all the corroborating testimony that Nobles had threatened, planned, and kidnapped my sons, all the documented violations of the previous injunction, the request was neither accepted nor denied. A hearing was scheduled for February 4 with Judge Goodman. I didn't know it that day, but Santurri had already signed the order to return Nobles' guns to him.

* * *

My DVI filing generated another DCF report, this one describing Toby's firing of a gun in the home of a convicted felon.

On January 30, Toby was interviewed by child protection investigator, Rick Karshna, who worked closely with Jennifer Clark and Heather Pagano under Donna Parish's supervision.

His arrival at my house was one of the most clownish, buffoonish moments of this entire story. He looked like he had just rolled out of bed. He barged into my house unannounced, throwing papers around, demanding that I sign them, and telling me I needed to get a divorce.

Then he took my sons upstairs to interview them. When he left, they were both crying and told me Karshna didn't believe them.

The DCF case file states: "[Toby] was happy and talkative. CPI spoke to him in the upstairs bedroom [of the Harris home]. He said he took a ladder [at Nobles house] and climbed up into papa's closet in master bath. He took a gun out and pointed it at a picture and pulled the trigger, breaking the glass. He did this one time. He said his mom was in the house at the time. He did not make statements about seeing other guns, or a secret room. He described the gun as short, most likely a handgun."

I'm offering some of Karshna's activities out of order of occurrence to illustrate just how blatant, pernicious, and incessant they were. In the fall of 2009, he falsified two reports that should have included disclosures of child abuse and endangerment. He also destroyed records provided to him by Dr. Fred DeShon and therapist Karleen Shuster. Later in 2009, he interviewed my mother, shouted at her, called her a liar, and hung up the phone leaving her in tears. He gave the same treatment to Toby's teacher, Bonnie Emmons, leaving her in tears and covering up what she told him about Toby's signs of abuse.

Rick Karshna was a washed-up ex-cop from Wisconsin who was fired for incompetence, outrageous misconduct, and psychological issues[1]. According to a 2004 article in Madison, Wisconsin's *Capital Times*,[2] Karshna was sleeping in his patrol car when he was awakened by a woman who needed transportation. As he tried to find the vehicle of a friend, she claimed would get her home, a man arrived and Karshna let her leave with him. Still groggy from his nap, Karshna didn't bother to run even a cursory background check on the man. Had he done so, he would have learned the woman had filed a restraining order against the man, and Karshna could have (should have) arrested him on the spot. Instead, the woman who sought Karshna's help was held captive and raped all weekend. He once had a slow-speed chase in which the woman he was chasing got out, went into a store, got back in her car, and the chase resumed. Repeatedly caught sleeping on the job, he was suspended several times and forced to go to counseling which I find particularly ironic, *as he tried to label me crazy.* An open records release later stated that Karshna "...demonstrated a complete lack of investigative initiative." *Does this behavior sound familiar?*

He was also a failed Republican candidate for the Wisconsin 58th Assembly District. After being fired from his law enforcement job, he washed ashore in Florida where he got a job with the Department of Children and Families. In terms of King Arthur's Court, I would name him the Court Jester. A perfect recruit to fix cases involving a bunch of crooked cops. As a DCF investigator, Karshna falsified reports, and destroyed records, buried gruesome disclosures by children, amassing a voluminous personnel file replete with complaints.

Also, on January 30 CPI Heather Pagano documented that Mike Nobles had surrendered his weapons and ammunition on October 1 to the Sheriff's Department when the restraining order was served. These weapons were a decoy for his secret arsenal, which Gabe had witnessed. She received this information from Joey Forgione. However, just days later, Joey Forgione seized the case from officer Joseph Kearnes, falsifying a report by claiming that Nobles possessed no weapons at all. These case files show that both Forgione and Pagano, in fact the whole DCF/EC-CAC team, knew Nobles was a felon, possessed guns despite the prohibition, and then covered it up. The case files also show communication between Pagano and a FBI agent Tim Kinard. Notably this shows that they all knew, and her notes show, that FBI agent Kinard knew about the guns at the Sheriff's Department *before* they were returned to him.

A Suspicious Death?

On January 31, 2009, a body was pulled from the bay, the remains of Bill Richey. Richey allegedly hurled himself from the Mid-Bay Bridge, leaving his car still running.

An attorney friend of mine found the whole thing smelled funny, so she called someone she knew in the coroner's office. She was told, "It would be in your best interest not to ask questions about things that don't concern you." This response rattled and frightened her.

Is this incident related to what I was going through? I can't say, but it does illustrate how things are run in Okaloosa County, heart of the Redneck Riviera. This was one of many suspicious deaths and murders around that time.

On January 31, I attempted to report to the Niceville Police. I called Tom Dunn's cell and told him I was going to the precinct to make a report, but he told me not to go there, instead to meet an officer at the children's park not far from there. I had no idea what kind of orchestration was taking place, and I couldn't be certain how much danger I was in, but I acquiesced. I met Officer Joseph Kearnes at the children's park. He let me talk, but he didn't file a report. His name shares space with Forgione on several falsified reports. When I told him about machine guns, cash, bars of gold, and explosives that Gabe said Nobles had, he literally said that he thought hoarding those things was a good idea. Welcome to lower Alabama.

I kept checking for Kearnes to file a report on the information I had given him, an articulate report three pages long, but he never did. On February 3, 2009, I contacted Officer Nelson of the Niceville PD. Officer Nelson took the case very seriously. He asked me an interesting question. Was Nobles connected? He knew how things worked. He wrote a detailed and accurate report. I point that out because it's important to note that not all cops nor all Florida cops are corrupt. In my case they were blocked by others from doing their jobs. The same would apply to the Florida DCF. Nelson immediately forced to give the case to Kearnes and Forgione, who then killed the case. Officer Nelson used the word "forced" repeatedly when he told me off the record what had happened. This crystallized the ongoing pattern – Forgione and Kearnes were seizing cases and fixing them. Nelson was gone from the department a short time later.

I discovered later that on this same day, something else happened. Heather Pagano's DCF case files describe a meeting between her and Joey Forgione in Forgione's car in the parking lot behind Food World in Niceville. What did they discuss? Difficult to prove but easy to surmise is that they were scheming to make this case go away. The fact that they had a meeting outside both of their offices certainly suggests they didn't want anyone overhearing.

The next day, Toby was interviewed by Heather Pagano the CPI from DCF. Her report states:

> We then discussed the guns. He stated that he found one gun in the closet and it was "this long" (he put his hands out to measure the size of the gun). He [stated] that he shot the gun and broke a picture. He [stated] that the [Mother] was there when this happened. He shot it w/the bullet that was already in the gun.[3]

A bullet hole was found in the wall and photographed by the DCF.

* * *

It was time for me to reach out and try to get some real law enforcement, to reach out beyond this cesspit of local corruption I was mired in. So, through an acquaintance, I reached out to Special Agent Tim Kinard from Pensacola. I gave him the story, and he agreed that it warranted investigation, and that he would come to Niceville.

Pagano's notes also show communication with Agent Kinard. Everyone involved knew that Nobles was a convicted felon. Everyone knew that he had surrendered firearms to the Sheriff's Office, and that they would be returned to him.

February 4 was the hearing on the injunction I sought against my wife for failure to keep our sons safely away from her father. While waiting in the witness room, Nobles saw me, flew into a rage, and lunged at me. Security stopped him before he could reach me.

As soon as the hearing opened, Judge Goodman announced that Judge Thomas Santurri had requested the case, and Goodman had acquiesced to the request. Judges don't get to choose cases, but it happened again and again. Every case was funneled to Judge Santurri, even after I filed a judicial complaint. And he would repeatedly make sure I never got a hearing.

In the parking lot, Nobles literally skipped to his car, gloating and smiling as he called someone on his phone. Nobles would continue in his ever-changing stories about his guns. Claiming that the weapons belonged to his son who sold them prior to moving to Guyana. This is even though the long rifle his son supposedly sold was a family heirloom, formerly belonging to Nobles' father. His would also claim they had been returned to the Okaloosa County Sheriff's Department; both cannot be true, just as his accounts that the guns were both his son's and his wife's can't be true, nor can the claim that this arsenal was in his clothes closet, yet he didn't know they were there. He attempted to distract from these inconsistencies with his claims about the status of my paternity, but fortunately that attempt failed. Yay for small victories.

A later hearing was scheduled. Santurri quietly dismissed the case five days later with no motion to dismiss and no hearing.

* * *

Outside the courthouse, Christy offered to let me come to the Nobles house on 1118 Rhonda Drive to see things for myself. She told me that her father wanted Joey Forgione to be there. This was, of course, a setup. I was being summoned to see that there was no substance to anything Gabe was saying. In my reports and discussions around the area, I was describing what Gabe told me, and this had no doubt gotten back to Nobles.

So, on February 5, I went to the Nobles home, but I was bringing a secret weapon, FBI agent Tim Kinard. I met him for the first and only time in person that day before he hung me out to dry. He looked the essence of the G-man, business-like suit, tall, medium build, about forty. A veteran FBI agent. A Special Agent, Joint Terrorism Task Force, Kinard was also a former Air Force Intelligence officer, part of a parade of ex-military men and military police that would engage in this cover up followed by ex-military doctors.

When we arrived at the Nobles house, however, for some reason Agent Kinard refused to go inside. When I prompted and urged him, I was dismayed that he steadfastly refused. I couldn't help but wonder what the hell he'd driven all that way for if he wasn't going to do any investigating. He remained outside chatting with Brian Riggs, Shelly's husband.

It was during this conversation I overheard between Kinard and Riggs, I discovered that Nobles' weapons had indeed been returned to him. I later followed up and obtained the records from the case file from the courthouse, the Evidence Custodian. They commented that Nobles and his attorney should be in jail, as Nobles was a felon.

I was left to go in by myself, camera in hand.

* * *

Entering the house, I looked in the front door closet and found the large control box for Nobles surveillance system. Inexplicably, the entrance to the attic that had been in the skylight of the master bathroom had been freshly and hastily drywalled over. It hadn't been thoroughly spackled, sanded, or painted. Oddly, there was no attic access now, aside from tearing it all back out again. Carolyn Palmer had lived here for a couple of years, and the Nobles had since booted her out and reclaimed the house. There was no way she'd have had the money or the reason to have any work done on the house. Both Gabe and Toby described seeing their grandfather do this work during their abduction. Toby and Gabe had previously described this in great detail. Toby had said that his grandfather had hurriedly put up a "piece of wall" (sheetrock) and then used "dry tape" (sheet rock tape) and afterwards painted it. Just one of many details provided by the kids confirmed by physical evidence.

The entire living room carpet had been removed; I believe because of what Gabe witnessed there. Carpet that the kids would later describe as being blood soaked from a murder they witnessed. The entire house was in disarray. Clearly some kind of clean-up was ongoing.

The entire back yard had been dug up into a muddy mess, a morass of deep tire tracks and disturbed earth. The vent pipes I had seen sticking out of the ground back there were gone. Even the shrubs had been removed. There was a new water connection on the back of the house that looked like a fire department connection. Tracks from my trailer led from the back yard to the road, but there was no sign of my stolen utility trailer.

The more I looked around, the more I recognized the destruction and burial of evidence, just like how his computer with the child porn had been swapped out. That computer might have been safely stowed in the walled-up attic. What was he destroying in the back yard?

* * *

In the coming days, my faith in even the integrity of the FBI was shattered. My secret weapon may well have been turned into a weapon for the forces protecting Nobles.

CPI Heather Pagano documented a conversation with Agent Kinard on February 10. Kinard claimed to have spoken with Mike Nobles the previous day, and Nobles claimed that the weapons he had surrendered and then reclaimed were hunting rifles belonging to his wife. They were registered in her name. Of course, they weren't registered at all, as Florida had no such firearm registration system.

Pagano also reported a communication with therapist Karleen Shuster in which:

> The boys did draw pics of the guns they saw at the [grandfather's] home and their play suggested that they were credible. Ms. Shuster [stated] that the boys were acting like they were shooting guns and that they had to kill the "bad guys" and that the bad guys were the police. The boys said that the [grandfather] had told them that the cops were bad guys.[4]

There is also a photo in the case file of the bullet hole in the wall.

On February 10, I received an email from Agent Kinard saying he had spoken to Nobles.

> I spoke with Mr. Nobles. He advised the home previously had two skylights, one of which leaked. When he had the home re-roofed several years ago, he had the leaking skylight removed and covered over with plywood and shingles on the outside. The "skylight" opening remained in place until he sold the home to Caroline [sic],

who had the skylight opening closed up and sheetrocked over. This took place approximately five years ago, and I confirmed this with Caroline who is now living out of state. I also spoke with two Child Protective Services investigators who have spent a great deal of time in the home throughout the past year. Neither of them recalls seeing an opening in the ceiling that would have recently been covered over as described by your son. My investigation is continuing.

Kinard never contacted Carolyn Palmer.[5] She was never contacted by the FBI at all.

Why in the hell was the FBI covering for a pedophile swindler and sexual predator? Why were all these law enforcement and child protective entities running around like Korrupt Keystone Kops destroying records and falsifying reports? It was unbelievable. Lying to the FBI during an investigation is a federal felony. *But the FBI can lie to you with no consequences.*

Agent Kinard then cut off all contact with me. He refused to talk to my son and refused to meet with me. He had been involved for all of a few days and stuck around just long enough to put a federal stamp of approval on the lies and corruption swirling around me.

* * *

My kids had affirmed the allegations in recorded interviews, and I had the sense that more would come out. A mental health professional and school administrator had sworn under oath that both boys showed unmistakable signs of sexual abuse and had described that abuse in some detail. Mike Nobles had admitted that child-on-child sexual abuse occurred in his sworn testimony, while blaming the victims with his next breath. The DCF, the ECCAC, and several law enforcement officers, including an FBI agent, were whitewashing and deleting reports, falsifying documents, and then charging me with filing spurious police reports. Church leaders were involved. A circuit court judge was involved, "losing" filings and falsifying records. A known felon was allowed to possess firearms, against law and common sense, and according to my son, possessed an arsenal of apocalyptic proportions. Christy's counseling records were destroyed by a "flood." The campaign to discredit me and get me to shut up was incredible, and all I wanted was safety for my kids and justice done on the man responsible.

Throughout all this I was increasingly in need of emotional and spiritual support, so I signed up for a one-on-one discipling program through my church called Iron on Iron. It was supposed to be an eight-week intensive bible study for men but ended up being just a kaffeeklatsch.

My first time, I was matched with a man named Dave Clark, a good man who later helped put me in touch with authorities who might be able to help me.

The next two times, however, I was matched "under the guidance of the Holy Spirit" with Jerry Williams from Alabama, another "patriot" Vietnam veteran and former member of the 82nd Airborne who had approached me on day one at church. The minister would stand ahead of the group and pray, and supposedly moved by the Holy Spirit, would assign mentors and disciples. Out of sixty men who took part, I was matched with Jerry Williams twice, which seems to me to be statistically unlikely, and if a spirit was involved it wasn't holy. The second time he supervised himself. Williams made a great effort at "helping" me. One time in the parking lot, knowing that I was struggling with finances, he shook my hand and slipped me a hundred-dollar bill.

Later, he gave me a cell phone that I could use at his expense.

My suspicions piqued when he began using these meetings to pump me for information and to pressure me into silence. He tried to convince me that Nobles was a confidential informant for the government, which made him all but immune to all sorts of legal proceedings. He also told me my life was in danger.

After a while, the phone that Williams gave me went haywire, just like the previous phone Nobles had insisted on giving me right before he cut off contact with me. After the way it became apparent that they always seemed to be a step ahead of me, I became certain it was being used to spy on me, maybe bugged, cloned, or with a GPS tracker, or all the above.

Over a few days and weeks, however, the boys began to talk more and more about what they had seen and undergone during their abduction. *The magnitude of it was far worse than anything I had imagined.*

Endnotes

1   Benson, Dan. "Cudahy police officer resigns, Charges by chief include sleeping while on duty." December 14, 2004. *Milwaukee Journal-Sentinel*.

2   https://www.newspapers.com/image/525977045/?match=1

3   Pagano, Heather. Case file report February 3, 2009. Department of Children and Families.

4   Pagano, Heather. Case file report, February 9, 2009. Department of Children and Families.

5   Carolyn Palmer, interview with the publisher, July 17, 2023.

CHAPTER TEN

LAWYERS GUNS AND MONEY

The corrupt intricacies of how all these public officials were running in circles to destroy me, discredit me and my sons, cover for Nobles, and then cover their own tracks could go on for chapters and chapters. And I do have documentation to show it all, at least the records that I managed to acquire before they were destroyed.

The bottom line was that terrible things had happened to my children, and Mike Nobles was not only responsible, but he also appeared to be at the center of a wide and expanding web.

The month of February 2009 was fraught with lies, stonewalling, and corruption as I pressed local officials hard on the issue of Nobles' guns.

Judge Santurri somehow "lost" my filings over Nobles restraining order violations. Santurri had unilaterally declared my address to be a nonsense address at an unpopulated intersection. Kearnes and Forgione were editing police records to describe me as "crazy," erasing the fact that they all knew Nobles was a known convicted felon. I was painted as some crackpot best ignored. My sons' honest accounts of what had happened to them were ignored, as were documented accounts of child pornography in the Nobles' home. The Okaloosa County Sheriff's Department and the Niceville PD were doing their best to spin me in circles. Three of my efforts to file reports were deflected and squashed. I went to the Florida Department of Law Enforcement, the Florida state police. They sent me back to the Sheriff. If you've ever sought justice in Florida, maybe you've played the Jurisdiction Shell Game, too.

Gabe and Toby had witnessed their grandfather killing numerous pets, one of the tactics he'd used to frighten his daughters throughout their lives. He tied a snake into a knot, shot Christy's cat, killed my son's pet rats. While Mike Nobles was giving statements that his daughters' hamsters died of "natural causes," Wanda Nobles was saying no animals died at all.[1]

Meanwhile, Nobles led the congregation of Destin Church of Christ in a prayer for the pastor.

* * *

On February 16, 2009, Michael Nobles entered the Okaloosa County Sheriff's Department to retrieve weapons he was prohibited by law from possessing. He produced the court order signed by Judge Santurri stating he was entitled to their return. He produced his driver's license, which was photocopied. He had submitted to and somehow passed a background check which concealed his 1986 conviction. He personally signed for and received three hunting rifles and a 12-gauge shotgun, plus 643 rounds of ammunition, which included .410 shotgun shells, even though no .410 shotgun had been surrendered. Testified under oath by Okaloosa County Sheriff's Evidence Custodian Mary Lou Collins, witnessed by and attested to by her assistant, who provided me with receipts signed by Michael Nobles. She was furious at the corruption of how this all went down, how a convicted felon could have guns returned to him, how everyone at every level was covering for him. At any mention of Joey Forgione, she simply rolled her eyes Local state and federal officials all knew this was happening and all lied to cover it up.

Nobles' son-in-law, Brian Riggs, later testified to hiding at least eight guns for his father-in-law. Billy Nobles occasionally tried to sell them. To make sure they didn't come up again, they were stashed at the Riggs' home. They called one of them a family heirloom, having belonged to Mike Nobles' father, who was murdered in the 1970s in a fight at work.

These guns were barely the tip of the iceberg, however.

* * *

It was like I could feel a freight coming at me at full speed, but I couldn't see it or know where it was coming from. I called everybody I could think of, knowing that my children had already been exposed to terrible danger and abuse and fearing that more was coming. I even called the office of George Sheldon, Secretary of the Florida Department of Children and Families. I was transferred in circles, repeatedly warned that my sons would imminently be abducted again to suffer more abuse, all because I was calling out local authorities for putting guns in the hands of a felon.

Gabe was describing rooms of military style weapons, stacks of ammunition, grenades, explosives, and weird occult symbols and paraphernalia. When I asked where all that was, he said it was all in "the gun room" at Paw Paw's house but was unable to articulate exactly where the access was.

"They had a bunch of trash cans and loaded them on the trailer," Gabe said. Then he drew that too, but on the sides of the trash cans were accurately rendered hazardous warning labels and symbols. He was describing 55-gallon drums. Toby confirmed having seen this too, as well as crates full of guns.

Anytime I asked Gabe about any of this, he got extremely nervous. After several gentle promptings, he confessed why. *"Because Paw Paw said he would shoot you if I talked about his guns or anything."*

* * *

After a couple of weeks of stewing, I met with Okaloosa County Sheriff's evidence custodian, Mary Collins, who was outraged at the blatant lies being perpetrated about Nobles' guns. She had been there. She gave me copies of the receipts that showed Nobles had signed for them. During our meeting she said, "His lawyer, Michael Gibson, should have been charged too." She refuted the absurd claims that someone else signed out the weapons. Her assistant was also present at this meeting and made clear her belief that Joey Forgione was a crook. "Everyone in Okaloosa County knows that."

Trying to maintain some degree of peace and civility with Christy as there was no custody arrangement, I entered into a fragile agreement with Christy that she would keep the boys while I was traveling for work, as long as she promised *never* to let her parents or younger sisters have any access to them. It was foolish of me, but I felt like I had no other options. Desperate times, desperate measures.

* * *

On February 27, 2009, Okaloosa County Sheriff Charlie Morris was arrested on federal racketeering charges. Morris, along with his secretary Teresa Adams, was convicted of conspiracy, theft, and money laundering in a kickback scheme where they stole department employee bonuses. Morris was sentenced to 71 months in prison.

Charlie Morris was an eighteen-year veteran of the Air Force in military security. Rumor had it that he was drummed out of his military career before retirement because weapons and materiel had a way of disappearing under his care.

This may sound conspiratorial, but I believe his arrest constitutes a "wag the dog" scenario, when public attention is diverted from something of greater importance by something of lesser importance.

In this case, Charlie Morris' office was largely responsible for how my case and the associated reports had been mishandled. As soon as I heard that Nobles had gotten his guns back, I began pushing hard against every institution and everyone involved that Nobles should be arrested. It was a mad scramble of epic ass-covering at the Niceville PD, the Okaloosa

County Sheriff's Office, the Emerald Coast Child Advocacy Center, and the Florida DCF.

I believe it was a wag-the-dog scenario, because a whole bunch of incidents happened on the same day – launch day for a massive cover-up. Arresting Morris was part of the cover-up.

All of my police and child abuse reports were quietly closed the very day of Morris' arrest.

Ed Spooner, from Quincy, Florida, and son of an Army Air Corp veteran was appointed interim sheriff and sent in to clean up the shit I was stirring up. His first act as sheriff was to shut me up – and my boys too.

I was traveling for work, coming home the same day. After all that happened, my anxieties were through the roof whenever I had to leave town. I was living in a swamp of desperation, fear, and anger.

When I was traveling the boys were in the care of a nanny, Marilyn, who had worked for us for about a year, an elderly African American lady with diabetes. During this trip, the kids were with Christy and were to be returned to me when I finished my trip. On this day, February 27, I had called Gabe's school, Calvary Christian Academy, and asked them to send him home on the bus. I was coming home and worried more and more about Gabe being mentally abused about guns again. I was also growing more anxious of Nobles putting the screws to Gabe to silence him. So, some trusted family friends from when I was in the military picked up Gabe at my request and took him with them to Pizza Hut for a birthday party for one of their sons. Toby was with Christy. Nobles called Marilyn and threatened her. Then the Okaloosa County Sheriff's Department called her and threatened to arrest her.

I was boarding a plane to come home when the Okaloosa Sheriff's Department called me, threatening to arrest me and the nanny if I didn't hand over my kids to them. They also called the nanny and made the same threats. They had no court order, no custody order, and no legal justification to seize my sons. I told them as much. Law enforcement can't just seize a child without a court order. I was the custodial parent in practice, and there was no custody order in place. They quizzed me about whether I was Gabe's biological father, the apparent go to position which was legally irrelevant. I had no legal obligation to tell anyone where my son was but did after the threats of arresting me and the Nanny.

Lacking any grounds to do such a thing, Sheriff's deputies crashed the birthday party and seized my seven-year-old son, falsely claiming he was "a missing child." They behaved like a white bubba goon squad from 1950s Mississippi. Gabe was dragged out of there like a criminal and put in the back of a patrol car. Gabe was taken to Mike Nobles' house and handed over to the monster. One of the first acts of the new Sherrif was to kidnap my son and deliver him to Mike Nobles.

When I arrived home, I couldn't reach Christy. Apparently, she had filed a "missing child" report, which was the tissue-thin pretense on which the abduction was based. I called her sister's home several times. Shelly Riggs told me over and over she didn't know where Christy was, even though she was living there.

Marilyn moved back to Louisiana shortly after this nightmare, and I went through two other nannies. One a nice Filipino lady from church who had her own nightmare story dealing with the local racists, then, the wife from a couple I knew from church. The husband had tried to help me once. He had a friend, an ex-con, who worked as a cook at a Waffle House in Santa Rosa County and knew a lot of cops. When asked about Mike Nobles he said, "If it's the Mike Nobles I know of, I don't want anything to do with this. He is in deep with the cops."

* * *

Six minutes after Gabe was abducted, CPI Heather Pagano closed out her report. It was filled with breathtaking fabrications, first about my mental health, suggesting that I was mentally ill but citing no evidence, and then suggesting that I was too dangerous and unable to take care of my sons. Here's the most egregious – and easily disprovable – lie: She claimed that Mike Nobles had "no guns at all and never had."

"The parents continue to battle over custody," her report said, painting all of this as a tiresome game of he-said-she-said, putting words in Christy's mouth, and ignoring Christy's documented history of mental illness.

Other quotes from her report show her concerted effort of fabrication and disinformation. Here are examples:

> 1. *There have been several reports recently with serious allegations of sexual abuse. None have been founded.*

Obviously, this is ridiculous, because *none of the allegations were investigated.*

> 2. *Mother has been seen and she is protective of the children. Mother denies being afraid of the father. CPI believes that she is trying to be cordial to the father to prevent aggressive behavior.*

I have never shown aggressive behavior towards anyone.

3. The father appears to be exhibiting behavior that raises questions regarding his mental health … The parents are separated, the mother appears not to have similar issues.

4. There are concerns for the father's future ability to provide for the care of the children. He is exhibiting behaviors that are beginning to raise concerns for his mental health. He has filed several reports and injunctions with similar allegations against his wife and father-in-law. The mother has been the primary caregiver for the past several months. The father only recently began having the children for overnight visits.

This is a great many lies to pack into a single paragraph. Of course, I was making consistent allegations because that's what the truth looks like.

5. Toby does make statements about firing a weapon at the Grandfather's house…

Which is true, and the DCF has a photo of the bullet hole to prove it.

6. The parents do not have a positive relationship, and the father appears to be unstable. There are 10 priors that repeatedly address sexual abuse of the children. Mother says she is protective of the children but CPI suspects that she is not able to protect herself or the children.

She then closed the case with "no indicators of sexual abuse as to both of the boys. These allegations have been reported numerous times. The allegations have been previously investigated and there are no new allegations of sexual abuse.… There are no indicators of family violence [threatening] children or inadequate supervision.… The parents have filed numerous DVI's against one another. All have been dismissed."[2]

The following note was entered by supervisor Donna Parish.

No indicators of family violence, inadequate supervision, sexual abuse, physical injury …. The Parents continue to battle over custody and visitation of the boys. CPI has filed a false reporting request with the DCF. The Niceville PD is also looking at filing for false reporting on this case.

Donna Parish again, a fellow Church of Christ leader of Mike Nobles, trying to label me crazy and have me arrested. Again. Repeating the Goebbels lie. A custody battle. Back and forth allegations. Very clever.

It was so insidious, relentless, and pervasive that at times it felt like an assault on my sanity. How could anyone blithely make all this shit up and still sleep at night?

Whatever sporadic "fighting" Christy was doing for custody of the boys, it was at the behest of her father. She was barely in their lives at all, of her own choice. She was coerced into being used as a pawn to cover for her father and the people who were covering for him.

Pagano then followed through and attempted to frame me, charging me with filing false police reports through the DCF.

Joey Forgione attempted the same through the Niceville PD.

Meanwhile, my kids were gone, and who knew what was being done to them.

I gave up on seeking any help from local law enforcement. It felt like I had a bounty on my head.

* * *

A few days later, on March 2, 2009, I sent certified letters to the new sheriff and to Governor Charlie Crist's office outlining the refusal by Niceville PD and Okaloosa County Sheriff's Department to investigate firearms possession, child endangerment, and kidnapping by a known convicted felon. The letter contained proof and witness statements. Some part of me must have believed that someone, somewhere would listen. Even though I knew the new sheriff was complicit, I was determined to hold his feet to the fire.

The same day, Christy tried to file another domestic violence injunction (DVI), based on the same fabrications she had made before, which she had subsequently denied under oath. The injunction was not immediately approved but set for a hearing.

* * *

On March 5, State Attorney Bill Eddins announced that his office would investigate the Okaloosa Sheriff's Department. Would this be a legitimate investigation or just another sham?

Nobles called me that night and left a creepy voice mail: "Hey Mark, this is Mike. Is there any way you can talk? You know what we've done so far has not accomplished anything in the world. I'd sure like to try and sit down and talk to you and see if we can work something out and change the status of our relationship and which won't hurt the kids and everything, so if you would give me a call you've got my phone number."

Gabe could be heard in the background, asking for his pillow, and the sound of it stabbed me in the heart. He had been delivered to a sociopath by a corrupt sheriff.

Gabe and Toby were held hostage in the Nobles' home for seven days, undergoing psychological torture as they had experienced before.

* * *

On March 8, I made a report to the National Center for Missing and Exploited Children (NCMEC). The next day, a woman named Julia returned my call and informed me that they had forwarded the report to the Niceville PD, to Joey Forgione.

"No, no, no!" I said. "Joey Forgione is a dirty cop and a mobster! He's part of this! He's running around in circles cleaning up after Nobles, threatening witnesses, destroying evidence, and falsifying reports!"

Later that day, I received a voicemail from Joey Forgione asking me to call him. I decided it was prudent not to return his call.

That evening, March 9, Christy called and told me to come to her sister's house. I roared across town. When I arrived, she brought out Gabe and Toby and once again, gave them back to me with no previous conversation, a whole four days after stating in a court filing that I was a danger to their lives. They were clearly overjoyed, but trauma was written all over each of their faces. She herself looked ashen, beleaguered, like she hadn't slept in weeks. I hugged the boys and told them to get in the car.

* * *

Christy said, "Joey Forgione called me looking for your number. You need to watch your back."

"Is that so?"

"They're out to get you."

"Who?"

"The cops. They told me to watch your back, you're digging a hole for yourself."

"I'll be careful."

She moved to get back in her car, then paused. "By the way, I won't be at the DVI hearing."

"You mean the one you just filed?" I said dryly.

"I don't have time." Then she turned and went back inside.

As we pulled away, Gabe started crying in obvious terror. I tried my best to console him, telling him I would always protect him.

"You can't protect me from what I see when I close my eyes."

* * *

Out of the mouths of babes. It took all my self-control to remain calm. "What do you see, Gabe?"

"Dead people."

That night, Gabe wouldn't sleep in his room. I let him sleep in my bed.

"What are you so afraid of?" I asked as we lay there with the lights on.

"Being crucified like Jesus."

"Why would you be afraid of that?"

"Paw Paw took me in the bathroom and nailed Faith's rag doll to the wall and told me he would crucify me like that if I talked about his guns or anybody messing with my weenie."

"Paw Paw is never going to hurt you or scare you again," I said. "I'll do everything I can to protect you."

"Who's gonna protect *you*?"

I didn't have an answer for that. All I could do was stroke his hair and tell him everything would be okay. I don't think either of us slept much that night.

* * *

Christy indeed did not show up for her DVI hearing, so the case was dismissed.

* * *

On March 16, 2009, the Okaloosa County Sheriff's Department received confirmation from the state of Florida that Mike Nobles was a convicted felon. Gasp! What a revelation! By this time, cynical sarcasm on my part was a reflex. This outcome was a result of a scathing letter I wrote to the Governor, including the documentation.

Instead of arresting him or seizing the guns again, the sheriff's department attorney, Steve Hurm, who had been installed alongside Ed Spooner, and a Florida Department of Law Enforcement attorney who had been sent by the governor's office in collusion with Mike Nobles' attorney, Mike Gibson, fabricated evidence. An affidavit was prepared by Gibson at Hurm's request stating the guns had been returned to Billy Nobles, which was of course ludicrous since there are plenty of records stating that Mike Nobles had signed for them. According to Gibson, this was requested by Hurm, the son in law of former Governor turned Senator, Bob Graham.

The banality – and stupidity – of evil just rings through this story over and over again.

Because all of this was a gross violation of legal ethics, not to mention a felony, I sent a letter to this effect to the Florida Bar Association. Gibson, in his response, cited all the false charges and fabrications entered against me by Forgione. He also claimed that he "forgot" his client was a felon. But the lies they were spreading had taken root in the legal system and had begun to solidify.

* * *

On a telephone call with my parents, Gabe disclosed to my mother some of the terrible things that had happened to them. He described Nobles forcing them to take naked pictures of each other. Nobles even showed them naked pictures of their mother at a young age to show them it was "okay." Nobles then killed two of Gabe's pet rats as an intimidation tactic, and he threatened him with crucifixion. These were events Gabe had described to me. Appalled, my mother made a complaint to DCF on April 8, 2009.

I still had the fragile agreement with Christy that the boys would stay with her while I was out of town. Christy was still living with her sister, Shelly Riggs, and her husband, Brian. One might question why I would ever allow them back into her care after what had happened to them previously in her care. I was out of options and trying to walk a very fine line. I was fairly certain that she herself wouldn't hurt them, although I couldn't say the same of Brian Riggs, who had punched Toby in the eye and subjected him to violent beatings with a belt. *I had been threatened with arrest if I withheld the boys from her.* The entirety of local law enforcement and the justice system had painted me as crazy, or worse, and had painted a bullseye on my back. I was barely getting by financially, with a job and career that often took me out of town. If I filed for divorce, everything I had reported would be painted as a "custody dispute," more so than it already had been. I have asked myself a thousand times what I could have done differently.

The next day, April 9, I left town for work and left the boys with Christy. During this visit, they were interviewed at the Riggs home by CPI Janelle Torres.[3]

Her report states:

> He stated he killed my rats. CPI asked him when this happened. He stated yesterday. He stated he has rats and his grandpa killed them and he was not sure why.... He stated that he [had] said ha ha I killed your rats.... CPI encouraged him to tell his mom if someone is telling him to lie. He stated that if he tells, then he will be crucified.... He [stated] that it meant you will get nails in your hands and feet. He [stated] he cannot tell his secret. He was very hesitant to be talking about this and in between all the answers he was talking about his pictures and the bad guys and the guns he was drawing. He confirmed his Paw Paw is the one telling him to keep the secret.... CPI asked him if his dad has ever asked him to lie and he [stated] no.

Her report was handed over to Rick Karshna, *who buried it.*

153

* * *

I was often accused of coaching them, when I did no such thing. Of all the boys' most damning allegations to investigators, none of them were made while they were in my care.

* * *

On April 9, just prior to Nobles arrest, in an incident that may or may not be related, a cache of World War II machine guns was found dumped in a creek under a bridge in Bibb County, Alabama, about two hours from Niceville.[4] An ATF agent described it as "a significant arsenal if it got into the wrong hands."[5] This made me wonder if Nobles' old cronies in the Patriot Network were getting nervous about the stink I was raising around his guns and everything else he had to hide, or even if this might have been part of the arsenal Gabe had described.

But then, on that same day, against all my deeply cynical expectations, lo and behold Nobles was arrested at his workplace by Okaloosa County Sheriff deputies on charges of weapons possession by a felon. Nobles had been chief of security at one of Constance Wayne Jones' condominium complexes. Jones had also built Nobles' house. Notably, Nobles arrest is absent from the Sheriff's log of events that day, a website that contains far more trivial and routine incidents and arrests. And good luck finding any mugshot.

Judge Patricia Grinsted set his bond at $5,000, a paltry sum, but that was overruled by Judge William Stone, a judge I had encountered before. Stone released Nobles on his own recognizance hours later, a release signed off by interim sheriff Ed Spooner.

The report was signed off by Deputy Robert Norris, the former OSI agent whose name appears on a series of related reports. It states that when the restraining order was filed, Nobles led Deputy Darr all over the house collecting guns, just as Gabe described, and that Nobles did in fact lie under oath. Throughout this trashy drama, Nobles had spun lie after lie about these guns. He surrendered the guns. Then he lied under oath saying he had no guns. Then he and his then attorney, Mike Gibson, submitted a filing to the court acknowledging he was their "rightful owner." He then signed them out at the Sheriff Department's evidence locker. Then he claimed they were his wife's guns. Then they were his, but he had transferred ownership of the guns to his son. They were his son's guns, and he didn't even know about them. I heard that he even once tried to claim I planted them in his house. One of the many ironies is that while all these cops were running in circles to protect Nobles and his guns, he told my sons that he had the guns to shoot cops.

Law enforcement with DCF executed a search of Nobles' house the next day. Wanda Nobles showed the officers the walled-up entrances to the attic and said that her husband had recently been up there but had walled it up. It should be reiterated that FBI Agent Tim Kinard stated in his email to me that the drywall had been installed years before when Carolyn Palmer lived there, which Kinard said he confirmed with her. Carolyn Palmer denies ever being contacted by the FBI. The officers decided to bring the fire department out to open those entrances, but this was never done. Gabe drew a map of the attic showing where a computer and a Russian RPG-7 – a rocket-propelled grenade – was hidden in the attic near the chimney. How would a seven-year-old know this incredibly specific detail unless he had heard it from his grandfather and seen it? Possibly most significant is that at this point in time, according to Gabe, this was where the big trophy was being hidden. The gun Mike Nobles alleged killed John F. Kennedy

During this visit by law enforcement and DCF, Mike Nobles returned from jail, with his son Billy, who had picked him up after only being held for hours (the record, however, says he was released days later). Both held a pity party and played the victim as Nobles concocted a new story about his guns, which Billy was hiding at his sister's home.

* * *

Recall that I had seen and reported evidence of child pornography on Nobles' home computer, when Christy and I were still together, and that my sons made detailed and graphic descriptions of Mike Nobles and accomplices using them and his own daughters in child pornography. Someone had tipped Nobles off that I had reported it, and that machine had been swapped out for Billy's computer. Tom Dunn and Joey Forgione were the only ones who knew about it.

The officers did, in fact, find a computer and several hard drives in the attic above the converted garage, the only part of the attic that was accessible. These were confiscated as evidence. The officers decided to send them to the FDLE for investigation.

A year later I called the FDLE (Florida Department of Law Enforcement) and was told they never received the computer. Now, a report claims that over two years later it was examined, that it was Roger Nobles' computer (who had never lived in Mike Nobles' house) yet the chain of custody of the computer has been destroyed.

No one ever returned to see what was in the sealed-up attic.

The whole visit was pure theater.

Neither my sons nor I were ever contacted or interviewed about Nobles' arrest, even though Toby had fired one of the guns inside the house. There was no mention in the media of a local church leader and pillar of the community being arrested for illegally possessing firearms, or for child abuse and endangerment. The *Northwest Florida Daily News* refused to cover the story. These refusals continue to the present day.

Meanwhile, the DCF and the Niceville PD – i.e. Forgione, Pagano, Karshna, Clark, et al. – were discussing having me charged with filing false police reports *for the very things Nobles had just been arrested.*

* * *

Today, as I lay out these documented facts and events, I'm forced to recall the emotional death ride I endured every day. I had few allies, and of those, none had any power to help. While the entire Nobles' family was telling everyone who would listen what victims they were, the only real victims – my sons – were traumatized wrecks, plagued by nightmares, increasingly unable to function at school or play with other kids. They had little appetite, and every time one of my sons spoke, fresh horrors were brought to light.

CPI Rick Karshna's notes in the DCF file case indicate a conversation with Toby's teacher on April 17, 2009, referencing the period of August 2008 to February 2009. "She said there were constant problems with Toby trying to touch boys' privates. She said it was almost a daily issue. He would reach for the genital area either outside the pants or try to put his hands down their pants." She also heard Toby say he "didn't like going to the grandfather's house." What his report doesn't state is that he left the teacher in tears, that he was abusive, treated her like a liar and an idiot, and made it clear that he didn't believe her. Karshna also called my mother, who had made the report, and screamed at her, calling her a liar. He touted his experience as a cop. Then he hung up the phone on her leaving her in tears.

There was nowhere to turn, nowhere to hide. All I could do was to continue to fight back, and there was plenty more fight coming

Endnotes

1   CPI Report, Jennifer Clark, November 2008.

2   Pagano, Heather. February 27, 2009, Department of Children and Families.

3   Case ID 80071, April 9, 2009.

4   Morton, Jason. "Historical firearms found dumped in river," *Tuscaloosa News.* April 13, 2009. https://www.tuscaloosanews.com/story/news/2009/04/14/historical-firearms-found-dumped-in-river/27798666007/

5   Stewart, Sherrell. "World War II era weapons pulled from Bibb County creek," *The Birmingham News.* April 13, 2009. https://www.al.com/spotnews/2009/04/world_war_ii_era_weapons_pulle.html

CHAPTER ELEVEN

WELCOME TO THE JUNGLE

It was a Tuesday night, April 21, 2009, and my sons' nanny, Marilyn, was at my home with the boys. I was traveling for work. She was awakened when the backyard security lights flashed on and frightened away an intruder who was trying to break in the back door. The man ran away and hid behind a tree in the dark, out of range of the lights. The following day, I returned home and found several cigarette butts behind that tree – Mike Nobles' brand, Doral.

That week I stumbled across a strange "yard sale." The manager of Nice Villa Rental Storage had a unit open and was selling things out of it. I had discovered the history of this property looking into the backgrounds of Nobles, McCormick and Osman and was curious what its real purpose was. Among the things offered for sale were piles of new-looking military clothing and gun paraphernalia. Not particularly alarming or unheard of given the proximity of so many military forces in the area, but what really piqued my interest was when the manager happened to open a nearby unit of things that weren't for sale, and I got a glimpse inside. Inside that unit was a row of new-looking, neatly pressed BDUs (military apparel), a whole militia's worth, right next to a brand-new-looking military shipping crate labeled to contain two-pound cylinders of TNT. The crate was empty, but crates like this are controlled items in the military, not as just munitions but also their containers are not for civilian use. Again, this one looked very new, immediately bringing to mind the "explode boxes" in Paw Paw's gun room that Gabe had drawn and described to me.

The owner of Nice Villa Rental was Jerry McCormick, Mike Nobles' old business partner. In 1988, McCormick had deeded one of the facility's three buildings to himself, separating that building from the business, presumably for his personal use. Leslie Michael Osman became a trustee of Nice Villa Rental in 1989, the same year that Nobles got involved with Osman and his many corporations.

* * *

As a result of Nobles' arrest, Christy called me out of the blue and told me she wants me to keep the children full-time. She said she's so afraid of her father that she and Shelly might move out-of-state. I told her about the intruder in my backyard, about her father stalking Gabe at school.

I said, "They have been through too much, more than any child should be." Her voice trembled. "Yeah, you're right."

I was astonished.

* * *

At this point, I did not yet know that Nobles had been out of jail for two weeks. He had been, if you recall, taken into custody at his workplace on April 9 by Okaloosa County Sheriff deputies on charges of weapons possession by a felon. He was released on April 10. When I spoke to Rick Karshna to tell him about the intruder in my back yard, he blithely dropped that nugget of information as if it were no big deal.

* * *

That same day I learned of the arrest, April 22, I received a call from Jerry Williams, one of my Iron-on-Iron mentors from Coastline Calvary Chapel. Jerry called to tell me that my kids were banned from Sunday School and that the pastors wanted to meet with me. So, I met with Pastors Dale Waltman, the youth pastor, and Joe Prestridge, the associate pastor who lectured me to shut up about the kids' abuse and submit to the church's "spiritual authority." They criticized my kids' behavior and my parenting suggesting I should beat my kids – who both suffered PTSD – with a belt.

Waltman described an incident when Gabe tried to run away from Sunday School during the church's big Christmas service featuring a prominent Christian pop artist, Phil Wickham. Waltman said there were other church-related incidents. He gave me an example of one of them grabbing a girl's privates in childcare at a church function. He made other vague insinuations of improper behavior and called Gabe "weird." If I wanted the boys to return to Sunday school, they would have to have counseling sessions with him for a set period of time. I reluctantly agreed to this.

* * *

At their first session, the boys disclosed, in great detail, that their grandfather had exploited them for child pornography. They even told Waltman, "Paw Paw said he needed really good pictures because he needed the money." They had never reported this to me or anyone else. Gabe would later tell a therapist that he was forced to take pictures of his own aunts and brother, and that he was shown pornographic pictures of his mother as a child in an apparent effort to convince him it was ok.

Waltman and the church refused to report it.

* * *

Over time, I realized that Jerry Williams had been playing both sides of the fence. He had already urged me to move away, get a divorce, and to date other women to "satisfy my physical needs." He told me to give up on pursuing justice against Mike Nobles because Nobles was some sort of confidential informant for the feds, which made him untouchable. Williams had bribed me with gifts and cash. He had insisted on giving me a cell phone to replace the one Nobles had given me a couple of years before, which had developed bizarre problems. The new phone from Williams had the microphone malfunction within a couple of months. I suspect both phones had been hacked and bugged.

Williams told the Cavalry pastors that I was trying to set the church up, that I wanted my sons to cause problems, had coached them to do so, and that the church could get in trouble for child abuse allegations.

To my face, Jerry expressed anger at how the church was isolating me, but I learned he was slandering me behind my back to other church leaders and members. He had used the Iron-on-Iron discipling program to pump me for information, which he then fed to Nobles and twisted facts in order to use against me with the church.

Years later after I exposed what Jerry had done his wife, Nancy Brown Williams, also from a right-wing Christian Crusader military family, spread rumors via social media that "Mark is apparently mentally ill." But where was this coming from? It was always right-wing religious fanatics. DCF supervisor Donna Parish. Nancy Williams. Mike Nobles and his family. Pastor and chaplain Brad Bynum and his deacon Ed Ferrell. And the parade of Christian nationalists and right-wing extremists and freemasons trying to frame and smear me would continue. And nearly all of them had military ties.

The church was supposed to be a community of healing and protection, but instead it was used for manipulation, coercion, and intimidation. Even George Bush's lawyer had been allowed to come there and con me. I often regret how hard it was for me to see that at the time, and to remove myself from that situation. Apparently, I needed some sense of community for the simple primal need that humans are social creatures, and I had nowhere else to go.

I didn't hang out with my old military friends much anymore. For years, all my energy had been funneled into trying to keep my family afloat, first into the bottomless black hole of Christy's psyche and then protecting my children. I sought justice for them, helped them heal from their trauma. I didn't have the energy, or even the desire, to make new friends.

Meanwhile, the cover-up was well underway.

* * *

On April 27, 2009, Assistant District Attorney LaShawn Riggans inexplicably dropped three of the four counts of weapons possession against Nobles.

On May 6, Mike Nobles no showed in Judge Santurri's court for a Show Cause hearing regarding his repeated violations of the restraining orders. This hearing was six months after the actual violations. Even though he is supposed to be under court supervision, out on bond awaiting trial for his arrest, he somehow avoided being served the subpoena. Somehow, he faced no consequences. He was neither held in contempt, nor was his bond revoked. The case was subsequently "lost."

* * *

On May 15, CPI (Child Protective Investigator) Karshna closed out his report with another series of glaring falsifications. There's no mention of Nobles' arrest, his abuses, or of child pornography. The report states, "The children were interviewed and did not give disclosure that supports the allegation.... The parents are going through a divorce and the children need counseling to help them through the divorce." Gabe had disclosed that his grandfather killed his pets and threatened to crucify him and Toby. Karshna was given a vivid and graphic description by Toby of finding a pistol and firing it in the house. Toby's teacher had told him Toby showed horrible signs of sexual abuse.

In mid-July, weeks after I had contacted the FDLE, Mark Perez, Chief Inspector in the Office of Investigations, responded to me. He said that my complaint regarding kidnapping, sexual abuse, organized crime, corrupt law enforcement officers, and corrupt child protection investigators had been forwarded to the appropriate agency – the DCF. I call this the DCF (Florida Department of Children and Families) dumping ground. The DCF was funneling all reports to the same three so-called investigators who falsified reports, retaliated, buried disclosures and signs of abuse, and destroyed any therapy or medical records provided to them. All this while blocking other investigators from completing any investigations into my case. Meanwhile local state and federal law enforcement authorities who had the actual jurisdiction refused to investigate. They too hid behind this charade. *Why?*

* * *

My sons and I were trapped in an elaborate shell game (confidence trick used to perpetrate fraud). Everyone I reached out to funneled my case straight back to the perpetrators.

During this terrible summer I tried to make life the best I could with the boys by trying to get them back into soccer and karate and taking them on outings, but they were too traumatized to interact well with other children. The entire world terrified them. Something would set them off and they would take off screaming at a dead run as if the hounds of hell were chasing them.

They stayed with their mother sporadically when I was out of town. Christy had once again promised she wouldn't let her father anywhere near them.

* * *

In August, subpoenas were sent out for Mike Nobles' weapons possession trial. I never received a subpoena, nor did the evidence custodian, Mary Collins, who had physically returned his weapons to him, even though we were listed as witnesses and were scheduled to testify. We were never given a chance to testify.

Something in the run-up to the trial sparked increasing desperation from Nobles.

On August 11, while the boys were visiting their mother, she allowed him to call and talk to them. In that phone call on speaker with Christy in the room, he threatened both of their parents with death if they talked about his guns. *"If you talk, I will shoot your daddy."* They described their *mother in a fetal position across the room while she allowed this.*

Nobles later tried to convince them that the man on the phone was a "bad guy talking through a speaker" pretending to be him.

My sense of alarm hit the roof when they told me about this. I reported it to FDLE agent Terry Thomas, then to Santa Rosa Kids House director Traci Ritchey. I then called the state attorney and left a message. My mother made repeated attempts, including sending a fax, to report this to the state attorney's office.

No one ever responded. My mother was told that the state attorney would "never have time" to talk to her. On August 17, 2009, Assistant State Attorney Lashawn Riggans offered Mike Nobles Pre Trial-Intervention (PTI). Nobles was not even eligible for PTI under Florida law, yet declined what amounted to a slap on the hand, knowing the case would be taken care of.

* * *

Then, on September 6, 2009, it was announced in the Destin Church of Christ bulletin that Mike Nobles was leaving the United States in one week's time for Guyana. It did not specify why. But Nobles put on some production called "plans for Guyana." He later tried to sell the claim that he was going to teach the locals how to raise rabbits. However, he told some that he was moving there because I was trying to "destroy his life," playing the victim again. Of note, this bulletin stated Nobles, Billy, and Rowena were leaving, and that Wanda and the girls would join him on January 10, 2010. This did not occur as he snatched them out of the country immediately following another abuse report, this one from a psychologist. When I heard that news, the sense of sick dread that had become so familiar washed through my stomach. He was still awaiting trial, released on his own recognizance, so obviously he already knew that the case was fixed, that it would never go to trial. No one awaiting a felony trial gets to skip the country with impunity. *I tried to report it to the State Attorney, who again refused to talk to me.*

* * *

I will never forget that day, because Nobles' announcement was only the first of two huge blows.

The second was when Gabe, amid drawing one of his many pictures at home after church, announced to me that: *"Paw Paw shot somebody."*

It took me a moment to register what he had said. But I had to coax him to say more without asking leading questions. "Oh? Shot somebody? How?"

"With a pistol. In the stomach. There was a lot of blood coming out of his mouth, and he made gurgling sounds."

"Are you sure, son? This is very serious."

He nodded and kept drawing as though he was talking about an every-day occurrence.

"Do you know who it was?" I asked, trying to compose myself.

"Jack Stephens." I didn't know any Jack Stephens.

"What happened to him, to the body?"

Gabe said, "They carried him outside in a body bag, and buried in the back yard." Gabe said Wanda scrubbed the carpet, but they ended up removing it. I had clearly seen that the carpet had recently been removed when I was there on Feb 5, 2009

* * *

Gabe was starting to become agitated, drawing more furiously. I thought it best not to push him, so I held off on more questions. Instead, I went to the Internet to search for a Jack Stephens who might be missing. I made some phone calls asking about missing persons' reports. As one might imagine, there are many Jack Stephens, but none of them had been reported missing. I included John Stephens in my search, remembering that Jack was often a nickname for John. Nothing came up.

The dilemma hit me like a brick. I was already under assault by law enforcement and child protection services seemed to be determined to

slander me or worse. Nobles and his enablers and cohorts had already issued death threats against me and the boys to keep us quiet about the gun
and sexual abuse charges. How much further would they go if the boys
started talking about murder?

* * *

On September 9, after nearly a month of waiting for a response, I contacted Okaloosa County Assistant DA LaShawn Riggans and was able to
speak to her assistant. I informed her of Nobles' death threats against me,
the patterns of stalking me and potential witnesses. I informed her of Nobles' weapons possession and gave her a list of names of people who could
attest to it. I told her about the recorded conversation with Christy, who
acknowledged her father owned those guns, always owning guns. He had
offered her one and gave a pistol to her sister. I also warned Riggans that
Nobles had publicly announced he was moving out of the country despite
awaiting trial. There was no response. I would learn later that I and the evidence custodian were to be subpoenaed to be deposed as witnesses, but
never were. The witnesses were handpicked and included Billy Nobles.

* * *

On September 10, at 7:18 P.M., I emailed Lt. Randy Sallee, Niceville Police Dept., to ask for an appointment to report a murder my sons say they
witnessed. I chose this officer because he was of higher rank than both Joey
Forgione and Joseph Kearnes and possibly could do something without
funneling the report directly into the black hole of Forgione's desk. The
number of lies, reversals, and deflections around Nobles' guns was already
far into the ridiculous. In the email, I reported what Gabe had told me, and
that out of the blue Nobles was planning to leave the U.S. for Guyana.

On September 11, Assistant District Attorney (ADA) Riggans abruptly dropped all the charges against Nobles. The same day I came to a difficult decision, concerned about further retaliation.

* * *

On September 12, Mike Nobles, along with his son Billy, Billy's wife
Rowena and Rowena's kids, all flew to Guyana to begin their "missionary
work." Wanda Faith and Emily did not go. It had been announced they
would go in January. This is important because they would be snatched
out of the country earlier to block another investigation.

My Iron-on-Iron study mate at Calvary Chapel, Dave Clark, put me in
touch with a friend of his at the federal Bureau of Alcohol Tobacco and
Firearms, an agent named Craig Roegner. Surely the ATF would have an

interest in a convicted federal felon possessing firearms since the state had refused to prosecute him.

I called Roegner and told him the whole story as best I could do. During our conversation, he said, "Everything you're telling me is consistent with Nobles' FBI file."

"The FBI has a file on him?"

"They sure do. Are you sure you want to go ahead with this?"

"Absolutely."

"I'll make some calls and get back to you."

By the end of our conversation, I felt hopeful. I was led to believe there was some sort of big raid coming. Roegner set up a meeting for me with an ATF agent named Randy Beach.

* * *

A few days later, Beach called me and scheduled an appointment at his office. There was a junior ATF agent present as well. Whatever hope I had felt after my conversation with Roegner was quickly dashed during my conversation with Agent Beach.

"Yeah, I talked to Donna Parrish at the DCF," Beach said. "She told me all about your little family squabble."

My heart sank. Another shred of hope bit the dust.

He went on to add, "Joey Forgione is a stand-up guy."

There would be no help from the ATF. This took place at the ATF office in Pensacola.

I then did some checking on Randy Beach. It turned out he was pursuing a master's degree in theology from the Augusta School of Biblical Studies in Augusta, Georgia. It seemed there was no end to these Christian Crusaders.

The school claimed to be accredited, but that fact has been staunchly disputed.

The teachers and administrators who ran Augusta School of Biblical Studies were neither certified nor qualified in Theology or Biblical Studies. The school is alleged to have openly discriminated against students and prospective hires based on race, often harassing them with racial slurs by phone. They are also alleged to have hire white sex offenders and felons, including a teacher who was arrested for murder.[1] The school is now closed.

* * *

Meanwhile, Gabe was dropping more trauma bombs about what he and Toby had experienced while they were abducted and held at Mike Nobles'.

Gabe described a biker they called "Tiger." Tiger wore a jacket with a skull wearing a top hat, an ace of spades stuck in the brim. This is a symbology that goes back to the Vietnam era, and it is used in gambling circles to invoke luck. Gabe said his grandfather killed Tiger in a junkyard with some sort of grenade or C-4 detonator, and that Tiger was driving a bulldozer at the time.

In all, Gabe described having witnessed five murders committed by Mike Nobles. In one case, he described being in the car while Nobles went into an "old warehouse" to meet with two men. Gabe then heard two gunshots, and only Nobles came out.

Gabe had previously described Wanda Nobles scrubbing blood off the floor after her husband shot Jack Stephens in the living room.

Gabe told how Wanda Nobles had stuffed tissues up his and Toby's rectums to stop the bleeding after they had been violated by "magic wands." I would learn later that Nobles' occultist brother made these and sold them online.

Gabe verbally portrayed a night-time ceremony in the woods that sounded like a cross between a lynching and a bizarre occult ceremony. A man's body was strung up in a tree and set ablaze. The tree itself was circumscribed with some sort of magic circle that was then set aflame. Gabe has talked about the terror of witnessing all this horror and breaking into a wild panic where he and his brother set off running full speed through the woods, falling and injuring himself for which he still has a scar on his knee. The body was burned to a crisp and the head separated as it fell.

Gabe also described Nobles using my utility trailer to transport the body and on another occasion, pulling teeth and dental gold out of burnt skulls in the back of the trailer.

All I could do was listen and try to write it all down.

* * *

Around this time, Billy Nobles had been trying to sell Mike Nobles' guns all over the area. When he tired of this, according to Brian Riggs' later testimony, he took "the rest of them" to the "police station" to dispose of them. Presumably the Niceville Police Department.

State Attorney Bill Eddins refused to press any charges claiming "no evidence" despite overwhelming proof.

The list of dirty cops and complicit lawyers kept ballooning.

* * *

Lt. Sallee finally responded to my "Hey there's been a murder" email on September 14 when Nobles and his family were already on their way to South America via Barbados. Sallee's email told me to call for an appoint-

What Gabe and Toby Saw

My sons, Toby and Gabriel Harris, told me they had witnessed the murder of a man by their grandfather, Michael Nobles, in their grandfather's living room in January 2009. The slain man's name was Jack Stephens. The motive for this murder appears to have been a dispute over money. Gabe said the victim's last words to Mike Nobles were, "Don't double-cross me." According to Gabe, Nobles shot him in the stomach.

According to the children, Nobles buried the body in his backyard at 1118 Rhonda Drive, Niceville, Florida. He was buried in the back corner of the yard near a flowering tree they refer to as a "rose tree." He forced Gabe to help him. The kids witnessed their grandfather place the body in a body bag and their grandmother scrubbing blood off the carpet.

In January 2009, I reported Mr. Nobles for possession of weapons as a convicted felon and child endangerment after my sons had told me about the arsenal of weapons in his home and about finding a handgun in the closet and firing it. Corrupt Niceville Police Officers, Joseph Forgione and Joseph Kearnes, seized the report from officer Nelson and shut down that investigation and falsified a law enforcement report.

Nobles later dug up the body and transported it with my utility trailer – which he had stolen in June 2008 – with the help of an unidentified member of law enforcement. My children accurately and graphically described the state of decay and the odor of the body. He tied branches to the bag and poured glitter glue on them to make it appear he was disposing of a Christmas tree. Gabe said the body smelled like "ten thousand rotten squid" and described the insects and decay in an accurate manner, consistent with scientific proofs and evidence. I consulted with Nancy Locke and Brad Dennis who train and use cadaver dogs, and they said my son's description of the decomposition was evidentially accurate. Locke and Dennis were subsequently blocked repeatedly from taking part in any crime scenes related to this case.

My sons describe a policeman with white hair and mustache, a description that closely matches that of Tom Dunn, Niceville police officer and child protection investigator at Emerald Coast Child Advocacy Center.

During the execution of this crime, my sons were taken into the woods, and they itemized the following specific details.

1. Traveling on a dirt road.
2. Crossing two sets of railroad tracks with gravel around them.
3. Turning left.
4. That road was a "white, sandy trail" only big enough for one vehicle.
5. A burnt tree where the body was burned.
6. That their grandfather had chopped at the base of the tree with an ax.
7. A sound my sons heard that night which terrified them.

Both children ran in terror and dread from the scene, falling repeatedly and injuring themselves. They were both bleeding. They both will forever be forced to endure both mental scars from the horror of that night and their attempt to escape. Gabe has a large scar on his knee.

On the way home, Nobles stopped at a car wash. He poured something from a gallon jug onto the trailer and spread it with a paintbrush. He then washed the trailer at the car wash. This sounds eerily akin to an attempt to destroy DNA evidence.

My sons witnessed their grandfather spray deodorizer in his vehicle to kill the odor and then wash his clothes.

I made repeated efforts to identify a site that matched my sons' description, including talking to the Division of Forestry and traveling to several locations, but was unsuccessful – for a while.

ment, but I didn't. By this time, I knew well all the ways they could say, "We're not going to do anything." And I didn't feel entirely safe walking into the Niceville Police Station.

Where did Nobles get the money to move so many people to another hemisphere on short notice? How did he get visas so quickly? Why Barbados, an infamous offshore tax haven? This was a guy who was so poor his defense attorney was a public defender.

I don't recall the exact date, but around this time my job took me on a trip to Nashville. There I was able to get an appointment with Greg Moore, an ATF intelligence officer. I told him the story, showed him my son's drawings. He identified Nobles as an Imperial Wizard of the Ku Klux Klan and said that my sons' account sounded credible. This was consistent with ATF Agent Craig Roegner's statement about Nobles' FBI file. He also identified the drawing of the gun as a Sentry gun, a gun with cameras that fires automatically, most likely a classified weapon.

This turned out to be yet another fruitless attempt at getting federal authorities involved. I made several attempts to involve the FBI and the ATF in what should have been an open-and-shut, slam-dunk case. But the cases went straight back to Tim Kinard and Randy Beach, who had already lied to cover for Mike Nobles. Tim Kinard refused any contact with me.

* * *

On October 14, 2009, the boys were visiting my parents in Georgia. He told them of horrific crimes they had witnessed and abuse they had endured. My sister, a schoolteacher and former foster parent, was outraged and dismayed that there had been no investigation and no forensic interview with the kids. She took them to a therapist, Dr. Elaine Woods, a PhD psychologist, who interviewed them. The boys told her the same story they had told me and my parents. Dr. Woods said she had never seen a case like this before, despite her lengthy experience, joining their principal, teachers, therapist, and doctor in believing the boys' accounts to be "credible and serious."

Dr. Woods reported this to the DCF on October 15 and was directed to Jennifer Clark and Rick Karshna. She included copies of Gabe's drawings, which would be omitted from the DCF case files. Pictures depicting Nobles and a masked man or men engaging in sex acts with his daughters and my son. People Gabe described as "bad guy officers" and "army men."

* * *

I left all this information for Okaloosa Sheriff, Ed Spooner, and asked for an appointment. He never responded.

This drawing shows Nobles daughters, one saying "stop" and someone wearing a ski mask and a holstered gun laughing at them.

Gabe said that the girl on the left, one of his aunts, was handcuffed. The perpetrator again is wearing a ski mask and a holstered gun.

This drawing shows Nobles' daughters and Toby forced to undress, with Nobles wearing a gun and holster. This is consistent with Gabe's repeated disclosures that he was forced to take pictures of the other children for Nobles.

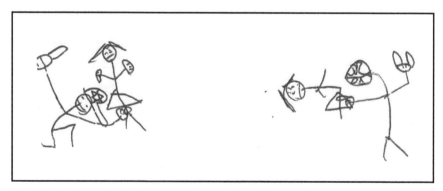

One of the graphic sexual abuse drawings that accompanied Dr. Wood's report. The victims in this picture are Nobles' daughters. One of the perpetrators appears to be wearing a law enforcement hat, and the other a ski mask. This and the other drawings were omitted from the DCF case files as were all incriminating records.

169

I received a flier on my door from the DCF that Rick Karshna has been assigned to the case. Furious, I called his supervisor and told them that this lying creep wasn't getting anywhere near my kids again, and that I had already filed a complaint against him, Pagano, and Clark for falsifying reports.

* * *

On October 16, corroborated by another witness who saw them, Christy told me that her parents had been back in the U.S. for about a week. I met with her to convince her to help protect our kids. She told me that he had traveled through Barbados, one the world's money laundering capitals, and that they had left the country again on October 15. She warned me again to "watch your back." It was clear during this meeting that her mental and physical health had deteriorated greatly since I'd last seen her. She looked like a ghost of the woman I married. I had grave concerns about her mental state, memory, and cognition.

* * *

On October 20, I spoke with Santa Rosa Kids house director, Traci Ritchey, expressing concerns about my sons' mental well-being and my fears that corrupt officials might attempt to take my children from me to silence them.

That same day I tried again for an appointment with the Okaloosa County Sheriff's office, but instead I received a two-minute call from the department's legal advisor, Steven Hurm, who told me to mail him the information. His tone was abrupt and hostile. For a year I had, in person, on the phone, and in writing, sought an appointment with the Okaloosa County Sheriff regarding not only Mike Nobles criminal conduct, but also that of law enforcement officers, child protection investigators, and the department chaplain, Brad Bynum. Hurm continually acted as a buffer and a deflector.

On October 21, Rick Karshna sent CPI Jennifer Clark the following email regarding the Nobles case:

> *Jennifer,*
>
> *call me when you get a chance on the above case, we are trying to do it differently this time*
>
> *rick*

That same day, CPI Jennifer Clark closed the sexual abuse case, designating Nobles' daughters as "no jurisdiction, the children are no longer in the country."

I would soon find out what their plan to "do it differently" was all about.

* * *

The next day, I learned from fellow church members that Wanda Nobles had been taken out of the country against her will.

* * *

Halloween season was a nightmare for my boys, especially Gabe. Whenever they saw decorations like skulls or masks of the Devil, he would suffer panic attacks, hyperventilate, and curl into fetal position in a corner. The day before Halloween, my sons and one of their friends wanted to go to the Navarre Fire Department Haunted House. I had concerns, but I was told it was "kid friendly." At one point, a make-believe corpse dropped down out of the ceiling on a hangman's noose, and they, in no uncertain terms, lost their shit and tore screaming out of that haunted house.

I could barely get Gabe calmed down, and through shallow, ragged breaths he started talking. He told me again about how Paw Paw had dug up the body from the back yard, and it smelled like "a thousand rotten squid," a description that would later be confirmed by cadaver dog trainers, Nancy Locke and Brad Dennis. He described the state of decomposition, how the eyes haunted him the most. The flesh had sloughed off the skull, but still had some hair on it. He told once more how the body was taken to the woods using my utility trailer, removed from the bag, and hung in a tree and burned by Nobles in front of my children. The boys told how they ran away, and heard the body fall, and they looked back and saw the head had come off. During their panicked flight, Gabe got a deep cut on his leg and has the scar to this day. Horrified, I comforted them and planned my next move.

* * *

Two days later, I took Toby and Gabe to the Santa Rosa Kids house for what I thought would be a forensic interview but was changed to an "investigative interview." Law enforcement refused to attend. DCF supervisor Connie Edgar wouldn't even look at me or speak directly to me. And I made it clear I wanted nothing to do with Rick Karshna. The air was tense, but Toby and Gabe were brave enough to tell the therapist about the sexual abuse they'd suffered at the hands of their grandfather. Regardless, therapist Leilani Mason and the Director, Traci Richey, advised me there wasn't enough evidence to bring charges.

Mason tried to smooth things over by telling me her report would indicate a "threat of abuse" and a recommended safety plan to prevent my sons from having contact with their grandfather. *Both she and Tracy Ritchey made sure that Edgar promised this would be the finding. Edgar sheepishly finally agreed. Despite promises from Edgar, that never happened.*

* * *

My frustration compounded when, shortly after this, I discovered that either *my wife or her sister had reported abuse that occurred when they were twelve years old and the investigation was shut down in 24 hours.* Simultaneously, friends of mine through the Niceville church disclosed to me that they had been handing over checks to Nobles' attorney, Leslie Michael Osman, to support a fraudulent foster care organization he had been running through the Hialeah Church of Christ. Osman had incorporated a company, Hialeah Christian Missions Inc.,[2] with himself as Director. It seemed obvious to me the foster children were being abused and the money taken. How long had this been going on?

Within a week, I was able to speak to Lt. Sallee about the murder and, now that the weapons and ammunition in Nobles' house had been documented, with Sgt. Gaiser about Nobles' firearms and child endangerment. Gaiser assured me he would pursue the matter and, after Sgt. Forgione declined to accompany me to retrieve the trailer Nobles used to transport the body, it was Gaiser who joined me instead.

With Gaiser's help, I brought the trailer back to the police department on November 13th so forensics could run tests. Sallee instructed Forgione to spray the trailer with luminol, a water-based solution capable of detecting blood, but Forgione refused, insisting there was no chance any evidence could remain on it, so I was instructed to take it home. Instead, Forgione seemed much more interested in grilling me about what my kids told their therapist. I gave him her name and phone number and he left in a hurry. He jumped into an unmarked police car and sped away. After bringing the trailer home, I later learned that forensic evidence could last 150 years, but my attempts to get the trailer examined were fruitless.

I'd have to do it myself.

Endnotes

1   https://www.complaintsboard.com/augusta-school-of-biblical-studies-augusta-ga-misleading-students-c624633

2   Hialeah Christian Missions Inc.

CHAPTER TWELVE

THE EVE OF (MY) DESTRUCTION

U ndeterred, I was still intent on going through official channels, and I returned to the Niceville police station to meet again with Lt. Sallee. Because I was running late, and Sallee was busy with another matter, I spoke to Sgt. Gaiser about the child endangerment charges. By this point it seemed obvious to me that my children were in danger: Nobles was a convicted felon illegally hoarding weapons in his home, and multiple therapists had confirmed that my children disclosed instances of abuse. This was specifically in regard to the kids finding a gun and firing it. It was also time, *again*, to report the murder my son had described, adding to my acute concern for my boys' safety. This would be my second effort to report the murder. I had emailed Lt Sallee who didn't respond until after Nobles had skipped the country in September. I finally decided to go in and make a formal report in November. This would be my first time visiting law enforcement about it.

I had now reached a new level of concern, a recognition that Mike Nobles was a very dangerous man.

But Gaiser informed me he'd been told not to pursue the matter further and insisted that Nobles wasn't a convicted felon – *Joey Forgione had told him so*. Despite my insistence that was not true (and it still didn't address the matter of child endangerment), my protests fell on deaf ears. Or worse, they heard me but protected Nobles anyway.

* * *

On November 18, 2009, I drove over to the Niceville CAC (Child Advocacy Center) to speak with the therapist Nicole Fryback. I called her while driving, and she suggested I ask the State Attorney to subpoena her report. She recommended I speak with her supervisor. I entered the building and talked to the receptionist who apparently knew of me and referred to me being the" squeaky wheel." But when I walked through the door I was instantly assailed by Tom Dunn, the same man who pressured me not to file any reports, the same man who matched the description my kids gave of the person who helped Nobles lynching/burning in Walton

County. He wouldn't even let me enter the building, to get past the lobby. Instead, he angrily shouted, red in the face, that *I* was the one under investigation. He escorted me to the parking lot.

So, I drove back to the police station. When I finally got a chance to talk to Sallee, I was ambushed this time by Kearnes and Forgione. I talked to Sallee who told me I would have to be interviewed by Forgione. I was furious as I had made it clear I didn't want anything to do with him; he had fixed previous related cases. *Sallee responded saying, "It has to be this way," and with no explanation, Forgione slammed a blank affidavit onto the desk threatening to arrest me if I filed a report.* Forgione admitted he knew Nobles was a felon back in April, but that didn't matter. I had given Sallee a lengthy report including Forgione's past and his ties to Jones etc. Forgione threatened to sue me and was out for blood. All the information about Ruckel, Wayne Jones, the strange property histories of 1118 Rhonda Drive in Niceville, and 2 Kathy Lane in Freeport – none of it mattered. They were going to make me the bad guy. Feeling exasperated and exhausted after wasting my day, I saw that it was time to pick up my kids, and I left.

I later learned that my wife met with Forgione the same day, and that he had "read her the riot act" and pressured her to take my children away and hide them again. He asked for the name and phone number of my employer saying he was going to call them and tell them I was crazy. Two months later, Mike Nobles called that employer claiming just that and other false information about me and used Forgione's name to back up his claims. On top of this, with encouragement from Tom Dunn, Donna Parish, and Jennifer Clark, the Department of Children and Families was demanding that I take a psychological evaluation. It would become clear to me that corrupt officials in Okaloosa were doing everything they could to block the investigation of the report made by a PHD psychologist. He then attempted to prevent the implementation of a safety plan for my children, blocking counseling services, just as Clark had done, and again labeling me as crazy.

But of course, I didn't know any of that yet.

* * *

Because the police had refused to examine my trailer, I ordered a luminol hunting product called Bloodglow, a substance that illuminates under blacklight in the presence of blood. There were spots on the surface that glowed but the main part that glowed was the bottom of the trailer. This is consistent with my son's account that Nobles poured a cleaner on it and washed it at a carwash. I called the manufacturer, who agreed that I'd likely found blood. With no help from the police, I eventually pried up the trailer's floorboards and discovered remnants of dental fillings and human hair. I sent a sample that glowed to Lt. Sallee with a sworn statement. He promised to forward them to the Florida Department of Law Enforcement for further testing, but I later learned they were never forwarded. Instead, Forgione and Kearnes would later try to use the evidence that I had found and that I had sent to them against me.

* * *

During this time, I was desperate to get in contact with Attorney Betty Thomas, who had previously warned me my life was in danger. But now, she wasn't returning my calls and refused to return evidence I'd shared with her. In fact, she played a role in getting Nobles' firearms returned to him and, when I was finally able to confront her about this, she hung up on me. The only result of my efforts was a threatening letter from Ed Fleming, George Bush's attorney, on Betty Thomas' behalf.

* * *

Several weeks before the winter holidays, I finally had a chance to spend some quiet time with Gabe and Toby. We were watching *Christmas Vacation* and, during the scene where Chevy Chase locks himself in the attic, Gabe mentioned that his grandfather's attic had similar floorboards. Gabe had tried to pull up the ladder in the skylight on his grandfather, just like in the movie. Gabe also drew a map from the skylight hole to a box of guns in the attic which I later provided to law enforcement. *It was never searched.* It seemed that everything continued to draw my mind to the horrendous things my sons had been exposed to in their young and vulnerable lives, ages.

But these were traumatic memories, and the shadow of what they endured darkened even our peaceful moments. As we talked about what was happening between their mother and myself, the boys suddenly erupted in an argument about whether the abuse, what had been done to them, hurt. Toby, ever the tough guy, insisted that it didn't. Gabe, meanwhile, recalled that Faith had worn a glove when she put her finger "way in there." They agreed that Toby had been made to take pictures, and suggested they'd met people they identified as buyers. Gabe described in graphic detail a sexual assault by Nobles and an accomplice upon his daughters, including the sights, odors, and the detail that they washed their hands afterwards. Details he could not have made up.

Dumbfounded, I emailed Lt. Sallee the next day to discuss these new revelations, but his reply was terse: "Call the police department and make an appointment."

* * *

In a series of events unfolding just days later, Rick Karshna emerged as a central player in a disconcerting scheme. Collaborating with Clark at the ECCAC, Karshna had engaged in a covert effort to manipulate records stemming from the October 15th complaint lodged by Dr. Wood.

Karshna's actions culminated in the misrepresentation of my mental health status and the distortion of facts surrounding the Child Protection Team (CPT) interview and Toby's disclosure of abuse. I should point out he wasn't there for the interview, had not had anything to do with the investigation, and I had not made the report. Most troubling was Karshna's endeavor to

KARSHNA HISTORY

As noted, Rick Karshna, a former law enforcement officer in Wisconsin and now a child protection investigator in Florida had a track record replete with negligence and incompetence. Instances such as a slow-speed chase where he allowed the suspect to re-enter their vehicle after fleeing into a store epitomize his ineptitude. Repeatedly reprimanded for sleeping on duty, then suspended and ordered to undergo mandatory counseling, Karshna's tenure in law enforcement ended when he was forced to resign for egregious misconduct that resulted in a victim's rape.

Karshna's incompetence was evident. His actions and their encounters with him left my family and witnesses, including my elderly mother and Toby's school teacher, worried and distraught. Handpicked to manipulate cases for Mike Nobles – including shredding documents, falsifying records, burying repeated disclosures of heinous abuse by my children, refusing to interview witnesses, and then burying the disclosures of the witnesses he did interview – Karshna was rewarded with a promotion to Program Manager, perpetuating this ongoing cycle of corruption.

However, it was his tenure as a DCF investigator in Florida that exposed the depths of his unethical and unprincipled conduct. Alongside accomplices Clark and Pagano, Karshna operated with impunity, engaging in a pattern of cherry-picking cases, tampering with evidence, and retaliating against whistleblowers. Departmental records painted a damning portrait of collusion and deception, implicating supposed responsible and trustworthy people up to the highest echelons of authority.

Despite the gravity of these revelations, I remained resolute in my commitment to transparency and accountability. Armed with evidence and resolve, I pledged to bring to light the systemic corruption plaguing the justice system in Florida and to seek redress for those wronged by its failings.

attribute the profound psychological distress suffered by my children to my own actions, implying of course that the boy's distress was my fault for reporting abuse and allowing them to be interviewed, despite overwhelming evidence to the contrary. He more than doubled the actual number of times my sons had been interviewed. Instead of a psychological assassination from some government hack protecting the state, In December, I sought an independent evaluation of my mental health from a Dr. Eric Goldberg, a psychiatrist, whom I had sought out on my own. It took several months, but here's what he found: "Partner relational problems. No need for treatment. Dated 3/16/10."

Despite Karshna's concerted efforts, his attempts to undermine my parental rights faltered due to the absence of substantive evidence. Karshna engaged Florida Legal Services to try to remove my kids from me and failed. It became clear that his motives were driven by a desire to discredit my kids. Karshna's checkered past, marred by allegations of misconduct during his tenure with law enforcement in Wisconsin, and subsequent involvement in politics as a failed Republican candidate, provided additional insight into his character.

You will recall that on December 12, 2008, Mike Nobles was called in for his deposition hearing regarding the restraining order against him I filed in October, and the restraining order Christy filed against me. Though previously discussed in Chapter Eight, I include excerpts of the deposition here to demonstrate that Nobles' own account, in his own words, contradicts what police and other officials kept telling me – namely that he'd never had foster children in his care and that he wasn't a convicted felon:

Q: Who lives with you in your home?

A: My wife and two youngest daughters.

Q: And that would be Emily and Faith?

A: Yes, ma'am.

Q: And what is your wife's name?

A: Wanda.

Q: And how long have you been married?

A: 32 years.

Q: Does Wanda, is Wanda employed?

A: No. She does some cleaning. She cleans the church building once a week, a few things like that, but not employment.

Q: She's never been employed?

A: Yeah, she was a schoolteacher.

Q: While married to you?

A: Yes.

Q: How long?

A: Seven years, I believe.

Q: Do you know why she quit?

A: We had two foster children, and she had decided – we'd had these foster – we wound up with these foster children for three years, and she decided in order to give them the same kind of care that our children received, she had to quit working. Because we were doing the daycare thing with them, and it just didn't seem fair to them.

Q: When you say foster children, when did you get in to taking foster children?

A: I don't remember the year. It's been many years. Well, let's see, wait a minute now. Faith is twelve years old, we'd been in it for three years. So it was sixteen years ago when we first got in it.

Q: And you stayed in it for how many years?

A: About four years. We had the two children off and on for three years, and then we just – for a while after that we didn't take any more children in, and that's when my wife became pregnant with Faith.

Q: Okay. When you say two children, were they the same two children or you had two children?

A: We had several children, but we had two pretty much the whole time for three years.

Q: Did you talk or discuss adopting those children?

A: When they terminated parental rights we were going to adopt them. There was seven children involved in this family. Some friends of ours had the sister and they had had her from birth. They also wanted to adopt the children. We felt in the best interest of the children, that it would be better for us to back out and let them have the three so they could grow up together.

Q: Did they adopt all seven children?

A: No, they adopted three.

Q: Okay.

A: They adopted the two – the three youngest of the children.

Q: And when you had children in and out, you had these two children that remained for two years, but how many children were in and out of your house in those four years.

A: One, two, three, I can recall four more.

Q: What's the longest they stayed?

A: Short periods, just a month or so.

Q: Explain foster care to me. What do you do, sign up for that, undergo some kind of background check?

A: Its [sic] a very extensive course you have to go through, I believe it was a six-week course we had to go to. Yes, there's all kinds of background checks and everything, fingerprinting, all of that.

Q: And what motivated you to do that?

A: The couple that had the children—

Q: These seven children we're talking about?

A: Yes.

Q: Yes.

A: –we went to church with. They had an altercation, she wound up with a broken arm. They called us and asked us would we come to the hospital and pick the children up so that they could take care of her broken arm, because they wouldn't give her any medication or anything until the children were taken care of because they were at the hospital with her. So we took the children.

Later, Children's & Family Services took the children away, and then they were ordered back into our care under court-ordered adjudication. Then when they were ordered into foster care, they contacted us and said, "If you'll go through this course, we'll let you go ahead and keep the children."

So we had the children the whole time we were going through the foster training.

Q: You said that she was a member of your church. What church do you attend?

A: At that point in time I was at the Niceville Church of Christ.

Q: And how long have you been in that church?

A: Let's see. I met my wife there in '76. We left and moved back to Alabama in '77. We moved back there in '85. I was there until about five years ago when I moved to the Destin Church of Christ.

Q: Why did you change churches?

A: We were just not happy there and was looking for something different and went to the Destin church and liked it there.

Q: And that was about five years ago?

A: Yes ma'am.

Q: What church is that?

A: Destin Church of Christ.

Q: It's still called Church of Christ?

A: Yes ma'am.

Q: Why were you unhappy with the Niceville Church of Christ?

A: There was an elder in that church that was a business partner of mine and he and I had had some disagreements in business, and I felt it was in the best interest of not causing any problem at the church for us to go ahead and move somewhere else.

Q: Who was the elder that you had the–

A: Jerry McCormick. [Note: Jerry McCormick is the brother-in-law of Nobles' attorney, Leslie Michael Osman]

Q: Do you know if he is still associated with the Niceville Church of Christ?

A: Oh, no. He moved to Nashville, Tennessee.

Q: What business were you in with him?

A: Subway Sandwiches.

Q: How long were you in business with him?

A: 18 years.

Q: Several corporations? What were those corporations?

A: Androgenous [sic] of Florida.

Q: What was it?

A: What was it? Oh, a C corp.

Q: But what did it do, what kind–

A: Subway. All of them were for Subway.

Q: Oh, I see. I see.

A: We had several Subways. We had ten Subways and we had—

Q: Okay.

A: Most of them had different corporations. Some were in a bind.

Q: But they all held Subways–

A: Yes.

Q: –and they all had different–

A: Yeah, some terrible names. We had an attorney that made the names up.

Q: Yeah. So they were registered corporations?

A: Yes ma'am.

Q: And when was the last that – when was the last one dissolved?

A: Probably first part of this year, I just chose not to renew it. It was the only one left.

Q: So you basically had difficulties with him five years ago, but stayed in business with him until just the first of this year?

A: No, ma'am. We dissolved – we split up and I still had that corporation. That became my corporation.

Q: I see. You divided the corporations?

A: Yeah, uh-huh.

Q: Have you ever been convicted of any crime?

A: Yes, I have.

Q: And what would that be?

A: Aiding and abetting.

Q: Tell me what it was.

A: It was a tax protest case. I was a tax protester, and that was the charge they chose to charge me with was aiding and abetting.

Q: What'd you do?

A: Well, they say I gave a piece of paper to allow someone to file for a return of money, and that was the aiding and abetting. I was aiding and abetting them in trying to get money back the government felt they didn't have a right to get back.

Q: When was this?

A: 1985. And I don't remember no dates.

Q: Who did you give this piece of paper to so that they could get a return of money that the IRS did not approve of?

A: I think Snyder was his last name, I'm not even positive about that, but I have no idea recalling what his first name was.

Q: It was a stranger?

A: Oh, no, no. It was someone that was in the tax protest group with me. It's just been a lot of years ago.

Q: A tax protest group?

A: Yeah, a patriot group, a patriot network.

Q: How long were you in that group?

A: Probably three years.

Q: And where was that group?

A: Scottsboro, Alabama.

Q: What happened with this aiding and abetting allegation, did you – you were convicted?

A: I was convicted.

Q: And what resulted.

A: I served three years' probation and then had all my rights restored by the Florida legislature.

Q: When? When you were off probation and had your rights restored?

A: '85 was when they convicted me, so it was '88. Now I'm guessing at that date. I mean, it was right around '88 or '89 would have been the three years I served.

Q: And then at that time all rights were restored automatically?

A: Yeah. I got a letter.

Q: You can carry a firearm?

A: Huh? No, not a firearm. Everything except firearms.

Q: And you don't have any firearms?

A: No.

In this short exchange, it's easy to see that what I was being told, and what was actually true, were two very different things.

On the one hand, DCF insisted my claims about the Nobles' foster children were false. They said the Nobles had never had foster children, but here is Mike Nobles not only admitting they'd had foster children for years, but that they'd done it at the urging of DCF.

Furthermore, police repeatedly told me that Mike Nobles wasn't a convicted felon, but on the other hand, here is Mike Nobles admitting he was a convicted felon who wasn't permitted to have firearms in his possession. Yet on January 30, 2009, the police confiscated four hunting rifles, one shotgun, two .22 rifles, and one .30-30 rifle from his residence.

Rick Karshna, who had, as you will recall, "...demonstrated a complete lack of investigative initiative," was insisting my children never admitted to sexual abuse, but there had been multiple reports from therapists saying they had. Furthermore, Nobles and Christy admitted it while trying to minimize it and the CAC therapist made a finding that it had happened.

Clearly, reality wasn't aligning with the fiction I was being fed. And all of this while the authorities were increasingly trying to paint me as the crazy one.

* * *

On January 15, 2010, the Judicial Qualifications Commission reviewed my complaint against Judge Thomas Santurri. Unsurprisingly, a week later, William Schneider, General Counsel for the State of Florida Judicial Qualifications Commission, claimed that Santurri's actions were "procedural errors." No, he repeatedly deflected cases and denied me and my sons our right to a hearing to obtain a restraining order.

Santurri had cases repeatedly funneled to him.

He dismissed cases on legally bogus grounds.

He allowed Nobles to flaunt the restraining order and repeatedly violate it.

He knowingly returned guns to a felon.

He should have been removed, disbarred, and prosecuted.

To this day, my son is disabled because of Santurri.

* * *

While judges continued to protect Nobles, he had been hiding in Guyana this whole time. I thought I was rid of him, at least temporarily, but even from a continent away, he continued to make our lives hell.

Though I wouldn't learn the details until weeks later, on Monday, January 25, Nobles emailed my employer claiming that I often came to work under the influence of alcohol. At his deposition hearing, Nobles had called me "a very moral man" and a "good father," but he told my employer I was mentally ill, regularly went to work drunk, lied on my job application, and had a "less than honorable discharge," claiming it was a result of a problem with "getting drunk and exposing himself to minors." All were total nonsense. Blatant lies. Nobles claimed that there were DCF reports in Santa Rosa County and Okaloosa County stating that I was "suspected of suffering from mental illness." He claimed that I came to work after drinking all night and that I called in sick from being hungover. To lend credibility to his claims, he cited Joey Forgione and threatened to go to both the FAA and the press if they didn't fire me.

* * *

On January 21, I emailed Lt. Randy Sallee again asking to come in and make a sworn statement regarding the murder my sons had witnessed. I provided him with some of the details my kids had described, including the location of where the body had been buried. He never responded.

On February 1, I left a lengthy sworn statement for Captain Hurm of Okaloosa County regarding what I knew from my sons about the murder they had witnessed.

* * *

On February 8, I was lured to work under false pretenses. I believed I was scheduled for a trip. But immediately after signing in, I was summoned to the Chief Pilot Brad Sheehan's office, who authorized this charade. From there I was escorted to the Manager of Human Resources James Brimberry. Jim Brimberry I now know was the son of a cold war era Navy veteran, and son-in-law of the former Chief of Police of Auburn, Maine, Richard Small. Small was a Shriner and Freemason, and the son of a Shriner and Freemason, and spent his entire adult life in law enforcement. Brimberry's aunt was a 50-year member of the Order of the Eastern Star. Other members of his family include founders of a ministry, a corrections officer, and right-wing MAGA Republicans. Brimberry lives in Newton County, Georgia where the Dukes of Hazard was filmed. The county is more than half black, as are the schools, but Brimberry sends his child to a practically all-white Christian school with a C-rating for diversity and some bizarre rules including banning males from having earrings, and approval for corporal punishment. Interestingly, Piedmont Academy was formed by a military veteran and Freemason (and Baptist church deacon) as a segregation academy in the 1970s in a reaction to desegregation.

It was then I learned my employer had received Nobles' email claiming I was mentally ill and implying I might harm myself or someone else. He had even called my employer from Guyana and pretended to have witnessed this behavior as a passenger on my flights. Only after three phone calls did he finally admit who he was. (He had never been a passenger on any flight of mine, and I had not seen him outside a courtroom in two years. More importantly, he had never seen me drunk.) *After being dragged into Brimberry's office on the word of a white supremacist child pornographer and murderer hiding in South America, I was suspended with pay and pulled from all flights;* I would eventually be suspended without pay after my medical was pulled.

Yet only three days before Nobles sent his emails, I had obtained an FAA medical certificate in the state of Florida by Dr. Reddoch Williams. This was on top of my independent evaluation from the psychiatrist, Eric Goldberg, who found no disorders – including any substance abuse disorders – and no need for treatment of any kind. At this time, I hadn't consumed any alcohol in approximately two years, having taken a break by choice, nor had I been accused by any coworker, supervisor, passenger, or anyone else of any alcohol issues or any other problems that might impair my ability to fly. But because of Nobles' email, I was forced to obtain another evaluation from the alleged "company doctor" as described by Brimberry, to address these allegations.

Additionally, the scheduling department was not notified for some time that management was forbidding me to fly, which resulted in me being accused of "no-showing" for flights. Nobles' motives and timing were obvious to me: flagrant witness intimidation and stalking.

* * *

Remember, Nobles had skipped the country immediately after I first informed the Niceville Police Department about the murder my sons witnessed. While hiding in South America, he was being fed confidential information to make these claims against me. He cited the falsified DCF reports by Heather Pagano, who tag teamed with Forgione to cover up state and federal weapons violations, both attempting to make "false reporting cases" and both covering up the fact that my sons fired a loaded pistol they had found in the Nobles' home. He also cited the falsified report Rick Karshna made after Tom Dunn and Joey Forgione had interfered. The same Forgione who threatened my job and threatened to arrest me when I tried to report that my sons had claimed to have witnessed a murder. They had described the event in great detail. But what was the source of Pagano's allegations? Ultimately it appears to go back to Dunn and Forgione, over and over.

* * *

During this time, I was still trying to get this murder investigated, and the trailer examined. Nobles knew the trailer contained human remains, which was why he fled to South America. I had tried to report the murder witnessed by my sons to law enforcement, and I was still trying to get the feds to enforce federal law regarding Nobles' possession of firearms.

Despite these setbacks, I wanted to try to figure out where exactly the lynching that my kids were describing had occurred. I'd made plans with Lt. Callahan of Range Patrol to search an area near Eglin that seemed to fit their description. The intention was to take Toby and Gabe to dirt roads that crossed certain tracks similar to what they had recalled and to see if they recognized anything. But scheduling conflicts and rumors of hunters shooting in the area caused delays.

* * *

Toward the end of February, I called Lt. Callahan, but he was out of the office. Fortunately, the officer on duty that day informed me of an area that matched the description – East of State Highway 285 and South of Highway 90, near the railroad tracks in Mossy Head, one of the scariest redneck parts of Florida. About half hour from Nobles' house, the area today has been built up with new pavement and a hotel, but back then it was all lonely roads and dense Florida scrub brush.

I took the children there and as soon as we saw a double set of tracks crossing the road, Gabe instantly identified it as the correct spot. He led me to the road on the left which was identical to the road he had described: a white sandy trail only big enough for one car. The highway roared with the sound of cars and trucks speeding nearby, just as Gabe had described. Beneath a nearby overpass, there were graffitied symbols of hate and occult imagery, including an upside down cross and a ram's head and what looked like a lynching with the n-word scrawled in spray paint. At the end of the road, we found the charred tree my sons had identified as the very one where the body was burned.

* * *

I notified Range Patrol as they had requested. I had asked them not to, but they went ahead and called Walton County Law Enforcement. An important point, as Walton County would later try to frame me for a false report even though I wasn't the one who contacted them. By now, I was well aware that these guys were corrupt good old boys, and I knew there were officers there who were allegedly involved in child pornography with Pentagon Freemason and occultist, RobRoy McGregor; Church of Christ minster, Bob Lewis; as well as Michel Barthelemy who lived right around the corner from Church of Christ leader Jerry McCormick.

* * *

A few days later, I was subpoenaed to the Santa Rosa County Courthouse, a squat yellow brick building along the Blackwater River, for a show-cause hearing on Nobles' DVI violations fifteen months after I filed them! Nobles should have been immediately arrested in November 2008, but Santurri sat on the files and refused to even record the violations for months. Nobles, who had moved his entire family to South America and built a house there after stopping in Barbados, was again provided a free attorney by the State of Florida.

In a move that shocked no one, Judge Santurri refused to hear motions I submitted requesting Mike Nobles return his firearms – firearms that Santurri ordered be returned to Nobles knowing full well he was a felon. When I raised the issue of the firearms, Mike Nobles yelled out that they weren't his and said they were "at the Okaloosa County Sheriff's Department." I noted that he had personally signed them out and he yelled, "That's a lie." I had the records in my hand that included his signature.

As I returned to my seat, he sneered at me across the courtroom and yelled out the words: "Failed again." Judge Santurri then denied any responsibility for arming a felon and washed his hands of the situation, refusing to make Nobles account for the weapons and allowing him to again commit perjury and make a mockery of the courtroom. Santurri dismissed the case saying, "that's taken care of."

After court I submitted another DVI against Nobles for stalking based on his email to my employer, the repeated DVI violations, the death threat on August 11, and his past pattern of conduct – including kidnapping my sons. My petition was denied by Santurri.

* * *

On February 26, despite my misgivings, I returned to the site of the burned tree with OSI Range Patrol, Security Forces, and the Walton County Sheriff's Department. The officer responding was James Lorenz, another Air Force Veteran and member of the Assembly of God. I made some calls before I went into the woods, fearing I would not come out alive given what I had learned about that department's involvement in human trafficking of foster children at Lake Sharon alleged by multiple neighbors. The site was seen by a small army of military and civilians who photographed it, and someone later marked it with surveyor's tape. Again, it was clearly and precisely as my son had described it. I made a recorded statement to an OSI investigator only to later learn my statement had been erased. (They claimed the battery was dead on the recorder. It wasn't as I saw the recorder operating).

Rather than using this new evidence to investigate Nobles, Joseph Kearnes and Joey Forgione drew up a law enforcement report to have me charged with obstructing justice. The Forgione-Kearnes tag team again. The timing of this couldn't be more obvious: I had attempted to report the murder four months prior, but no report was taken or made. Now that proof was found in the case of the tree, and Forgione knew that there were human remains in the trailer – a trailer he had defied orders to examine – the lying son of a mobster and military veteran pulled the trigger and tried to frame me once again. This was the third time they were behind plots to frame me on false charges and obviously a result of finding the proof we needed. A lynching tree.

I went back to Walton County where Lorenz claimed that "higher ups" and the Niceville Police were pressuring Walton County to not investigate. He admitted it was Forgione and his sidekick, Kearnes, who were seemingly plotting my arrest. After lengthy discussion, I was promised my trailer would be inspected and was asked to call as soon as I returned from a trip to Atlanta the following day to arrange a sworn statement.

Dunn's name was on the sign in log to visit the Walton County Sheriff that very morning. Dunn and Forgione had already shut down cases of

189

sex abuse and child pornography in which there was absolute proof; child endangerment with loaded weapons in which there was also absolute proof; and weapons possession by a felon in which there was again absolute proof. Coincidentally, Dunn had the same gray hair and mustache as Gabe described in his testimony about the body being burned. The Dunn-Forgione shitshow had struck again.

* * *

To recap: I had reported signs of sexual abuse and child pornography as related to my sons to Tom Dunn in 2008. He told me not to talk to anyone but Joey Forgione, the son of a known associate of Santo Trafficante who had a long personal relationship with the Master Mason and Knight Templar leader who built Mike Nobles' house, Constance Wayne Jones. My sons had been victims of repeated sexual battery, and Robert Norris and the Okaloosa County Sheriff's Department had forwarded my report to Forgione, who along with Kearnes, never investigated and made the report go away.

I was forced to file a restraining order; Mike Nobles' arsenal of weapons was revealed. My sons were kidnapped and, when they were returned to me, they told me they had seen an arsenal of machine guns and explosives in a "gun room." They had also seen a drug lab and more. I tried to report all this and was intercepted by Kearnes who never took the report. I then reported it to Nelson, who had the case, but it was seized from him by Forgione and Kearnes. Forgione then tried to frame me on false reporting and colluded with DCF investigator Pagano. The Niceville Police Department said they would investigate my statements that my sons had found a loaded pistol and had fired it, but the investigating officer was blocked by Forgione. Computer equipment was found in Nobles attic, but Forgione made it disappear.

As I've said, I tried to report the murder my sons witnessed but was tag teamed by Kearnes and Forgione who took no report and refused to investigate or have my sons interviewed. Forgione then threatened my job and grilled me about the interview of my sons in Santa Rosa County by Dr. Woods and had filed a report. Once he realized the Dr. Woods' potential threat, the case was flipped on me, and Karshna falsified a report. Nobles stalked me all the way from South America at my work, and he provided Forgione's name and number to my employer, you may recall, to give his claims credibility.

* * *

Once I had found the tree in the woods, Forgione plotted to also frame me in Okaloosa County. In Walton County, Lorenz admitted that Forgione had interfered in the investigation of the tree site, and Dunn made a visit to the Walton County Sheriff. Then Walton County tried to frame me as well. Over and over, Forgione/Dunn/Kearnes ran around like keystone cops cleaning up after Nobles and with immunity, targeted me. Because Nobles was protected, if not explicitly by the mob, then at least it could have been the Federal Government covering for one of their informants. The common link? Make your conclusion. Here are clues surrounding Mike Nobles that could be considered – put together – when attempting to make sense of all this colluding I've described so far:

- His house and the names on property records from 1986.

- His deal with the government in 1986.

- The Osman web in Miami.

- Dirt on public officials and the military.

- Missing kids.

- And the supposed "national treasure," the gun Nobles claimed killed JFK.

* * *

These are merely highlights of a complicated web of criminal activity.

I sent a letter via UPS to the Walton County Sheriff urging a proper investigation of the crime(s) committed in their county and asking that the trailer finally be examined and my children interviewed in an appropriate setting per their reporting of abuse, of murder they witnessed and of overall terror experienced at the hand of their grandfather. I also sent a letter to the Niceville Police Chief urging his department's cooperation, that my sons be interviewed in a respectful and safe situation, and that they accept an offer by a nationally certified cadaver dog team to examine the alleged murder site that included a lynching and corpse defilement. I sent another letter to Chief Deputy Larry Ashley informing him that his department had violated the civil rights of my sons and myself, as well as those of Faith and Emily Nobles for failure to protect. The very next day, citing "personal reasons," Forgione dropped out of the sheriff's election race.

* * *

I filed a Bar complaint against Michael Gibson for his part in knowingly arming a convicted felon. The Bar covered for him as the Judicial Qualifications Committee had done for Santurri, claiming Gibson had prevented the guns from being returned to Nobles (which is laughable since the guns had been returned to him). The Florida Bar Association also claimed that Gibson "forgot" his client was a felon. It is also notable that Gibson, at the Sheriff's Departments request (attorney Steve Hurm), had created a false affidavit signed by Nobles claiming that the guns had been returned to Billy Nobles and that Mike had transferred ownership of the guns to Billy). Another case of one hand dirtying another.

* * *

Before we move on, I will explain my history with alcohol. In our world, the one we call reality, it doesn't figure in. But since the topic turned into a major influence in my battle with Mike Nobles, let me provide you with the facts. I had my first beer at the age of 16 when a coworker offered me one after work. In high school, my friends and I – much like many teenagers at this time, and other times – would drink when we got together on weekends if we could get our hands on alcohol, which was very rare. Like most high school kids who drink, we drank to get drunk. In college I was working two jobs, making straight A's and maintaining a scholarship. I didn't drink very often as I didn't have time. When I joined the Air Force, I quickly learned of the military's culture of alcohol. I am not making excuses, I gladly and willingly participated.

Starting at Officer Training School, where unlimited free beer was provided every Friday, I participated in the drinking culture. For the most part, I was responsible. It never affected my performance, which records show was superior, and I would say was limited to blowing off steam at the end of a stressful week. This continued into pilot training where it was a normal event for someone to buy a keg and put it in the flight room on Fridays ... followed up with heavy drinking at the officer's club later in the evening. It shouldn't surprise you that I could tell you many drinking stories about my friends and me during this time. Silliness, foolishness, and male bonding. And yes, drinking to excess.

As ridiculous as the movie *Top Gun* was, the drinking and bar scene was pretty accurate. There is a name for this, binge drinking. According to the Alcohol Rehab Guide studies show about 35% of military members engage in binge drinking as do 50% of college students. As an example, when I left the Air Force in 1999, the wing commander and his chief enlisted advisor had seven combined DUI convictions between them. I remember one change of command ceremony, where Air Force Special Operations Command Commander, General Holland, described pulling pilots out of the bar and found the least drunk among them to fly a mission during an ensuing military crisis. My last squadron in the Air Force had a full-blown bar upstairs, something not uncommon in the military.

In the summer of 1998, I was stationed in a beach resort town, single, and had single friends who liked to party and drink. I probably drank more that summer than any other time in my life. We had good times, sure, but sometimes we were irresponsible. After a wakeup call from the incident described in the appendix, "Military Madness." After that, I quit drinking for a while and cut back when I resumed. I have never drunk on the job or before work, never neglected my work or family duties because of alcohol, never had withdrawals or cravings, and never had a problem with setting alcohol aside.

As a matter of fact, I can tell you that I did not drink for ten years between 2008 and 2018. No one other than Mike Nobles, not a coworker, passenger, family member, or otherwise, has ever raised questions about alcohol affecting my role as a husband and parent or in the course of my job. I was evaluated in 1999 because of this one incident which led to the military board of inquiry detailed in the appendix "Military Madness." I was found to be free of any alcohol use disorders. Case closed, or at least it should have been.

Between 2010 and 2012, I was subjected to six alcohol evaluations, none of which concluded that I met any criteria for treatment. What happens next in this saga was a case of digging for dirty laundry, pouncing on a point of perceived weakness – an old arrest from a decade prior – and exploiting it to the max to discredit me and control me. They used these old stories, but only the parts that bolstered their goals, to paint me as an alcoholic to discredit and silence my kids as victims and witnesses. Only after numerous failed efforts to frame me on false charges, failed efforts to label me crazy, and failed efforts to take my kids away. When you put all the tales I've shared here, their motivation, hopefully, will be obvious in the light of day.

* * *

In March, I received an email from Jim Brimberry, the manager of HR at my airline, demanding I submit to an evaluation with "our doctor." The company didn't have a doctor. This was a set up from the start. He demanded a copy of Dr. Goldberg's report, which hadn't even been written yet. A second email from Brimberry was sent – to "All" – stating that Brad Sheehan (Flight Ops) and the Air Line Pilots Association (ALPA) were backing the decision to force me into an illegal evaluation, citing Mark

Wollman, an attorney and ALPA representative, as claiming the contract allowed it. The email he sent to me making false allegations regarding my military service and false claims I had lied on job applications was attached and available to whomever was included in this email. "Wollman advised that we set up an appointment and direct Harris to show up for it. A phone call from the CP (Chief Pilot) telling him we have set up an appointment, etc., might take the "directive" sting out of the conversation. If we know this is the net outcome, then why continue to wait on this other material. This is becoming very untimely."

Wollman, a Union representative, knew this was illegal and baseless and he had no permission from me to talk to management. I had previously gone to Wollman for legal advice because my job had been threatened by Forgione and Karshna. Now, it appeared, he was colluding with management and violating attorney and union confidentiality. After a decade of being a model employee and one of the most respected pilots in the company, I was fed to the wolves when Wollman took that confidential information straight to management without my consent. Instead of helping me, the union later circled the wagons and tried to bully me into silence.

There are four types of substance abuse tests authorized by the FAA: pre-employment, post-accident, random testing, and reasonable suspicion testing. Reasonable suspicion testing requires *two* specially trained supervisors to make a conclusion based on smells, eyes, and/or behavior, that an employee, a pilot, is on duty and under the influence. Of course, none of these statements were true in any way. Furthermore, the testing must be performed within 8 hours, not two months after the malicious and transparently motivated allegations. Also of note, it is illegal for an employer to ask an employee about the reason for his military discharge. I was grilled on this subject repeatedly and then there was false information regarding my service and medical history spread all over the country.

I was about to be unknowingly introduced to the "Berry Scheme," as labeled by the *Washington Examiner*.

But what could I do? On March 4, 2010, I was forced to submit to an illegal urinalysis with Dr. Charles Richard Harper, a man who my employer claimed was the "company doctor," but in fact was not. A Navy veteran, former head of the FAA's accident investigations, and former United Airlines Medical Director, Dr. Harper's sole business by the time I met him was performing FAA medical examinations for a fee – cash only. His office was in a seedy run-down office building in Doraville, GA. According to him, he performed four to five of these examinations a day, three days a week. Upon entering his office, I discovered he had John Birch Society and other right-wing literature in his lobby and Egyptian art on the walls. Pyramids and the god Anubis that Gabe had drawn. (I would learn much later he was also a member of the Roswell Masonic Lodge as was his future attorney Clifford Hardick, an Army veteran.) An old cold warrior, his obituary makes him out to be some Indiana Jones, dancing with headhunters, fighting off tigers on the Ho Chi Min trail, and treating malaria. Ironically, given what was about to happen next, Dr. Harper was an alcoholic with a DUI conviction.

Had I not complied with this exam, I could have been fired. The stated excuse made by Jim Brimberry for this violation of my employment contract and violation of FAA regulations, not to mention an illegal search and seizure, was the "issue" of my military discharge. There had never been an issue. He talked about "how my application was marked." This is important because I was falsely accused of lying on my job application when I could not have been more honest. I have never and still have never met the criteria for substance dependence, nor have I remotely met the criteria for substance abuse as defined by the DOT and FAA. To this day I have never had a single incident reportable to the FAA.

My urinalysis came back negative.

* * *

Regardless, based on the questionable word of a pathological liar and federal convict hiding in South America, Dr. Harper forced me to obtain what is deemed a Psychological and Psychiatric evaluation with Dr. Michael Haberman. So, under duress, I left my kids with a nanny in Florida and traveled all the way to Atlanta, where Dr. Haberman ordered I take a full battery of psychological tests. After being deliberately deceived by Dr. Harper as to the purpose and intent of this evaluation, I had no choice but to comply if I wanted to return to work. In retrospect, Haberman was just checking the boxes of requirements for a special issuance medical certificate, a medical certificate that allows a pilot to fly, after jumping through certain hoops.

Like so many other people I encountered during this time, Dr. Haberman, I would later learn, was a right-wing extremist who spread racist propaganda on Facebook where he used his medical degree to diagnose Barack Obama as a narcissistic sociopath because of his parents' "mixed-race marriage."[1] There, he also referred to the Guantanamo Bay attorneys as "enemies of the state." The source of this tirade was an Islamophobic blogger and a Russian Psychiatrist who suffered narcissistic personality disorder. Haberman was also the author of a letter to the editor opposing universal health care. But I was getting used to this pattern, and I wasn't concerned about the psychological tests. I returned home, hopeful I could get back at least one small sliver of my normal life.

I was arrested the next morning.

Endnotes

1   https://www.facebook.com/TheNarcissistSeries/posts/10152271783909639/?paipv=0&eav=AfbXfmxhD-nlEJcLBchrmxUEAihYlMRaP0VysNeux19-aUxl4qL7n2VsG3N83AqZsP8&_rdr

CHAPTER THIRTEEN

DIRTY DEEDS DONE DIRT CHEAP

I woke to a Santa Rosa Sheriff Deputy knocking on my door. I was shackled, strip searched, booked in Santa Rosa County Jail, and then transferred and booked in Okaloosa. Interim Sheriff of Okaloosa County and a future US Marshall, Ed Spooner – who had personally bailed Nobles out of jail when he was arrested for firearms violations – signed off on the warrant. The charge was "providing false information to a law enforcement officer of a capital offense." This was based on the shit-show back in November when Forgione – who had threatened to arrest me if I filed a report and threatened to go after my job – refused to examine evidence of murder while the Niceville Police Department and other agencies refused to interview my sons. Among the litany of lies, Forgione claimed he examined the trailer and claimed I refused to let my kids be interviewed claiming I "got nervous" and hurriedly left the Department. I had, again, sent a certified letter to his Chief requesting an interview and did the same in Walton County accompanied by a notarized sworn statement that refuted falsified reports in both jurisdictions. Forgione is a bully and coward who threatened women and children while trying to portray *me* as crazy and a coward.

The arresting officer in Santa Rosa knew something was wrong with the case and even apologized to me and let me use my cell phone – which may have saved my life – before putting me in my cell. I was quickly (unusually quickly) transferred to Okaloosa County jail. A day later, at my first appearance before Judge Jim Ward, I was informed I needed to see someone before he'd agree to set bond. That "someone," I'd come to find out, was yet another psych eval. But the psych eval never happened and for the next six days, I was left in a holding cage twenty-three hours a day like an animal, with no change of clothes or chance to shave and blocked from receiving visitors. My fellow inmates, and even one guard, told me that was not possible. I believed then and believe now the plan was to kill me and stage a suicide, but someone got their wires crossed or cold feet. An Epstein scenario to cover up missing children to protect the military, clergy, and law enforcement involved in human trafficking and drug trafficking. To stop an unravelling that could lead to the grassy knoll. A later review of the records showed no evidence whatsoever to support a psychological evaluation, and I never received one. While incarcerated, I learned in a call with my mother that Sgt. Lorenz in Walton County was plotting to frame me as well. He told my mother that, "There's a lot you don't know." The real problem was what I did know. And what my sons had seen.

* * *

Finally, on March 24, I was released on bond. My elderly, hardworking, poor father had to borrow money to hire an attorney. My cell phone, which had been confiscated, was returned to me. but when I tried calling for a ride home, I discovered it didn't work. The battery was charged, and I'd never had any problem with it until then. I opened it up and found the sim card installed backwards. Someone had searched it – without a warrant.

The nanny took care of my sons the entire time I was incarcerated. Their mother never bothered to pick them up. More charges were filed against me by Detective Lorenz, who denied the existence of the burnt tree and omitted details about evidence found in the trailer. He omitted even the existence of the trailer. It was never even logged in by the evidence custodian.

He said I had filed false police reports because, he claimed, I told him I was in an "ongoing custody battle with my soon to be ex-wife." I never said any such thing, and there was no custody battle. Not only did she fail to get our children while I was in jail, by Christmas she took off entirely, leaving me to raise them alone for the next two years. If she and her family truly thought I was mentally ill and dangerous, why did she leave the kids with me? But this was the game. Portray it all as a "domestic dispute."

* * *

Shortly after my release, I received a response to a complaint I had made to Okaloosa County Sheriff Larry Ashley asking for an appointment to file complaints against not only Mike Nobles, but also Case Advocate Tom Dunn, DCF investigators Jennifer Clark, DCF Heather Pagano, and Rick Karshna, Detective Joey Forgione, and Chaplain Brad Bynum. All had committed documented crimes. The letter was dated March 8, 2010, but not mailed until I had spent six days of psychological abuse while illegally held in an Okaloosa County holding cell. The letter was signed by Steve Hurm. As a reminder, Steve Hurm is the son in law of former Governor turned Senator, Bob Graham. His wife is Gwendolyn Graham, a former Congresswoman and then assistant secretary of the United States Department of Education. Hurm, who had solicited a false affidavit to cover Mike Nobles tracks as well as the Sherrif's Department's tracks, after they knowingly armed a dangerous felon, denied knowing the outcome of that case. He, like others, hid behind the Florida Department of Children and Families who do not investigate crimes against children. He cited Jennifer Clark's complaint to the Sheriff's Office as evidence, a complaint Clark and her supervisor denied making. Oh, what a tangled web of lies.

Hurm:

> ... to the best of my knowledge, and a review of our historical records, no child has asked this agency for help from that household for two decades. The only allegations of wrongdoing have been from you. As far as your allegation that our agency has violated the civil rights of you, Gabriel Harris, Toby Harris, and Emily Nobles, see nothing in your correspondence to justify such a claim. First, you do not have the legal basis to make such a claim on behalf of Faith and Emily Nobles since you are neither their parent nor guardian. Second, there is no evidence that the Okaloosa County Sheriff's Office has done anything other than respectfully listen to you, review your complaints, and investigate whether criminal wrongdoing occurred in our jurisdiction. Your dissatisfaction with the outcome of those investigations does not equate to a civil rights violation
>
> If you have any new allegations of criminal wrongdoing, we will investigate those with the professionalism and alacrity that has marked our previous efforts. We will not, however, investigate old allegations that have already been reviewed and closed as unfounded.

Once again, as the Sheriff's Department was violating my civil rights through false imprisonment, the Sheriff was hiding behind a lying lawyer, Steve Hurm, who had fabricated evidence in the firearms case against Nobles. The only allegations were from me, he said, despite the documentation otherwise that I sent to him and undoubtedly ended up in the shredder

Repeat a lie often enough they say. *Professionalism and Alacrity? Please.* Making reports go away, arming a felon, falsifying records, kidnapping my son from a birthday party and delivering him to a monster? Refusing to investigate crimes including a murder with two eyewitnesses?

* * *

Then what, in retrospect, was likely a preplanned maneuver occurred. Joe Figueroa, an acquaintance from Calvary Chapel (also a new member) showed up at my door and told me he was thrown out of his house, getting a divorce, and needed a place to stay for a couple of days. Joe, I would learn later, was an ex-Air Force OSI agent and *ended up staying two years and took over the childcare job while I was at work.* I ended up sharing everything with him and he would gently prod me to back off investigating Nobles, but he wanted to know every detail. He tried to convince me that there was a "spiritual cloud of darkness" over the panhandle and even claimed to see spirits floating around our house. He would lay hands on me and the kids and pray for us.

* * *

Come April, I was required by my company and Dr. Haberman to obtain the psychological testing ordered by Dr. Haberman. I met with Dr. Fiona Hill in Atlanta; a respected psychologist known in Washington D.C. for her work. While none of this had any real justification behind it – the ultimate purpose was to discredit me, and by extension, the testimony of my autistic child (he had not yet been diagnosed with autism but had an uncanny photographic memory and artistic skills) – I made the trip and took the tests. Dr. Hill's report stated, "Mr. Harris does not appear to be experiencing any cognitive or emotional problems that would impair his capacity to operate an airplane safely. Cognitively, he demonstrates skills that are even more impressive given the stress he has been under. At this time, Mr. Harris appears capable of resuming his duties as pilot."

The stress I was under. You could call it that.

Only a week before I'd been in county jail after my father-in-law tried to get me fired in coordination with a police officer who had mob ties. My children had been kidnapped and assaulted. They had witnessed a murder, and I was arrested when I tried to report it. Yes, I was under stress, but again and again I passed every damn test they threw at me. "The airman appears fit to fly," Dr. Haberman put in his report. "I am not recommending any additional treatment at this time."

* * *

This, of course, would not do. Dr. Berry and Dr. Harper had other plans. So, Dr. Haberman did a cut and paste job and conjured up a "history of alcohol abuse from the '90s in full remission." Again, this simply wasn't the case. There was no alcohol abuse as defined by the FAA, which required multiple DUI convictions, and this vague opinion of alcoholism – opinion, not diagnosis – was irrelevant under FAA regulations, even if it were true, because of the time frame. (Even with a previous diagnosis of alcoholism, being alcohol free for 2 years eliminates any action against a medical certificate).

And, not to beat a dead horse, but entirely of my own volition I hadn't had a drink in two years! It was all smoke and mirrors.

* * *

My own court date was scheduled, conveniently, on my 43rd birthday. Only days before my arrest, I had brought Gabe and Toby to our church's family camp where we'd enjoyed a pleasant, quiet weekend with members of the church. It felt like we were in the eye of a hurricane swirling around us. Tom Read, the Ministry Assistant at Calvary Chapel wrote me a nice letter in which he called me a fine man and wonderful father. Steve Ward, of The Most Excellent Way chapter from Calvary Chapel, also wrote me a supportive letter, describing me as a loving father truly concerned for my sons. And Joanna Morris, owner of Lighthouse Private Christian Academy, wrote a "To Whom It May Concern" letter regarding Toby's "inappropriate behavior" back in 2008. Her letter made clear that Toby's therapist had also reported the suspected abuse, and that their reports were ignored or obstructed by authorities:

> Based on concern from a teacher, I made a call to abuse hotline to make a report concerning Toby Harris. Someone returned the call and told me that the case had already been reported and was in the system. Therefore, I contacted Toby's therapist, Karleen Shuster and told her what they told me. She said she had just reported it and that is probably why it was already in the system. She informed me that DCF would probably be coming to see me at the school. Over the next two weeks, no one ever came to speak to me at the school and then Toby and Gabe were removed from my school at the end of October. [Refers to when they were kidnapped on Halloween.]
>
> Toby Harris returned to LPCA in February of 2009. After his return, a gentleman named Rick [Karshna] (from DCF) did stop by my school to speak to Toby's teacher, Ms. Emmons. I was not at the school that day. However, the teacher, Ms. Emmons stated that he asked her just a few questions about Toby's behavior. Ms. Emmons said, "I am worried about Toby so please check into the Grandfather." But, she said that the gentleman's response was as if he didn't believe that Toby had been abused.
>
> My notes indicate that when he was in his father's care, his behavior was calm and secure. When he was in his mother's care, or

away from his father, his behavior was radical and insecure. Mr. Harris, the father, has displayed good parenting skills. Since Toby and Gabe have been in his care and have now both returned to school, their behavior and their academics have improved significantly.

After so much stonewalling and gaslighting, I can't say how much these kind words of support and validation meant to me. They were few and far between in coming.

I spent my birthday in court, not with friends, not with family, but with my attorney, Glen Swiatek. Not just my birthday but also Hitler's birthday, revered by white supremacists. As we waited to plea "not guilty," a familiar figure in a t-shirt barged into the courtroom, motorcycle helmet in hand, and plopped down in the seat next to me: Mike Nobles had returned from South America to harass me in court. My attorney was livid and let the state attorney have it, telling him to keep Mike Nobles the hell away from his client. *Happy birthday to me.*

* * *

On May 4, Dr. Harper sent a letter dated April 30 to the FAA claiming a "history of alcohol abuse and/or dependence" that is "well documented." Dr. Harper followed up these fabrications with claims that I had been the subject of "chronic" complaints during my time as a pilot. The only complaints I ever received in my professional career came from one man and one man only: Mike Nobles. All of this without my knowledge or consent and in violation of HIPAA laws, he recommended I be issued a special issuance medical certificate and be put in a monitoring program, with him as my sponsor of course.

On May 4 a mysterious DUI from 1998 appeared in my records. I later found a note in my files stating, "Releasing to DUI as requested," written by a Sandy Clymer at the FAA in Oklahoma City. (Clymer appears in an obituary of a relative, Donna Fitzgerald, a Navy wife, former Rainbow Girl, and leader in the Order of the Eastern Star and member of the Church of Christ. In this obituary Clymer claims she saw angels take her father-in-law to heaven.[1] Her father-in-law was a military veteran and 32 or 33 degree Freemason.[2]) This record has since been removed from my file to cover their tracks.

The next day an FAA doctor in Oklahoma City, William Mills, signed a letter for a Dr. Silberman, an FAA official in Washington D.C., stating that my application for a medical certificate dated January 22 was denied because it disclosed a history of "alcohol abuse." This was a bold-faced lie. There was no outstanding application, and nothing disclosed on the application referenced as there was nothing to disclose; I already had a valid medical certificate that couldn't legally be rescinded because, even if all the charges against me were true, more than sixty days had passed since I'd received it. This was all smoke and mirrors. My medical had been effectively and illegally "canceled" in an illegitimate game that avoided the revocation process required in which I would have had a right to appeal. After I received this letter, I ordered my FAA medical records, which would ultimately shed light on this Orwellian scheme, but too late.

Both Clymer's note and Dr. Harper's letter were recorded in my FAA records on the same day: May 5, as was the bogus denial letter. Dr. Harper's letter stated I needed monitoring and a special issuance medical certificate. Let me be clear, I never got a DUI in 1998 or any other year, and it's no coincidence that this forgery showed up when it did. I was caught in the middle of the "Berry Scheme" through Dr. Michael Berry's pal, Dr. Harper.

Even if the story of a DUI in 1998 were true, under the FAA's AME guidelines a single incident more than five years old requires an examining AME to issue a medical certificate and document the incident. So, had there been a ten-year-old DUI – there wasn't – I still would have been fully qualified to hold the first-class medical certificate required to fly a plane.

* * *

My employer stopped paying me, but the scheduling department kept calling me to say I'd missed flights. Each time I "missed a flight" I was no longer supposed to be on there, the "missed flight" was added to my record. (I have no doubt that some of these flights were delayed or canceled due to the chain reaction of events caused by Nobles' email and Harper's report.) Desperate, I reached out to the Air Line Pilots Association which had been taking 2% of my salary for over a decade to allegedly represent me, but they only threatened to have me terminated for not paying union dues during a time I wasn't getting paid.

* * *

I was unemployed with steadily rising legal and medical debts. During all this, I was still the sole caregiver of two children with disabilities from mental injuries they'd suffered at the hands of their grandfather. My wife – who should have been gravely concerned about the kids if she believed I was the alcoholic, mentally ill monster her family had painted me as to our friends, the courts, and my employer – was nowhere to be found.

I survived by doing odd jobs, including ditch digging, during a time I was required to have a double hernia operation. An ex-coworker, Mike

Montamat, tried to start a fundraiser to help me and my kids, but he was stopped by Brad Sheehan at Flight Ops. One day I woke up to find the power had been cut off.

* * *

Knowing this scheme couldn't withstand scrutiny, and having already "canceled" my medical with a fake DUI and smoke and mirrors, Dr. Harper and his pals in Washington started an illegal fishing expedition to justify their actions. Dr. Harper told me he had an old friend in Washington who could clear up this whole mess. He later called and told me that his pal Dr. Berry was demanding my military Board of Inquiry records. He said I would never go back to flying if I didn't and that Berry had threatened to have some military General friend of his get them for him if I refused. This was all illegal of course. A classic shakedown. I now had to relive that nightmare again. I copied the entire file, over 300 pages. But Harper didn't want them. He only wanted excerpts, the finding of the board, for his cut and paste assassination.

On June 2, 2010, Dr Harper sent these Privacy Act protected, extremely sensitive records to Dr. Charles Chesanaw, the FAA's Chief Psychiatrist, with a note documenting that Berry had requested them. I never signed any release of these records and had produced them out of coercion and blatant extortion.

* * *

On June 22, 2010, Dr. Alan Sager, a consultant who has an exclusive multimillion dollar contract with the FAA, wrote a bizarre cut and paste report. The report opened with the claim that I was "applying for a special issuance from a history of alcoholism under the sponsorship of C.R. Harper, MD." I had never filed any such application, had not authorized Dr. Harper to give my information to Dr. Sager or anyone else, and certainly never requested he be any kind of sponsor. I was being steam rolled by Dr. Harper and his pals. The report claimed I had a DUI in 1998 (a total fabrication), that I had quit drinking after separating from my wife because I couldn't drink and raise my kids (which I never said to anyone and wasn't true) and referred to an evaluation in the Air Force that found me free of any substance abuse issues as "weeklong outpatient treatment." He went on to claim I had received civilian treatment as well, also a total fabrication. I now had a fake DUI and a fake medical history along with a fake request for a special issuance medical certificate.

On July 14, 2010, Dr. Stephen Goodman, a crony of Dr. Berry, sent me a letter denying my "request for reconsideration." (Goodman was later

The Berry Scheme

Dr. Berry had been accused of this before. In 2009, The Washington Examiner wrote:

"A former Continental Airlines pilot who was medically grounded after complaining about safety problems in the cockpit told *The Examiner* that "the dreaded Dr. Berry," as he is known among some pilots, falsified his medical records by telling the FAA he had "a neurological condition (seizure)" that ended his 17-year flying career.

"Dr. Berry found me 'unfit for duty' with no corroborating medical evidence, based upon a phone call to the pilot about whom I had complained … and then had the audacity to ask me for money to pay him to take care of it. He even wrote this in his notes…. If I decided to work with him, he'd have to charge me for his time.

In a written complaint to the FBI, the grounded pilot outlined what he called "The Berry System:" The following list describes/defines the Berry System? This part of the newspaper article?

1.   An airline pilot falls into disfavor with his employer, often for voicing safety concerns.

2.   The airline tells the pilot he will be fired if he doesn't go see Dr. Berry.

3.   Dr. Berry reassures the pilot, saying he can't do anything to get the pilot grounded.

4.   Dr. Berry informs the pilot that the exam results are all "perfectly normal" and asks why he's there.

5.   The pilot complains about somebody and/or something at the airline.

6.   Dr. Berry falsifies a story based partly upon statements made about the pilot by fellow crewmembers.

7.   Ignoring any clinical evidence and opinions of other medical specialists, Dr. Berry finds the pilot "unfit for duty" and begins lobbying the FAA (paid for on an hourly basis by the airline) to begin the process of revoking the pilot's medical certificate.

8.   Dr. Berry fraudulently alters the pilot's past medical history.

9.   Dr. Berry refuses to send a copy of the fraudulent report to the pilot.

10.   Dr. Berry calls the pilot and makes ambiguous statements about his report, then attempts to extort money from the pilot to "take care of it."

11.   If the pilot rejects his "offer," Dr. Berry sends his fraudulent reports to the FAA, deliberately excluding all data that is in the pilot's favor (in violation of 18 U.S. Code Sec. 1001:3571).

12.   A friend of Dr. Berry's at the FAA (Dr. Warren Silberman, DO) revokes the pilot's FAA medical certificate via letter and immediately faxes a copy of the revocation letter to Dr. Berry.

13.   When the airline gets hit with a lawsuit, Dr. Berry sends them a copy of the FAA's letter which is nothing more than a product of his fraudulent scheme.

14.   The airline uses the FAA's letter to affect the outcome of the lawsuit (and various other legal proceedings/investigations) in its favor.

> 15. If the pilot complains to the State Board of Medical Examiners, Dr. Berry uses the FAA's letter as "evidence" that he has done nothing wrong.
>
> 16. The pilot becomes both unemployed and unemployable – without any hope of legal recourse."
>
> "Berry would harass the complaining pilots by sticking them with needles to draw blood and poking his finger up their anuses, with the message being clear: we can do whatever we want with you.
>
> "If the pilot complained further, Berry would make up an ambiguous story and try to get the pilot to pay him not to send it to the FAA. If the pilot wouldn't pay him, he'd send it to his friend at the FAA, who would revoke the pilot's medical certificate.
>
> "Berry made a lot of money doing this and was financially protected by us using the same arrangement he had at other airlines. Berry became very conceited and left a substantial paperwork trail. You need to investigate this."[3]

promoted to Deputy to Dr. Berry in DC.) I had never made one, nor did I have the opportunity to do so. I had never been told I was under investigation nor advised of my rights, which is required. This letter changed the allegation from alcohol abuse, previously justified with a fake DUI, to alcoholism, now justified with a fake medical history in Dr. Sager's report. It was again bizarre. And even more bizarre that Goodman was the Senior Regional Flight Surgeon for the Western Pacific Region where I neither lived nor worked. And the Regional Flight Surgeon's office where I worked and lived had been completely bypassed.

* * *

Meanwhile, Dr. Harper informed me that if I was going to return to flying, Dr. Berry would require me to attend a relapse prevention aftercare group. Aftercare is for individuals who have been diagnosed with alcoholism and completed treatment. I would learn two years later from the head of a substance abuse program that forcing someone who had never been treated nor had any diagnosis to attend aftercare was unethical.

There was a group that met at my church which was recognized nationally as well as by the court system and I asked that I attend this group for my requirement. I sent Dr. Harper a packet of information about the organization. He informed me that Dr. Berry had denied my request. Dr. Harper and Dr. Berry demanded that I attend a shady, for-pay group that met in a strip mall in Pensacola. *Control the message by controlling the messengers.*

The man who ran this group was a convicted cocaine trafficker with some apparent ethical issues. During my attendance in this group, he lost his contract for a group of nurses with addiction issues after sleeping with one of them. My intake assessment at this group consisted of him taking an assessment of another client, cutting his name out, and inserting mine and changing the date. He did this in front of me. This was similar to a practice Dr. Harper would engage in with his annual evaluations, which were pre-filled out forms stating that (fill in the blank) was in compliance with the program. He would insert the name and date fax them to the FAA each year. They had quite a racket.

* * *

Dr. Berry has held many lofty positions, including President of the Aerospace Medical Association, and Chief of Flight Medicine at the Johnson Space Center for NASA, a role once held by his father. Before that he was an Air Force Flight Surgeon. Part of a parade of old cold war ex-military relics who have messed with my life over the years. Dr. Berry's father, Charles Alden Berry, was the Director of Life Sciences for NASA. He provided support for the Apollo space program and was a member of the Mercury Astronaut Selection Committee. According to an interview with Berry, Freemason James Webb, the NASA administrator, chose him for his role. Previously, Webb participated in the "Lavender Scare" in which 5000-1000 gay employees of the State Department lost their jobs. Who did he pick for these roles at NASA? White male Freemasons. All of them except a few, and those few were the sons of Freemasons. In an interview on NASA's website, Berry's racism exudes.

> BERRY:" We had some interesting things during the Kennedy administration. Deke and I both got a call from Bobby [Robert F.] Kennedy. This was when we were going to do – I can't remember if it was the second or the third selection. But we got a call, and he said, *"We want to assure that there is an African American in the next selection.* I did not know that he had called Deke at that time. I got his call, and I said, well, at that time we already had a list of the people that were really going to be looked at. We culled the group down. I don't remember what the total number was now, but it seems to me it was something like sixty that we had culled it down to.
>
> "So I said, Well, I don't know that I can – I certainly can't guarantee that, that we're going to have an African American. As a matter of fact, there are two African Americans, I think, in the group, in this group that *we've done some culling already.* But to tell you that we're going to select one of those, I can't do that. We're going to go down and they're going to be selected based upon the merit, the way we've been doing it. Whether there's going to be one of them, I don't know."
>
> He said, "You did not hear what I said. I said we want to assure – and you will assure – that *there will be an African American.*"

Then Deke came to me and said he'd gotten a call. So, we talked about this, and we ended up making our list. We'd always end up having to take the list, after it was done at the Center, we'd end up having to take the list to Washington [DC]. So, we took the list to Washington, and *the two blacks were way down*. You'd have had to take another – I don't remember, something like fifteen or something more to get to the first one, and you'd probably have had to take another thirty more or something to get to the second one. And we left the list as it was with them graded.

Took it up and said, "If there's going to be any change in this list, it's going to have to be done somewhere else. *We're not going to change the list*. And the President didn't change it, wouldn't change, so that wasn't done. But there's a lot of political things."

"Absolutely. Well, I don't think people can really understand today, in our world today, the things that were going on in the world at that time and how important it was to have something good happen, something that was a human accomplishment, when we were doing so much to tear everything down. *Gee, we were having riots.*

BERRY: "Before we launched Apollo 11, I was going to the Cape from the motel at about – oh, I think it was something like one in the morning. I drove up to the gate, and there *were a bunch of African Americans marching back and forth in front of the – Reverend [Ralph] Abernathy and all his people were marching in front of the gate. I stopped the car. I went through the gate and then I stopped the car and got out, and I went back, walked back. I saw Abernathy in this group, and I went up to him* and I said, 'You know, I do not understand why you would come and try and demonstrate and say that we ought not to have this flight to the Moon. Do you have any concept at all about what this can mean to the world and to us as a nation, having the capability to do this?'"

Reverand Abernathy said: "It's really not about the capability to do this, it's this money that's going to the Moon, this money's going to be on the Moon, and it should be being spent on these people down here on the Earth."

"And I said, there isn't a single dollar going on the Moon. Not one dollar going to be on the Moon. Every one of those dollars that's gone to this program, and a lot of this nation is involved in that, and every one of those dollars is going to somebody down here on the Earth. If some of your people wanted to be working on some of that, they could have done it. I'm sure that jobs are there. So, I said, You could work on it, and you could be getting some of that so-called moon money, if you want to call it that.

REVERAND ABERNATHY: "'That's not what I'm saying,' he said. 'The thing is, that money ought to be spent on these people right down here.'

"I (Berry) said, well, you obviously don't understand what is happening here, and it's being done for your good and for everyone's good. If a nation is great, it's my view that that nation ought to be able to do both things, and we ought to be able to do the things that are necessary here. We need the science and the technology on the cutting edge if we're going to be a nation that's going to progress. If you don't, you're going to die as a nation and you're not going to solve any of the problems here on Earth or anywhere else.

Well, he didn't believe that. I don't think I made any headway with him whatsoever, but I felt better, anyway, afterwards.

But that sort of thing went on. There were a lot of things happening in our world. I tell you, I was really privileged to see a lot of the things that President Johnson and – well, clear up – President Nixon understood that, too. All of those three Presidents certainly utilized the space program as a diplomatic tool for our country, and it worked.

In a racist referenced to Africans BERRY said: "In Africa, you'd open the aircraft door and you'd be at the top of the stairs, *and all you can see is a mass of nothing but black,* as far as you could see, *and people with spears and fur, animal fur* and what have you. Amazingly, even in these places, people had radios and things, and they knew what we were – and they were excited and thought it was absolutely wonderful. We were mobbed, absolutely mobbed, wherever we went. I saw that time after time."

Dr. Charles Berry was really a grotesque racist at heart. A cold war era monster. In fact, test pilot Edward Dwight, a black test pilot, had been handpicked by Kennedy for the Apollo missions. According to Dwight, "racial politics had forced him out of NASA." During his training he was isolated and harassed by Freemason Chuck Yeager, who didn't want him in the program. Dwight was cut from the program just weeks after the murder of the president. The legacy of the Lodge is a Legacy of Hate.

On Sept 10, after receiving my records, I sent a letter to the FAA informing them that there had been no DUI.

* * *

I did my best to fight for my children. Despite the costs, I continued to take them to their appointments with therapists and other doctors. That May, upon referral by my lawyer, Glenn Swiatek, the boys began sessions with Kelly Beck, a psychotherapist in Fort Walton Beach. She recommended further evaluations under the supervision of Dr. Marianne McCain. After careful testing, Gabe was diagnosed with PTSD as a result of the abuse he had endured, which we would learn about slowly over time.

A few weeks later, I agreed to take a polygraph test with an independent Polygraph Examiner regarding my children's claims about witnessing the murder of Jack Stevens. The examiner asked me three questions:

1. Are you deliberately lying when you say that your children told you that their grandfather had murdered a man in Niceville, Florida?

2. Have you in any way encouraged your children to lie about that murder?

3. Are you deliberately lying just to get your father-in-law in trouble?

The conclusion? "After careful analysis of the polygraph charts it is the opinion of this Polygraph Examiner that Mr. Harris was truthful when answering "No" to the above listed relevant questions."

* * *

My medical certification had been denied, but a follow up letter from the FAA told me they would reconsider this decision if I joined an aftercare group for alcoholics referred to by my sponsor. That's when I learned I had a sponsor, and that my sponsor was Dr. Harper. Of course. I was never told there were over 40 sponsors available, including two in my area of Florida. Dr. Harper was handpicked for me. By Dr. Berry.

In August, my children were subpoenaed to testify in detail regarding the murder they witnessed, the gun Toby fired in Nobles' home, the other weapons Mike Nobles possessed, and in Gabe's case, the incident in which Nobles threatened Gabe with "crucifixion" if he told the truth. I drove them to ECCAC, despite my objections, but I was not allowed to stay during their testimony.

Though I've edited sections in the following testimonies where one or the other child went on unrelated tangents – they're children after all – I think it's important to hear the story in their own words. Gabe was the first to be grilled by the Assistant State Attorney, Christopher Smith.

G.S.H. DIRECT EXAMINATION

MR. SMITH: All right. Where are you – will you say what your name is?

GABE: (Witness says first name).

MR. SMITH: And what's your last name?

GABE: (Witness says last name).

MR. SMITH: Okay. And how old are you, G.H.?

GABE: No. I have a second name.

MR. SMITH: What is it?

GABE: (Witness says middle name).

MR. SMITH: (Repeats middle name and full name).

GABE: Yeah. And my mom used to say, G.S.H. when – she's like, G.S.H., when I'm in trouble. I'm like–

MR. SMITH: I know.

GABE: I'm like, I'm so busted.

MR. SMITH: I know. My mom would do the same thing to me and my sister, would say the same thing to me.

MR. SWIATEK: And I used to hear it every single day.

GABE: I used to hear it every single day when I throw something out the window. Like, a CD, I thought it was a frisbee.

…

Q: And who do you live with, G.S.H.?

GABE: My dad. My mom, she didn't die. Well, she actually – actually –

MR. SWIATEK: Does she live somewhere else?

GABE: She's far, far away.

MR. SMITH: Do you know where she lives?

GABE: Like, in Fort Walton, or something like that.

MR. SMITH: Oh, okay. Who told – did somebody tell you that she died?

GABE: No. Well – no.

MR. SMITH: Nobody told you that? Okay…. Does your little brother live with you?

GABE: I have a little brother.

MR. SMITH: What's his name?

GABE: Six-years old.

MR. SMITH: What's his name?

GABE: T.H.

MR. SMITH: And he does live with you guys?

GABE: Yeah.

MR. SWIATEK: How old are you?

GABE: But he sure is rough. He gave me this scar.

MR. SWIATEK: Oh, no. How'd you get that?

GABE: On the way to vacation Bible school, he just scratched me. And I was like (makes noise), and he just got away. It wasn't bleeding.

…

MR. SWIATEK: How old are you, G.S.H.?

GABE: Nine years old.

MR. SWIATEK: Nine?

GABE: I just turned nine on May 15th.

…

MR. SWIATEK: Okay. Well, where are you in school, G.S.H.?

GABE: The Zoo, Lighthouse Christian Academy.

…

MR. SWIATEK: Do you like your teachers?

GABE: Yeah.

MR. SWIATEK: Nice so far?

GABE: Yeah.

MR. SWIATEK: Awesome. Well, I'm going to ask you a couple questions, and you can just, you know, just be honest with us and tell us the truth. G.S.H. have you ever seen anybody with guns at any - -

GABE: Yeah. My mom's dad.

MR. SWIATEK: Really? When did you – when did you see him with guns?

GABE: Like, long – when I was, like, four, three, something like that.

MR. SWIATEK: When you were three or four years old?

GABE: Yeah.

MR. SWIATEK: Okay. What did – what was he doing with guns?

GABE: Actually, he murdered a guy named Jack Stevens.

MR. SWIATEK: When–

GABE: Murdered at his house.

MR. SWIATEK: When did that happen?

GABE: Like, like, I drew a picture of it.

MR. SWIATEK: Uh-huh. Is this – when did you – when did you draw – is this the picture right here?

MR. SMITH: *We'll mark this as Exhibit 1.*

MR. SMITH: Is that one of the pictures?

GABE: Yeah.

MR. SMITH: Really?

GABE: Yes, it was.

MR. SMITH: When did you draw these pictures?

GABE: Well, those one when I was eight....Oh, that one I just drawed when I was nine before.

MR. SMITH: You just drew this one – when did you draw that one?

GABE: Like, Tuesday night.

...

MR. SMITH: Did your dad tell you to draw these pictures?

GABE: Yeah.

...

MR. SMITH: So Tuesday night, did your – what did – what did your dad ask you when he asked you to draw that? Do you remember what he said?

GABE: No.

MR. SMITH: You don't? He just asked you to draw a picture. What did he ask you to draw a picture of?

GABE: This.

MR. SMITH: Do you know–

GABE: Because when Jack Stevens got murdered–

MR. SMITH: Okay.

GABE: –this is a part, and it's true.

MR. SMITH: Okay. And so you – so you saw your grandfather hurt somebody with the guns?

GABE: Yeah.

MR. SMITH: What did he do?

GABE: Well, my little brother – well, playing with a pistol, he – he accidentally pulled the trigger, and it (makes noise). And there was, like – then it made a hole in the wall. I was like, so – we're so busted.

MR. SMITH: So your little brother did that?

GABE: Yeah. I was, like – I was thinking of what I was going to say. I was going to say, like, he didn't know; I didn't; I'm busted; I didn't do it.

MR. SMITH: Did you tell anybody when that happened?

GABE: Yeah. My brother did. He said, G.S.H. did it. He lied. He said, G.S.H. did it. No.

MR. SMITH: Tried to blame it on you?

GABE: (Witness nods head).

MR. SMITH: Yeah, that happens sometimes.

GABE: At least my grandfather believed me. I said, no, I didn't. He did.

MR. SMITH: So did your dad tell you to tell other people that your grandfather killed Jack Stevens?

GABE: Well, yeah, that's what he wanted me to tell you guys about mostly.

MR. SMITH: That's what – you talked to – what did you talk – you talked to him about it before today, this morning?

GABE: Hmm. I don't understand.

MR. SMITH: Okay. Did you talk to your – did your dad talk to you about what was going to happen today, like, what we were going to do in here?

GABE: Not exactly.

MR. SMITH: Not exactly?

GABE: What all he said is we're going to look at the fish and play with toys. That's what he mostly – that's what he–

MR. SMITH: And that's what you're going to get to continue to do, definitely. So did you actually see your grandfather kill Jack Stevens, or did your dad just tell you to tell everybody that?

GABE: no, no, he didn't tell me to do that. But it's true. He did – no, not dad. Well, my grandfather did murder Jack Stevens.

MR. SMITH: And you saw this happen?

GABE: Well, at first I heard it. And then I peeked, and then I saw it. And then I saw Jack Stevens was just laying on the floor, not breathing. I was like – then he caught me awake. I saw he didn't see me, so I ran – so I ran–

MR. SMITH: Okay.

GABE: – into bed, falling – trying to pretend. And he said, can't you help me? Wake up T.H. And I just didn't.

MR. SMITH: Did you ever see your grandfather dig up anything in the ground?

GABE: Actually, I did.

MR. SMITH: You did?

GABE: It was him –

MR. SMITH: What did you see?

GABE: He actually buried it for, like, a couple days. Then he wanted to throw it on a tree, tie it on a tree and burn it.

MR. SMITH: Really?

GABE: Until it fell and scared us all.

MR. SMITH: Really? And where was – was that in your grandfather's backyard?

GABE: Well, he buried it in his back yard, for sure, but he actually – well, we ran for a forest. Not exactly a forest. Well, like a ton of woods. There was this old dead tree. Well, the leaves were, like, falling off, and they were not green. They were, like, brown, like fall.

…

MR. SMITH: All right. Let me ask – I need to ask you another question. How long was it – did you then – did you tell your daddy that you saw your grandfather kill Jack Stevens?

GABE: Yeah. Yes, I did. Wait. What?

MR. SMITH: Did you tell your dad about what you saw your grandfather do to Jack Stevens?

GABE: Yeah.

MR. SMITH: You did?

GABE: Yeah

MR. SMITH: Do you know how long it was after you saw that before you told him, before you told your dad?

…

GABE: I don't remember.

MR. SMITH: That's okay.

MR. SMITH: I don't think I have any other questions.

CROSS - EXAMINATION

MR. SWIATEK: When you were talking a couple of minutes ago about the forest, where – where is the forest?

GABE: Not exactly a forest, but I forgot where it was.

MR. SWIATEK: Is it, like, the woods around here, when you're driving around Niceville and Navarre and all that? Was it very far away?

GABE: Pretty much. It took, like, two hours.

MR. SWIATEK: Okay. And why – why were you in the forest?

GABE: My brother was, too. We were – I don't really like to talk about this, but we were actually gone, if it's thrown away, to get all this stuff, getting rid of. We were just – just, like–

MR. SWIATEK: Did your grandpa bring you to the forest?

GABE: Yeah. It was, like – well, it didn't seem like a forest. All I could hear was frogs, and that's it. It wasn't pretty scary. All I could hear was frogs…

MR. SWIATEK: …When you went to the forest, was it daytime or nighttime?

GABE: Nighttime. And, like, a field behind me was frogs, frogs, frogs, frogs, frogs, frogs. Well, I saw this mosquito. And I've been bitten. Yeah, I've been bitten. I'm bitten a lot. But what I mostly saw was frogs. It was the weirdest thing I ever did.

MR. SWIATEK: When you went to the forest, who was with you?

GABE: My grandfather, and my brother, and – you know how bad guys dressed as a police officer? Well, we had one of them with us.

MR. SWIATEK: Do you know who that was?

GABE: I don't remember his name.

MR. SWIATEK: What did he look like?

GABE: Well, he got my dad in jail for six days. He had a white mustache, white hair, and that's all I recognized him from.

MR. SWIATEK: Okay.

GABE: He looked like a good cop, if there was a good guy.

MR. SWIATEK: Did anybody – do you know what a threat is?

GABE: Yeah.

MR. SWIATEK: What's a threat?

GABE: Like, something like murder, or, like, being mean to someone. Like, throwing their shoes on a power line. Like, something like that.

MR. SWIATEK: All right. So if I threaten you, like, if you don't–

GABE: What you said?

MR. SWIATEK: – your homework–

GABE: Yeah, homework. Ew.

MR. SWIATEK: – you're going to bed–

GABE: That's it.

MR. SWIATEK: – Is that a threat?

GABE: Well, not – no. It's like, just life.

MR. SWIATEK: It's just life?

GABE: Yeah. It's just life. I don't understand much about life. I let this frog free. It was like, oh, a froggy. And then it just hopped into the water. It didn't swim very fast. I got him. And I caught some guppies that day, too. And then my dad told me to let it free. And that's when we found this big fish that Dad almost caught. It would be a great fish to put with the African cichlids. [Gabe had pet fish at the time.] And, well, when we let the frog loose, chomp, chomp, chomp. The fish just ate it. And the fish brought it with him, spit it out. I was like, a frog? And then I just about run into the water. I didn't have any socks on. I had a rock accident that day.

MR. SWIATEK: Let me ask you another question. Did your dad tell you to make this stuff up about Jack Stevens?

GABE: No, no, not at all. It's actually, like, true, true, like, very true.

MR. SWIATEK: Okay. Did anybody – remember when I was talking about a threat, like if I, you know, tell Chris that, you know, unless he buys lunch for me, I'm going to bop him in the mouth –

GABE: That is a threat.

MR. SWIATEK: That's a threat, right? Did anybody threaten you?

GABE: Or hang him on a tree.

MR. SWIATEK: Did anybody threaten you about this story about Jack Stevens?

GABE: Oh, yeah. My Pa – my uncle said he was going to, like, hang me on – nail me on something.

MR. SWIATEK: Was he going to nail you?

GABE: Yeah. But I ain't afraid.

MR. SWIATEK: If you told this story about Jack Stevens? Is that it?

GABE: Yes. I already did it, so he ain't going to do nothing. Because I know he doesn't going to mean it, because there's thousands of police searching for him. And he's up in the air protecting me, in the heavens. It's God, and I know he'll protect me from being killed. And Papa threatened us to be killed, sort of.

MR. SWIATEK: What did he – what did he say?

GABE: Well, I don't know, but my dad knows. Exactly knows what he says.

MR. SWIATEK: Okay.

GABE: I think he forgot.

MR. SWIATEK: All right.

GABE: Are we done?

MR. SWIATEK: Yeah, I think I'm done. Are you done, Chris?

MR. SMITH: Yeah, we're finished.

(WHEREUPON the deposition was concluded at approximately 10:08 A.M.)

* * *

Toby's deposition began shortly after:

VIDEOTAPED DEPOSITION OF T.H.

MR. SMITH: We're here today, we're just going to ask you a couple of questions. And we want you to tell the truth to us. You know the difference in a truth and a lie?

TOBY: Uh-huh.

MR. SMITH: Okay. Will you say – when I ask you a question – she's going to write down and type down everything that we say in here, and so if when Glenn [Swiatek] and I asks you a question, if you'll just say yes or no. Can you do that for me?

TOBY: Yes.

MR. SMITH: Okay. Awesome. Very, very good. Okay. So, like, the difference in a truth and a lie, if I told you that, you know, I'm wearing a red tie, would that be a truth or a lie?

TOBY: Lie.

MR. SMITH: Exactly. But if I said my piece of paper here is yellow, would that be a truth or a lie?

TOBY: Truth.

MR. SMITH: There you go. So you understand the difference in a truth and a lie?

TOBY: Uh-huh.

MR. SWIATEK: Is a lie right or – is it right or wrong to tell a lie?

TOBY: Bad.

MR. SWIATEK: Why is it bad?

TOBY: Because – because it's a sin.

MR. SWIATEK: Because it's a sin? Is that what you said? Okay. How old are you?

TOBY: Six.

MR. SWIATEK: How long have you been six?

TOBY: I don't really know.

MR. SWIATEK: No? When are you going to be seven?

TOBY: October 25th.

MR. SMITH: Oh, that's pretty close. It's, like, two months away.

TOBY: Uh-huh.

MR. SWIATEK: Is that the truth?

TOBY: Yes.

MR. SWIATEK: Are you sure?

TOBY: Yes.

MR. SMITH: Good deal. Okay.

MR. SWIATEK: How old do you think I am? Twenty.

TOBY: I don't know.

MR. SWIATEK: No? You think I might be fifteen? If I told you I was fifteen, what do you think?

TOBY: I think it would be a lie.

MR. SMITH: There you go.

MR. SWIATEK: You know what you're talking about.

MR. SMITH: We're ready. Good to go.

... :

MR. SMITH: Okay. And what's – what is your full name T.H.?

TOBY: (Spells first name).

MR. SMITH: (Spells first name)? And what's your last name?

TOBY: (Spells last name).

MR. SMITH: Wow. Smart. I – I couldn't spell when I was your age. Very, very good.

MR. SWIATEK: That's why he went to Ole Miss.

MR. SMITH: That's right.

MR. SMITH: Do you know a man named Jack Stevens?

TOBY: Uh-huh.

MR. SMITH: How do you know him?

TOBY: Because he got killed.

MR. SMITH: Who killed him?

TOBY: A bad guy named Papa.

MR. SMITH: Really? When – when did you see that happen?

TOBY: About, like, three years ago.

MR. SWIATEK: Well, did you see it happen?

TOBY: Yes.

MR. SWIATEK: Okay.

TOBY: I was there. Me and my brother were there.

MR. SMITH: And did your – did your grandfather – have you ever seen anybody with guns?

TOBY: Not that much.

MR. SMITH: Not that much? Have you ever?

TOBY: Uh-huh.

MR. SMITH: Who?

TOBY: Papa.

MR. SMITH: And who is Papa? Is Papa your grandfather?

TOBY: Uh-huh. Used to, but he's not anymore.

MR. SMITH: Used to be your grandfather? Why is he not your grandfather anymore?

TOBY: Because he's mean now.

MR. SMITH: Okay. Do you think he's mean?

A: Uh-huh.

MR. SMITH: Why do you think he's mean?

TOBY: Because killing someone, murder.

MR. SMITH: And he did – okay.

MR. SWIATEK: Have you ever shot a gun?

TOBY: Once.

MR. SWIATEK: Once? Tell me about that.

TOBY: It was when – I can't think of it.

MR. SWIATEK: But you know you did it, huh?

TOBY: Uh-huh.

MR. SWIATEK: Anyone see you do it?

TOBY: What?

MR. SWIATEK: Did anyone see you do it?

TOBY: Huh-uh. But they saw the bullet.

MR. SWIATEK: Where was the bullet?

TOBY: In a picture. It hit a picture. It was flying across the room.

MR. SWIATEK: And where did it go?

TOBY: It hit a picture.

MR. SWIATEK: It hit a picture? On a wall?

TOBY: Uh-huh.

MR. SWIATEK: Wow. How old were you when that happened?

TOBY: About five.

MR. SWIATEK: Where was that?

TOBY: At my Papa's house.

MR. SWIATEK: At Grandpa's house, Papa. All right. Go Ahead.

MR. SMITH: All right. Who do you live with now, T.H.?

TOBY: My dad.

MR. SMITH: Does anybody else live with you?

TOBY: No. Just me and my brother and my dad.

...

MR. SMITH: Okay. Did your – did your – did you and your dad and your brother talk about what we were going to do here today?

TOBY: Uh-huh.

MR. SMITH: And what did you all talk about?

TOBY: About, like, people are going to be here and talk about the bad stuff.

MR. SMITH: Bad stuff? Did your dad tell you what to tell us in here?

TOBY: Uh-huh.

MR. SMITH: What did he tell you to say to us?

TOBY: Tell the truth.

MR. SMITH: Okay. And did you ever see – did you ever see your grandfather dig up anything in the ground?

TOBY: I don't really know.

MR. SMITH: You don't know? And that's fine. If we ask you a question and you don't know the answer, you can just say, I don't know, because I don't know everything either. And if you – if there's a question that one of us asks you and you don't really understand it, you can just say, I don't understand, or could you ask it – ask it again. You know what I mean?

TOBY: Uh-huh.

MR. SMITH: Okay. Great. Did you tell anybody about when you saw your grand – your Papa hurt Jack Stevens?

TOBY: I didn't, but my dad did.

MR. SMITH: You didn't? Who did – so how did your dad find out about it?

TOBY: Because we tell him.

MR. SMITH: You and your brother told him?

TOBY: Uh-huh.

MR. SMITH: Okay. Did you know who – how did you know it was Jack Stevens that your grandfather hurt?

TOBY: Because–

MR. SWIATEK: Well, did you know his name?

MR. SMITH: Did you know his name before that?

TOBY: Uh-huh.

MR. SMITH: How did you know his name?

TOBY: Because he told me.

MR. SMITH: You met Jack Stevens before?

TOBY: (Witness nods head).

MR. SMITH: Okay. Do you know why your grandfather hurt him?

TOBY: Huh-uh.

MR. SMITH: You don't? He just did it?

TOBY: (Witness nods head).

MR. SMITH: I got you. Did you ever go into the woods with your brother and grandfather?

TOBY: Uh-huh.

MR. SMITH: Where did you all go? Why did you go in the woods?

TOBY: Because Papa didn't want their – Jack Stevens' mom or dad or brother to know that they were there, so they just took him to the woods and hanged Jack Stevens onto a tree, fire him, and then he went away.

MR. SMITH: Okay. Okay. And do you know how long ago this was?

TOBY: I told you, it was, like, three years ago.

MR. SMITH: Like, three years ago? Okay. That's fine.

MR. SWIATEK: Yeah, listen up. He told you already.

MR. SMITH: I know. I know. Sometimes – I have bad, bad hearing, and so sometimes I can't hear what people say. And so if I ask you a question more than once, please don't be mad at me, okay?

MR. SWIATEK: You just tell him, you say, Counsel, asked and answered. You know how to say that? Okay. Go ahead.

MR. SMITH: That's okay. I actually don't have any more questions right now.

CROSS-EXAMINATIONS

MR. SWIATEK: I got a couple, all right? When you shot the gun – do you remember shooting the gun?

TOBY: (Witness nods head).

MR. SWIATEK: What kind of gun was it?

TOBY: A pistol.

MR. SWIATEK: What's a pistol look like?

TOBY: Like, sort of like your fingers, like that (demonstrating).

MR. SWIATEK: Okay. Are there other types of guns?

TOBY: Uh-huh.

MR. SWIATEK: What other types of guns are there?

TOBY: Machine guns, pistols – no. I said that.

MR. SWIATEK: Machine guns is one. Pistols?

TOBY: Shotguns.

MR. SWIATEK: What's a shotgun?

TOBY: I don't really know. I don't really know about – I just know that name.

MR. SWIATEK: What does it look like? Do you know what it looks like?

TOBY: Uh-huh. Bad. I can't show it with my fingers.

MR. SWIATEK: Why can't you show it with your fingers?

TOBY: Because it's not – it's long, and I don't have, like, long fingers.

MR. SWIATEK: Oh, okay. Have you seen shotguns before?

TOBY: Uh-huh.

MR. SWIATEK: What other kind of guns have you seen?

TOBY: I can't think of any.

MR. SWIATEK: All right. Where does – when you saw this with Jack Stevens, where was that at?

TOBY: At his house.

MR. SWIATEK: At Jack Stevens house?

Toby then went on to positively identify that it was at his Papa's house, that Papa was now gone, and that his mother lived there now.

TOBY: No, no. At their Papa's house.

MR. SWIATEK: Okay. Do you know where Papa's house is?

TOBY: Yeah. He's – he's gone – our Papa's gone, so–

MR. SWIATEK: When was it then? When you saw all this, where was Papa living, do you know?

TOBY: Yeah. My mom's living it (sic), so I don't know.

MR. SWIATEK: Okay. So do you know – where is that, do you know?

TOBY: Nope, don't really.

MR. SWIATEK: All right. That's cool.

MR. SWIATEK: All right. I don't have any more questions for you. ... Chris do you have any more questions?

MR. SMITH: No, I don't. We're done, buddy.

(WHEREUPON the deposition was concluded at approximately 10:21 A.M.)

* * *

That afternoon, the boys' psychotherapist sat down for her own deposition.

A: No, it's not ... the possibility of confabulation is there, because–

MR. SMITH: What does that mean?

A: Putting things together, bringing things together, just because of – we have so many issues at hand, and one issue would be that his mother suffers from some mental illness issues. And then we have, in the past, exposure to ... horror movies, and exposure to R-rated video games, extreme violence, and those types of things. So the possibility that this could be a name that's grabbed from one of those situations, or something that he has just picked up from some scenario – children are wonderful observers, but poor interpreters. He could have just brought that in. So I don't think that he's … made it up on purpose if it is not a real name. I can't say whether it's a lie or not.

Then questions about me:

MR. SMITH: How many times did you meet with him?

A: My policy is, when I meet with a child, I always bring that parent in in the initial session; so typically, anywhere from ten to fifteen minutes. Sometimes I will meet with the father and child together. And I've met with him I think at least two times on an individual basis for a full hour to discuss his perspectives on the children, to gather background information, and kind of make my own decision about what is going on with him.

MR. SMITH: Did you ask him [*the father*] about this incident, the alleged murder of Jack Stevens?

A: Well, I didn't ask but it was told yes.

MR. SMITH: What did he tell you about it?

A: He has told me what the children have allegedly witnessed and what the children have told him… they witnessed an alleged murder; that there was a body that was, I guess, hung and later burned, which G.S.H. has told me about. So those are things that have been relayed to me.

MR. SMITH: Okay. Is there any indication – what, in your opinion, what kind of control does the father have over the children?

A: I had to laugh because I thought, not enough, in my waiting room. I–

MR. SMITH: Mental control?

A: – if you're thinking about that. I don't believe so. I think that these children are pretty strong. I would say that, is he an influence? Absolutely. But any parent would be. He seems to be pretty appropriate when he – what I have observed. He doesn't speak of these things in front of the children. And he's very appropriate about what he says when the children are around, as to not lead them. So that is what I have witnessed. So I don't think he has fed them any information, in my opinion.

MR. SMITH: Did you have an occasion to talk with Mr. Harris about his prior dealings with Mr. Nobles in regards to a – I want to use the right words – a Florida – south Florida organized crime and Alabama militia activities?

A: Yes.

Mr. Smith: What did he tell you about that?

A: Basically what you've said . . . Mr. Harris, in my opinion – now, again, I am not his psychologist, so I cannot speak to what his psychologist believes, but he does have an obsessive-compulsive quality, so to really tell you what he has told me would be quite difficult, because it's very expansive.

Mr. Smith: Certainly. And I think, not to – I'm not meaning to confuse you. I think that both of us here are trying to figure out what's happened. I know I am. And that's why I asked you about that.

A: He has spoken of it, and in quite detail. And, certainly, he has quite a bit of information, you know, that he feels supports [his] statements.

Mr. Smith: Okay.

A: And, again, not with the children present. I do want to–

Mr. Smith: Okay. And that didn't have anything to do with the children, necessarily. So did both – both children voluntarily give you the information about the alleged murder of Jack Stevens, or did you ask them about it?

A: Yes. As far as the murder, they did that. Now my policy always is, is when I interview children, in the beginning I will ask them, you know, of course, good touch/bad touch/secret touch kind of questions. They did not want to talk about it in the beginning. They eventually began to talk about the sexual abuse allegations. But as far as the allegation of murder, that was unsolicited.

Mr. Smith: Did they ever mention talking to their father about it?

A: Yes, because of nightmares that they both had.

Mr. Smith: Did they tell you what they told their father?

A: They have told their father about – G.S.H. has told me and drawn pictures of, you know, the body burning, the head – I guess the body falling on the ground, and things like that.

Mr. Smith: Okay.

A: Now, G.S.H. will speak more of it, more than the younger brother.

Mr. Smith: Who gave you more information about the incident?

A: G.S.H.

MR. SMITH: What did T.H. tell you about it?

A: T.H. has talked a little about it. He feels embarrassed by the incident because in – to his – the information that he's provided me is that he was sexually abused, whereas G.S.H. was not sexually – he was not a victim. He was a victim, but not as a direct of sexual abuse. He was put more in an aggressive role, in his mind. So he didn't talk about it as much because he feels very embarrassed by it.

Then the cross examination:

CROSS-EXAMINATION

MR. SWIATEK: We were talking about pictures and the grandfather. Can I flesh that out a little bit? Pictures were directed by the grandfather, or–

A: The photographs, yes. According to G.S.H., he says that his Papa had him take pictures of the other children, and had him dance naked, and that–

MR. SWIATEK: And the other children were doing what?

A: They were naked, and I guess being forced to participate in acts. But I've never received those details of what those acts were.

MR. SWIATEK: Okay. I've got kind of a two-part loaded question, I guess.

A: Uh-huh.

MR. SWIATEK: One, how do you know when kids are telling the truth or not?

A: Uh-huh.

MR. SWIATEK: Number two, the story, you know, the Jack Stevens story, and the murder at the grandpa's house, and then the subsequent burning out on the reservation, all that, is that story true in the minds of both of those kids? Whether it's alleged – you know, we're saying alleged and all this. Whether it's true or no–

A: Yes.

MR. SWIATEK: – in their minds, is that story true?

A: Yes, in their minds, it is true, especially in the mind of G.S.H. And I will say that–

MR. SWIATEK: And how do you know that? How do you come to that conclusion? That's–

A: Well, certainly, building trust and rapport; but consistency over their statements over a period of time. I don't know how – any other way to answer it but just by gut, and knowing, and asking them do they know the difference between right and wrong, do they know the difference between lie and truth, which I always ask them that.

MR. SWIATEK: Well, let me ask you this. You just mentioned that there was consistency in the stories over a period of time. What would be some of the indicators – maybe this is easier to tell us. What would be some of the indicators to you if they were not telling the truth?

A: Certainly, the story would change. I think that the brothers would diverge in what they're stating, or you would notice a divergence … usually children will – I've had children in the past that have eventually told me, this is not the truth, because I do have a background in working with abused and neglected children … in the few cases that I have worked where they were false allegations, they have admitted it at some point … you said, is it true in their minds? Yeah, I do believe that they believe it's true in their minds, whether or not this really happened or not.

MR. SWIATEK: What are the chances – now, you've mentioned abuse of the children by the grandfather–

A: Uh-huh.

MR. SWIATEK: – and probably T.H. directly, G.S.H. indirectly.

A: Uh-huh.

MR. SWIATEK: What are the chances, or can you even say, that the children are fabricating this story to get back at grandpa for abusing them?

A: I don't believe so.

MR. SWIATEK: Are they too young for that?

A: I think so, yes … quite frankly they don't have the intelligence level to do that. G.S.H., the older one, who, again, takes the lead in more of these things, he has a low average IQ. So it would require someone of a higher intelligence, and to be further along socially and emotionally.

MR. SWIATEK: Yeah. I noticed – I met them for the first time today. G.S.H. said he was nine–

A: Yeah.

MR. SWIATEK: – and T.H. was six, going on seven. When I looked at them physically, and just talking to them for a couple of minutes when we were getting started, I mean, it appeared that maybe T.H. was, like four, G.S.H. six–

A: Six or seven.

MR. SWIATEK: –or seven.

A: Exactly. And their behaviors are consistent with that age frame.

MR. SWIATEK: Is that any – is that any indicator of any type of abuse, sexual or otherwise?

A: Yes and no. It's – one, it's a function of their – well, of G.S.H.'s, you know, IQ level being low average. I think it's also a function of maybe limited exposure because of where they go to school. And their high anxiety level, especially with G.S.H., Dr. McCain noticed a very high anxiety level, and that will reduce social skills, concentration, memory, focus, distractibility.

MR. SWIATEK: Were you or Dr. McCain able to come to any type of conclusion or educated guess as to where the high anxiety level came from?

A: We believe it's probably due to whatever trauma exposure that they have. We can, without a doubt, say that these kids have been exposed to trauma; but to directly say, okay, we know for sure that this is what it is, other than taking their word for what it is, that's it. So the anxiety comes from the trauma. There probably is a genetic component. You know, the biological mother, she does have previous diagnoses, you know, by historical comments of the father, that she's been diagnosed with bipolar and some other disorders, so there is that genetic component. But, certainly, that genetic component gets triggered, and so–

MR. SWIATEK: All right. Given your educated conclusion about my client, Mr. Harris, being obsessive-compulsive, what are the chances that the story has been fabricated by the children because he's so obsessive-compulsive that he just puts it in their minds that this is the story, and you're going to go with the story to vindicate Dad with a custody battle, or for whatever other reason out there there may be?

A: I don't see that kind of maliciousness with Mr. Harris. Again, I'm not his therapist, so I can't speak to – but I have spoken to Dr. Donner, and I have spoken to Dr. Goldberg quite frequently about Mr. Harris because this is such an involved case and has so many different planes. But I will say that one thing that I have observed and that has been consistent in every single observation of him with these children, is that he is highly attached to them. He has a high level of empathy and caring, and he's extremely nurturing with these children. So, you know, I just don't see that happening, because I don't think that he would put his children through this. If anything, I think that he feels like he's, you know, championing them and protecting them, but carrying it to the nth degree.

MR. SWIATEK: So your conclusions about Mr. Harris are based on other professionals' conclusions?

A: That, and my own, and my own observations in family therapy, and I've met with him for historical gathering information.

MR. SWIATEK: Either based on your own observations, or the observations of the other two doctors, does my client meet any criteria for being legally insane as far as McNaughton?

A: No. And that's one thing that I found to be consistent. Mr. Harris has been very forthright and has allowed me to look at all providers' information. I have spoken with Dr. Donner and Dr. Goldberg. Dr. Goldberg even wrote a letter on Mr. Harris' behalf to – it escapes me, but his employment, whichever airline that was, stating that he was, you know, sane within the limits and not a risk factor, in his opinion. I have also reviewed the psychological testing that was done by the airline, and the neuropsychological testing that was referred out, and neither one of those conclude that he is not of sound mind.

MR. SWIATEK: All right. Let me ask you this … switch gears a little bit. Now, as far as Mike Nobles –

MR. SWIATEK: And I'll get to the relevancy on this.

MR. SMITH: Okay.

MR. SWIATEK: Would it be your conclusion that it's unhealthy for the kids to be around Mike Nobles?

A: Yes. Not because of – because I have not met Mr. Nobles … it is based on the anxiety level that these children have, the frequent nightmares, and their perceived reality, absolutely, because it retraumatizes them and they feel unsafe.

MR. SWIATEK: And I don't know if we've made this a part of the record or not, but Mike Nobles is the individual we know as Papa.

A: Correct.

MR. SWIATEK: All right. Given that, I mean, that would be in line with Mr. Harris' conclusions, as well, as to Mike Nobles.

A: Yes.

MR. SWIATEK: Would Mr. Harris go to the extent of fabricating the story and reporting it to law enforcement to keep those kids away from Mike Nobles?

A: I mean, certainly, that is a possibility, but I do not believe so.

MR. SWIATEK: And why not?

A: One, because I think that he is so highly attached to these children, that he has a good understanding that that would be emotionally psychologically harmful to put them through this just for that.

MR. SWIATEK: Okay.

A: And that's not his goal.

MR. SWIATEK: Do you think that it was in the children's best interest for Mr. Harris to report these events to law enforcement?

A: Yes. I will say yes. And the reason being ... he thought he was doing what he should do to protect his children. And I think that he felt that nobody was listening. And, certainly, there are some avenues that could have been taken to prevent some of these situations. I think, quite frankly, more services could have been offered at the onset, in the beginning of this, and it would not have gotten to this level as far as him being arrested and things like that. Certainly, there are services available.

MR. SWIATEK: And the children, prior to today, had both been over at the CAC because of the sexual abuse allegation; is that correct?

A: It's my understanding that they were interviewed, but I have not seen records in regard to the Child Protection Team records. I have not received copies of those.

MR. SWIATEK: Did Mr. Harris indicate to you his dissatisfaction as to the interviews at CAC, or, you know, just generally law enforcement, or–

A: Yes, he has.

MR. SWIATEK: In regard to the sexual abuse?

A: Yes.

MR. SWIATEK: So is it a surprise to you that he may have pushed this too far because of past history?

A: No, it is not a surprise at all. And given his own kind of obsessive nature with things, certainly, he would. And if he felt, you know, he needed to protect his children, which he did feel the need to protect his children, absolutely. I think that probably in the very beginning – and, again, services are certainly available – the children could have been referred to mental health counseling within the Children's Advocacy Center. And that's a free service. But, for whatever reason, there was something that did not happen with that. And, certainly, the mental health advocate of the CAC, there's something there that didn't flow with the services that could have been offered, and maybe could have prevented some of these things.

MR. SWIATEK: And just to clarify the record, the CAC that we've been talking about is the Children's Advisory Center up in Niceville, right?

A: Yes, correct.

MR. SWIATEK: Okay. Those are all the questions that I have for you.

REDIRECT EXAMINATION

BY MR. SMITH:

Then there was a lot of back and forth about whether the kids had been coached, or memories planted which Kelly Beck said, if it occurred at all, it would have only been indirect, from hearing my conversations. Then in her re-cross examination she made it clear that she didn't believe I did or would plant information in my kids' heads, and reaffirmed the definite trauma and sexual abuse, contrasted with the Florida DCF's repeated claim of "no indicators."

RECROSS EXAMINATION

MR. SWIATEK: Probability-wise, did that happen here?

A: The indirect?

MR. SWIATEK: Yeah.

A: Yes, probably. My gut feeling in this case is that there's definite trauma, there's definite abuse. There are abandonment issues because of not – having very little contact with their mother, and it is not routine contact. So we have a lot of things, and exposure to things that they probably should have never been exposed to. And, you know, more than likely – and the allegations go that that happened at Grandpa's house, at Papa's house. So we have a lot of things that have come together. And I don't think there was anything purposeful. There's definite abuse, there's definite neglect, there's definite trauma, there's definite indicators. What that was, I'm not sure. But there is – I will tell you that in their language and in their drawings, subjective drawings, especially with G.S.H., there is a lot of indicators of sexual abuse, a lot of phallic symbols, a lot of things that would – a lot of themes of sexual abuse. And, certainly, I'd be happy to share those. I've been given full consent to do that.

MR. SWIATEK: Let me flesh this out a little bit, because I'm not sure that your answer that you have just given us about whether or not this Jack Stevens story was implanted in their head or not –

A: Uh-huh.

MR. SWIATEK: – jibes with what you told us earlier in your testimony. To the kids, it's real.

A: Yes.

MR. SWIATEK: The father acted appropriately, based upon what the kids have told him.

A: Absolutely.

MR. SWIATEK: But if the father implanted this into the kids' head, then he acted inappropriately.

A: Correct.

MR. SWIATEK: And can you say which way the wind blows on this?

A: I cannot. I mean, you know, it's very hard to tell. I can tell you that I don't believe that Mr. Harris did that. And that is based upon the psychological testing that I have reviewed, and the conversations and treatment planning that I have had with Dr. Donner and Dr. Goldberg. I think out of – I have reviewed numerous records on Mr. Harris, and I have also spoken with three professionals that are his treatment team or, you know, that have provided services to him, and there's not anything that would indicate that.

MR. SWIATEK: So those acts, if he did do what I'm saying, he implanted it, would be contrary to his psychological profile as you have assessed, and the other two doctors have assessed; is that what you're saying?

A: Yes.

MR. SMITH: That's – I don't have anything else.

MR. SWIATEK: Okay. I've got a few.

REDIRECT EXAMINATION

MR. SMITH: Could this have been coached? Like, the murder, could it have been coached into them by their father, repeated? Could it have been?

A: Sure. Absolutely.

MR. SMITH: If something was continuously repeated to these – to children of this age, would it almost become that they believe it? Could that happen?

A: Absolutely, yes. You always have to ask yourself, what would the goal of that behavior be, and what is the underlying – and, certainly, that is a real possibility.

MR. SMITH: And I have an idea of what it could be in this situation, but we discussed that.

MR. SWIATEK: When you give that response, are you talking in generalities, or are you talking in specifics to this case?

THE WITNESS: Generalities, with any – absolutely.

MR. SMITH: Do you think that happened here?

A: If it did, it did not happen directly. The children have poor boundaries and really poor social skills. So, like, for example, when you tell a child, I'm in a grown-up conversation and you need to go into the other room, most children will do that. But given the situation and kind of some of the chaos that has happened between the separation, the divorce, and all of this other chaos, those kinds of things have been absent, so it is possible that they have had indirect exposure to overhearing Mr. Harris. I don't think that he sat down and directly coached them with that purpose. If it is the case, then it would be my belief that it was an indirect.

MR. SMITH: Okay. That's it. That's all I have?

(WHEREUPON the deposition was concluded at approximately 3:50 P.M.)

* * *

As I waited in the hall of ECCAC, the Assistant DA stormed past me, red in the face. My kids, who were supposed to be witnesses to the prosecution, told the truth and undermined their whole narrative.

That night, Glenn Swiatek called to let me know the case was probably over. Two weeks later, the State Attorney entered *Nolle Prosequi* – a Latin phrase that indicates a prosecutor has decided to abandon prosecution – in the case against me. I asked Attorney Swiatek what he recommended I do now the case was over. He replied, "move to Mexico." I don't think he was joking. I'd been locked up and dragged through the mud, but the plot to frame me backfired again.

Nevertheless, it was far from over.

The rights of every man are diminished when the rights of one man are threatened.

– John F. Kennedy

Endnotes

1   https://www.legacy.com/us/obituaries/oklahoman/name/donna-fitzgerald-obituary?id=27307847#:~:text=Donna%20Jurhee%20(Jackson)%20Fitzgerald%2C,OKC%2C%20 OK%20to%20Edgar%20A.

2   https://www.findagrave.com/memorial/157488490/bobby-wayne-clymer

3   https://www.washingtonexaminer.com/news/2035492/update-dot-ig-urged-to-investigate-one-of-faas-top-docs/

CHAPTER FOURTEEN

AND JUSTICE FOR NO ONE

The very next day, we were back in court. Betty Thomas, my former attorney, sued me claiming I owed her what I believed were inflated legal fees after she had abruptly quit the case and left me hanging out to dry. After I gave her over $3000 to retain her services, I refused to pay her more because she had violated our verbal contract, withheld information from me, hung me out to dry, and conspired to arm a felon behind my back. To prove this, I subpoenaed the Okaloosa County Sheriff's Department Evidence Custodian, Mary Lou Collins – who hadn't been allowed to testify previously – so she could finally speak honestly about the facts of the case:

Thus, on August 27, Collins told the court that Mike Nobles did in fact enter the Niceville Police Department on February 16, 2009 with a court order from Judge Santurri; that Nobles produced a photo ID, which was copied and filed; and that Nobles submitted and received the firearms and ammunition he'd surrendered after they were found in various locations of his home on October 1, 2008. Collins identified all the documents with Nobles' signature that confirmed these facts, and she also testified that she was lied to by a lieutenant in the Sheriff's department who told her the guns were in the possession of the Santa Rosa County Sheriff's department.

None of it mattered. The court sided with Thomas.

* * *

Throughout this period, the only community my boys and I had was the church. Despite all the hypocrisy I had already seen and experienced, I found a modicum of comfort in going to church, perhaps only for the routine and community aspect. I still took them to Sunday school. I still knew there to be good people there. I still tried to give everyone the benefit of the doubt. And it seemed my attempts were appreciated, since that September the Calvary Chapel sent me a thank you letter for helping with the children's ministry.

Friends became a rare commodity when the entire community seemed to have turned on us. I continued to take the boys to therapy and counseling. Meanwhile, I couldn't take the boys to activities like soccer anymore, because they were so traumatized they were trapped in "flight or fight" mode. Gabe exhibited this behavior increasingly at school and elsewhere. Something would set them off, and they would break into a deer-like run. I would have to chase them down myself and restrain them. On one occasion, another boy pushed Gabe, and Gabe fell upon him and beat the crap out of the poor kid.

* * *

Toward the end of September, I received a call out of the blue from Diane Gaston, an acquaintance who claimed concern for what had happened to the kids. She offered to put me in touch with Senator Durell Peaden, a Republican who represented our district at the time. She told me that Peaden sat on a committee that oversaw the Florida DCF, and he'd be interested in my story. Gaston's friend, the go between, oddly felt the need to volunteer that he was not a member of the Ku Klux Klan. Apparently, he had appeared in a newspaper photo with Klan members restoring the flagpole on city property in Crestview where the Confederate flag flew. After some odd cloak-and-dagger planning arranged by Gaston and her friend, I met for three hours with Peaden's secretary in Crestview, and I provided her with numerous documents on disc as well as my son's videotaped testimony for her to give to Peaden's office.

I only learned later that Peaden's time working with DCF was marred by the 2003 case of Rilya Wilson, a four-year old girl whose disappearance while in Florida foster care went unnoticed by authorities for two years. In the wake of that scandal Peaden suggested reorganizing DCF and told reporters, "I want to do anything I can to make sure that children and families are the focus of that agency."[1]

But Peaden, with help from Governor Rick Scott and Sheriff Larry Ashley, had created the *"Stand Your Ground Law"* used to justify the Trayvon Martin murder, was just a good old boy from DeFuniak Springs. He'd groomed Freemason Congressman Jeff Miller for politics before Miller hired Judge Santurri's wife as his District Representative. Miller, in fact, referred to Peaden as "my mentor,"[2] at the Senator's funeral in 2015. He also made a point to enter into the Congressional Record the obituary of Charles Walter Ruckel, whose name appears on the property records of Nobles' house in 1986, and the military service record of Charles Merkle, owner one of the mystery house previously owned by Nobles' own mentor, Jerry McCormick, in the creepy Sharon Lake subdivision where foster children were being exploited by government officials and are now missing.

It turned out Peaden's office was just fishing for information and, once I handed over the documents, I never heard from Gaston or Peaden again. Retaliation would begin four days later.

* * *

On October 3, the Destin Church of Christ announced the arrival at their church of two new deacons. The first deacon was David Lamon, Jerry McCormick's son-in-law from Decatur, Alabama, the city where my children were to be held after their kidnapping. And the second deacon was Mike Nobles.

That same day, my sons and I were banned from our church.

This may have been orchestrated by Randy Lamon, a strange character who appeared at church after I ceased contact with Jerry Williams, due to his own suspicious behavior – pumping me for information, giving me cash gifts and a cell phone, and constantly trying to convince me my life was in immediate danger. Once I distanced myself from him, Williams called me over and over and, when I didn't answer, he called my friends, and he demanded I resume meeting with him on a weekly basis.

Given Lamon's surname, I suspect he's related to the same Lamon family connected to McCormick. When I stopped responding to Williams' calls, Lamon started pouring on the charm, offering to pray for us and then invited us to join their small prayer group. I had cut off ties with Jerry [Williams] and was now getting a handoff. After the second week in the new prayer group, my kids were accused of jumping on the bed (when left alone with other kids watching cartoons) – hardly a serious offense – and we were thrown out of the group.

The following Sunday, Lamon's wife – a Sunday school teacher – accused Toby of grabbing a girl in class. This was an accusation on which she later backpedaled. I was told that there were other allegations but could never get specific details. Gabe and Toby were not only banned from Sunday School but banned from sitting in church. We had no choice but to leave. Maybe Williams and Lamon got the information they needed?

We had been very involved with the church for more than two years, volunteering for everything we could. Despite all our troubles, or perhaps because of all our troubles, we had never missed a service. I went home that night and explained to my sons that they couldn't go back to the church they loved, the church where they thought they had friends and family. They were heartbroken. No one ever bothered to call us to ask what happened.

We were more isolated than ever.

* * *

Within weeks, an FAA employee named Tammy Brown, lacking any authority to do so that I know of, signed an authorization for Dr. Warren

Silberman (whose name is on the signature block) for a special issuance medical certificate forcing me to obtain unwarranted monitoring and services from Dr. Charles Harper. I had never requested such a special issuance and didn't need one. Dr. Harper requested this without my knowledge, and of course with him as my sponsor. I was fully medically fit to fly and had been for my two decades of flying up to that point, thanks to the interference by these strange people with whom I had become mysteriously involved, including the Nobles Family. My existing pilot's certificate had never been revoked, and there was no basis to revoke it.

Simultaneously, FAA Doctor Warren Silberman, the former chief flight surgeon for the Oklahoma Air Guard, signed a fraudulent special issuance medical certificate. He knew that I was fully qualified for an unrestricted medical certificate, and he also knew that my valid and unrestricted medical certificate had never been revoked. (I had not applied for this, nor authorized Dr. Harper to apply on my behalf. I never filled out an application and did not receive an examination). My valid certificate was "canceled" in a cagey and puzzling game of smoke and mirrors. I was required to enter a substance abuse program at work with nothing in my history to justify it, and Harper was handpicked as my sponsor despite a long list of available sponsors in Florida that I was never made aware of. My kids had been kidnapped by a cult on Halloween. I had been arrested on the anniversary of the execution of Knight Templar martyr, Jaques De Molay. Now I was issued a fake medical certificate marking my career for death on the anniversary of the order to round up and execute the Knights Templar, October 13, the original Friday the 13th. Was this a federal curse?

* * *

Due to the complexity of the tangled webs here, I will summarize some of the facts.

Mike Nobles, while a leader in a white supremacist neo-confederate group in Alabama, made a deal with the government in 1986 to avoid prison. The same year, a Freemason Knight Templar leader built a house under a permit he and his wife obtained numbered 1118 for the year the Knights Templar were founded. Also, the same year, he entered into a partnership with fellow Church of Christ elders, Jerry McCormick, McCormick's brother-in-law, and Leslie Michael Osman, a connected attorney in Hialeah Florida. Osman created numerous corporations for him and his brothers (and Nobles) with occult/masonic/Knight Templar names.

Fast forward to 2008, the Knight Templar builder and his associates are on the board of trustees of the Emerald Coast Child Advocacy Center. Joey Forgione is tied to the Knight Templar builder of Nobles home and is a Niceville Florida police officer. Beginning in 2008, there were at least 18 reports of sexual abuse against Mike Nobles, whose brother is an outspoken occultist. These reports included ritualistic abuse. Some of the acts are spelled out in Aleister Crowley's *The Equinox*. The reports are all dispensed in an elaborate shell game involving the Emerald Coast Child Advocacy Center and Forgione.

* * *

The refusal to enforce the law forced me into filing a restraining order (which was repeatedly violated with immunity). This led to Nobles kidnapping my sons, also with immunity on a cursed day, October 31st. This also led to the surrender of a small arsenal of weapons by Nobles, a felon. Nobles tried to groom Gabe during the three months he was held hostage. While looking for answers I found myself in the neighborhood of Nobles' partner, McCormick, and learned of foster children exploited through human trafficking tied to another Church of Christ minster, and more prominent military Freemasons.

A judge tied to a prominent right wing Freemason congressman took care of the restraining order and gave the guns back to a felon [Nobles] then lied to cover his tracks. The imminent return of my sons led to a cleanup operation and ultimately to murder and an occult lynching, both witnessed by my sons. Forgione covered up the murder and the firearms violations and repeatedly tried to frame me, as did state officials at the Emerald Coast Child Advocacy Center. My sons, returned, described a Knight Templar temple on Nobles' property as well as how they had been sexually abused and exploited as part of child pornography produced by Nobles. All efforts to get these investigated were blocked and I faced repeated retaliation and efforts to frame me by the same people.

* * *

Nobles eventually fled to South America. Having failed at repeated efforts to frame me in Florida, a new path was found. Nobles contacted my employer with a litany of false allegations. The manager of Human Resources at my airline, who happens to be the son in law of a multi generation Freemason/Shriner and a police chief forced me into a substance abuse evaluation with a man he claimed to be the company doctor, but who was really an ex-military Freemason crackpot, Doctor Charles Richard Harper.

After I passed an illegal urinalysis, a psychological evaluation, and a full battery of psychological tests, another crackpot in Oklahoma City who worked for the FAA planted a fake DUI in my records "as requested." This woman, Sandy Clymer, believes she has seen angels and comes from a military family of Freemasons and Order of the Eastern Star. My medical certification was then "canceled" illegitimately with the fake DUI for "alcohol abuse."

When I realized something was wrong, FAA Doctor Michael Berry stepped in. He was NASA's former doctor as was his racist father, Dr. Charles Alden Berry. Charles Berry chose an all-white and all male Freemason cadre of astronauts for the Apollo missions, defying the orders of the President. Dr. Berry, creator of the "Berry Scheme," then went on an illegal fishing expedition and demanded and illegally obtained some of my military records. Those records are distorted to make the claim that I was treated for substance abuse in the military. The allegation of alcohol abuse was changed to alcoholism with no evaluation or diagnosis.

Having had my medical canceled with a fake DUI for alcohol abuse, changed to alcoholism, using a fake medical history, I was then issued a fake "special issuance" medical certificate I never requested nor had an exam for on a cursed day, October 13th. I was then forced to use the very man responsible for this fraud, Dr. Harper, as my sponsor, and to pay him for it. Before it was all over, a church tied to a Freemason Sheriff would threatened to burn my house down if I didn't shut up about all the allegations.

* * *

After this charade, I was then assigned a peer monitor, Brad Secker, another right-wing Christian Crusader from a military family who was fond of his guns. Secker used his position to pry information from me and pressure me to remain quiet about how and why I was placed in this bizarre charade. I was then required to attend "relapse prevention" meetings. Secker would frequently offer to pray for me. When I told him about Nobles' guns and surveillance system, he said it was a good idea, and he did the same thing at his gated home in rural North Carolina.

Dr. Harper specifically requested that I be forced to use him as a sponsor and conveyed false information to the FAA claiming I requested this. The Special Issuance limited me to a second-class medical certificate, preventing me from upgrading to captain. Again, I had done nothing wrong, passed all tests, never had an alcohol related incident, nor violated any rule or regulation and I had no diagnosis of any alcohol use disorder. This was about control and punishment, a way to contain and discredit my autistic son by discrediting me after all the efforts to frame me and seize my kids in Florida had failed.

It was only at my first appointment in January 2011, that Dr. Harper smugly informed me that I had to pay him for these services. Until this time, I thought this was an FAA funded program. He laughed and said he was giving me the "ASA discount" and, after performing a quick, cursory FAA exam, he handed me a bill for $210.00 – more than twice the standard rate. He performed a total of four so-called examinations for this fee, though I refused to pay for the last one after his conduct during that evaluation and subsequent conduct.

Harper, knowing that I was only required to obtain one examination from him per year, then dated my medical certificate to expire in six months to require an extra evaluation for double the going rate.

All this followed a lengthy investigation, including a review by the FAA Chief Psychiatrist, which found that I wasn't mentally ill. (Glaringly absent from all the FAA reports was my false arrest and the murder my sons witnessed while their trauma was described as just back and forth allegations.) I returned to work in October 2010.

* * *

That November, I received an email from Brad Dennis, the director of Klaas Kids, a non-profit whose "mission is to stop crimes against children."

> Mark, I have not forgotten you!! I was called to the capital in Tallahassee early last week. I had several meetings with FDLE on unrelated cases. It was not the time to answer your calls or return your calls while I was with them. This weekend we had a search for another missing child (already scheduled). I have a couple of K-9 teams that will go with me to Eglin to check out this area we have discussed. As soon as we finish that I will get back in touch with you.
>
> In Hope,
> Brad Dennis

Dennis promised to examine the tree in the woods – the tree the Sheriff's department insisted wasn't there – with his nationally recognized cadaver dog team. He and his team did. He acknowledged that the tree was bizarre and highly suspicious, particularly as Gabe had described it in detail in advance. He also told me that his dogs reacted to the tree, and that their reaction was consistent with a reaction to an accelerant. He made a detailed report and promised to provide me with a copy. Then poof. He stonewalled me and never gave me the report. Dennis, like so many others in this coverup, is a preacher, and the pastor of Eden Fellowship Church in Pensacola.

Frustrated, I emailed the Walton County Sheriff's Department demanding they release my trailer. Finally, in the second week of December, I was allowed to pick it up. The evidence custodian didn't know the trailer had been there and he told me it had never been logged in as evidence or even examined. *It seemed the charade never ended.*

* * *

With the holidays upon us, I must admit I felt anything but festive. On Christmas Eve, I made dinner for the boys, helped them leave some cookies and milk out for Santa, then put them to sleep for the night. While my kids slept upstairs, all snug in their beds, I went out to the yard where I'd parked the trailer. The radio played softly–

And when those blue snowflakes start falling
That's when those blue memories start calling
You'll be doing all right
With your Christmas of white
But I'll have a blue, blue, blue, blue Christmas

I spent Christmas Eve scraping and vacuuming every crack and crevice in that trailer. By the time I was done, I found burnt dental remains (including a titanium post from a burnt dental implant), nine pieces of dental gold, and human hair. I carefully bagged and photographed each one.

That morning, for only the second time that year, my wife showed up to spend time with the boys. We agreed we wanted them to have a nice Christmas morning. She got there early before the kids were up to help prepare Santa Claus. It was sort of sad and surreal.

I could tell she was pregnant, but she didn't say anything about it to me, and I just hoped the boys wouldn't notice. After a little more than two hours, she left. Citing concerns for the kids' safety from her own family, she disappeared. Although contact was minimal both before and after, my children didn't see their mother for almost two years. She emailed my mother in June 2012 and then visited the kids briefly in Georgia that fall.

It was a blue, blue Christmas indeed.

* * *

On the morning of December 29, I left some of the samples from the trailer with the Escambia County Medical Examiner. I also attempted to provide this evidence to the FBI at their Pensacola office, but they refused to accept it, claiming they had no jurisdiction.

I don't remember the exact date but back in 2009, Nancy Locke, the cadaver dog trainer who worked with Brad Dennis, arranged a secret meeting with me. She asked for all the information I had, and we copied it together at a local Office Depot. She gave them to someone in the Santa Rosa Sheriff's Department she trusted with a handwritten note: "Turn over to Feds (FBI St AG) if Mark Chapman Harris dies."

A female deputy later met me at a convenience store and returned the copies with no comments. Philip Dixon, a member of Calvary Chapel who had introduced us, told me a short time later that she was withdrawing from the situation out of concerns for the safety of her family. He told me that she had seen evidence of what I had uncovered and that she had told him that she had grandchildren to think about. That evidence was dead kids. This was my last meeting with Dixon as well. He cut off contact and unfriended me on Facebook. He was rattled by the entire situation, particularly the murder and missing foster children.

* * *

In a last-ditch effort to protect myself and my sons, a second restraining order was served on Mike Nobles by a Deputy Darr. Judge Santurri who was no longer in Santa Rosa County.

And so, with a "Temporary Injunction for Protection Against Repeat Violence" to protect my family, if only temporarily, I rang in the New Year alone.

I tried to view 2011 as a fresh start. I won't lie, after so many setbacks and so many hardships, it was difficult to keep going, but I tried to remain optimistic and pressed on. Considering the mountains of evidence and testimony I had gathered over the past few years showing an elaborate web of lies and crimes perpetrated by public officials covering up for Mike Nobles, paper files were growing unwieldy, so I had them professionally digitized on compact discs. On January 11, I reached out to two officials who I hoped might help me.

The first was Janine Williams at the Florida Department of Law Enforcement. We were able to briefly meet, and I gave her an overview of what had happened to my children and myself. I provided her with two copies of the discs I had made, and she assured me she'd be in contact by the end of the month.

The second was the office of Governor Rick Scott, which I hoped might be able to take a closer look at the good ol' boy network I'd been dealing with for so long. In my desperations, I laid it all out for them to see:

Governor Scott,

I have repeatedly appealed to the former Governor for assistance. He passed the buck.

My two sons, and other children, have been raped and tortured and exploited in child pornography. My sons witnessed the perpetrator commit murder. They have testified to this. There is overwhelming evidence the murder occurred. There is overwhelming proof the sexual abuse occurred. The perpetrator of these crimes is well connected, and all of these cases have been taken care of.

Abuse reports have been made regarding my sons at least twelve times including three by two child therapists. Most of these reports were deliberately falsely closed out as "duplicates." In each of the cases in which this did not occur, children disclosed horrific abuse including sexual abuse, having pets killed and being threatened with death.

I can document that these disclosures were made. Each child protection report was falsified to claim these disclosures were not made. In almost every investigation there were efforts by local DCF investigators and law enforcement to bring false charges against me, the father, for false reporting, even when child therapists reported it and the children said they were abused when interviewed.

The offender is a convicted felon with a federal record. He was caught with a small arsenal of weapons and ammunition including a pump shotgun. He has threatened to shoot and kill me and my sons who saw him shoot another man. The Okaloosa County Sheriff's Department returned these weapons to him, then refused to investigate the weapons matter until I contacted the previous governor. They then fabricated evidence to exonerate him. The record shows he still has those weapons. He has committed approximately 40 acts of stalking against me and my sons in the last two years. The Sheriff himself has refused to document or investigate and has engaged in false statements.

My nine-year-old is diagnosed with Post Traumatic Stress Disorder from his abuse and every day of his life is a struggle. His mother, my wife, has abandoned her children and has diagnosed psychological problems from her own childhood abuse. Friends, family and multiple mental health professionals have repeatedly encouraged me to leave the state. Running is not my nature.

I am an airline pilot and have to leave my sons for days at a time. At this point I don't see much choice but to leave this cesspool of corruption that won't enforce the law or protect my children, where I have been repeatedly threatened and harassed by a member of law enforcement. I have appealed to the former Governor, the FDLE, the DCF IG, the FBI, the ATF, the state attorney and the Sheriff's Department. The latter two have refused to talk to me and the others all forward it back to a corrupt DCF, specifically circuit one administrator Janice Thomas who has refused to discuss the matter.

These are matters for law enforcement anyway. There has never been a law enforcement investigation of the rape of my sons or of the murder they witnessed. I was arrested and falsely charged when I told law enforcement about it. I was punished by being held in a holding cell for 6 days, denied bond without cause, denied an attorney, denied visitors, denied a bible, and denied a change of clothes. I spoke with investigator Janine Williams of FDLE yesterday. I ask that your office follow up and ensure these matters are addressed.

I hope my seven- and nine-year-old sons aren't forced to leave their home for their safety and that you will take action.

Thank you and God bless,
Mark Harris

After specifically stating that DCF and Sheriff's Department were part of the problem, here is the reply I received:

Thank you for contacting Florida Governor Rick Scott.

The Governor understands your concerns and asks me to respond on his behalf. Because you mention possible child abuse, I forwarded your email to the Florida Department of Children and Families Child Abuse Hotline and Inspector General for review and response. If you want to contact that Department directly, please use the information provided below:

Florida Department of Children and Families
Building One, Room 202
1317 Winewood Boulevard
Tallahassee, Florida 32399-0700
(850) 488-4306

You may also want to contact your local Sheriff's Department. Please be aware that alleged or suspected elder/child abuse should be reported to the Florida Department of Children and Families' toll-free Abuse Hotline at (800) 962-2873.

Thank you for contacting Governor Rick Scott.

I was back in the DCF dumping ground – the same dumping ground used by the ATF, FBI, and the FDLE. And even as I was trying to find allies in law enforcement like Janine Williams, telling me to contact the

Sheriff's department after I just pointed out the crimes committed against me by the Sheriff's department only goes to show the amount of consideration I was given. Meanwhile, when Janine Williams did get back to me, she told me that the discs I gave her were blank (they were professionally made) and her superiors had instructed her not to investigate my claims.

It felt like being trapped in a giant shell game, a pattern of lies and plausible deniability that wound its way through multiple state and federal agencies. Every record I provided to a local state or federal agency seemingly disappeared into a black hole, which is why I want to make all these records public. Because, as I noted in my letter to Governor Scott, I eventually did have to leave the state due to the stalking and threats by the Nobles Family, compounded by the efforts to frame me and harassment at the hands of local and state officials. I don't want this to happen to anyone else.

On January 12, 2011, I had my hearing on my latest effort to get a restraining order, again with Judge Goodman, who again passed the buck.

Nobles continued to lie about his felony gun possession while the court continued to let the charade play out. Here is a brief excerpt of the stonewalling I encountered day after day:

IN THE CIRCUIT COURT IN AND FOR SANTA ROSA COUNTY, FLORIDA

MARK HARRIS on behalf of GABRIEL HARRIS, Petitioner
Vs.
MICHAEL NOBLES, Respondent.

THE COURT: I just want to know about the firearm.

MICHAEL NOBLES: The weapons belonged to my son.

THE COURT: Is that where they are?

MICHAEL NOBLES: My son disposed of it. Sold them. He is presently in Guyana. This has been tried in Okaloosa County and was dismissed for lack of evidence.

THE COURT: Okay. So you don't have any weapons at your house?

MICHAEL NOBLES: And I did sign a statement–

THE COURT: Okay. That's all I need.

MICHAEL NOBLES: –on the injunction that I did not.

THE COURT: That's all I need.

MARK HARRIS: Your Honor.

MICHAEL NOBLES: And the other–

MARK HARRIS: Your Honor, the respondent testified in February of last year that the guns were back at the Okaloosa County Sheriff's Department. In August of last year the evidence custodian testified that that never occurred. The respondent has repeatedly – I can document that he lied to the FBI–

THE COURT: Okay. There's nothing I can do, sir. If he says he doesn't have weapons at his house–

MICHAEL NOBLES: And I challenged to produce what he is saying.

THE COURT: What is, what is the next date?

MICHAEL NOBLES: Your Honor, before–

THE COURT: Yes, sir.

MICHAEL NOBLES: Before you rule on that–

THE COURT: I'm not ruling on anything; I'm just continuing.

MARK HARRIS: May I ask–

MICHAEL NOBLES: But before we even continue I'd like to address case number DF2-2649-DR-01-DV. Mr. Harris is not the father of this child. This Court has already ruled once that he has no standing to file anything on this child's behalf. He is holding this child against the mother's will. He has–

THE COURT: Are you the father of Gabriel Harris?

MARK HARRIS: Your honor, I am the legal biological father, claimed through the affidavit of paternity, filed by the Court. The respondent has already tried to rebut that and found out he couldn't do it. My name is on his birth certificate.

THE COURT: Okay. Your name is on the birth certificate, then he's the father.

MICHAEL NOBLES: Ma'am, he filed an acknowledgment of paternity.

THE COURT: Okay.

MICHAEL NOBLES: He has sworn under oath through deposition that he is not the biological father of this child. The mother of this child is present here, ready to testify that he is not the biological father.

THE COURT: Okay. But this– That's not going to be sufficient. If he's done an affidavit of paternity and that has gone to the state–

MARK HARRIS: And the mother also signed it.

THE COURT: If he is on the birth certificate, he is the father of the child.

MICHAEL NOBLES: but he was not on the original birth certificate. He got a secondary birth certificate issued through perjury.

THE COURT: Well, if he signed it and the mother [signed] it, then he is the father of the child.

MICHAEL NOBLES: Your Honor, may–

THE COURT: What's the date, please?

THE CLERK: January 26 and February 23.

THE COURT: Let's do it February 23rd which will give everyone enough time to get everything together. Anything else?

MARK HARRIS: No, Your Honor.

THE COURT: Okay. Thank you very much.

(PROCEEDINGS CONCLUDED)

* * *

On January 13, 2011, I had to have Gabe involuntarily hospitalized, or "Baker Acted," at Emerald Coast Behavioral. He was overheard talking about harming himself, and Kelly Beck determined he was in a temporary dissociative state. Even though his hospital was two-and-a-half-hours away, I assured Gabe I was there for him and visited as often as I was allowed. There was no support or help from anyone. Over the course of his stay, therapists at the hospital found him suffering from acute PTSD that they attributed to the abuse Gabe had suffered at Nobles' hands. After five days, his condition stabilized, his medications were adjusted, and he was allowed to return home with me.

But this wasn't a simple fix. Nothing about this situation was simple. My request for Legal Services of Northwest Florida was denied due to a "conflict of interest" that was never fully explained but probably because Rick Karshna and the DCF had tried to use them to take my kids away previously. Because the medical bills were stacking up, I attempted to get them subsidized by a crime victims compensation program which had evaluated the kids' cases and found them to be eligible. The DCF repeatedly tried to block my access to this program for some reason, but the kids' former therapist, Kelly Beck, signed a letter affirming the kids had

PTSD related to their grandfather, and confirmed they should have no contact with him. With this, I was able to get the kids into new psychiatric care provided by Pamela Powers of Lutheran Services.

But Gabe continued to lash out, sometimes violently. His fight or flight response – a reaction of the nervous system to acute stress – had become fight *and* flight, so these outbursts were often followed by attempts to run away from school. This may have been related to the therapy work they were both undergoing, which seemed to be unlocking old, often painful memories. For instance, during one therapy session, Gabe suddenly and unexpectedly remembered an incident where his grandfather violently pinched his genitals and anal penetration by an object he drew resembling some sort of magic wand, which I would later learn was identical to ones that Nobles occultist brother made and was selling on the internet.

* * *

On April 4, the kids' family doctor, Dr. Perez, from Sacred Heart Medical Group, reported on Gabe:

SUBJECTIVE: *"The patient is now in specialized counseling regarding suspected child abuse/sexual abuse. He recently reported to his counselor recalling an object was placed in his rear-end and he had bleeding afterward. This apparently occurred two years ago. His aunt, who is the perpetrator, was 12 years old at the time … and this occurred in front of the grandfather per his history given today. He reported that the grandmother stopped the bleeding with paper towels. Apparently this had been reported three times in the past to different therapists, without actual details, only that there was abuse."*

ASSESSMENT AND PLAN: *"Child abuse/Sexual abuse. Advised I would like to report this as details of the matter have not been evident. He is apparently having increased recollection of events with his current counseling. He is seeing counselor Pamela Powers through Lutheran Services in Fort Walton. Advised that there would likely not be any physical signs two years after the abuse mentioned. This will be reported through Florida Department of Children and Families abuse hotline."*

There would be no investigation until August when it was subsequently shut down.

* * *

While waiting on my rescheduled hearing for another attempt at a restraining order, I found myself on an overnight work trip in Romulus, Michigan. During this time period, former Air Force OSI Agent Joe Figueroa was living with us and taking care of my kids when I was away.

It had been a long day, and I was trying to fall asleep in my hotel room by mindlessly scrolling the Internet, when a message from Billy Nobles appeared in Facebook messenger. With a bit of distance from the event now, I half-jokingly call it the "Fredo" message because Billy, still living in South America, threatened to send professional killers from Guyana with "open ended visas," and are "good at what they do," to take me on a fishing trip from which, he promised, I would not return. Considering what I'd been through already, I didn't see any reason not to take that threat seriously, so around 11:00PM I filed a report with the Romulus Police Department. They took down the information, but with so many jurisdictions involved, there wasn't much they could do.

Following the threats from Billy Nobles, I was exhausted and suffering from severe anxiety. After I returned home, I took a rare sick day off work to get my head on straight, but what little rest I got quickly evaporated when I learned I wasn't the only person getting threats.

* * *

Shortly after returning from Michigan, I had a long discussion with Sherry Taylor, the nanny who Christy tried to hire when the Nobles kidnapped my kids back in 2008. I caught her up on what had been going on since the kidnapping and discussed the upcoming injunction hearing. The entire conversation was cordial and friendly, and by the time we said our goodbyes she gave me her address so she could be served a subpoena to testify on my behalf.

Less than a week later, she called me in a panic. Before I could even get a word in, she began screaming at me.

"I don't want to go to your court case! If I come, I am going to say I don't know anything about you and your situation and that you are harassing me so leave me the fuck alone!"

The call lasted ten seconds. Then she hid from being served.

* * *

At the same time, I received a call from the boys' old babysitter, Mary Smith. She wasn't screaming, thankfully, but she wanted to let me know that her daughter and elderly mother had been getting creepy messages from Nobles now that he was back in the area. Mary was so freaked out by the situation that she moved into a hotel right before the injunction hearing, hoping that Nobles wouldn't be able to find her.

* * *

Every previous effort to obtain a restraining order against the Nobles had been blocked by Judge Santurri as case after case had been reassigned to him. Santurri, however, was now on the bench in Santa Rosa County and this time the case was reassigned to his right-wing ex-military friend. The hearing took place on April 20 (another important event scheduled on Hitler's birthday), in the courtroom of Judge Gary Bergosh, the balding former military JAG and George Bush crusader. Bergosh had displayed his racism and narcissism in an earlier case by lashing out at an African American man for not calling him "sir" or "your honor." He went on a bizarre tirade rambling about marching on Baghdad as a Marine executive officer. He had the poor young man handcuffed and jailed for contempt.

Even though Sherry Taylor refused to show up and sounded terrified, four witnesses showed up for me. Therapist Pamela Powers of Lutheran Services, Mary Smith, and therapist Nicole Fryback – the fourth, Nobles' son-in-law, Brian Riggs, a hostile witness. Nobles had only one witness that day, Christy, but she mysteriously had a "medical procedure" that prevented her from being present (I am guessing giving birth). He appeared with no attorney. The judge would act as his attorney. Initially, the court wasn't going to provide a transcript of the hearing, but a court reporter who had transcribed previous related cases, and whom I had spoken to about this hearing, appeared unexpectedly. She did this for free, because she knew what I was up against.

Nobles engaged in a flurry of stalking and witness intimidation leading up to the hearing, including having his son threaten to murder me. But it didn't end there. He and his son in law parked beside Mary Smith in the parking lot, and they followed my witnesses around the courthouse property – in a creepy manner – during breaks.

* * *

The first witness, Nicole Fryback, was the therapist at the Emerald Coast Child Advocacy Center who had interviewed my sons back in 2008 after they were kidnapped. She also interviewed Faith and Emily Nobles, and she was the one who allowed Nobles to come into her office while he was under investigation. She provided him – as the alleged perpetrator – with graphic details of his victims' play therapy. Of interest, Tom Dunn had previously physically blocked me from meeting with her at the ECCAC. As a side note, a quick view of social media at the time showed Fryback as Facebook friends with Joey Forgione, Jennifer Clark, Heather Pagano, and Rick Karshna. Each one had falsified reports for Nobles. Again, her testimony has been summarized here to the relevant portions.

NICOLE FRYBACK,
Having been duly sworn, testified as follows:
EXAMINATION BY THE COURT:

[...]

THE COURT: Ms. Fryback, where do you work?

THE WITNESS: I work for the Child Protection Team in Niceville, Florida.

THE COURT: And specifically, do you work for the state, or who do you work for?

THE WITNESS: Our contract is through the Department of Health, and we work – it's given to Families Count.

THE COURT: Do you work for Families Count?

THE WITNESS: Uh-huh, yes.

THE COURT: Okay. You've been subpoenaed here by Mr. Harris. Is that correct?

THE WITNESS: Yes.

THE COURT: There's some allegations he's seeking an injunction against his father-in-law, Mr. Nobles, Michael Nobles here. [...] Are you able to testify ... one of the reasons I brought you here. Are you – did you interview a child for an alleged sexual abuse report?

THE WITNESS: Yes.

THE COURT: Are you able to testify about that absent a court order?

THE WITNESS: You would have to order me.

THE COURT: All right ... do you actually work at the children's house?

THE WITNESS: At the Children's Advocacy Center.

THE COURT: And there was a DCF investigation into these allegations?

THE WITNESS: Yes.

THE COURT: And you know what the results of that investigation were?

THE WITNESS: Yes.

THE COURT: What were the results of [the DCF] investigation? Are you able to tell me what that is, without me ordering you?

THE WITNESS: There were ... seven investigations within a five-month period of time.

THE COURT: Okay.

THE WITNESS: And they were all no indicators of sexual abuse.

THE COURT: Okay. Mr. Harris has told me that there was some indicator of child-on-child and specifically ... Mr. Nobles' teenage daughters were the on–

THE WITNESS: That was the case I specifically worked.

THE COURT: Was there any indicators or was it insufficient, or was that the investigation, did it show any indications of that?

THE WITNESS: ... did not work it as a DCF case ... not a caregiver perpetrator.

THE COURT: I understand.

THE WITNESS: It's child-on-child. So there were no DCF findings, since there was no DCF case. But they did turn it in to law enforcement.

THE COURT: And there was no case that – law enforcement didn't pursue a case there?

THE WITNESS: Correct.

THE COURT: All right.

MR. HARRIS: Your honor.

THE COURT: Let me do just this before I let you ask the questions. You said there were seven investigations; is that correct?

THE WITNESS: That was when I first – when I had this case, that was the history I went into the case with.

THE COURT: Is there anything else I need to know about that to make my decision here on whether a domestic violence injunction should be entered, or not, that you can tell me without violating any of your confidentiality with kids? And if there is, let me know, and then I'll make a determination whether I'm going to order you to divulge that, if I need to make the decision here. Is there anything I need to know? Let me go this way. Were the allegations legitimate?

THE WITNESS: I can't answer that without going into an explanation.

THE COURT: There were seven of them.

THE WITNESS: Yes.

THE COURT: Were any of them frivolous? Can you answer that? Or mean spirited or–? I understand he and Mr. Harris and his wife, Mr. Nobles' daughter, are going through some sort of divorce or separation. Any indication of retaliation or anything like that? Anything I need to know in that regard?

THE WITNESS: There were findings on my case pertaining to Child-on-Child sex abuse

THE COURT: There were findings on – on some of the cases?

THE WITNESS: On mine. On just specifically my child-on-child case.

[...]

THE COURT: Okay, what about the other cases

He is referring her to the 7 or 8 other reports that were not investigated.

THE WITNESS: They were all not indicated, no findings.

THE COURT: Okay. So there may have been legitimacy at least to one. And how was that found, but it was not pursued because it was child-on-child, no caregivers involved?

THE WITNESS: Right.

THE COURT: Basically keep the kids apart?

THE WITNESS: Right.

THE COURT: As to the other ones, were they any legitimate cases or no, or can you?

"Repeat a lie often enough and it becomes the truth." There are several of those in this story and here comes one of the biggest:

THE WITNESS: I can say that when I did my interview, I interviewed Toby and ... Gabriel, ... against standard procedure. The only reason I interviewed them and the only reason that the other two girls were brought in on that very last and seventh case for interviews was because a string of reports were being called in September, October, November, six of them. DCF would go out, the children would not make any disclosures of abuse at all, and then the reports would keep coming in and the DCF would still have to keep going out. And we were to the point where we felt it was getting mentally injurious to these children to be constantly asked over and over again about sexual things.

And so, we decided – we usually don't interview children unless we have a disclosure … to bring them in and get them videotaped, all four children, to ask them, hopefully for the last time, if anything happened to them of that kind of a nature, and to get it on video, so we wouldn't have to – so Department of Children and Families wouldn't have to keep going out and asking them about it.

The reality is that the stated purpose of the interview, per DCF supervisor and fellow Church of Christ leader, Donna Parish, was to "make sure nothing happened." Something basic is reiterated here. Not to get to the truth. The Goebbels lie that the kids had been interviewed seven times is beyond outlandish. My kids had spent five minutes with Sarah Johnson who then washed her hands of the case. After the kidnapping of my sons by the Nobles, Jennifer Clark responded and found my son beaten black and blue, and both kids were asking to see their father; then she falsified a report and tried to frame me for false reporting on a report that wasn't false, and I did not make the report in the first place. That was it. Two encounters with DCF and no real interview. In terms of the Nobles kids, the record is clear that they were only interviewed once, assumed a fetal position, and were unresponsive, showing severe signs of abuse. This would continue with Rick Karshna who later exaggerated further, claiming 13 interviews. And when my kids affirmed the allegations on tape, the DCF and law enforcement buried it. When I tried to introduce these disclosures, documented in a law enforcement report, Judge Bergosh refused to allow it, calling it "hearsay."

The next relevant testimony was when *I confronted Fryback regarding a meeting with Nobles while he was under investigation, providing him with details of his victims' play therapy. Something Nobles had testified to.* Her response?

THE WITNESS: I don't remember. I don't recall.

NOBLES: Have I met you?

THE WITNESS: No.

NOBLES: I didn't think so. I've never laid eyes on you. Okay?

The web of lies was now expanding, so I tried to redirect, but I was blocked by Judge Bergosh. Note that both Nobles and I are representing ourselves here.

MARK HARRIS: *May I redirect based on his testimony?*

THE COURT: Well, I don't need to hear any more from her. I think I've got it on this. Ma'am, you're free to go. Thank you.

THE WITNESS: Thank you.

THE COURT: Let me bring the next one. Pamela Powers.

(Witness takes the stand.)

[...]

THEREUPON:

Next was Pamela Powers of Lutheran Services who had been treating my kids for some time.

PAMELA POWERS,
Having been duly sworn, testified as follows:
EXAMINATION BY THE COURT:

THE COURT: Ma'am, your name is Pamela Powers?

THE WITNESS: Yes, Your Honor.

THE COURT: And you're a counselor with Lutheran Services?

THE WITNESS: Yes.

THE COURT: And in your capacity what do you do?

THE WITNESS: I'm a program therapist for the sexual and physical abuse treatment program. I work specifically with child sexual and physical abuse in individual capacity.

THE COURT: All right. And when did you start seeing them?

THE WITNESS: Mr. Harris arrived middle of February, and I did testing on all three of them, and began services with all three on the 22nd of February.

THE COURT: Okay. How long – your degree is what?

THE WITNESS: I have my bachelors in psyche [sic], a master's in education and master's in clinical social work, and I'm also certified to treat depression. I've been a therapist for 20-plus years.

THE COURT: So you've worked in this area for 20-plus years?

THE WITNESS: No, actually. I'm also retired military. I worked with posttraumatic stress disorder when I was active duty. I worked with rape crisis and rape victims, adult male rape victims, I've worked with teens at risk. I retired the military in 2005.

THE COURT: What rank were you when you retired?

THE WITNESS: Navy chief. And I have my one Master's, and I returned to school to complete my second Master's and I've been with Lutheran Services for the last four years.

THE COURT: So I can at least focus. Now we'll go to the two boys. And I know you may have some sort of privilege. Is there anything you can speak about here or no?

THE WITNESS: Well, I can. And I will be very clear about this. Knowing that this hearing was coming up ... I gathered information from the boys, and I asked them what if anything I could share with the judge. And they agreed to ... some very specific information. And I would like to present some of their work if you would allow it.

THE COURT: Let me ask you this. Based on what you've learned from the boys, have you made a subsequent report to the Department of Children & Families? Is there a new report to them?

THE WITNESS: No additional reports. I have not made additional reports, because I'm dealing with things that to my understanding have obviously been reported, if that goes to your question.

THE COURT: Someone in your – okay. So when you learn something, and I think it applies to judges and law enforcement and therapists and teachers, if there's an allegation of child abuse, sexual abuse or physical abuse, you have to – you are a mandatory reporter?

THE WITNESS: I am. If it's new information. If it's previously been reported, in my understanding of it from everything, the allegations had been previously reported. So I didn't make specific allegations.

THE COURT: So what happens in your line of work, let's just say you learn that there's been previous reports made, DCF comes out. I just heard from a lady, Pamela Power – I'm sorry, Nicole Fryback, who stated there were seven allegations back in 2008, October, November, December, January, February, whatever. I'm bringing – she said, "We bring the kids in every single month," and said, "they're not reporting, they're not." She goes, "At some point we said, "Look this is enough. We're going to get this done." Interviewed the kids. She said there was some indication of sexual contact between kids, nothing with adults, so the cases were all closed. Knowing that history, the cases closed, DCF says no findings of adult-on or caregiver-on children, yet you, let's say, get a subsequent report that may add to it. Do you report that?

THE WITNESS: I would, yes, sir, Your Honor. And I will say this: I have not made additional reports because my understanding of it is that the reports have been made. Now if there is any question as to whether or not these reports have been made, I am glad and will do so.

THE COURT: Let me ask you this. Is there with what you've been allowed to share from the boys, and I don't want to go into it in great depth, I need to know–

THE WITNESS: I promise no traumatizing details. You don't want to hear it.

THE COURT: Right. And I don't want – I've got to make this determination if I'm going to grant some sort of an injunction here. What is it I need to know the boys have said that they can – that you can release? What is it I need to know?

THE WITNESS: both boys identified a grandfather as having sexually offended them. Both. Both boys also identify having witnessed significant violent episodes. And I am not at liberty to any more than that.

THE COURT: How old are the boys right now?

THE WITNESS: 7 and 9.

THE COURT: And what years, how old would they have been when this alleged abuse occurred?

THE WITNESS: 6 and 4, 2008.

THE COURT: 6 and 4. Let me ask you this. With the number of interviews they have had with Department of Children & Families, is it possible that these memories could have been suggested to them–

THE WITNESS: Let me give you more.

THE COURT:– a la the McMartin preschool?

This was a tell for Judge Bergosh. An indication that he may have really knew what was going on at 1118 Rhonda Drive. Although ritualistic abuse had occurred, none of those details had ever been reported to the court, the DCF, or law enforcement. As I feared, it would be used to discredit the kids. But here Judge Bergosh was invoking McMartin preschool, where 41 children testified they were victims of ritual abuse.

THE WITNESS: Let me give you more of a characterization. Okay? The boys are terrified of the grandfather. This would not come – and when I say terrified, I mean terrified. Part of posttraumatic stress disorder, if you think of it from the perspective of the fight or flight base concept. If a person, any person, veterans or children, are overwhelmed with the amount of threat to self or perceived threat to self or a witness to threat or harm to others, they're overtaken with this comprehensive fear. I mean, that's the foundation of it. From that then comes a variety of symptoms. Both boys display significant posttraumatic stress disorder symptoms. There is no question. And they both identify; I mean I'm glad to show you the DSM criteria and I'm glad to tell you how in my true professional observation each one of these boys meets the criteria.

THE COURT: So, they're posttraumatic stress because of yelling, screaming?

THE WITNESS: No, sir.

THE COURT: Because of sexual – what you believe was sexual contact?

THE WITNESS: Because of their reports of sexual contact, sexual abuse. One of the boys described it he was made to bleed, and the other boy witnessed that.

THE COURT: Made to bleed?

THE WITNESS: Yes. Anal penetration, sir.

THE COURT: Okay.

THE WITNESS: Very specific about that. He was also very specific that the grandmother got him a tissue. Very specific detail.

THE COURT: All right.

THE WITNESS: This is not the kind of thing that would be, even if from repeated interviews. Forensic interviews are not conducted on a weekly basis, and I'm familiar with forensic interview process. And when I do an assessment on a child, I don't – I ask open-ended questions. For example, and this is one of the things that the boys allowed me to share, and I'll just give you a concept on that. I asked them, because they both present with so much fear, and one of the – there are a few tools that can help me learn about that. They see nothing changed her. So I have some Easter eggs, empty Easter eggs. I say, "Okay, we're going to write down the things that you're afraid of." Very open ended. I didn't say anything as to what these fears were about. "We're going to write down the things that you're afraid of and we're going to put them in this egg, so you don't have to carry it with you everywhere. We're going to pick it up when you come here and we're going to help you with them one at a time." Both boys, the most significant fear they identified was fear of the grandfather.

THE COURT: Let me ask you this. Has the grandfather, as you understand it, have the boys had any contact with the grandfather recently?

THE WITNESS: Not that I am aware of.

THE COURT: Okay. I understand your testimony. Anything else I need to know, Mr. Harris? I think I understand what her testimony is.

MR. HARRIS: *Your Honor, only that there is significant corroborating testimony.*

THE COURT: From what?

MR. HARRIS: Ms. Kelly Beck testified in a peripherally related case.

THE COURT: Which case was it?

MR. HARRIS: It was not sexual abuse, it was the false report he threw out at the last hearing and my arrest in – last year.

THE COURT: Well, I'll let you argue that later. Let me – any questions of this last, Mr. Nobles?

MR. NOBLES: Yes, Your Honor.

CROSS-EXAMINATION

MR. NOBLES: So you've been seeing the boys since the 22nd of February of this year?

THE WITNESS: Yes, sir.

MR. NOBLES: Are you aware or did the boys – maybe – maybe you're not going to be able to answer this, but.

THE WITNESS: I'll answer it if I can.

MR. NOBLES: Are you aware of the boys claiming that they witnessed me committing murder? Did they reveal anything or anything you could answer?

THE WITNESS: That's my information the boys told me that I could disclose, and out of respect for their safety, their emotional safety, I won't disclose the content. I can say that they are terrified for several reasons. And can I add a couple, also, recommendations, Judge?

THE COURT: Meaning what? What does that mean?

THE WITNESS: Not in answer to your question. How about I will answer your other questions first, and then I will come back to that.

THE COURT: Okay.

MR. NOBLES: Have the boys revealed anything to you about a supposedly hidden room in my home that had automatic weapons and double-barreled shotguns, you know, specifics? You said that they have been very specific details that they have revealed.

THE WITNESS: They have revealed some details, but I cannot say given the length of time that I've seen them that they have yet revealed all details.

MR. NOBLES: No, no. I'm not asking there all on it. I just – I guess what I'm trying to get to is, the murder charge, there was very specific– Your Honor, you have a copy of it, I don't have a copy of it. The name of the person that I was supposed to have murdered, the relationship of this person.

THE COURT: Well, I'll let you ask the question. If she can answer it, she can answer it; if she can't, she can't. So, ma'am, do you know about anything specific to the murder?

THE WITNESS: Yes, I do.

THE COURT: Are you able to speak about it or no? I mean, have they given you permission to speak?

THE WITNESS: The boys have not given me permission to share or disclose that, they have disclosed some content around that.

THE COURT: All right.

MR. NOBLES: Have you ever talked with the mother of these children?

THE WITNESS: No, sir, I have not.

MR. NOBLES: In your profession, can terror be instilled in a child against someone other than the person that the fear is of? Can someone else – can I instill in this child fear of their father?

THE WITNESS: Not PTSD, not to the severity I see, not with the specificity of detail that I see, no.

MR. NOBLES: Okay. The DCF report, I know you said you filtered them out. But did you – did you realize how many there is? I keep hearing six, there's fifteen of them. Have you reviewed these reports?

THE WITNESS: I have reviewed the overall DCF papers, but again, because there was so much, because it was so complex, my focus was not on corroborating the validity of those, my focus was on determining the clinical condition of my clients and developing appropriate treatment for them. So have I looked at all the information on these DCF reports? No, I have not.

MR. NOBLES: Okay. But the important, outstanding things, have you looked at those?

THE WITNESS: The outstanding – the outstanding information that I have from previous reports is that the boys alleged that there has been genital fondling, play is the way the boys would phrase it, from two preteen aunts, that I think were twelve or so at the time, I believe. And that there had been anal penetration. That there had also been being forced to witness that. And one of the boys actually drew a picture that he did give me permission to share, where he drew 9 points of fingers where he was held down. Inside he felt that his head was going to explode.

The boys have not yet, because I am seeing them – and I would like to address one piece on that. Avoidance of – this is one of the things that is so compelling for me as a therapist. Avoidance of specific cues that trigger the level of trauma that the boys have experienced, avoidance of that, and physiological response and physiological signs of psychological distress and exposure, cues of that is very consistent with posttraumatic stress.

[...]

THE COURT: Let me just see if he's got any more questions, ma'am. Do you have any more questions, Mr. Nobles?

MR. NOBLES: Yes, the one I was talking about before she went off on that. Something that stands out. This is a report from DCF, it's a sort of a summary, one of the latter reporters [sic]. It says there have been several reports recently or there have been several reports recently with serious allegations of sexual abuse, none have been founded. The father appears to be exhibiting behavior that raises questions regarding his mental health. Would that stand out, tell you something really important? Because I understand you're saying that your client is Mr. Harris and Tobe [sic] and Gabe – Gabe. And here there are a lot of concerns about his mental health. And there is also concern for the children because of the repeated nature of the reports over and over, these same things.

THE COURT: So let me understand your question. So, ma'am, were you aware of that statement from DCF or no?

THE WITNESS: I'm not aware of that specific statement, but I can speak to what my observations have been of the family as a unit and of my experience with Mr. Harris and my clinical impression of Mr. Harris.

THE COURT: Is there any – okay. What is your opinion of Mr. Harris?

THE WITNESS: Like many that come to see me as a nonoffend-
ing caregiver, the concept of dealing with knowing that or believing
it or whatever, I don't want to get into fact truth of this, because I'm
not the one deciding on that.

THE COURT: I understand.

THE WITNESS: It is a significant traumatic event for any parent to
find out that their child has been offended. So that's a piece of it. I
have seen that Mr. Harris has struggled with this entire process as
complex as it has been. He has been working on improving his focus
with that, to be able to filter out things that require prioritization.

THE COURT: Well, let me ask you this. I'm going to cut to the
chase. Any issue as to his mental stability?

THE WITNESS: No, sir.

THE COURT: Okay.

THE WITNESS: As a matter of fact, the boys very clearly define
him and easily identify him as safety.

THE COURT: Well, what about you as a therapist and his – your
observations of him, any issue as to his competence or mental
health issues? No?

THE WITNESS: No, none at all. I mean, there are stressors that go
along with this, and I think people are human. But what I have also
seen from him, and I did a family session specifically to watch for
this, this was right after I had done the assessments, I wanted to see
how the boys and he functioned as a unit. And what I found is that
he is child focused, meaning that he attends to the concepts of the
boys, when they have concerns, he listens to what they're saying.

THE COURT: That's fine. That's fine. I've got to get through this.
For the–

MR. NOBLES: One more thing that I think's really important,
Your Honor.

THE COURT: Yeah.

MR. NOBLES: Are you aware of the former criminal history on
Mr. Harris that has to do about exposing himself to minors?

*And there it was again. The go-to dirty-laundry card. Of course there was
no criminal history. No conviction of anything because there was no crime.
And a sealed record.* But I would have to hear this for years like a broken

record as this violent child rapist would use projection and try to label me a pedophile. She wasn't buying it.

THE WITNESS: They identify him as safety ... and I see him providing parenting for the boys.

THE COURT: Okay. All right. I appreciate that. I don't need to hear any more from her, I think I understand the testimony. Is there any other questions you have to get out or–?

DIRECT EXAMINATION

MR. HARRIS: Would it be harmful for these children to be around the respondent?

THE WITNESS: Absolutely, unequivocally. It would risk re-traumatization, and it would halt the progress we're making. In order for the children to work to recover from posttraumatic stress, they need two forms of safety, emotional and physical. To be in an unsafe atmosphere or even one that they perceive as unsafe would absolutely result in progress reversal and–

THE COURT: Okay, I understand. Thank you, ma'am, you're free to go.

[...]

THE COURT: All right. Mr. Harris, any other witnesses?

MR. HARRIS: No, Your Honor.

[...]

Next was Brian Riggs. I called Brian, husband of Christy's sister, because it was his house where my kids stayed during the kidnapping, and he'd been privy to the Nobles' conversations and actions, and he had hidden Nobles' guns in his home, obstructing justice.

DIRECT EXAMINATION

The testimony began with Nobles lying again about the skylight hole, claiming it was covered when Caroyln lived there, something she refuted, and official records refute as well. Then Nobles and Riggs claim that the FBI searched the house. Another lie, as they never entered the house. The lies would just continue.

MR. HARRIS: Did your father-in-law, the respondent, possess weapons in his house?

BRIAN RIGGS: Did he? No, sir.

THE COURT: I'm sorry, what was the answer?

BRIAN RIGGS: No, sir, he did not.

MR. HARRIS: He did not? Who had those weapons?

THE COURT: Who did?

BRIAN RIGGS: His son Billy did.

MR. HARRIS: His son Billy possessed weapons?

BRIAN RIGGS: Yes.

MR. HARRIS: Okay. Were you aware that if he told the FBI and DCF and law enforcement that those weapons were his and they were registered in his wife's name?

THE COURT: Who is he?

MR. HARRIS: The respondent.

BRIAN RIGGS: All I know is what his son Billy told me, that they belonged to him and when he–

MR. HARRIS: Have you ever seen the respondent handle a weapon in his home?

BRIAN RIGGS: No.

MR. HARRIS: Did you tell the FBI Agent Kinnard [ph] on the day mentioned previously that you were familiar with those weapons, that they belonged to your father-in-law?

BRIAN RIGGS: This was three years ago; I seriously doubt that.

MR. HARRIS: And that, in fact, did you not tell the FBI agent that there was a, quote, long rifle that he had inherited from his father?

BRIAN RIGGS: Not offhand, but that is true.

MR. HARRIS: That is true?

BRIAN RIGGS: That is true. He did inherit one and he's already passed it on.

MR. HARRIS: Okay. And he surrendered those, and the weapons and they were returned to him according to the records, but however, he also surrendered a shotgun with .12 gauge shells, a .12 gauge shotgun, along with .410 shells. The children both say he had a double-barrel shotgun. Did you ever see a double-barrel shotgun in his home?

BRIAN RIGGS: No double-barrel shotgun was ever present. Billy actually gave me a 12-gauge shotgun, which my grandfather now possesses.

THE COURT: Is that a double-barrel or not?

THE WITNESS: No, sir. It's a single barrel.

[...]

Then I asked about the kidnapping of my sons in October 2008. His response reflects another mantra by the Nobles family, the DCF, and even the Okaloosa County Sheriff's Department. *The claim that I was not the father of my sons.*

BRIAN RIGGS: I'm not even aware they are your children, to be honest with you.

When pressed about why my sons were at his home in 2008, the flurry of phone calls, and so forth, he lied three times with the same answer:

BRIAN RIGGS: I don't remember the circumstances.

Then I questioned him about the guns.

MR. HARRIS: Were you aware that Billy Nobles, the one who gave you the shotgun, has threatened to kill me last week?

BRIAN RIGGS: Billy's in Guyana.

MR. HARRIS: That's right. That's where he is. That's where he says he'll bring the hired killers from.

THE COURT: Do you know Billy?

THE WITNESS: Yes, sir.

THE COURT: What does he do in Guyana?

THE WITNESS: As far as I'm aware, he teaches computers to the locals.

THE COURT: Is he a gun aficionado?

THE WITNESS: I don't think he would know how to load a gun.

THE COURT: He's got the guns that the grandfather, this gentleman here, has given him or–?

THE WITNESS: Billy gave me the guns and he came over and sold a few of them. What was left over he told me to do what I wanted with. My grandfather possesses both of those weapons.

Correction. I actually possess one of them as a family heirloom that's supposed to go to my son when he turns 18.

THE COURT: All right.

[...]

MR. HARRIS: Your Honor, that I think now is the eighth story regarding the guns, but it is very concerning because clearly this is the respondent's guns, not Mr. Riggs' guns. The respondent testified–

THE COURT: Well, let me ask– let you ask your questions, I'll let you argue later.

MR. HARRIS: All right.

MR. HARRIS: So it is your claim – now, how many of these guns do you currently possess?

BRIAN RIGGS: One.

MR. HARRIS: And who has the other guns?

BRIAN RIGGS: My grandfather has a rifle and a .12-gauge shotgun.

MR. HARRIS: A rifle and a .12-gauge shotgun, and you have the long rifle?

BRIAN RIGGS: I don't know what you call rifle – the long rifle, but I have a .22 rifle.

MR. HARRIS: You have a .22 rifle. Okay, there was a 30/30 and two .22s

THE COURT: Let me cut you for one second, I need to check something. All right, I've got a twelve o'clock meeting. Let me just get through this witness here and then we'll take a lunch break and come back. Yes. Any other questions?

MR. HARRIS: One quick question:

MR. HARRIS: How did you acquire these weapons?

BRIAN RIGGS: Billy brought them to the house and asked me to store them initially.

MR. HARRIS: Then what happened?

BRIAN RIGGS: He came periodically to bring them to try to sell them to different individuals. Then when it was time for him to leave to Guyana he took what was left we rode up to the police station with them.

Riggs testimony ended with a bombshell. *He and Billy were hiding Nobles guns at his home during the so-called investigation and prosecution of those guns, felony obstruction of justice.* While Nobles was facing prosecution for guns that the Sheriff's Department had stored for him, gave back to him as a felon, then lied to cover up, his son in law was admitting that the police disposed of some of these guns for Nobles just prior to him fleeing the country. Evidence destruction and obstruction of justice by the police.

(Lunch recess taken 11:56 to 1:14 p.m.)

The final testimony was from Mary Smith whose family has been relentlessly harassed by Nobles, his church, his family, and local officials.

THEREUPON:
MARY SMITH,
Having been duly sworn, testified as follows:
EXAMINATION BY THE COURT

Mary's testimony began with background. How she knew the Nobles and me. How she had attended church with the Nobles had known their kids since childhood. She then reiterated her testimony from 2009. She told how Mike Nobles had used her to threaten to kidnap the kids and about the meeting with Christy:

> MR. HARRIS: Okay, do you recall if at any point in time Mr. Nobles had requested to meet with you and threatened to take my children away?
>
> MARY SMITH: Yes, yes.
>
> MR. HARRIS: What were the reasons he threatened to take my children?
>
> MARY SMITH: To shut you up. That was his exact words, to shut you up."
>
> MARY SMITH: Yes, he did say to shut you up.
>
> MR. HARRIS: "If he had to use the children to shut you up, he would."
>
> MARY SMITH: Yes, he did say to shut you up. You are correct.
>
> THE WITNESS: I will tell you; I spent the night in a hotel last night because I'm terrified to death. If anything's going to happen to me, I wanted it to happen to me and not my children.

Mary then went on to describe the harassment she and her family had received, targeting her, her children, and even her elderly mother. And the threats made to her by Joey Forgione.

> MR. HARRIS: So have you and your husband been concerned for your safety and the safety of your children from the respondent because of your testimony?

> MARY SMITH: Yes.

> THE COURT: Why?

> MARY SMITH Because he's got some pretty powerful friends.

> THE COURT: Like who?

> MARY SMITH: No. Like sheriff's department, police department, Department of Children & Families.

> THE COURT: But you don't know if that's true or not, you just have heard this?

> MARY SMITH: Oh, I know he knows them.

> THE COURT: Who is it that he knows?

> MARY SMITH: I know that he has some dealings with Forgioni [sic].

> THE COURT: Who is that?

> MARY SMITH: It's a police officer.

> THE COURT: Okay. I understand.

> MARY SMITH: Uh-huh.

> THE COURT: He's never made any threats to you?

> MARY SMITH: The only thing he said to me was that he was – that this case was going to have to go away.

> THE COURT: All right.

> MR. HARRIS: Did Joey Forgioni [sic] ever threaten to arrest your foster child if you made more allegations of corruption?

> MARY SMITH: Yes.

> THE COURT: And who is this, the deputy?

> MARY SMITH: Uh-huh.

> THE COURT: And what did he – how is he related, because he knows this gentleman? I don't understand the tie in.

> MARY SMITH: I just know that he told me–

THE COURT: Who's he?

MARY SMITH: Mr. Forgioni [sic] told me that he could make my life very difficult.

THE COURT: If what?

MARY SMITH: If I continued to press the fact that I wanted this family – because I wanted this family investigated as well.

[...]

THE COURT: All right. Any other questions?

MR. HARRIS: No, Your Honor.

At this stage, I was feeling confident that we'd made a convincing case for the injunction against Nobles. In addition to the testimony, I submitted the transcript of Kelly Becks testimony, the psychological evaluation and diagnosis of PTSD by Dr. McCain along with a letter from her recommending a restraining order, the transcript of the testimony of therapist Shuster, and statements from the kids' school.

Brian Riggs' testimony about the guns had more holes in it than the walls of Nobles' house. DCF itself reported that on January 30, 2009, police confiscated four hunting rifles, one shotgun, two .22's, and one .30-.30 rifle from Nobles' bedroom closet. If they were Billy's guns, why didn't Billy have them? If they were Billy's guns, why did Riggs testify, "I don't think he would know how to load a gun?" According to Riggs, Billy, and Nobles, the long rifle was a gift that Nobles inherited from his father and gave to Billy, but Oscar Nobles passed away in 1978 and Billy didn't turn 18 until 1998, so this admission alone meant Mike Nobles was in possession of a firearm for over a decade after his arrest in 1985 – clearly a felony.

Mary Smith, who, as I mentioned, was terrified and testified she'd received threats from Nobles "to shut me up." She said she felt Nobles' threats were also conveyed through Officer Joey Forgione who had repeatedly shut down investigations into reports I'd made.

Nicole Fryback testified that she found evidence of child-on-child abuse, and even though these findings were turned over to police, there had been no investigation. She admitted to violating procedures in an effort to prevent future investigations, and she blatantly lied about the number of times the kids had been interviewed.

Pamela Powers testified to the horrifying abuse that, with proper investigation, she determined had taken place, and that it would be "absolutely, unequivocally" harmful if Mike Nobles was permitted to be around my children. Although I had done my best to keep him away, there was the constant fear that he could re-enter their lives at any time. But the fix was in. Again.

> THE COURT: Let me ask. The reason I'm asking these questions, if I dismiss the injunction, he's the grandfather, he doesn't have a right to see them unless you take them there. You understand that? I mean, he's not a parent. Do you understand that? So how would he see them if I dismiss the injunction?
>
> MR. HARRIS: Your Honor, with all due respect, I don't feel like the court understands. He was held–
>
> THE COURT: Let me just tell you what I understand. I understand I've heard from a mental health professional, and I'm not being pejorative towards her, I understand that she had a career in the military, she's got two master's degrees, but I've been around the block long enough to know that, I don't know if he's got the money but he could probably hire another psychologist with a Ph.D. to come in here and say, "Well, somebody could suggest this to the kids." What I perceive is that they are afraid of him, for whatever reason I do not know. I know there's an allegation that you've made, DCF has investigated, they found no corroboration or no – let me be precise with the words – they didn't go forward with it for whatever reason. So, I've got to determine whether I'm going to grant an injunction based upon things that I can't know. I mean, I'm never going to be able to know things for certainty. So, the question I'm asking you is: If I have to dismiss, what contact is he going to have with the kids?
>
> MR. HARRIS: Your Honor, I've been able to work to the best that she will agree, with my wife when he doesn't interfere and insists on being around the kids. But she's been up and down. DCF actually did ask her over and over again, we have documentation here, to sign a safety plan. She refused. It is not just a matter – the children are witnesses. They may testify someday. I'm not going to push them; I've talked to their therapist about this yesterday. She said they're not ready but they're close.
>
> THE COURT: Well, let me just – let me just go here. I'm inclined not to grant injunctions today. But I'm concerned for the kids, the children's mental well-being. And I think the mental health person you brought in today said it would be harmful to the children if they see him.

MR. HARRIS: So did Dr. McCane [sic], Your Honor.

THE COURT: Let me do this. So what I'm going to do is I'm going to have this hearing transcribed and I'm going to send the transcribed copy, and I'll do it – the court's recording this, I know you're having the court reporter, private court reporter doing this as well or – I'm going to have the court transcribe this and I'm going to send it to the Department of Children & Families, and I'm going to say, "There seems to be an issue with these children. I don't know if it's been planted in them," which he [Nobles] believes, "I don't know if it actually happened," which you [Harris] believe. All I know for the safety of the children and their mental health, something needs to be looked at. Now, that's the most I can do. As far as an injunction, I don't see where I can grant it. I don't think I've got enough to do it. Obviously, you and he are not going to ever see eye to eye. You believe something happened, and for that I'm sure you probably hate him. He believes you made false allegations against him, he probably hates you for that. I don't know where the truth is here, it's hard for me. I can't read minds, I don't have the wisdom of Solomon, I can't – I don't know, I can't figure it out. *So what I'm going to do is I'm going to deny all the injunctions. I'm going to just dismiss them all.* And you're free to refile, but I'm going to have this hearing transcribed and I'm going to send it to the Department of Children & Families and instruct them to review the case, and to the extent they can be involved with the children's mental health, let them do that. You're free to refile. You don't have to have contact with this gentleman. Obviously, he may want contact with the grandchildren, but you control them, so he may not be able to have that. So it is what it is. All right, so I've dismissed it. I'm going to give you guys paperwork on that. I know you want to say something, but there's nothing to say, I've dismissed it. Okay? All right, good luck to everybody.

Hearing concluded at 1:39 p.m.

* * *

I shouldn't have been surprised. After everything I'd been through, I shouldn't have been, but the swiftness with which Judge Bergosh said, "I'm going to deny all the injunctions. I'm going to just dismiss them all," hit me like a ton of bricks. And based on what? Not on the testimony given. Not on the evidence presented. Bergosh heard testimony from multiple witnesses who corroborated my claims and presented solid reasons for why I needed an injunction against Mike Nobles. Instead, Bergosh fabricated a hypothetical "psychologist with a Ph.D." who might hypothetically testify in Mike Nobles' defense. Bergosh based his ruling on non-existent evidence that was never presented in court, that only existed in his own imagination. It was as though Bergosh was acting as Nobles' defense lawyer.

After hearing the most damning testimony imaginable and viewing the most damning records imaginable – including a diagnosis of PTSD for both of my kids and a death threat in writing by Billy Nobles, Begrosh dismissed the cases and claimed he would have the hearing transcribed and sent to – guess who? The Florida DCF. The dumping ground of plausible deniability. This included a restraining order I had filed against Billy Nobles for repeatedly threatening to murder me. What was the DCF was going to do to prevent that?

As I walked out of the courtroom that day, *the court reporter approached me and touched my arm, stopping me before I left. "I just want you to know, I've never seen anything like that,"* she said.

If I hadn't asked her to transcribe the hearing that day, I'd have no record of it at all.

Then things got weirder still, if you can imagine.

* * *

That night, I texted Christy to find out what medical reason she had for missing her appearance in court. An hour later I received a call from a blocked number with only background noise followed by a click. My elderly mother received a similar call with only the sound of breathing. Two days later, Christy's number called me back, but this time all I could hear was a male voice yelling incoherently in the background before the call was hung up.

Only days later, Gabe and Toby came home after school to discover their pet mice had all died, apparently poisoned. I can't know for sure, of course, but although the poor mice had food and water, their bodies were desiccated as though they'd been fed rat poison. Was it a coincidence? A warning? It wouldn't have been the first time my kids' pets met a mysterious end during this whole bizarre affair.

* * *

One night we were driving home from church, and we were pulled over in Gulf Breeze for no apparent reason. After checking my ID, the officer pointed his flashlight at my terrified kids and said: "take care of dem boys." And that was it. He left. No explanation as to why we were pulled over.

And then, one day in early May, I stopped at Tom Thumb, a regional chain in Gulf Breeze. Gabe was inside using the bathroom and Toby and I were waiting outside on the sidewalk. A Santa Rosa County sheriff's deputy was inside. A total stranger – who looked like a skinhead no less – left the store and got in his pickup truck. Then he pulled up beside me and rolled down his window. Leaning out the window, he looked right at me and said, *"They're on to you, man. It's safe in Canada."*

"What?" I asked, trying to understand.

He just repeated himself, *"They're on to you, man. It's safe in Canada."* And then he drove off. I ran back into the store and asked the manager for the security tape from the parking lot, but no one would help me.

Did the sheriff's deputy put him up to it?"

Should I have been surprised?

> *A democracy cannot thrive where power remains unchecked, and justice is reserved for a select few. Ignoring these cries and failing to respond to this movement is simply not an option – for peace cannot exist where justice is not served.*
>
> – John Lewis

> *If one really wishes to know how justice is administered in a country, one does not question the policemen, the lawyers, the judges, or the protected members of the middle class. One goes to the unprotected – those, precisely, who need the law's protection most! – and listens to their testimony.*
>
> – James Baldwin

Endnotes

1   https://www.gainesville.com/story/news/2003/01/19/lawmakers-talk-change-at-dcf-two-years-after-rilya-disappearance/31625068007/

2   https://www.nwfdailynews.com/story/news/2015/06/28/1-494490/33881639007/

CHAPTER FIFTEEN

PATRIOT GAMES

I'll admit, the situation made me feel like I was going crazy. But why would all these different groups go to such extreme lengths to cover for someone like Mike Nobles? There had to be a reason. Who was the puppet master?

I suspected it had something to do with the circumstances of Nobles' involvement in the tax protest group, the Patriot Network. Because when you understand who the Patriot Network was, what it stood for, and who it was connected to, the other pieces of the puzzle come into focus.

On May 31, 1986, *The Birmingham Post-Herald* reported that "…three North Alabama men who authorities say are leaders of a tax-protest organization have been indicted by a federal grand jury on charges that they told people their wages are not taxable.… The three men – Timothy Yarbrough, 31, Hillsboro; Tony L. DeMurray, 34, Huntsville; and Michael Nobles, 34, Scottsboro – were charged with a total of 17 felony counts alleging conspiracy to obstruct the IRS, filing false returns and aiding others in filing false returns."[1]

For years, Yarbrough, DeMurray, and Nobles had been holding Tax Saving Seminars across Alabama.[2] Topics included "The Truth About the Income Tax Law" and "You Can Stop Tax Withholding," in addition to advice about forming tax shelters. (The concept of the "tax shelter" was invented by William Casey,[3] a conservative attorney who headed the CIA under President Ronald Reagan.)

In light of their activities, Nobles and DeMurray were facing eleven years and fifteen years in prison respectively, with each possible sentence topped off with a $210,000 fine. Yarbrough, who faced forty-one years and a $1.2M fine, fled the country.[4] And the IRS wanted him back.

Back when I helped flip houses alongside him, Nobles would tell me stories about how during the time he was stationed in Germany he worked at the Base Exchange where he ordered merchandise, then marked it undelivered and sold it on the streets. This "black-market" "rip-off-other-taxpayers" behavior appears to have never stopped.

After separating from the military, he got a job painting a nuclear reactor built by the Tennessee Valley Authority, and he bragged to me about how they would paint the same areas over and over to keep the taxpayer-funded contract open and the taxpayer money flowing. Nobles had no problem with taxes at all – if other people's money landed in his pockets. It was during this time in the early '80s that he was recruited into the Patriot Network.

No one likes paying taxes, but the Patriot Network was much more than a "tax-protest" group. And when you start peeling back the layers, things get real strange real quick. While I started trying to figure out who the Patriot Network really was, I noticed that they always seemed to go hand in hand with other organizations I'd never heard of.

* * *

For instance, a 1984 newspaper article titled "IRS AGENTS FEAR VIOLENCE FROM TAX PROTESTERS" reported, "Various tax protest organizations such as Posse Comitatus, Patriot Network, and Life Science Church, have distributed homemade arrest warrants for IRS officials and filed frivolous lawsuits against them.... The agents say threatening literature has been placed in their mailboxes, that tax protesters in parked cars have watched their homes, that farmers have posted signs threatening to kill agents who enter their property, and that they are often threatened verbally. 'These guys are weapons nuts,' said one IRS agent."[5]

What would a church have to do with a tax protest group? And what was Posse Comitatus?

* * *

It turns out Life Science Church was headed by Archbishop William Drexler out of San Diego. He was more than happy to give interviews in 1980, and he told one journalist how he happened to become a man of the cloth. Twenty years earlier, Drexler was working as a lawyer in Minnesota when he took on a client named Archbishop Cruikshank. (Conveniently, Drexler couldn't remember his first name.)

Cruikshank was apparently so happy with Drexler's legal work that, "...the grateful archbishop offered to ordain Drexler as a Life Science Church minister so that Drexler could reap some of the advantages of the religious life, such as reduced fares on airlines. Drexler accepted the offer and says he began researching the tax status of clergymen. By 1973 he was so impressed with the latter that he bought the whole church from the then-ailing Cruikshank, relocated it in Minnesota, and set himself up as a bishop (or was it as an archbishop?) and one of the church's trustees."[6]

Who was this Archbishop Cruikshank? Again, I had to do some digging. And by looking at Cruikshank and Drexler's histories side by side, it's easy to see there's nothing holy about them.

Drexler said Cruikshank was based out of Chicago when he met him in 1969. I found Gordon Cruikshank – a painter – who had moved to Rolling Meadows, Illinois with his wife in 1960. An article welcoming them to the neighborhood noted that neither he nor his wife "cared for organizations or clubs."[7] Their new home was directly across the street from the Cardinal Drive Church of Christ.

In 1964, Cruikshank wrote an angry op-ed in his local paper, saying "The reference to this country as being a 'Christian' nation is thoroughly repugnant to an agnostic like myself. Perhaps if a few basic 'Christian' principles were taught less, and more emphasis placed on the teachings of human rights and human dignity, the whole country would be better off." The same letter went on to remind readers that Billy Graham always printed his own name "ten times higher than Jesus Christ. This is humility?!! I will close thanking you for reading my vitriolic blast."[8]

Maybe I had the wrong Cruikshank? I was confused. How could this agnostic painter be the archbishop of a church only five years later?

In 1966, Cruikshank wrote more op-eds, this time upset that the city council had approved the placement of Christian crosses on city vehicle stickers. It was his view that the city should discontinue services to churches and parochial schools unless they were fairly taxed. He went on to contend that "…the cross is a Christian symbol and not of all religions, and therefore it is discriminatory."[9] He continued, "This is the first step toward fascism in allowing a city or government to establish or support a religion."[10]

Later that year, he attended a city council meeting to oppose a 3% utility tax increase and suggested people should pay their bills "by check and under protest."[11] The following year, he ran for mayor of Rolling Hills on a platform calling for the explicit separation of church and state.[12] He didn't become mayor, so he made himself an archbishop instead.

In February 1967, Gordon Cruikshank aligned himself with Reverend Garry DeYoung of the Life Science Center in Cass Lake, Minnesota, to continue his opposition to the placement of Christian symbols on Rolling Hills' civic seal. Cruikshank announced he was now a minister, and the Life Science Church would operate out of his home on Cardinal Drive.[13]

In May, Cruikshank was facing jail because he refused to get the city license sticker with the Christian cross on it. His stance apparently attracted national attention, since an op-ed written in from Laguna Hills,

California, described Cruikshank as "patriotically standing up for the Constitution."[14]

It must have been around this time that Cruikshank required the services of a lawyer, and somehow, he found William Drexler. The first mention I can find of Drexler is from St. Paul, Minnesota in 1965 when he and a fellow attorney, Jerome Daly, were sentenced to six months in prison for cashing a forged check and hiding their client's money from his ex-wife.[15] Drexler said Cruikshank made him an archbishop in 1969, and that same year Jerome Daly was publishing *The Daly Eagle*, a tax revolt newsletter that argued The Federal Reserve wasn't allowed to issue paper money[16] and that the only legal tender was gold and silver.[17] Daly would be disbarred by the end of the year,[18] while Drexler was disbarred in 1971 after he was indicted for bribery.[19] The bribery charges were dropped when the witness failed to show up, but he was ultimately disbarred for "tampering with a jury, concealing a client's assets, and perpetrating a fraud on the court."[20]

Cruikshank may have needed Drexler's legal services because the authorities realized he had turned the Life Science Church into a diploma mill. For $25 and a short essay, Cruikshank would make anyone a minister. His motivations, aside from money, seem to have been driven by the same agnostic fury he had for Christian symbolism on government property; in 1972, he said he had applied for state certification to issue degrees, but then realized it wasn't necessary for religious institutions. "There are no state statutes or minimum educational standards for religious schools. … The state won't accept anything but Christianity or whatever the state religion happens to be at the time."[21]

By November, a reporter in Rochester, NY, wrote an expose on Cruikshank and the Life Science Church. In an article titled "Just Call Me 'Reverend'" the reporter described how she became a Doctor of Divinity after filling out a little paperwork and sending in a check. She noted that middle schoolers down the street from her had also become ordained ministers and deacons in the same way.[22]

On the other side of the country, in Riverside, California, a Reverend Sean Longacre was running "God's House," a halfway home for runaway teenagers. The glowing article mentioned that Longacre received his theological training while studying at the Life Science Church Seminary in Rolling Hills.[23] But as we now know, there was no seminary and there was no training. Before the end of the year, Longacre was arrested for bigamy when it was revealed he had married as many as eight girls who he'd brought under his wing while pretending to be a reverend.[24]

By the latter half of 1973, the Illinois attorney general filed a lawsuit against Cruikshank,[25] and nine months later a warrant was issued for his arrest when he fled to California after being held in contempt of court.[26] Where exactly he was at this time, I can't say, but Cruikshank's name appears on the letter-head of The Tax Rebellion Committee, out of Fresno,[27] an organization to which William Drexler also belonged. Both Drexler and the Tax Rebellion Committee's head, James Scott, were being indicted on four separate federal charges of tax evasion.[28] Before the end of the year, Drexler and Daly were disbarred, but their work in the tax protest movement was just beginning.

* * *

Meanwhile, The Tax Rebellion Committee was being investigated by the FBI for its relationship to the rightwing paramilitary terrorist group, Secret Army Organization, as well as to the antisemitic vigilante group, Posse Comitatus, which was headed by William Potter Gale, a Nazi sympathizer who once belonged to the John Birch Society.

Since 1971, William Potter Gale had been promoting the "sovereign citizen movement," which taught a pseudo legal theory "...that an illegitimate, usurper federal government had taken over, and that [sovereign citizens] don't have to pay taxes, pull over their cars for police or obey any other law they don't like."[29] Because Gale also taught that income tax was part of an "international banking conspiracy" used by "Jewish satanists" to exert control over the United States, the very foundation of his tax theories were rooted in antisemitism and White Christian nationalism.

Gordon Cruikshank, who publicly started his tax protests in opposition to the idea of Christian imagery on government property, now found himself in bed with a group that wanted the entire U.S. government based on biblical precepts. While Cruikshank himself died in 1976, the movement he helped create spread across the country and joined forces with various "religious" organizations that inspired lawlessness and violence.

* * *

It was violence, and the threat of violence, that played an important and always present role in the group's messaging. According to James Scott, "We would have to be so organized that when the revolution comes, all the social science professors and government bureaucrats could be rounded up and liquidated with as little killing of the populace as possible."[30] Scott was armed and dangerous, and he was just one of many.

Among the members of the Tax Rebellion Committee was Church E. Murdock, a physician from Mobile, Alabama. By 1973, Murdock was calling himself "Reverend Murdock of the Ministry of Christ's Church," which sounds innocent enough except that the "Ministry" was founded by William Potter Gale to spread a religious doctrine – called Christian Identity – to advocate "white supremacy and violence against non-white races. The movement's ideologies have led it to promote paramilitary and racist activities in the name of fighting Satanism in contemporary life."[31] According to an FBI source who attended this group's meetings at the time, the Ministry of Christ Church was a "cover for an underground army."[32]

That same year, a pizza shop owner in Michigan (who was also a Reverend in Gale's church), armed himself with "shotguns, carbines, and teargas masks" after state officials closed his business for owing thousands of dollars in back taxes. He refused to pay them, he said, because the money wasn't being used "... for Christian people. You know, some of the taxes go to niggers and Jews."[33] When the pizza shop owner and his friends were finally arrested, police received death threats from the Ku Klux Klan.[34]

As the movement grew, it overlapped with different organizations. These relationships were often secretive and intentionally unofficial because, as the FBI reported, "... [they] had to stay in an informal connection with each other so that when the big revolt came, they could all unite; but they should not be too closely united yet or they would be caught and thrown in jail."[35]

During 1974, Posse Comitatus held events in Oregon and Wisconsin with William Drexler and Jerome Daly as honored guests. Drexler and Daly weren't "members," of course, they were just "guests" – plausible deniability. Also in attendance at these events was a Gordon Kahl and Thomas Stockheimer. Kahl, told the crowd he hoped Posse Comitatus could be "like the Klan," joined Patriot Network around the same time Nobles did, and became a right wing folk hero after he murdered two federal marshals.[36] Stockheimer, meanwhile, became a Reverend in the Life Science Church and went on the run after he kidnapped and assaulted an IRS agent in Wisconsin.[37] He was eventually caught hiding on a paramilitary compound in West Virginia. Who was his lawyer? Jerome Daly.[38]

By 1980, Drexler opened the Freedom Foundation in San Diego. Or rather, he asked someone else to open the Freedom Foundation, but he wasn't "officially" connected to it. He just had an office there and all the employees ran their own independent Life Science Churches. And it was just a coincidence that the Freedom Foundation paid for Drexler and Daly to hold tax avoidance seminars like the ones Nobles was arrested for three years later. According to an article written at the time,

"...This is how the church ploy works. First Joe Taxpayer walks into the office and fills out an 'Application to Qualify as a Minister,' a one-page form which asks for one's vital statistics (name, address, marital status), then poses six questions that your average tax dissident isn't very likely to stumble over:

"Do you believe in and adhere to the principles set forth in the Declaration of Independence and the U.S. Constitution?

"Do you believe in the Free Enterprise Capitalistic System as opposed to the Collectivist systems of Socialism and Communism?

"Will you perform the duties of a Minister?

"Keep in touch with the head office of the church?

[and]

"Furnish the head office with a report at least once a year?'"[39]

All Joe Taxpayer had to do after that was pay $1000 to the Freedom Foundation and they were officially ministers or reverends of their own tax-exempt church. *According to Drexler, the New York branch was signing up approximately thirty people per day at $3500 each – over $100,000 daily from one branch alone, or $381,000 daily when adjusted for inflation.* The new religious leaders were given a choice as to what denomination they wanted to be affiliated with. Non-Christians often chose the Life Science Church. But good Christians, like Mike Nobles, could become leaders in their very own Church of Christ.

When the reporter interviewing Drexler in 1980 expressed skepticism at the legality of it all, "Drexler fixed me with those dark, cold pupils and said, "All you have to do is ask yourself why hasn't the IRS from 1973 up to the present time said, 'Bill Drexler, your church is no good. You got airplanes. You got automobiles. You got big checking accounts, bank accounts in Switzerland. You got all these things swinging for you. We're going to say no to you.' If they are on any good ground at all, why haven't they come after me?' Good question. 'They know I'm right,' he answers himself. 'Hey, we're in fat city.'"[40]

On November 26, 1981, William Drexler, his son, and four others were convicted in federal court of conspiracy to defraud the government. "The six persons were accused in connection with an alleged scheme in which persons operating under the name of 'Life Science Church' and the 'Church of Christ' for about the last five years sold about 3,000 packets throughout the United States which included documents showing the purchasers were 'ministers,' allegedly helping them to illegally avoid paying taxes."[41]

* * *

But while Drexler may have finally faced justice, the structure of his scam continued unabated. It had grown too big. It was too easy, too profitable. It was cloaked in religion and wrapped in the flag, and easy marks eagerly handed over their money to new conmen who happily exploited their faith, patriotism, prejudice, and greed. Because in addition to the tax-avoidance-paramilitary-antisemitic-racist-Nazi angle to the whole thing, it also functioned like a pyramid scheme: "... a Life Science Church Minister could become a millionaire in one year by recruiting new Ministers, who in turn would recruit new Ministers thereby receiving commissions on all recruitments at an ever-increasing level." Everyone involved got their hands dirty.

In the midst of all this, the Patriot Network formed under the leadership of Robert Clarkson, a onetime secretary of the South Carolina Libertarian Party who worked as an attorney until he was accused by the federal government of filing false tax returns for his clients.[42] His law career came to an end in 1978 when he pleaded guilty to the charges and got disbarred.[43] Three years later, Clarkson was leading tax seminars on Constitutional law in front of Patriot Network members from all fifty states.[44]

There were at least 104 groups like Patriot Network operating around the country in 1981 alone. Using names like "We the People," "Committee of Correspondence," and "Constitutional Rights and Protection Association," Clarkson and others inspired thousands of people like Mike Nobles to not file their taxes, and to tell others to do the same. A judge that year called the groups, "nothing but unadulterated snake oil."[45]

Another judge added, "Self-proclaimed constitutional lawyers hold seminars across the country, while their only real goal is to help people falsify tax returns and line their own pockets. Such scams make a mockery of the vast majority of honest, tax-paying Americans who must bear the added tax burden."[46]

By 1983, Clarkson was facing jail time for his scams. Legal trouble followed him for the remainder of his life. He would become the head of the neo-confederate Southern Rights Association, later marched with Klan leader David Duke in South Carolina in support of the Confederate flag,[47] and his sidekick was the prominent white supremacist, Nelson Waller.[48] Waller was a member of two hate groups, Council of Conservative Citizens and League of the South. *In 2008, while facing domestic violence allegations in court, Clarkson blurted out that he had gotten his wife hooked on cocaine and methamphetamine and blamed her for selling his possessions on Ebay to feed the addiction he created*.[49] Today, the Patriot Network website reminds visitors: "Disclaimer: Robert B. Clarkson is not a lawyer. He is not licensed to practice law in South Carolina or in any other state or jurisdiction."[50]

While Clarkson faced jail, Timothy Yarbrough, Tony DeMurray (the son of a Freemason and Shriner), and Mike Nobles joined Clarkson's Patriot Network and began holding snake oil tax seminars at the Western Sizzlin' in Scottsboro, Alabama. Steakhouses and barbecue joints appear to have been the preferred locations for promoting and learning misinformation about the Constitution. Yarbrough told a newspaper, "More Americans are studying the Constitution and getting fed up with the fact that the IRS is confiscating about 70% of what everyone makes."[51]

(The rate he's referring to was for households making, when adjusted for inflation, over $700,000 in 1981. The actual rate for farmers and other people attending these seminars was probably closer to 14-28%.[52])

* * *

That same month, just two states over, U.S. Marshals tracked down Patriot Network and Posse Comitatus member Gordon Kahl to a rural Arkansas farmhouse where he was being hidden by sympathizers after murdering two marshals in North Dakota. Kahl shot a county sheriff, Harold Mathews, through the heart at the farmhouse, just as Mathews squeezed off a shot at Kahl's head, killing him instantly. Mathews crawled back to his cruiser and gasped, "I got him." He died of his injury later that night at the hospital.

A week after the shootout, the *Birmingham Post-Herald* published an exposé on the Posse Comitatus and its shadowy presence in Alabama, noting that little was known in the state about membership in the Posse Comitatus. Police said they were unaware of any Posse activity, but locals recalled "a Mobile physician who passed out handbills to recruit members." I assume this was "Reverend" Church Murdock, who spent a year in prison for tax evasion. The article continued to remark on the irony that Posse Comitatus, which recognized county sheriffs as the only legitimate law enforcement officials in the country, had just killed a county sheriff for attempting to enforce the law.[53]

Rather than dissuading people from joining Posse Comitatus, Kahl's death caused a surge in membership. In a newspaper interview, Yarbrough suggested the incident was intended to make them look bad, and others suggested that like-minded patriots "arm themselves, not with pistols, but with bigger guns, in preparation for the coming battle."[54] The leader of the group at that time was James Wickstrom – or "Reverend James Wickstrom of the Life Science Church." The Posse compound in Wisconsin, where Wickstrom lived in one of 26 trailer homes, had been officially declared a church.[55]

* * *

Again, this was the exact same time period when Mike Nobles joined the Patriot Front. Back when he used to brag about his activities with them, he told me how members of Posse Comitatus showed him counterfeiting plates used to make fake currency with which they'd purchase weapons. I knew nothing about it at the time, but in 1988, James Wickstrom went on trial for, among other things, "... [providing] the blank paper for the manufacturing of ... counterfeit currency. The bogus bills were to have been exchanged for foreign currency through an intermediary, an Irish national, and the foreign money was then to have been exchanged for American money on the legitimate exchange market."[56]

That fall, the Patriot Network declared President Reagan "too mainstream," the John Birch Society "too wishy-washy," and income tax to be a "Marxist infringement on personal freedom."[57] On October 22, 1983, Patriot Network member Charles Harris, an unemployed alcoholic upset because of a late tax return, crashed his truck through a fence at a golf course in Augusta, Georgia while Reagan and his cabinet were playing a round there. Harris took seven people hostage at gunpoint, including two White House aides. Harris gave up after two hours of convincing by his mother. He ultimately received ten years in prison, while other members of the Patriot Network's Augusta branch – where a sign on the door read "If you've come to harass us ... no trespassing. Survivors will be prosecuted," – were prosecuted for tax evasion and sentenced to prison as well.[58]

Meanwhile, with Yarbrough acting as regional director, and Nobles and DeMurray acting as directors of the Scottsboro and Huntsville chapters, the Alabama branch of the Patriot Network continued holding meetings at local steakhouses. Though they were billed as "tax seminars," according to court transcripts:

> There was a standard agenda for Patriot Network meetings and Nobles learned by observing Yarbrough, DeMurray and other group leaders. Meetings began with "a very patriotic activity" which was designed to generate popular interest in the Patriot Network. Constitutional history and principles were discussed, and then the discussion turned to the Sixteenth Amendment and income taxes. The

Patriot Network's basic "theory" was that wages are not taxable income. The final portion of a Patriot Network meeting was designed to show people what the Patriot Network could do for its members; specifically, to show them how to stop paying taxes and having taxes withheld, and how to get refunds of taxes paid and withheld in prior years. It was "standard procedure" at Patriot Network meetings to demonstrate how to file exempt withholding certificates (Forms W-4) with one's employer, and to advise filing amended returns (Forms 1040X) to claim refunds for prior years.[59]

Additional transcripts I located from the Federal Archives in Atlanta describe how Patriot Network leaders insisted at these meetings that all payments and dues be paid in cash only. Nobles testified that this was in service of the Patriot Network's real goal: to overthrow the government. (An interesting goal considering DeMurray was employed as an engineer at NASA in Huntsville and worked on the Space Shuttle program.) And, of course, the main goal was to line their own pockets.

Q: And did [Yarbrough] say why he preferred cash?

A: Members were encouraged to get out of the banking system. So this was a step towards doing that. By not using checks, you would be getting out of the banking more feasibly.

Q: Why were members encouraged to get out of the banking system?

A: To prevent any records from being kept on financial transactions.

Q: Why would they not want records to be kept?

A: You couldn't be traced.

So where was the money going? Much of it was pocketed by the Patriot Network leaders, but money also flowed up – like a pyramid scheme – to the national group and the informal umbrella organization that was controlling them. In April 1985, several neo-Nazis in Alabama were arrested after they were found distributing documents calling for a white revolution to overthrow the U.S. government.

With titles like "Principles of War and Rules of Engagement," the documents praised Gordon Kahl as a "stout Aryan yeoman who loved his family. Government agents shot him in the back."[60] (He was shot in the head by a county sheriff trying to arrest him for murder.) The documents went on to describe the behavior expected of Aryan warriors: "Any traitor in our midst who betrays us will be hunted down like a dog and have their head removed from their body.... When the day comes, we will not ask whether you swung to the right or swung to the left; we will simply swing you by the neck."[61] In other words, traitors would be lynched.

As it turned out, these documents were being printed and distributed by The Order, an umbrella organization for "anti-tax groups" like Patriot Network and Posse Comitatus, as well as the KKK, and the American Nazi Party,[62] The Aryan Nation, The Right Arm of God, and The Christian Patriots.[63] Apparently scamming people out of money with tax scams and fake church documents wasn't cutting it, because in April of 1985 The Order was found responsible for "two murders, armored car robberies, and counterfeiting schemes to advance their right-wing revolution."

The 93-page indictment also accused The Order of being responsible for bombing an adult theater and a Jewish synagogue. Murder victims included a Jewish, liberal radio host from Denver, and a member of their own "Aryan Nations Church of Idaho" who disappeared under mysterious circumstances. Arrests took place in twelve states, stretching from Washington to Georgia, and FBI agents "…seized an arsenal of weapons … and a small part of the money believed stolen in a number of robberies – including a $3.6M armored car heist July 19 in Ukiah, California and a $500,000 armored car robbery last April [1984] in Seattle."[64]

Officials at the time found a common thread running through all these groups: "…evangelical interpretation of the Constitution, a moral mandate from a Christian god; [and] an adversarial relationship with establishment authority, whose members are viewed as pawns in a larger conspiracy. Some of these groups are considered zealously antisemitic. Others are thought to be dangerously paramilitary. All of them are set on society's fringe."[65]

Meanwhile, amid all this madness, I made a disturbing discovery, closer to home in none other than Niceville Florida. Like so many other hate groups, the World Church of the Creator (COTC), a neo nazi group, was founded by a former member of the John Birch Society and former Florida Congressman, Bernard Klassen. Klassen, a George Wallace supporter, also founded the Nationalist White Party. Klassen referred to black people as "niggers" and promoted a Racial Holy War (RaHoWa). Klassen, who also wrote "The White Man's Bible" formed a compound and boys' school in Otto North Carolina. In 1992, a COTC minister, George Loeb, murdered a black Gulf War veteran in Florida. The Southern Poverty Law Center filed and won a lawsuit seeking $1 million in damages against the CTOC. Klassen panicked, anticipating this lawsuit, and sold his compound in North Carolina to White Supremacist Willam Luther Pierce.

Pierce, another John Birch Society member and George Wallace support-er. Pierce was the founder of the National Alliance, a white supremacist group responsible for bombing plots, racially motivated murders, and bank robberies. His book, the Turner Diaries, inspired Timothy McVeigh and the Oklahoma City bombing. The book was found in McVeigh's car days after the attack. The book also inspired the formation of The Order. Two bombing sprees by members of the CTOC were averted in Califor-nia, including a plot to bomb a black church and assassinate Rodney King, which makes the following particularly disturbing.

Shortly before committing suicide in 1993, Klassen handed over the reins of the COTC to Rick McCarty who moved the headquarters to none other than Niceville Florida. McCarty, like Nobles, was the son of an Army veteran. He attended school in Niceville then moved to Birming-ham Alabama. After reading about all of this and seeing the link between this group and the John Birch Society, I decided to do some research. I discovered that McCarty registered the neo nazi organization at 1030 Al-derwood way in Niceville, just 2 miles from Nobles' house. I looked up the property records and discovered the owner of that property, built near the same time as Nobles' home, was a man named Steven Dayle Whitney. Further digging revealed he was active-duty Air Force at the time. If this wasn't disturbing enough, it turns out that Whitney, a native of Missis-sippi and the son of an Assembly of God pastor, has a degree in chemical engineering and was doing research on RDX (TNT) at Eglin AFB. Now he was linked to a neo nazi group that planned bombings. A recent look at Whitney's Facebook page reveals that he is a religious zealot, anti-im-migrant, a gun fanatic, and supports protecting Confederate statues. Yet another link to white supremacy, terrorism, the military, and particularly Eglin AFB as well as Niceville Florida, a City of Lies and center of hate.

* * *

That August, state and federal authorities discovered two bodies bur-ied on a Posse Comitatus survivalist compound outside Rulo, Nebraska.[66] The owner of the farm, Rick Stice, had traveled to meet with Posse Co-mitatus leader James Wickstrom in 1983 after his wife died of Hodgkins disease. Stice was struggling to keep his farm afloat, and when a Posse member, Michael Ryan, told him that "...he communicated directly with God ... the Jews were to blame for their financial problems ... and An-glo Saxons, white people like themselves, were to rule the world..." Stice believed him. He gave his family farm to Ryan, and Ryan transformed the property into a paramilitary training ground in preparation for the Battle of Armageddon.

Ryan also married multiple women living on the property, including Posse member James Haverkamp's mother and two sisters. Haverkamp was arrested in June when he was found transporting a stolen "sprayer rig" to the compound. Authorities raided the property and located "...40 rifles, 150,000 rounds of ammunition, and $125,000 in stolen goods." And then they found the bodies.

Rick Stice, once considered a "five-star general" in Ryan's make believe army, had fallen out of favor with Ryan and was sentenced to live in a trailer with his five-year old son, Luke Stice, and another man, James Thimm. Ryan declared they were "his slaves" and forced them at gunpoint to pound their heads against a wall as punishment. On March 10, Rick Stice fled the farm left to him by his father. As for his own son, Rick left Luke behind.

Thimm was chained to a post in the trailer, whipped, sexually abused, and sodomized with a shovel handle by Ryan, Haverkamp, and three other men. They forced him to have sex with a goat and shot off his fingers one by one. He died before they could skin him alive.

Five-year old Luke was beaten, pistol whipped and shot in the arm with a .25-caliber pistol. Ryan used Luke's mouth as an ashtray and forced him to stand in the snow in nothing but his underwear. During one of Ryan's beatings, Luke's head hit a filing cabinet. Luke died convulsing on the floor.

James Thimm and Luke Stice were found in unmarked graves. Ryan was sentenced to the electric chair. Other members were given life sentences. Rick Stice, who gave his farm to the man who abused and murdered his son, was charged with "interstate transportation of stolen cattle."[67]

These were the people and groups that Mike Nobles was working with and sending money to for several years – at minimum. So, when he told the courts in 2008 that he was just "a tax protester," his response covers up his role as the local director of a group with national and international ties to organized crime, robberies, torture, and murder. And his own connections extended out of Alabama, down to Florida, and into the Caribbean.

In 1985, a year before Nobles was caught, newspapers reported that the "tax shelter industry" had become a "billion dollar disappearing act," with several of the schemes connected to the Patriot Network.[68] One of the crimes Nobles was charged with was "aiding and abetting."

Q: What'd you do?

A: Well they say I gave a piece of paper out to allow someone to file for a return of money, and that was the aiding and abetting. I was aiding and abetting them in trying to get money back; the government felt they didn't have a right to get back.

Q: When was this?

A: 1985. And I don't remember no dates.

Q: Who did you give this piece of paper so that they could get a return of money that the IRS did not approve of?

A: I think Snyder was his last name, I'm not even positive about that, but I have no idea recalling what his first name was.

Q: It was a stranger?

A: Oh, no, no. It was someone that was in the tax protest group with me. It's just been a lot of years ago.

I believe the person Nobles is referencing here was Kenneth Snyder, a construction consultant who worked on condo developments in Miami and other areas of Florida throughout the '70s and early '80s.[69] (According to reports, Patriot Network members were specifically encouraged to target workers in the construction industry for recruitment.[70]) In addition to his work in construction, Snyder was an associate of the Florida Chapter of the American Patriots Association, a Texas-based survivalist group that called tax-payers "sheeple,"[71] and instructed its members to stockpile weapons.[72] (Other sources argued that the APA was just a front for the Patriot Network.[73])

And Snyder was also, of course, minister of the Basic Bible Church,[74] another tax-scam spinoff created by Jerome Daly that let anyone become a minister for the low price of $750.[75] From the pulpit in his own house, Snyder taught "how Christian doctrine applies to the Florida Patriots' philosophy on federal income tax."[76] Snyder, authorities said, was a leader in the movement, not "just some guy who got sucked into this. These people are out pulling other people in (to the tax protest movement).... He's a major tax evader."[77]

* * *

During the period that Mike Nobles was "aiding and abetting" construction consultant Snyder, Nobles' Florida attorney and Church of Christ leader, Michael Osman, was incorporating the multiple shell corporations with "terrible" names that Nobles and Osman's siblings used to franchise a chain of Subway restaurants. Knight Templar names. The only public information I can find related to what these corporations were possibly for is ... property development and construction.[78] This makes sense, because a January 27, 1985, *Miami Herald* article describes Osman as "one of Hialeah's busiest zoning lawyers."[79]

Osman's biggest client during this period was Silvio Cardoso, a former University of Miami running back who turned to real estate when his football career didn't take off. At the time Osman was working for him, Cardoso was, "next to Mayor Raul Martinez, Hialeah's most powerful politician,"[80] and sat on the city's zoning board (with Mayor Martinez) voting to approve the very projects that Osman was developing. Both Osman and Cardoso denied there was any conflict of interest, but the entire point of the article was to expose the kickbacks and bribery taking place between politicians and real estate developers in Florida. "The amount of corruption is awesome," said City Councilman Paulino Nunez. "There's a tremendous cover-up going on. It's bad. It's real bad."[81]

Silvio Cardoso made his transition from football to real estate with help from Vincent Leal, a land speculator who had been "arrested but never convicted of numerous offenses ranging from alleged drug dealing to shooting his ex-wife's husband;"[82] Osman sold a house in Hialeah to Leal in 1982.[83] Cardoso's friend and business partner was Anthony Mijares Jr., a Miami businessman with extensive ties to real estate dealings.[84] Together, Cardoso and Mijares would own "about a dozen" or more corporations together over the ensuing decades.[85]

In 1979, Mijares was indicted alongside four other men for stealing "thousands of shares of Westinghouse Electric Stocks at Chicago O'Hare Airport"[86] worth over $4,000,000.[87] His partners in this scheme were:

- Arnold F. Seltzer, ex-president of the North Miami Junior Chamber of Commerce,[88] and Vice President of the Miami Savings and Loan Association.[89]

- Tito Carinci, a former football star and underworld figure from Kentucky who, in 1961, had once been tried for drugging and framing a sheriff's candidate to "control" the candidate's efforts at cleaning up organized crime.[90] He was later charged for racketeering while working for Florida Senator Dick Fincher,[91] and charged another time for credit card fraud. At the time he was indicted for stock theft, Carinci fled his home in Miami to the Bahamas when it was revealed he was also trafficking "the largest heroin shipment to reach the country since The French Connection."[92]

- Alva Johnson Rodgers, a lifetime criminal with burglary,[93] car theft,[94] and armed bank robbery[95] charges going back decades. Authorities caught him in Santa Monica after the 1960 bank robbery, and he spent 11 years in prison.[96] That's the last he was heard of publicly until he popped up working with Mijares in 1979.

- And lastly, Marshal "Shoes" Caifano, another underworld figure with a decades long rap sheet dating back to 1929, was charged for counterfeit stocks, extortion, interstate fraud, and "several murder investigations." Investigators described Caifano as "upper middle management" under mob boss Sam Giancana in The Chicago Outfit,[97] a violent mafia group that was allied with the Gambino crime family. (Giancana himself had been murdered in 1975 shortly before he was scheduled to testify in front of the Church Committee about his alleged role in the Kennedy assassination with Tampa kingpin, Santo Trafficante.) It turned out Caifano, who once told an associate, "All I know how to do is kill, and I do it well,"[98] had been working with Alva Rodgers and other Chicago mafioso, Anthony Accardo and Joey "The Clown" Lombardo[99] to distribute pornography for the mob since 1974.[100]

(Coincidentally, Accardo had other Florida connections were helping him with both pornography and cocaine trafficking. The first was Arthur Randall Sanders, who was found distributing the hardcore porno, David's Boys, through underground channels using shell corporations.[101] The second was Daniel Forgione, father of Joey Forgione, the police officer who helped bury my reports about child abuse, as well as, weapons possession and murder. Ironically, Daniel Forgione was suspected of shooting at police in 1978, but while his car could be traced to the scene, witnesses couldn't put him there personally.[102] Forgione's name came up during wiretap surveillance when the federal government was investigating a $2,000,000 kickback scheme involving labor unions and drug dealing. That investigation led to the indictments of both Santo Trafficante and Anthony Accardo,[103] but Forgione was still under investigation when he was shot to death while sitting behind the wheel of his 1984 Cadillac in the parking lot of The Shrimp Boat, a restaurant and lounge in Margate, Florida.[104] Forgione's murder was later ascribed to his activities with other mob associates who were kidnapping, torturing, and murdering each other in connection with drug money being laundered by a corrupt lawyer through a chain of Atlanta restaurants. Specifically, Forgione performed a hit on Ku Klux Klan member and drug dealer on behalf of his partner in organized crime, Carl Louis Coppola. After a dispute over payment for the murder, Coppola had Forgione killed. During Coppola's prosecution he plotted to murder the prosecutor. It's notable that this was an example of an alliance between the Klan and the mob, just as I believe was going on in Niceville Florida.[105/106])

Caifano, Carinci, and Rodgers were both sentenced to prison for their role in the stock scheme.[107] Arnold F. Seltzer received a $10,000 fine and five years' probation. While Anthony Mijares was convicted,[108] it's unclear what his exact sentence was, but he was back doing business in Florida with Silvio Cardoso not long after.

* * *

In 1986, Mijares was an executive at a company called Swissco, which was owned by the Chilean born "millionaire entrepreneur-turned-capitalist" Carlos Cardoen. Cardoen earned his fortune through weapons manufacturing, including a very profitable plant that created 24,000 cluster bombs, which he built in Baghdad for Saddam Hussein. The company who provided them was Teledyne, a Defense contractor with contracts with the DOD and NASA.[109] It was founded and run by Henry Singleton, a former OSS agent.

Documents turned over in a sworn affidavit by former National Security Council member, Howard Teicher, "gave a detailed description of how President Reagan and former CIA director William Casey carried out a policy during the '80s to ensure that Iraq was equipped to win the war against Iran."[110] Sources told the news program, *Nightline*, that in 1986, CIA deputy director Robert Gates, "had personally supervised a shipment of materials from the United States to Industrias Cardoen in Chile to make cluster bombs for Iraq."[111] Teicher's declaration in the United States District Court Southern District of Florida clearly states, "Under CIA Director Casey and Deputy Director Gates, the CIA authorized, approved, and assisted Cardoen in the Manufacture and sale of cluster bombs and other munitions to Iraq."[112]

Cardoen was known as Augusto Pinochet's favorite arms dealer. Pinochet was a brutal right-wing dictator and ally of the CIA. He was responsible for the murders and imprisonments of tens of thousands including the murder of 60,000 during the CIA-approved Operation Condor. And according to a 2002 expose on Cardoen: "Court records show that the money Iraq was paying Cardoen for cluster bombs was passing through Geneva, Switzerland, and ending up in several accounts in Miami, Fla. There, a Cardoen-owned company called Swissco would invest the money in Florida real estate. At the time, Cardoen and his Swissco associates were friendly with at least one prominent southern Floridian. In August 1986, Cardoen helped organize a fund-raiser for U.S. Sen. Robert Graham, a Democrat from Florida, at the Miami home of Swissco executive Anthony Mijares.

The event raised about $50,000 for Graham's 1986 campaign and got Cardoen added to the Friends of Bob Graham, a group of top supporters."[113]

(It should be noted again that Graham was the father-in-law of Captain Steve Hurm, the Okaloosa County Sheriff's Department attorney who I believe blocked me from filing law enforcement reports and personally obstructed justice by fabricating evidence in Mike Nobles' firearms case.)

Graham's house was located in Miami Lakes, a development he personally built in 1961 on "five square miles of pastureland" once owned by his father. Along with his brother, Philip Graham, owner of the *Washington Post* and *Newsweek*, they created Sengra Corp. to oversee the site's construction. Coincidentally, the Swissco offices were located in Miami Lakes, at 15485 Eagle Nest Lane, Suite 200.[114] Osman's office was down the street at 6447 Miami Lakes Drive East, Suite 212.[115] Mijares' home address, at 15300 Turnbull Drive, was listed during the 1979 stock swindling scandal – all within the same development built by Graham, all within blocks of each other. As far as I can tell, Osman has a home there, too.

A December 1, 1985, article titled "You Can't Hide From Drug Dealers" noted, "Every neighborhood, it seems, has its resident drug smuggler. Governor Bob Graham's home in Miami Lakes is ringed by the former residences of several drug dealers. Cocaine dealer John Ruffino lived five houses away from Graham's place on Aberdeen Way in a $475,000 house once owned by Graham's mother."[116] On December 28, 1980, less than a year after he was indicted for the stock theft, Anthony Mijares purchased a $475,000 house in Miami Lakes from a Mr. and Mrs. John Ruffino.[117] And in January 1986, Carlos Cardoen bought his own home in Miami Lakes for $575,000 directly from Bob Graham.[118]

* * *

In March 1988, an officer at Swissco, Augusto Giangrandi, sold a warehouse in Hialeah located at 335 W 74th street to a company called Caidoz Inc.[119] Caidoz had only been formed that year, and was owned by Anthony Mijares.[120] Its mailing address was the exact same as Swissco's in Miami Lakes, down to the suite number. A month later, the entire Miami Lakes Corporate Center was sold for $8,750,000; the sellers were Anthony Mijares and Augusto Giangrandi.[121]

Augusto Giangrandi, meanwhile, would be revealed in 2004 as "a Chilean arms dealer currently the subject of half a dozen US and international investigations" for his role in an oil-for-food scandal in which he acquired "cheap Iraq oil in violation of UN rules" with help from a Dallas-based oil company. The owner of that company, "David Chalmers ... was served with a subpoena [in 1993] by the US district court of the southern district of Florida to testify about his role in the sale of cluster bombs to Iraq by Mr. Giangrandi and an associate. That trial ended before he had to give evidence."[122] (The alleged recipient of the illegal oil was Vladimir Zhirinovsky, a Russian right-wing extremist and white supremacist known as the "Donald Trump of Russia." The intent was to bribe the Russians into dropping sanctions against Iraq, and according to a 2005 report released by the investigations subcommittee for the U.S. Senate Homeland Security and Governmental Affairs, "Zhirinovsky received Iraqi oil allocations worth $8.7 million under the oil-for-food program.")

All of this is to say that Michael Osman's client, Silvio Cardoso, was involved with some exceptionally shady people at the exact same time that his other client, Mike Nobles, was involved with some exceptionally shady people. That's not unexpected. I understand that lawyers are obligated to defend criminals. But Osman was helping Cardoso just as I believe he was helping Nobles, and in both stories, there can be seen repeated instances of corrupt land deals, money laundering, corruption, and coverups.

You see, in 1987, Cardoso declared he wouldn't seek a third term on Hialeah's city council.[123] One of his closest associates over the years had been Sergeant Leo Thalassites, president of Hialeah's Fraternal Order of Police. "He is the finest individual I know," said Cardoso.[124] But an undercover investigation by the FBI discovered that Thalassites was taking orders from a man named Alberto San Pedro, a real estate developer whose projects were approved by the zoning board that Cardoso sat on.[125] An account on San Pedro says, "[His] father was a delegate to the 1984 Republican National Convention, and Alberto San Pedro was cleared for an audience with Ronald Reagan in Tampa in 1985. The son told all inquisitors that in addition to his activities as a developer, he was also a bookkeeper and salesman for his father's business, the San Lazaro Racing Stables at Calder Racetrack."[126]

San Pedro built a six bedroom, eight and a half baths, mansion with bulletproof windows in Hialeah. It was in his office at this mansion that the FBI recorded meetings between Alberto San Pedro, Sergeant Leo Thalassites, Hialeah Police Chief Cecil "Whitey" Seay, and Silvio Cardoso. Other recordings captured San Pedro meeting with Joseph Paterno, a known *capo* in the Gambino crime family.

...These tapes, the police say, show that Alberto San Pedro was a major corrupter, a fixer, the classic cacique who works behind the scenes to secure power and wealth and enforces his presumed right to both with fear and violence. Among the institutions he is accused of corrupting is the Hialeah police department. It was a task he had trained for all of his life.

Since the early '70s, San Pedro had been arrested for stabbings, armed robbery, and intent to commit murder. Thalassites was San Pedro's karate instructor and, according to reports, acted as his "bag man," telling one officer, "You know, a bag man. I collect money for San Pedro and if people don't pay, I beat them up and make sure they pay, and I make sure the people do what San Pedro wants them to do."[127]

One of the tasks San Pedro wanted police to do was erase records of his criminal history: "San Pedro's file had disappeared three times from [Hialeah's] police department. A narcotics intelligence file on San Pedro also disappeared. And his records were missing from the Dade Circuit Court clerk's office and the State Attorney's office. San Pedro was clearly attempting to create a new personal history through elimination."[128] (Just as I have experienced, the police department wasn't above misplacing or altering public records for their friends.) When these allegations were brought to the mayor's office, Raul Martinez said he stood by Seay and Thalassites.[129]

* * *

When asked about his relationship with San Pedro, Cardoso told a reporter, "We used to fight together in junior high school and shit, so we've been together for a long time, and before then, before I was councilman before any of that shit."[130] San Pedro kept in close contact with another high school friend, Ricky Prado, who he met after their families "had fled Cuba following the revolution. Prado would later join the Air Force, though he never saw service in Vietnam, and returned to Miami to work as a firefighter. But he kept moonlighting as a hitman for San Pedro, who had emerged into one of Miami's most formidable cocaine traffickers."[131]

San Pedro was tied to the Medellin cartel through cocaine cowboy, Jon Roberts.[132] Roberts started as a Gambino crime family soldier, joined the Army, committed war crimes in Vietnam murdering women and children and skinning victims alive, then began trafficking cocaine with San Pedro and the brutal Panamanian dictator, Manuel Noriega. He later turned government informant after making over $100 million.

Prado attempted to join the CIA but was initially rejected when he couldn't pass a background check. However, he was later "admitted after the Reagan administration opened up a covert offensive against leftist Central American militants, where he reportedly served training the Contras." While he was employed by the CIA, Prado continued his job as a hitman for San Pedro, allegedly killing another cocaine distributor in Colorado with a car bomb and the stepson of mobster Meyer Lansky in Miami.[133]

By 1996, Prado "was a senior manager in the CIA's Bin Laden Issue Station," and went on to "build up a network of foreign shell companies" for Blackwater, the mercenary contractor owned by Erik Prince, brother of Trump's Secretary of Education, Betsy DeVos. According to author Evan Wright in *How to Get Away With Murder in America*, this "marked the first time the U.S. government outsourced a covert assassination service to private enterprise," and in 2008 the unit began "whacking people like crazy."[134]

Today, Alberto San Pedro is nicknamed "The Great Corruptor" and is remembered as among the top ten cocaine traffickers of the 1980's. The investigation into his activities caused both Cardoso and Mayor Martinez to resign amidst allegations about their corrupt behavior. In 1991, Martinez was tried for extorting "almost $1,000,000 in cash and property from developers in exchange for favorable zoning approvals," in connection with three real estate developments that Cardoso owned.

* * *

Osman testified that he helped Cardoso at an undisclosed date in the mid-1980s to bribe local officials as part of this deal, and admitted giving Thomas Chamberlain, a Major in the Hialeah Police Department, $5,000 for bringing customers to Cardoso.[135] Four months after Osman's testimony, it was revealed that Chamberlain's son belonged to The International Posse, a Miami street gang affiliated with Folk Nation, a "union" for gangs originating from Chicago[136] that specialized in "drug trafficking, homicide, theft, burglary, and extortion."[137] On June 19, Sean Thomas Chamberlain gunned down Justin Cortes, an 18-year old junior from Hialeah High School, when Cortes stopped at a red light. Cortes, also a member of Folk Nation, had threatened to leave the gang.[138]

Osman also testified that he "personally oversaw" a 1984 transaction in which Cardoso had "gifted" $45,000 worth of property to Martinez.[139] Among the 50 people who wrote letters of support for Cardoso during this time were: Anthony Mijares, Thomas Chamberlain, and Arnold F. Seltzer.[140]

Cardoso, who acted as a city councilman from 1979 to 1988, had already pleaded guilty in another case, "but agreed to cooperate with the government in return for a reduced sentence." No article I can find says this, but I interviewed the former federal prosecutor on the case, Bruce Udolf (later picked to investigate Bill and Hillary Clinton during the Whitewater investigation[141]), who verbally confirmed to me that Osman also made a deal and testified for the government.

There's at least some evidence to back this up, because both Cardoso and Osman's testimony was included in a 1988 document titled *Materials Relating to Wiretap Disclosure: Hearings Before the Subcommittee on Criminal Justice of the Committee of the Judiciary House of Representatives* that examined "bribery, payoffs, illegal zoning variances, and activities of political corruption in the city of Hialeah." Within a few years, Cardoso was again working with Anthony Mijares, and today they head the United Homes Group, which reported over $100,000,000 in sales for the first quarter of 2024.[142] Martinez was convicted in 1991 on six counts of conspiracy, extortion and racketeering. He was sentenced to 10 years in prison. After an appeal and a new trial, he was acquitted. The Clinton Justice Department then went after the prosecutor in the case, and he resigned. Martinez ran for congress in 2008, and Hillary Clinton attended a fundraiser at his home.

* * *

Back in 1985, Nobles was still learning the ropes. As regional director of the Patriot Network, Yarbrough "had become overburdened"[143] by the work involved and it was he who invited Nobles into the group to ease the load. Under Yarbrough's leadership, Nobles helped collect $200 initiation fees and annual dues from members. On one occasion, witnesses later testified observing Nobles collecting somewhere between $4,000-6,000 in cash, which he then handed over to Yarbrough at their Saturday morning meetings in DeMurray's apartment.[144]

Court documents state, "Yarbrough and DeMurray represented [to Nobles] that a percentage of fees and dues were converted into silver and held in reserve to fund Patriot Network members' legal defense against criminal tax charges," which mostly corroborates what I heard directly from Nobles himself, except he told me the cash was supposed to be converted into gold bars. Whatever the truth of the matter, this echoes both Jerome Daly's claims in 1969[145] and Yarbrough's claims in 1984 that "gold and silver" are the only real forms of currency.[146] In both versions,

Nobles grew frustrated when Yarbrough and DeMurray "always neatly sidestepped" his requests to see the supposed legal defense fund.[147] This frustration may have been just one of the reasons he eventually became an informant against them.

* * *

Over an 18-month period spanning 1984-85, a Special Agent of the Internal Revenue Service Criminal Investigation Division, James Testasecca, "was involved in the active investigation of ... 'Patriot Network', an illegal tax protester organization operating in Northern Alabama under the leadership of Timothy J. Yarbrough, Tony L. DeMurray, and Michael S. Nobles." [148] As this investigation came to its logical end, a strange timeline of events occurred:

- On October 17, 1985, Androgyny Corporation was incorporated by Michael Osman and his brothers, Craig and Ty. The registered mailing address was 1474-A West 84th Street, Hialeah, Florida – Osman's small law office across the street from the Miami Lakes development where he also had an office.

- On March 24, 1986, Androgynous Corporation was incorporated by Michael Osman, his brother-in-law, Jerry McCormick, and Michael Nobles. The address given, 21 Eglin Parkway SE, Fort Walton Beach, Florida, was the first of many Subway restaurants they would open together over the years.[149]

- On April 23, 1986, Androgyn Corporation was incorporated by Michael Osman, his wife Phyllis, and brother Craig.

- On May 29, 1986: Timothy Yarbrough, Tony DeMurray, and Michael Nobles were indicted in Alabama on seventeen felony counts of "conspiracy to defraud the United States Government and substantive income tax violations arising from their activities as leaders of the Patriot Network."[150]

- On June 5, 1986, Michael Nobles and Tony DeMurray were arrested by U.S. Marshalls. Timothy Yarbrough, however, went on the run.

- On June 12, 1986, Special Agent Testasecca interviewed Yarbrough's wife, Deborah, and advised her that he had a warrant for her husband's arrest. Testasecca "informed her that Yarbrough's arraignment was scheduled for June 13, to which she remarked that she was aware of the arraignment date."[151]

- On June 13, 1986, Nobles and DeMurray were arraigned in Birmingham, Alabama. Yarbrough did not appear for the arraignment.

- On June 16, 1986, Androgynal Corporation of Florida was incorporated by Michael Osman, Ty Osman, Craig Osman, and Michael Nobles.

- On June 18, 1986, Special Agent Testasecca met with Deborah Yarbrough again, and "advised her to tell her husband that he was making matters worse by fleeing from prosecution." That same day, a neighbor informed Testasecca "it was common knowledge that Yarbrough had been in the Bahamas for a couple of months."[152]

After issuing a subpoena to Eastern Airlines, Testasecca learned that on April 16, Tim and Deborah "Yarbrow" had purchased two tickets to Nassau in the Bahamas. Further investigation of phone records revealed that the Yarbroughs' landline in Alabama made 42 calls to the Nassau Life Insurance Company between April and June, and that Yarbrough himself was working there as a "paralegal" under the assumed name, "Robert Morris."

I believe Yarbrough was using the name of one of his heroes, Robert J. Morris. Morris was an anti-communist zealot who served as chief council for the United States Senate Subcommittee on Internal Security. Morris was behind McCarthyism more than McCarthy himself. Neo-Confederate Yarbrough was a member of the Chalcedon Foundation, funded in part by Nelson Bunker Hunt, a peer of Charles Walter Ruckel on the John Birch Society's Executive Council, who owned Nobles property during its construction. Morris was an ally of the John Birch Society's General Edwin Walker, who some researchers like Dr. Jeffrey Caufield, author of *General Walker and the Murder of President Kennedy: The Extensive New Evidence of a Radical-Right Conspiracy*, believe was the man in Dallas behind the curtain in the Kennedy assassination. Walker and his aid Robert Surrey were responsible for the distribution of 5000 "Wanted for Treason" flyers in Dallas, targeting Kennedy the day before his assassination. Morris served as Walker's attorney when he was fired by Kennedy. Author James Lateer believed Morris was a major player in the Kennedy assassination. Yarbrough had apparently been calling himself a paralegal for years, because of his "extensive research" on behalf of the Patriot Network. Yarbrough was not a paralegal.

On July 25, 1986, Special Agent Testasecca asked Michael Nobles – the new co-owner of several "androgynous" corporations with a shady lawyer and an elder in the Church of Christ who were opening Subway franchises across Florida while he simultaneously faced four years in prison and a $210,000 fine for conspiracy and tax evasion – to help capture his friend and fellow patriot, Timothy Yarbrough. Only days later, Nobles started wearing a wire for the federal government.

* * *

Investigations revealed that Nassau Life Insurance was incorporated sometime in the early 80's by Robert Chappell, a land developer from Indiana, and Norman Paul Cowart, an insurance agent from Texas. The first reference I can find for it is on May 16, 1984 in Salisbury, North Carolina: "A Church Freedom Seminar will be held at Cornerstone Christian Ministries ... [by] Paul Davis of Fayetteville, a full-time evangelist and pastor of 20 years. ... He is director of The Freedom League, a tax education service, and education officer for foreign trusts with the Nassau Life Insurance Co."[153] Topics of the seminar included "The Now and Coming Persecution of Churches in America and How to Prepare," "How America is now a Part of the One-World Government Conspiracy," "The Bible, Taxes, and The Constitution," and "Learn How to be Untouchable by Any Government Agency."[154] As it turned out, both Chappell and Cowart had been touched by government agencies many times.

In the mid-1960's, Chappell was president of the Air & Space Manufacturing Co. in Muncie, Indiana, but he resigned after his gyrocopters killed several people. By 1967, he was indicted for defrauding 6,500 investors of $9,000,000 but was acquitted the following year. Between 1975 and 1977, he defrauded 64 farmers of nearly $1,000,000 as part of an oil drilling scheme in Pennsylvania. Chappell ran off with the money to the Bahamas, but was arrested a year later when he was recognized from his "Wanted" poster by a policeman while taking night school classes in Hollywood.[155] During that trial it was discovered that he had once stolen an 8-foot tall Mayan statue from an archeological site in Guatemala.[156] Cowart, meanwhile, was arrested for burglary in 1960 when he was just 18-years old.[157] Over the years he was charged with forgery,[158] insurance fraud,[159] felony theft,[160] perjury,[161] and then another insurance scheme in 1974 that targeted elderly victims.[162]

Both Cowart and Chappell hopped in and out of prison over the decades but managed to form Nassau Life Insurance during one of their windows of freedom. Much like the Patriot Network's tax seminars, "investors were told that by setting up offshore trust companies and naming Nassau Life Insurance Co. as their trustee, they could eliminate income and inheritance taxes, avoid probate, and enjoy tax-free investment for life. It was alleged that Cowart and Chappell sold insurance policies, annuity contracts and securities, and shares in Nassau Life, Caribbean Express Airlines, and an oil-drilling venture in Guyana."[163] Other associated companies included Dunn Management Co., The International Society of Independent Business Administrators, The International Society of Senior Citizens, and the Swiss American Financial Exchange Assurance Co.[164]

Among Nassau Life Insurance's many clients who decided to "Keep [Their] Wealth in the Family,"[165] was Reverend Everett Sileven, of the Louisville Nebraska Faith Baptist Church, which "opened an uncertified school in its basement for 17 students in August 1977. Nebraska law then required even private school teachers to be certified by the state, and a judge issued an injunction to close the school. Maintaining that 'this school represents our right to exercise our religion,' and that 'the state is in violation of God's law,' Sileven, who as a high school student opposed the senior prom because dancing supposedly inspires lustful thoughts, began a long legal battle." According to the Southern Poverty Law Center, it was this conflict that inspired the "ideology and structure of today's unregistered churches movement,"[166] but Gordon Cruikshank had been making the same argument five years earlier when he noted, "There are no state statutes or minimum educational standards for religious schools."[167] Sileven's bold vision to run unregulated schools in church basements made him a martyr in conservative Christian circles.

In February of 1986, Sileven declared he was running for governor of Nebraska. When filing his bid, he stated that as pastor of Faith Baptist Church, "he attested to having no property, income, checking, or savings accounts, stocks, bonds or securities with a value of more than $1,000 and nor has he received gifts of over $100 in value."[168] This, of course, was exactly what William Drexler and Jerome Daly taught people to do to avoid taxes; the movement had spread beyond their own obviously fake churches and into the broader evangelical movement itself.

Newspapers noted at the time that Sileven's tax forms "listed him as a non-exclusive agent for International Leasing Co., Ltd. and the Coalition for Religious Education Co., Ltd., both foreign companies affiliated with Nassau Life Insurance Co., Nassau, Bahamas."[169] Miraculously, International Leasing Co. bought a brand new Buick Park Avenue in June 1985 and, purely out of the kindness of its heart, donated the car that same day to Sileven's Faith Baptist Church.[170] Sileven, who drove the Buick, was flabbergasted that anyone might think this constituted fraud, but the Justice Department argued it was clearly "only done to avoid paying taxes."[171]

Sileven would eventually change his name to Everett Ramsey and run a company called American Financial Services that helped clients launder money through a fake Canadian bank by making non-existent donations to Faith Baptist Ministries.[172] In the midst of the many lawsuits resulting from his criminal behavior, Sileven was ardently defended by Jimmy Swaggart, Jerry Falwell, Tim Lahaye, Orrin Hatch, and other notable Christian figures who argued in letters to President Reagan that Sileven and his employees were "in jail only because of their religious beliefs and we are convinced that you and millions of Americans are deeply grieved at the plight of these God-fearing people."[173] The truth, of course, is that religion and patriotism were being used to mask theft, money laundering, fraud, and a host of other crimes.

Which brings us back to the summer of '86. That August, Nobles strapped on a "concealed recording device" and drove over to Yarbrough's house to meet with Deborah. With the tape recorder secretly running under his shirt, Nobles' feigned concern for his friend's wellbeing, and Deborah informed him that "Tim was fine," and the "government knew where he was but could not touch him." That same day, the Honorable Judge J. Foy Guin inspected written, video, and audio materials related to the case, and instructed the proceedings "SEALED - Do Not Publish."

(On August 29, 1986, Michael Osman incorporated Androken Corporation with his brothers Ty and Craig. Even more companies formed the following year: Androgyny Management Corporation on April 23, 1987, and Androkam, Inc. on July 2.)

* * *

Shortly after the judge reviewed the collected evidence, Nobles' sentencing hearing was scheduled for October 24, 1986. Nobles' conspiracy charges were dropped and he was put on three years' probation for tax evasion; that same day, down in Niceville, Constance Wayne Jones finalized the purchase of land from Ruckel Properties that would eventually become Nobles' home at 1118 Rhonda Drive.[174] (Coincidentally, on the other side of the country that very same day, William Potter Gale and two other associates were arrested in California for threatening to kill multiple IRS agents, judges, and a magistrate judge, whose house they intended to burn down with his family inside.[175])

Over the course of the next year, Chappell, Cowart, and Yarbrough were also arrested one by one. Chappell, identified as "one of Indiana's most notorious con men," was picked up in December of 1986 at Miami International Airport,[176] and was sentenced to five years in a New Mexico prison. Cowart was apprehended in January of 1987 in Texas and was ultimately sentenced to 22 years in prison for his role, with Chappell, in stealing over $1,500,000 from elderly residents in several states.[177] Cowart was free by 2006, when he was again arrested for selling fake securities to the elderly, a third-degree felony for which he received another ten year sentence.[178]

Yarbrough, expelled by authorities in the Bahamas while using the name "Timothy Armbrecht," was subsequently arrested by IRS agents in Miami on May 15, 1987.[179] On July 13, a jury found DeMurray and Yarbough guilty on all counts. DeMurray was sentenced to two years in prison and fined $2,500. Yarbrough got five years and a $10,000 fine.[180] Today, Timothy Yarbrough and his son are ministers of the Trinity Free Presbyterian Church in Alabama,[181] and the head pastor, Reverend Myron Mooney, acts as the chaplain of a group called Sons of Confederate Veterans, "a neo-Confederate nonprofit organization of male descendants of Confederate soldiers that promotes the pseudo-historical Lost Cause ideology and white supremacy."[182]

(His son, Ernie Yarbrough, is an Alabama State Senator.[183] It is worth noting that in this position, Ernie has supported legislation that would impose the death penalty on women who get abortions or even have a miscarriage; supported banning books as well as prosecuting librarians in libraries with books containing LGBTQ content. The Yarbroughs and Trinity maintain a cozy relationship with pastor John Weaver of the League of the South and Council of Conservative Citizens, a vile racist who preaches the praises of slave trader, Freemason, Confederate General, and first Grand Wizard of the KKK, Bedford Forrest, teaches gun classes, and promotes another civil war.)

But after months of legal troubles, Nobles walked away. He bought a house at 1118 Rhonda Drive in Niceville and became the owner of Subway sandwich shops with Jerry McCormick, who was an elder in the Niceville Church of Christ alongside Nobles' father-in-law. *Nobles became a reputable business owner, a church elder and, eventually, my father-in-law.*

That he was embroiled with a money laundering domestic terrorist organization for several years didn't seem to be a problem, and the records clearly show that Michael Osman kept setting up these "androgynous" corporations at the exact same time that Nobles was under investigation. Why? As a resident of Alabama, why was he working with a Miami lawyer to open restaurants in the Panhandle? Franchise rights for a Subway at the time were about $65,000 per store[184] – or roughly $180,000 adjusted for inflation today. Where did Nobles get that kind of money? And why, aside from some familial connections in church, were McCormick and Osman working with him? Is it possible they were working with him not in spite of his connection to a money laundering domestic terrorist group, but because of it? With the hundreds of thousands of dollars and back taxes ignored after he put on a wire, did he have Patriot Network cash that needed cleaning?

* * *

The answer to some of those questions, I think, ties back to Michael Osman, Jerry McCormick, and the Church of Christ. See, Jerry McCormick and Michael Osman grew up together.

When Osman was just four years old, his uncle, Joseph Albert, was shot to death after an enraged husband discovered he was having an affair with the man's wife.[185] Albert, living with the Osmans at the time and working at their family grocery store, had only recently beaten a conviction for brutally murdering a local doctor during a break-in, and subsequently gained notoriety in the newspapers for his ability to repeatedly escape from the Dade County jail.[186] The woman Albert was having an affair with was the first cousin of Fred and Virgil Cash, brothers who once led a gang that terrorized Miami.[187] Osman, of course, was responsible for none of that, but considering his later business associates, it was an auspicious start and perhaps indicates a proximity to Miami's criminal world from an early age.

As children, Michael Osman and Jerry McCormick both attended Miami Springs High School[188] during the week and the Hialeah Church of Christ on Sundays.[189] Osman actually made the papers in 1969 because he never missed a single day of school except for graduation, which "he just couldn't get excited about."[190] In 1973, Osman married Jerry's sister, Phyllis McCormick, in the Hialeah Church of Christ where their father, Daniel McCormick, was an elder.[191]

In the summer of 1979, Osman was hired by the Hialeah Housing Authority but was fired within six months for "giving bad advice." Osman argued that he gave "confident legal advice. The law is an imprecise science."[192] The subtext of the article seems to be that Osman gave them questionable legal advice and they were in a hurry to be rid of him.

But in no time, Osman became a lawyer for his in-laws, the McCormick family. Because the McCormicks were Miami-based property developers, contractors, church goers, and politicians. And they figured out how to use each of those roles to make serious money.

The Hialeah Church of Christ was incorporated on August 25, 1971.[193] While Osman's name and address are on the paperwork now,[194] he almost certainly didn't have anything to do with that original arrangement since he'd only graduated high school two years earlier. (Interestingly, the principal address listed on the paperwork belonged to Andrew Capeletti, a contractor and horse racing enthusiast[195] who sat on the board of directors of Sengra, the company founded by the Graham family to build Miami Lakes.[196]) The incorporation date was only six months before the Church of Christ moved to a newer, bigger location.

Back in 1966, Jerry's father, Daniel McCormick and another church elder, Nile Songer, signed the deed for 9.8 acres of land in Hialeah-Miami Lakes on behalf of the church for $60,000 – or half a million dollars today. Only six years later, they sold that land for $500,000; a good turn of events which caused the local paper to note, "Occasionally parties outside the normal circle of real estate investors enjoy the profits produced from timely action in the markets."[197]

The purchasers of the property were Burl and Gerald McCormick, Daniel's brothers, who took out a loan of $350,000 to do so.[198] Coincidentally, Burl was also an elder in the Hialeah Church of Christ,[199] and I can only assume that Gerald was, too. McCormick Enterprises, as their company was called, built a 288-unit apartment complex on the land and sold it for $4,950,000 in 1974[200] – or approximately $31,500,000 adjusted for inflation today.

At the same time, the Hialeah Church of Christ announced in September of 1972 that they were breaking ground on a new complex of buildings that would include classrooms for a private Christian academy, Atlantic Christian Schools, and an auditorium that could accommodate up to 1250 parishioners.[201] The initial cost of construction was estimated to be $600,000, but by the time the building was finished in 1974, that number had run to over $1,000,000[202] – or, $6,300,000 today. The builder of the project was McCormick Enterprises.[203] Through these financial and business arrangements, The Hialeah Church of Christ, a tax-exempt religious organization, and the McCormicks, were turning a tidy profit.

It didn't hurt that while all this was going on, Burl McCormick had been elected mayor of Hialeah Gardens in 1972. By 1974, the "little known millionaire mayor" quit his job as mayor of Hialeah Gardens to be the running mate on Lt. Governor Tom Adams' campaign for Governor of Florida: "[McCormick] is 33, a land developer, builder, investor and a self-made rich man who likes people and politics."[204] Among his other qualifications, Burl McCormick was director of the Atlantic Christian Academy and sat on the advisory board of Freed-Hardeman College in Tennessee.[205] McCormick told reporters that "as many black students as want to come"[206] could attend the Academy, though a 1972 report noted that "one could usually identify a segregation academy by the word 'Christian' or 'Church' in the name."[207] Freed-Hardeman, a private university associated with the Churches of Christ, accidentally allowed black students to attend beginning in 1964 when, according to the school's president, it "made the mistake of accepting federal funds."[208] In 2016, Freed-Hardeman was allowed an exception to Title IX so that it might discriminate based on sexual or gender identity.[209]

* * *

Tom Adams, a Baptist deacon,[210] was unfortunately defeated after it was revealed he had been censured the previous year for using government employees to handle leasing arrangements for his 1,000-acre farm in Quincy, Florida.[211] After this devastating loss, the "deeply in debt" Adams formed a business partnership with Burl McCormick in land development.[212] In a 1998 interview, Adams admitted borrowing $70,000 from Santo Trafficante to finance his 1962 campaign debts, which he allegedly paid back through state contracts, and said that after losing the Governor's race he "spent the next five years 'getting rich' in the construction industry... [when he] and McCormick created and dissolved a series of corporations in the Miami area."[213]

In 1975, Daniel McCormick, now a construction developer, won a seat on the Hialeah city council with a campaign focused on "a sound economic plan for South Florida."[214] And guess what? Silvio Cardoso and Raul Martinez sat on the board with him.[215]

* * *

In January of 1980, a month before Michael Osman was fired by the Hialeah Housing Authority, Silvio Cardoso and Burl McCormick ended up on opposite sides of the table when each wanted to annex a "5 ½-square-mile tract of mostly undeveloped land in unincorporated Dade County."[216] Cardoso wanted the land for Hialeah, while Burl wanted it for Hialeah Gardens. Burl won his 1981 re-election campaign for mayor, and, in the end, he also won the land battle, nearly tripling the area of Hialeah Gardens. His differences with Cordoso appear to have eventually been put aside, since Osman soon acted as lawyer for both.

And both, it turned out, would need a lawyer who viewed the law as an "imprecise science." That May, Hialeah Gardens police responded to a "general complaint" about activity at 11750 NW 87th Place, a warehouse, and discovered over 200 people placing bets on "two cocks with spurs mutilating each other."[217] A sign in front of the warehouse read, "Another development by Adams-McCormick,"[218] and after officer Edward Mees called the fight in, Burl himself showed up at the scene in no time.[219] Burl later argued that the building was being rented by Perez Construction Co., and he knew nothing about the cock fights.[220]

The leader of the cockfighting ring was Ramon Benitez, a bulldozer operator who worked for Maule Industries,[221] a real estate and construction company owned by Maurice Ferre, the Mayor of Miami.[222] Benitez had been charged with first degree murder in 1975 after he got into a fight with a rival cockfighting promoter.[223] Those charges were dropped, and then in 1981 Benitez provided testimony during a bribery investigation in which he and another business rival accused each other of running their gambling rings with help from different factions within the police force; his rival's cockfighting arena was owned by a Miami Detective.[224]

Burl angrily demanded Mees come to his office the next day; Burl, "a builder with no law enforcement experience,"[225] had recently appointed himself acting Chief of Police when the real one quit – or was forced out[226] – a month earlier.[227] Mees was suspended and then fired almost immediately because, Burl said, Mees had accumulated sixteen citations in his file during the short time he'd worked there and the disciplinary actions against him were unrelated to the cock-fighting ring.[228] But Mees told reporters, "I believe the reason I've been suspended is because I'm getting too close to something I shouldn't be close to,"[229] and the previous police chief said Mees had only one citation in his file when Burl took over a few weeks before – yet another instance of the police altering files to suit their own ends. Mees later said, "After the raid, I knew I had stepped into a real rotten bag of dirty politics."[230] In light of these accusations, members of the city council, and especially City Attorney Jerald Rosen, came to Burl's vigorous defense.[231]

Mees was fired, then cleared of all charges a year later, and given $10,000 in back pay.[232] (Burl cost Hialeah Gardens another $50,000 when he re-hired Nick Small, an officer who had been fired for police brutality. During the cock-fighting investigation, Small pointed a loaded shotgun at Edward Mees and Burl took no action against him.[233]) Charges against Ramon Benitez were dropped, and his animals were returned to him.[234]

On April 16, 1982, Osman filed a $1,000,000 defamation of character suit on behalf of Mayor Burl McCormick against a political rival who accused him of "unethical, improper, unprofessional and alleged illegal actions in conducting the public's business."[235] Councilman Greg Read said in the past three years alone, McCormick had "manipulated an election, meddled in the operation of the police department, promoted the construction of a new City Hall despite citizen disapproval, and worked secretly for the construction of federally subsidized housing."[236] In June, Burl filed another lawsuit, this time against a city clerk who created a recall petition that threatened his job.[237] By the end of the month, a Circuit Court judge threw out Burl's defamation suit against Read, while the city council dismissed Read's allegation.[238]

Burl then spent seven months preparing a "temporary injunction" against the clerk's recall petition, and members of the city council came to his defense: "Sickening! Ridiculous! A joke!" said Councilman Daniel Riccio. "The man is innocent of all charges!"[239] Before the recall could move forward, Burl decided not to run for reelection and, as a result, another Circuit Court judge "ruled the case moot and irrelevant."[240]

After Burl's announcement, Greg Read decided to run for mayor, but he was defeated by a candidate with endorsements from both the Hialeah Gardens Fraternal Order of Police[241] and outgoing mayor Burl McCormick. The new mayor was Councilman Daniel Riccio, who won by only 24 votes.[242] Only three days before the election, Michael Osman and Jerry McCormick incorporated the Majestic Development Corp. with an address registered at 10595 NW 87th Avenue, Hialeah Gardens, Florida[243] – a building constructed "without the necessary permits from the state"[244] on a parcel of land that Mayor Daniel Riccio would later approve to purchase through Osman from the McCormick family for "22 times" what they paid for it in 1972.[245] According to an article on March 10, 1983, Burl was "ecstatic," at the election's outcome: "It's like I won."[246]

* * *

Not long after, Burl McCormick, who had lived in Miami since he was seventeen,[247] packed up his bags and moved back to DeFuniak Springs[248] in Walton County – half an hour from Niceville – where he bought back his parents' farm with other family members[249] and began developing real estate as the new president of Landever Properties.[250] Landever Properties had been incorporated in 1981 by his outspoken defender, Hialeah Gardens City Attorney Jerald Rosen.[251] The following year, they began construction on a 16,500 square-foot building for the Walton County government.[252]

By August of 1986, while Mike Nobles was under indictment in Alabama and Michael Osman was setting up the "androgynous" corporations with his wife and brothers, Mike Nobles, and Jerry McCormick, Burl McCormick made one last attempt to restart his political career when he ran for a seat on Walton County Commission District 4.[253] Though he outraised and outspent every other candidate running for office that year,[254] he couldn't escape the reputation he'd created for himself during his "six controversial years" as mayor of Hialeah Gardens. An article titled "Political Rumors Trail McCormick"[255] would go on to win the reporter an award for investigative journalism exposing Burl's political spending.[256] The truth was, Burl McCormick outraised the other candidates because "$12,000 of his $13,000" came from loans he gave himself.[257]

Burl's opponent charged that "McCormick was principal in a long list of corporations that had been 'involuntarily dissolved,'"[258] but Burl countered by saying that companies like Student Loan Fund, Housing for the Elderly, and Food For Starving Children had simply been dissolved after using all the funds available to them. Additionally, he wanted to emphasize that he had been actively working to help the elderly for many years. The public didn't find his arguments convincing, and Burl McCormick's political career came to an end on October 1, 1986, when his opponent beat him with nearly twice as many votes.[259] By March of 1988 he was under investigation for corruption yet again,[260] and that September he abruptly died of cancer.[261]

But at least one of the corporations he dissolved during his final campaign provides some insight into the way things would continue long after his death. In 1976, Burl McCormick and his business partner, Robert E. Forcum, franchisee of a string of Burger King restaurants across Florida,[262] incorporated Christian Food for Starving Children in the World, Inc., with a registered address at 14161 Leaning Pine Drive, Miami Lakes, Florida[263] – a 3-bedroom home with an indoor pool and waterslide owned by Forcum.[264] During the early 80's, Forcum used funds from the U.S. Department of Housing and Urban Development (HUD) to run a 128-unit low-income housing project for the elderly in Hialeah that was plagued by delays in construction and cost overruns. Robert Forcum Towers were supposed to open in August 1980, but many elderly residents were left waiting with boxes packed for over a year. One hopeful resident, 72-year-old Grace Chapman, first heard of the project at Central Church of Christ, where Robert Forcum was an elder.[265] And in 1981, just as Burl was surrounded by allegations of police corruption, Forcum appointed himself vice president of Police Recognition in Dade Everywhere, or PRIDE for short.[266] "He's the church's fair haired boy," said Chapman.[267]

Forcum wasn't the only one in Burl's circle who was interested in profiting from government funding for low-income housing. During the 1991 corruption investigation in which Osman had admitted bribing police on behalf of Silvio Cardoso, Cardoso himself admitted that in 1984 he, Mayor Raul Martinez, and a developer from Coral Gables named Jorge Perez had all "conspired to obtain a federal housing contract [from HUD] ...which they hoped to reap $1.2M in profit."[268] Cardoso, Martinez, and Perez plotted to split the profits evenly three ways. (Perez, the vice president of a New York firm interested in building low income housing in Miami, was well known for his large political contributions to local politicians like Maurice Ferre.[269]) During this testimony, Cardoso also described "dozens of episodes" in which Martinez and members of the city council "demanded or received" cash in exchange for political favors while he was actively working with the cocaine trafficker, Alberto San Pedro.[270] According to Cardoso, he had been a government informant since 1986.

In 1990, Osman incorporated Fountain Park Village Homes, Inc. for Silvio Cardoso and Jorge Perez[271] from offices located in Miami Lakes. Today, after creating the largest affordable housing company in Florida, Perez is number 316 on the Forbes 400 list and is worth $2.6 billion. Perez was an advisor to President Clinton and a big fundraiser for both Hillary Clinton and Barack Obama. Known as "the Donald Trump of the tropics,"[272] Perez was also a friend and former business partner to the CEO of the Trump Organization, and Trump himself wrote the foreword to Perez's book, *Powerhouse Principles: The Ultimate Blueprint for Real Estate Success in an Ever-Changing Market.*[273] In 2014, Osman helped Perez and his wife, Bienvenida, incorporate another Miami Lakes development, Bienvenida Apartamentos, LLC.[274]

* * *

Other businesses formed with similar patterns and similar relationships: The Darlington Church of Christ for Daniel McCormick in 1992;[275] a $120,000 land sale in 2014 for Palindrome Development Corporation,[276] for which he was president, his wife was vice president, and the Hialeah Church of Christ was director;[277] a $14,000,000 land sale for the Hialeah Church of Christ in 2021,[278] on behalf of RPRT, LLC, for which he was an officer along with a company called Redound Corp.,[279] for which he and his brother Craig were also officers.[280] Redound Corp., meanwhile, managed Alchemy, LLC,[281] which managed Eruditional, LLC.[282] Corporations within corporations. The list goes on and on.

* * *

While he was working as a lawyer and church elder, Osman began a long-term business relationship in the mid-90's with Frank Ippolito, a Miami based property developer. Together, they formed Unit Development Corp. in 1997,[283] Spring Hill Bluffs, Inc. in 2001,[284] Trend Corp. in 2001,[285] Hidden Cove of Davie Condominium Association, Inc. in 2004,[286] The Ippolito Family Limited Partnership, Ltd. in 2012,[287] and 1439 Oceania, LLC in 2017.[288] It was a long and seemingly mundane partnership, perhaps made more interesting by the fact that Ippolito had ties to the mob going back decades. As far back as 1962, Frank Ippolito and his construction company were linked to corruption in Philadelphia City Hall,[289] before they expanded their business into New Jersey and down to Florida. Reports in 1973 describe him as a condo developer with links to the Angelo Bruno crime family, which was working closely with the Gambinos at the time.[290]

Coincidentally, during the 1980's and 90's, another Ippolito with family ties going back to the New Jersey area was making headlines in Tampa – whether he was a direct relative or distant cousin, I can't quite tell. Emilio Ippolito's father was a simple cigar maker,[291] but by the middle of the century the Ippolitos were somehow "the largest landholders in Hillsborough County."[292] Among the family's planned projects was a $150,000,000 self-contained community in 1974 to be financed by investors who Emilio refused to identify.[293] But the Ippolitos were better known for the low-income housing they built or purchased throughout Tampa, which they rented to desperate residents who complained the buildings were poorly maintained and falling apart. Housing code violations began racking up in the 1970's, and Emilio Ippolito began a legal war against the city that would go on for decades.[294] By 1995, Ippolito belonged to a string of anti-tax, anti-government militias in Florida,[295] with ties to Greater Ministries International, a "Ponzi scheme" church with its own ties to The Church of the Avenger, a neo-Nazi inspired religious organization buying properties across the country.[296] In a few short years, it was estimated that Greater Ministries and affiliated groups had perpetrated $1.3B in fraud against 40,000 "people of faith,"[297] while Ippolito and his friends reportedly sent threats to state and federal judges.[298] When Emilio Ippolito, "the slumlord's slumlord, who for decades rented out sleazy decaying apartments that offended even the cockroaches,"[299] was finally sentenced to 11 years in prison, his final words were: "I don't ever want to see another legal document again."[300] At least we can agree on something.

* * *

Mike Nobles, of course, ran his Subways with Jerry McCormick and other elders in the Church of Christ. He was never a big shot, or the man in charge, but I believe he played a role worth protecting and there were plenty of connected people who had interest in protecting him. Money flowed through these systems, made clean by the appearance of religion or legitimate businesses and real estate transactions, and ended up in the right pockets along the way. It's certainly a strange coincidence that Nobles and Cardoso became government informants at the exact same year their lawyer, who may also have been a government informant, was furiously incorporating similarly named corporations within the restaurant industry.

This time period in the mid-80's was exactly when the walls were closing in and they may have all been all dealing with large sums of dirty cash that needed to be cleansed or hidden. Mike Nobles had Patriot Network money that couldn't be deposited in a traditional bank. Cardoso was up to his ears in bribes and payoffs. Burl McCormick, no longer mayor, was facing a lawsuit brought by South Florida Savings & Loan. Allegations in a complaint … charge the project promoter, Morocco Inc., with default. … The lender holds mortgages including one for $315,000 on offices in a commercial condominium at 9500 NW 77th Ave., Hialeah Gardens."[301] Osman, of course, incorporated Moroco Inc. for Burl a few years earlier.[302] And the address, 9500 NW 77th Ave., was the same address Church of Christ elder Robert Forcum used to run his low income housing project for the elderly, Robert Forcum Towers.[303]

I believe Osman set up the "androgynous" corporations for members of his own family, as well as the McCormicks, and others to help shuffle all this dirty cash around until it became clean again. Kieran Beer, the chief analyst of the Association of Certified Anti-Money Laundering Specialists explains, "Restaurants are a classic way to move money… pretty much any cash-intensive business can be used to launder money – laundromats, used car dealerships, taxi services – but restaurants tend to crop up again and again in money laundering cases."[304]

That Nobles, the Osmans, and the McCormicks were also deeply involved with multiple branches of the Church of Christ, another business with untraceable donations and tax exemptions, only created another possible avenue for dirty money to get laundered. In an article by the Organized Crime and Corruption Reporting Project, Mark Califano, a former assistant U.S. attorney and chief legal officer at Nardello & Co, a global investigative firm, stated, "Over the years, religious institutions have been repeatedly used ... to launder money.... And their special and protected place in most countries and societies has allowed that to happen." Marci A. Hamilton, a professor at the University of Pennsylvania who studies religion, continued that thought, saying that the reason the reason "religious groups are so convenient for money laundering, parking proceeds, is that for federal tax files you don't have to specify where your money came from and what you do with it.... It's this untouchability aspect that we have unintentionally crafted in the U.S. through several different mechanisms.... There's this black box quality to their public space."[305]

In the case of Nobles, the Osmans, and McCormicks, the money could go through any of their Subway restaurants, incorporated with multiple companies with similar names and various combinations of the same directors and officers; then that money gets donated as a large cash gift to any of the churches they run across the state; then the church could order meals that never get made from different restaurants owned by Androgyn, or Androgyny, or Androkam, or Androken. Who knows? With a lawyer already experienced in facilitating bribes and cash payoffs through long lists of shell corporations, it's that easy.

Is it possible that because of Nobles, Osman, and Cardoso's roles as informants, the government was willing to just look the other way? After all, Nobles and Cardoso kept doing business with Osman for years.

* * *

By the time I came along, the pattern of criminal behavior had been repeating itself for so long that no one knew exactly when it began or where it could possibly end. Corruption was woven so tightly into every aspect of life that it was a part of the fabric itself. Though it now seems obvious in retrospect, I didn't realize until well after the fact that some of the real estate dealings in which Christy and I had taken part were varying degrees of scam and tax evasion.

For instance, after Wanda Nobles' parents passed away, Mike Nobles convinced me to buy his in-laws' house, renovate, and flip it, as we'd done several times already with other properties. But the heirs of the house were Wanda Nobles and her brother. The house was sold to me at a *deflated* price, with part of the profits from that sale going to Nobles' brother-in-law as his inheritance. But not long after I bought it, we sold it again at an *inflated* price, thanks to the white-hot real estate market. Nobles pocketed 80% of the profit, Christy and I the rest. Then Nobles "borrowed" an equal sum from one of his shell corporations so that he could explain to the IRS where the big stack of cash came from.

I now know that this is called a loan-back scheme: "Money can be laundered using various methods which vary in terms of sophistication and complexity. Loans and mortgages are usually taken as a cover to launder money proceeds, and lump sum cash repayments are used to repay the loans or mortgages."[306]

* * *

A few years before Christy and I broke up, Nobles informed us that he had quit-claimed[307] a share of a condominium to us without explanation. We never received a key, never spent a night there, never had any use or access to this condominium, the building of which he owned with several other leaders of the Niceville Church of Christ. A couple of years later, he asked us to sign a quitclaim deed returning the property to him. We signed it back over to him despite serious misgivings on my part that we were being used for something shady.

Years later, during a period of serious investigations into Mike Nobles' business dealings, researching the records I discovered that he hadn't quit-claimed the property to Christy and I at all. Don Sublett, who was an elder in both the Niceville and Destin churches, had "sold" the property to me for $30,000 – on paper. I never gave him a cent nor had any knowledge of this transaction. At the same time, Mike Nobles was being sued for $30,000. So, in effect, he had "bought" some property from one of his cronies among the church leaders to hide $30,000 from his creditors and used Christy and I as middlemen to hide it. This was a clear case of fraud.[308]

Nobles was adamant that only my name appeared on all the documents of these transactions, which led to me being the only party with any tax liability. He kept assuring me that his lawyer Leslie Michael Osman was "running everything through these shell corporations, so I don't have to pay taxes on it."

My ignorance in these matters made me an easy pawn in these corrupt games. As I pieced together what was really going on, time and again I was told by respected men in the community to back off, stay out, and don't make trouble. When Mary Smith dared to ask questions, she was told by church elders to "walk away... move on and leave it alone... shut up." Even the Bible itself says "You must not eat from the tree of the knowledge of good and evil, for when you eat from it you will certainly die."

Speaking to me years later, Mary confessed, "I'm still terrified of these people."[309]

It took me years to figure out what I was pulling at, and what I threatened when I did.

Forget it Mark, it's Florida.

Endnotes

1   https://www.newspapers.com/image/795074538/

2   https://www.newspapers.com/image/1026676123/

3   New York Magazine. October 15, 1990.

4   https://www.newspapers.com/image/106614528/

5   https://www.newspapers.com/image/320710506/

6   *The San Diego Reader.* "Bill Drexler's way for you to avoid taxes: This man wants to sell you a church." April 10, 1980.

7   https://www.newspapers.com/image/44509160/

8   https://www.newspapers.com/image/74299238/

9   https://www.newspapers.com/image/44578372/

10   https://www.newspapers.com/image/44581160/

11   https://www.newspapers.com/image/44586113/

12   https://www.newspapers.com/image/44514379/

13   https://www.newspapers.com/image/44517842/

14   https://www.newspapers.com/image/71910466/

15   https://www.newspapers.com/image/188324313/

16   https://www.yumpu.com/en/document/read/4530185/the-daly-eagle-fights-4-rights

17   https://mn.gov/law-library/assets/1969-06-26affidavitofJeromeDaly_tcm1041-115941.pdf

18   https://www.newspapers.com/image/1025935585/

19   https://www.newspapers.com/image/190505239/

20   https://www.newspapers.com/image/186143174/

21   https://www.newspapers.com/image/44772128/

22   https://www.newspapers.com/image/136833919/

23   https://www.newspapers.com/image/61297868/

24   https://www.newspapers.com/image/61860024/

25   https://www.newspapers.com/image/376845591/

26   https://www.newspapers.com/image/45846200/

27   https://archive.org/details/SecretArmyOrganizationHQ157235771264pp/page/n315/mode/2up?view=theater&q=cruikshank

28   https://www.newspapers.com/image/703552151/

29   'Sovereign citizens' plaster courts with bogus legal filings--and some turn to violence

30   https://archive.org/details/SecretArmyOrganizationHQ157235771264pp/page/n319/mode/2up?view=theater

31   https://www.ojp.gov/ncjrs/virtual-library/abstracts/christian-identity-movement-analyzing-its-theological

32   https://archive.org/details/galewilliampotterministryofchristchurchlosangeles1577775/page/n99/mode/2up?q=alabama&view=theater

33   https://www.newspapers.com/image/208336335/?terms=%22Christian%20Posse%20Association%22&match=1

34	https://www.newspapers.com/image/206156886/?terms=%22Christian%20Posse%20Association%22&match=1

35	https://archive.org/details/SecretArmyOrganizationHQ157235771264pp/page/n197/mode/2up?view=theater&q=tax+rebellion

36	https://www.newspapers.com/image/190623046/?terms=%22Patriot%20Network%22&match=1

37	https://www.splcenter.org/fighting-hate/intelligence-report/1998/hate-group-expert-daniel-levitas-discusses-posse-comitatus-christian-identity-movement-and

38	https://casetext.com/case/united-states-v-stockheimer-2

39	https://www.sandiegoreader.com/news/1980/apr/10/cover-this-man-wants-to-sell-you-a-church/

40	https://www.sandiegoreader.com/news/1980/apr/10/cover-this-man-wants-to-sell-you-a-church/

41	https://www.oklahoman.com/story/news/1981/11/26/four-guilty-in-document-fraud-case/60364715007/

42	https://www.newspapers.com/image/746047928/?match=1&terms=%22Robert%20Clarkson%22%20misconduct

43	https://www.newspapers.com/image/750629283/?match=1&terms=%22Robert%20Clarkson%22%20misconduct

44	https://www.newspapers.com/image/469150046/?match=1&terms=%22Robert%20Clarkson%22%20%22Patriot%20Network%22

45	https://www.newspapers.com/image/99044564/?terms=%22Patriot%20Network%22&match=1

46	https://www.newspapers.com/image/283756201/?terms=%22Patriot%20Network%22&match=1

47	https://www.foxnews.com/story/supporters-defend-confederate-flag-in-s-c

48	https://www.splcenter.org/fighting-hate/intelligence-report/2004/anderson-county-sc-law-enforcement-takes-antigovernment-extremists

49	https://www.newspapers.com/image/814416244/?match=1&terms=%22Robert%20Clarkson%22%20anderson%20city%20cocaine

50	https://www.patriotnetwork.info/

51	https://www.newspapers.com/image/112359554/?terms=%22Tim%20Yarbrough%22&match=1

52	https://files.taxfoundation.org/legacy/docs/fed_individual_rate_history_nominal.pdf

53	https://www.newspapers.com/image/794835068/?match=1&terms=%22William%20Potter%20Gale%22

54	https://www.newspapers.com/image/974132508/?terms=%22Tim%20Yarbrough%22&match=1

55	https://www.newspapers.com/image/794837780/?terms=%22Life%20Science%20Church%22&match=1

56	https://www.nytimes.com/1988/07/03/us/panel-considering-currency-charges.html

57	https://www.newspapers.com/image/399442491/?terms=%22Patriot%20Network%22&match=1

58	https://www.newspapers.com/image/974561224/

59	UNITED STATES OF AMERICA, PLAINTIFF-APPELLEE V. TONY L. DEMURRAY AND TIMOTHY J. YARBROUGH, DEFENDANT-APPELLANT

60	https://www.newspapers.com/image/794840308/

61	https://www.newspapers.com/image/794840308/

62	https://www.newspapers.com/image/455398463/?terms=%22Posse%20Comitatus%22&match=1

63	https://www.newspapers.com/image/455477093/?terms=%22Posse%20Comitatus%22&match=1

64	https://www.newspapers.com/image/455398463/?terms=%22Posse%20Comitatus%22&match=1

65   https://www.newspapers.com/image/455477093/?terms=%22Posse%20Comitatus%22&match=1

66   https://www.newspapers.com/image/455535709/?terms=%22Posse%20Comitatus%22&match=1

67   https://www.newspapers.com/image/989288075/?match=1&terms=%22James%20Thimm%22

68   https://www.newspapers.com/image/257778034/?terms=%22Patriot%20Network%22&match=1

69   https://www.newspapers.com/image/227514036/?match=1&terms=%22Kenneth%20M.%20Snyder%22

70   https://www.newspapers.com/image/795074555/

71   https://www.newspapers.com/image/624599494/?terms=%22American%20Patriots%20Association%22&match=1

72   https://www.newspapers.com/image/624598458/?terms=%22American%20Patriots%20Association%22&match=1

73   https://www.newspapers.com/image/1026024919/?terms=%22American%20Patriots%20Association%22&match=1

74   https://www.newspapers.com/image/129550437/?terms=%22Basic%20Bible%20Church%22&match=1

75   https://www.washingtonpost.com/archive/local/1978/09/22/tax-court-rejects-donation-to-church/d6c08db6-7560-4d5b-a1f3-70b24f106825/

76   https://www.newspapers.com/image/642925197/?match=1&terms=%22Kenneth%20M.%20Snyder%22%20

77   https://www.newspapers.com/image/130727683/?match=1&terms=%22Kenneth%20Snyder%22%20%22Basic%20Bible%20Church%22

78   https://www.newspapers.com/image/112228262/?terms=%22Androgyny%20Corp%22&match=1

79   https://www.newspapers.com/image/631549162/?match=1&terms=%22Michael%20Osman%22

80   https://www.newspapers.com/image/631549162/?terms=%22Michael%20Osman%22

81   https://www.newspapers.com/image/631548975/

82   https://www.newspapers.com/image/631549173/?terms=%22Michael%20Osman%22

83   https://www.newspapers.com/image/630084037/?match=1&terms=%22L.%20Michael%20Osman%22

84   https://www.newspapers.com/image/624652227/?match=1&terms=%22Anthony%20Mijares%22

85   https://www.newspapers.com/image/643192935/?match=1&terms=%22Silvio%20Cardoso%22%20%22Anthony%20Mijares%22

86   https://www.newspapers.com/image/302044693/?match=1&terms=%22Anthony%20Mijares%22

87   https://www.newspapers.com/image/302463117/?match=1&terms=%22Marshall%20Caifano%22

88   https://www.newspapers.com/image/618775315/?match=1&terms=%22Arnold%20F.%20Seltzer%22

89   https://www.newspapers.com/image/628146514/?match=1&terms=%22Arnold%20F.%20Seltzer%22

90   https://www.newspapers.com/image/102677557/?match=1&terms=%22Tito%20Carinci%22

91   https://www.newspapers.com/image/628245362/?match=1&terms=%22Tito%20Carinci%22

92   https://www.newspapers.com/image/629508502/?match=1&terms=%22Tito%20Carinci%22

93   https://www.newspapers.com/image/638935427/?match=1&terms=%22Alva%20johnson%20Rodgers%22

94   https://www.newspapers.com/image/636272765/?match=1&terms=%22Alva%20johnson%20Rodgers%22

95   https://www.newspapers.com/image/516755217/?match=1&terms=%22Alva%20johnson%20Rodgers%22

96   https://www.newspapers.com/image/305661336/?match=1&terms=%22Alva%20johnson%20Rodgers%22

97   https://www.newspapers.com/image/628275417/?match=1&terms=%22Alva%20johnson%20Rodgers%22

98   https://www.newspapers.com/image/335465445/?match=1&terms=%22Marshall%20Caifano%22

99   https://www.chicagotribune.com/2007/06/28/witness-says-he-worked-in-outfit-for-lombardo/

100   https://www.newspapers.com/image/305661563/

101   https://www.newspapers.com/image/398632628/?terms=%22Arthur%20Randall%20Sanders%22&match=1

102   https://www.newspapers.com/image/235629122/

103   https://www.newspapers.com/image/235629092/?terms=%22Daniel%20Forgione%22&match=1

104   https://www.newspapers.com/image/630984733/?terms=%22Daniel%20Forgione%22&match=1

105   https://www.newspapers.com/image/238297173/?match=1&terms=%22Daniel%20Forgione%22%20%22Carl%20Coppola%22

106   https://www.newspapers.com/image/214616119/?terms=%22Daniel%20Forgione%22&match=1

107   https://www.newspapers.com/image/235421165/?match=1&terms=%22Marshall%20Caifano%22

108   https://www.newspapers.com/image/234761297/?match=1&terms=%22Anthony%20Mijares%22

109   https://www.latimes.com/archives/la-xpm-1993-05-27-mn-40477-story.html

110   https://www.sfgate.com/magazine/article/THE-CHILEAN-CONNECTION-Carlos-Cardoen-arms-2667085.php

111   https://www.sfgate.com/magazine/article/THE-CHILEAN-CONNECTION-Carlos-Cardoen-arms-2667085.php

112   https://nsarchive2.gwu.edu/NSAEBB/NSAEBB82/iraq61.pdf

113   https://www.sfgate.com/magazine/article/THE-CHILEAN-CONNECTION-Carlos-Cardoen-arms-2667085.php

114   https://www.newspapers.com/image/229500654/?match=1&terms=%22Swissco%22

115   https://www.newspapers.com/image/174534945/?match=1&terms=%22Michael%20Osman%22%20

116   https://www.newspapers.com/image/631893148/?match=1&terms=%22John%20Ruffino%22

117   https://www.newspapers.com/image/629160159/?match=1&terms=%22Anthony%20Mijares%22

118   https://www.newspapers.com/image/636830702/?match=1&terms=%22Swissco%22%20%22Bob%20Graham%22

119   https://www.newspapers.com/image/633359840/?match=1&terms=%22Swissco%22

120   https://search.sunbiz.org/Inquiry/corporationsearch/SearchResultDetail?inquirytype=EntityName&directionType=Initial&searchNameOrder=CAIDOZ%20K006521&aggregateId=domp-k00652-41d13798-4fa1-4fe6-bdfe-410d9523fbd3&searchTerm=CAIDENCO%2C%20LLC&listNameOrder=CAIDENCO%20L120001075430

121   https://www.newspapers.com/image/633345870/?match=1&terms=%22Anthony%20

Mijares%22

122   https://www.ft.com/content/1fe7932c-4311-11d9-bea1-00000e2511c8

123   https://www.newspapers.com/image/633459369/?match=1&terms=%22Silvio%20cardoso%22

124   https://www.newspapers.com/image/632885685/?match=1&terms=%22Silvio%20Cardoso%22%20%22Thalassites%22

125   https://www.newspapers.com/image/631345369/?match=1&terms=%22Alberto%20San%20Pedro%22%20%22Silvio%20cardoso%22

126   https://www.villagevoice.com/white-line-fever/

127   https://www.newspapers.com/image/632885685/?match=1&terms=%22Silvio%20Cardoso%22%20%22Thalassites%22

128   https://www.villagevoice.com/white-line-fever/

129   https://www.newspapers.com/image/642608642/?match=1&terms=%22Silvio%20cardoso%22%20police%20chief

130   https://www.newspapers.com/image/632333278/?match=1&terms=%22Silvio%20Cardoso%22%20%22Alberto%20San%20Pedro%22%20%22high%20school%22

131   https://www.wired.com/2012/06/cia/

132   https://www.npr.org/2011/10/30/141696333/from-mafia-soldier-to-cocaine-cowboy

133   https://palmbeachartspaper.com/journalist-wright-tells-miami-hit-mans-story-on-by-liner-site/

134   https://www.wired.com/2012/06/cia/

135   https://www.newspapers.com/image/635631298/?match=1&terms=%22Michael%20Osman%22%20%22Silvio%20Cardoso%22

136   https://www.newspapers.com/image/634207763/?match=1&terms=%22International%20Posse%22

137   https://unitedgangs.com/folk-nation/

138   https://www.newspapers.com/image/635529043/

139   https://www.newspapers.com/image/635628291/?terms=%22Michael%20Osman%22%20%22corruption%22&match=1

140   https://www.newspapers.com/image/635191399/?match=1&terms=%22Thomas%20Chamberlain%22

141   https://www.miaminewtimes.com/news/witness-for-the-prosecution-6360557

142   https://ir.unitedhomesgroup.com/news/news-details/2024/United-Homes-Group-Inc.-Reports-2024-First-Quarter-Results/default.aspx

143   https://www.taxnotes.com/research/federal/court-documents/court-petitions-and-briefs/brief-for-the-appellee/144jp

144   https://www.taxnotes.com/research/federal/court-documents/court-petitions-and-briefs/brief-for-the-appellee/144jp

145   https://mn.gov/law-library/assets/1969-06-26affidavitofJeromeDaly_tcm1041-115941.pdf

146   https://www.newspapers.com/image/112352945/?terms=%22Tim%20Yarbrough%22&match=1

147   https://www.taxnotes.com/research/federal/court-documents/court-petitions-and-briefs/brief-for-the-appellee/144jp

148   Patriot Network file

149   https://www.newspapers.com/image/268447531/?match=1&terms=%2221%20Eglin%20Pkwy%20SE%22

150   Patriot Network file.

151   Patriot Network file.

152   Patriot Network file.

153   https://www.newspapers.com/image/1027931812/?match=1&terms=%22Nassau%20Life%20Insurance%22

154   https://www.newspapers.com/image/1027931812/?match=1&terms=%22Nassau%20

Life%20Insurance%22

155   https://www.newspapers.com/image/250260575/?match=1&terms=%22Robert%20 S.%20Chappell%22

156   https://www.newspapers.com/image/312587462/?match=1&terms=%22Robert%20 S.%20Chappell%22

157   https://www.newspapers.com/image/639736038/?match=1&terms=%22%20Norman%20Paul%20Cowart%22

158   https://www.newspapers.com/image/762633931/?match=1&terms=%22Norman%20 Paul%20Cowart%22

159   https://www.newspapers.com/image/762518329/?match=1&terms=%22Norman%20 Paul%20Cowart%22

160   https://www.newspapers.com/image/762432090/?match=1&terms=%22Norman%20 Paul%20Cowart%22

161   https://www.newspapers.com/image/762469188/?match=1&terms=%22Norman%20 Paul%20Cowart%22

162   https://www.newspapers.com/image/48847869/?match=1&terms=%22Norman%20 Paul%20Cowart%22

163   https://www.newspapers.com/image/431588247/?match=1&terms=%22Nassau%20 Life%20Insurance%22

164   https://www.newspapers.com/image/430989252/?terms=%22Nassau%20Life%20Insurance%22&match=1

165   https://www.newspapers.com/image/401154169/?terms=%22Nassau%20Life%20Insurance%20Company%22&match=1

166   https://www.splcenter.org/fighting-hate/intelligence-report/2001/seizure-indianapolis-baptist-temple-ends-standoff-%E2%80%98unregistered%E2%80%99-church-movement-continues

167   https://www.newspapers.com/image/44772128/

168   https://www.newspapers.com/image/556681924/?match=1&terms=%22Nassau%20 Life%20Insurance%22

169   https://www.newspapers.com/image/556681924/?match=1&terms=%22Nassau%20 Life%20Insurance%22

170   https://www.newspapers.com/image/888877479/?terms=%22Nassau%20Life%20Insurance%22&match=1

171   https://www.newspapers.com/image/888877479/?terms=%22Nassau%20Life%20Insurance%22&match=1

172   https://law.justia.com/cases/federal/appellate-courts/F2/985/962/206389/

173   https://www.reaganlibrary.gov/public/digitallibrary/smof/publicliaison/blackwell/box-035/40_047_7007844_035_025_2017.pdf

174   https://okaloosacountyfl-web.tylerhost.net/web/web/integration/search?field_bookPageID_DOT_Page=1391&field_BookPageID_DOT_Volume=1367

175   https://archive.org/details/gale-william-potter-hq-100-487547-100-a-80325/page/n1/mode/2up

176   https://www.newspapers.com/image/312865771/

177   https://www.newspapers.com/image/300011334/?match=1&terms=%22Norman%20 Paul%20Cowart%22

178   https://www.newspapers.com/image/649917359/?match=1&terms=%22Norman%20 Paul%20Cowart%22

179   https://www.newspapers.com/image/261662671/?terms=%22michael%20s.%20nobles%22&match=1

180   https://www.taxnotes.com/research/federal/court-documents/court-petitions-and-briefs/brief-for-the-appellee/144jp

181   https://tntrafficticket.us/2020/12/taking-back-our-town-taking-back-our-county-yarbrough-rebuilds/

182   https://www.fox5atlanta.com/news/sons-of-confederate-veterans-gather-again-for-

memorial-day-at-stone-mountain-park

183   https://ernieyarbrough.com/

184   https://www.sun-sentinel.com/1987/11/09/appetite-for-expansion-south-florida-fits-in-founders-plan-to-make-subway-the-worlds-biggest-fast-food-chain/

185   https://www.newspapers.com/image/298709914/

186   https://www.newspapers.com/image/620131425/?match=1&terms=%22Joseph%20Albert%22

187   https://www.newspapers.com/image/298681996/?match=1&terms=%22virgil%20cash%22

188   https://www.ancestry.com/discoveryui-content/view/578848973:1265

189   https://www.newspapers.com/image/622139353/?match=1&terms=%22Hialeah%20Church%20of%20christ%22

190   https://www.newspapers.com/image/622139353/?match=1&terms=%22Leslie%20Osman%22%20%22high%20school%22

191   https://www.newspapers.com/image/622759449/?terms=%22Leslie%20Michael%20Osman%22&match=1

192   https://www.newspapers.com/image/628248360/?match=1&terms=%22L.%20Michael%20Osman%22

193   https://bisprofiles.com/fl/hialeah-church-of-christ-721584

194   https://bisprofiles.com/fl/hialeah-church-of-christ-721584

195   https://www.newspapers.com/image/301998571/?match=1&terms=%22Andrew%20Capeletti%22%20

196   https://www.newspapers.com/image/619386602/?match=1&terms=%22Andrew%20Capeletti%22%20

197   https://www.newspapers.com/image/625352868/?match=1&terms=%22Hialeah%20Church%20of%20christ%22

198   https://www.newspapers.com/image/625352868/?match=1&terms=%22Hialeah%20Church%20of%20christ%22

199   https://www.newspapers.com/image/624985877/?match=1&terms=%22Burl%20McCormick%22

200   https://www.newspapers.com/image/626179465/?match=1&terms=%22Gerald%20McCormick%22

201   https://www.newspapers.com/image/625825924/?match=1&terms=%22Hialeah%20Church%20of%20christ%22

202   https://www.newspapers.com/image/622325747/?match=1&terms=%22Hialeah%20Church%20of%20christ%22

203   https://www.newspapers.com/image/625825924/?match=1&terms=%22Hialeah%20Church%20of%20christ%22

204   https://www.newspapers.com/image/624985877/?match=1&terms=%22Burl%20McCormick%22

205   https://www.newspapers.com/image/332266462/?match=1&terms=%22Hialeah%20Church%20of%20christ%22

206   https://www.newspapers.com/image/332266462/?match=1&terms=%22Hialeah%20Church%20of%20christ%22

207   https://archive.org/details/ERIC_ED065646/page/n141/mode/2up?q=christian

208   https://lsupress.org/9780807172742/race-and-restoration/

209   https://www.campuspride.org/worstlist/

210   https://www.newspapers.com/image/124926855/?match=1&terms=%22Tom%20Adams%22%20quincy%20lease

211   https://www.newspapers.com/image/264763910/?match=1&terms=%22Tom%20Adams%22%20quincy%20lease

212   https://www.newspapers.com/image/227301124/?match=1&terms=%22Burl%20McCormick%22

213   https://www.newspapers.com/image/175072602/?match=1&terms=%22Burl%20Mc-Cormick%22%20

214   https://www.newspapers.com/image/626849557/?match=1&terms=%22Daniel%20Harold%20McCormick%22

215   https://www.newspapers.com/image/627461952/?match=1&terms=%22Daniel%20H%20McCormick%22

216   https://www.newspapers.com/image/301216387/?match=1&terms=%22Burl%20Mc-Cormick%22%20%22Silvio%20Cardoso%22

217   https://www.newspapers.com/image/628742490/?match=1&terms=%2211750%20NW%2087th%20Pl%22

218   https://www.newspapers.com/image/628744893/?match=1&terms=%22Edward%20Mees%22%20cock%20fight

219   https://www.newspapers.com/image/267082515/

220   https://www.newspapers.com/image/628742490/?match=1&terms=%2211750%20NW%2087th%20Pl%22

221   https://www.newspapers.com/image/629155684/?match=1&terms=%22Ramon%20Benitez%22

222   https://www.newspapers.com/image/627089359/?match=1&terms=%22Maule%20Industries%22

223   https://www.newspapers.com/image/626449567/?match=1&terms=%22Ramon%20Benitez%22

224   https://www.newspapers.com/image/629155684/?match=1&terms=%22Ramon%20Benitez%22

225   https://www.newspapers.com/image/628985869/?match=1&terms=%22Burl%20Mc-Cormick%22%20%22Edward%20Mees%22

226   https://www.newspapers.com/image/628744893/?match=1&terms=%22Edward%20Mees%22%20cock%20fight

227   https://www.newspapers.com/image/267082515/?match=1&terms=%22Burl%20Mc-Cormick%22%20

228   https://www.newspapers.com/image/628969899/?match=1&terms=%22Edward%20Mees%22%20%22Charles%20Forrest%22

229   https://www.newspapers.com/image/301475494/?match=1&terms=%22Edward%20Mees%22%20cock%20fight

230   https://www.newspapers.com/image/628715373/?match=1&terms=%22Ramon%20Benitez%22

231   https://www.newspapers.com/image/629253158/?match=1&terms=%22Jerald%20Rosen%22

232   https://www.newspapers.com/image/629515150/?match=1&terms=%22Edward%20Mees%22

233   https://www.newspapers.com/image/628985869/?match=1&terms=%22Burl%20Mc-Cormick%22%20%22Edward%20Mees%22

234   https://www.newspapers.com/image/628699237/?match=1&terms=%22Burl%20Mc-Cormick%22%20%22Edward%20Mees%22

235   https://www.newspapers.com/image/630038713/?match=1&terms=%22McCor-mick%22%20%22Michael%20Osman%22

236   https://www.newspapers.com/image/630038713/?match=1&terms=%22McCor-mick%22%20%22Michael%20Osman%22

237   https://www.newspapers.com/image/630059052/?match=1&terms=%22Burl%20Mc-Cormick%22

238   https://www.newspapers.com/image/630043319/?match=1&terms=%22Burl%20Mc-Cormick%22

239   https://www.newspapers.com/image/630039950/?match=1&terms=%22Daniel%20Riccio%22

240   https://www.newspapers.com/image/267082515/?match=1&terms=%22Burl%20Mc-Cormick%22%20

241   https://www.newspapers.com/image/630032134/?match=1&terms=%22Daniel%20 Riccio%22

242   https://www.newspapers.com/image/624584202/?match=1&terms=%22Burl%20Mc-Cormick%22%20%22Silvio%20Cardoso%22

243   https://search.sunbiz.org/Inquiry/corporationsearch/SearchResultDetail?inquiry-type=EntityName&directionType=Initial&searchNameOrder=MAJESTICDEVELOPMENT%20 G324710&aggregateId=domp-g32471-8ce8a444-e7fd-4587-a87a-c9bc8a8ef915&searchTer-m=MAJESTIC%20DEVELOPMENT%20&listNameOrder=MAJESTICDEVELOPMENT%202409771

244   https://www.newspapers.com/image/633321709/?match=1&terms=%22Burl%20Mc-Cormick%22

245   https://www.newspapers.com/image/632728626/?match=1&terms=%22McCor-mick%20family%22%20%2222%20times%22

246   https://www.newspapers.com/image/624584202/?match=1&terms=%22Burl%20Mc-Cormick%22%20%22Silvio%20Cardoso%22

247   https://www.newspapers.com/image/624985877/?match=1&terms=%22Burl%20Mc-Cormick%22

248   https://www.newspapers.com/image/267082381/

249   https://www.newspapers.com/image/633879652/?article=6a0e-c0b8-656e-406f-b468-8ddbbaf44aa1&terms=%22Burl%20McCormick%22

250   https://waltonclerk.com/vertical/sites/%7BA6BED226-E1BB-4A16-9632-BB8E-6515F4E0%7D/uploads/07-31-1984RegMinutes.pdf

251   https://search.sunbiz.org/Inquiry/corporationsearch/SearchResultDetail?inquiry-type=EntityName&directionType=ForwardList&searchNameOrder=LANDEVERPROPERTIES%20 F395880&aggregateId=domp-f39588-970bebc1-e991-483f-8f32-91e74d9c3fb4&searchTer-m=LANDE%20TRANSPORT%2C%20INC.&listNameOrder=LANDEVERMORTGAGE%20G646460

252   https://www.newspapers.com/image/267383126/?match=1&terms=%22Burl%20Mc-Cormick%22

253   https://www.newspapers.com/image/267049961/?match=1&terms=%22Burl%20Mc-Cormick%22

254   https://www.newspapers.com/image/267174213/?match=1&terms=%22Burl%20Mc-Cormick%22

255   https://www.newspapers.com/image/267082381/

256   https://www.newspapers.com/image/267624765/?match=1&terms=%22Burl%20Mc-Cormick%22

257   https://www.newspapers.com/image/267082515/

258   https://www.newspapers.com/image/267082515/

259   https://www.newspapers.com/image/267097835/?match=1&terms=%22Burl%20Mc-Cormick%22

260   https://www.newspapers.com/image/267584753/?match=1&terms=%22Burl%20Mc-Cormick%22

261   https://www.newspapers.com/image/633879652/?article=6a0e-c0b8-656e-406f-b468-8ddbbaf44aa1&terms=%22Burl%20McCormick%22

262   https://scholarworks.harding.edu/oral-history/8/ (57:20)

263   https://search.sunbiz.org/Inquiry/corporationsearch/SearchResultDetail?inqui-rytype=EntityName&directionType=Initial&searchNameOrder=CHRISTIANFOODFORSTARV-INGCHILDR%207351170&aggregateId=domnp-735117-965ecec5-ad87-4ac8-95f7-fe9eb13d-9d78&searchTerm=CHRISTIAN%20FM%20NETWORKS%2C%20 INC.&listNameOrder=CHRISTIANFMNETWORKS%20N070000094470

264   https://www.newspapers.com/image/301409912/?match=1&terms=%22Robert%20 Forcum%22

265   https://www.newspapers.com/image/629498379/

266   https://www.newspapers.com/image/629584625/?match=1&terms=%22Robert%20

Forcum%22

267   https://www.newspapers.com/image/629498407/

268   https://www.newspapers.com/image/635659257/?clipping_id=152014789&fcfToken=eyJhbGciOiJIUzI1NiIsInR5cCI6IkpXVCJ9.eyJmcmVlXZpZXctaWQiOjYzNTY1OTI1NywiaWF0IjoxNzIyODc0NTQ2LCJleHAiOjE3MjI5NjA5NDZ9.zPnh4mOCHwWngDySdheGLLqJeDOlaxEHpliryphHnphl

269   https://www.newspapers.com/image/629154386/?match=1&terms=%22Jorge%20Perez%22%20%22maurice%20ferre%22

270   https://www.newspapers.com/image/635659303/

271   https://search.sunbiz.org/Inquiry/CorporationSearch/SearchResults?InquiryType=OfficerRegisteredAgentName&InquiryDirectionType=ForwardRecord&SearchTerm=cardoso%20s&SearchNameOrder=CARDOSOSILVIO%20L240002704434&ListNameOrder=CARDOSOSILVIO%206875491&Detail=FL.DOS.Corporations.Shared.Contracts.FilingRecord

272   https://content.time.com/time/specials/packages/article/0,28804,2008201_2008200_2008208,00.html

273   https://penguinrandomhousehighereducation.com/book/?isbn=9780451227058

274   https://bisprofiles.com/fl/bienvenida-apartamentos-l14000119055

275   https://www.newspapers.com/image/227301124/?match=1&terms=%22Burl%20McCormick%22

276   https://www.newspapers.com/image/651095218/?match=1&terms=%22PALINDROME%20DEVELOPMENT%20CORP.%22

277   https://bisprofiles.com/fl/palindrome-development-p05000073785

278   https://www.bizjournals.com/southflorida/news/2021/05/26/church-sells-hialeah-development-site-for-14m.html

279   https://bisprofiles.com/fl/rprt-l16000203984

280   https://bisprofiles.com/fl/redound-p01000084973

281   https://bisprofiles.com/fl/alchemy-l04000087495

282   https://bisprofiles.com/fl/eruditional-l14000055759

283   https://search.sunbiz.org/Inquiry/corporationsearch/SearchResultDetail?inquirytype=EntityName&directionType=PreviousList&searchNameOrder=UNITDEVELOPMENT%20P970000208160&aggregateId=domp-p97000020816-494af3e3-633a-4f29-b286-b1b50a-0ba528&listNameOrder=UNITCONSTRUCTION%20P010000308620

284   https://search.sunbiz.org/Inquiry/corporationsearch/SearchResultDetail?inquirytype=EntityName&directionType=Initial&searchNameOrder=SPRINGHILLBLUFFS%20P010000089410&aggregateId=domp-p01000008941-b3489934-84d0-46d7-a70b-a8f0c567f-11b&searchTerm=SPRINGHILL%20BAY%20INVESTMENTS%20LLC&listNameOrder=SPRINGHILLBAYINVESTMENTS%20L190000881460

285   https://bisprofiles.com/fl/trend-p01000060268

286   https://search.sunbiz.org/Inquiry/CorporationSearch/ConvertTiffToPDF?storagePath=COR%5C2004%5C0219%5C50306155.Tif&documentNumber=N04000001572

287   https://bisprofiles.com/fl/the-ippolito-family-limited-partnership-ltd-a12000000967

288   https://bisprofiles.com/fl/1439-oceania-l17000252882

289   https://www.newspapers.com/image/184795422/?article=10ab3070-cd0a-48a5-91a1-109b92c5d862&xid=4716&terms=Frank_C_Ippolito

290   https://www.newspapers.com/image/623141739/?match=1&terms=%22Frank%20C.%20Ippolito%22

291   https://www.ancestry.com/discoveryui-content/view/103000782:6224?tid=&pid=&queryId=c5e2f899-21c6-498a-a501-7134cf6cde40&_phsrc=hYq2143&_phstart=successSource

292   https://www.splcenter.org/fighting-hate/intelligence-report/2001/false-patriots

293   https://www.newspapers.com/image/333887815/?match=1&terms=%22emilio%20ippolito%22

294   https://www.newspapers.com/image/332838590/?match=1&terms=%22emilio%20ip-

polito%22

295		https://www.newspapers.com/image/238664695/?terms=%22ippolito%22&match=1

296		https://culteducation.com/group/949-greater-ministries-international/8927-charity-group-linked-to-militia-organization.html

297		https://www.newspapers.com/image/1074707969/?match=1&terms=%22Greater%20Ministries%20International%22%20%22Church%20of%20Christ%22

298		https://www.newspapers.com/image/340590637/?match=1&terms=%22emilio%20ippolito%22

299		https://www.newspapers.com/image/340593179/?match=1&terms=%22emilio%20ippolito%22

300		https://www.splcenter.org/fighting-hate/intelligence-report/2001/false-patriots

301		https://www.newspapers.com/image/630493119/?match=1&terms=%22Burl%20McCormick%22%20

302		https://search.sunbiz.org/Inquiry/corporationsearch/SearchResultDetail?inquirytype=EntityName&directionType=Initial&searchNameOrder=MOROCO%206838930&aggregateId=domp-683893-c50829be-332d-4edb-afc5-97ee27ca3053&searchTerm=MOROCO%20LLC&listNameOrder=MOROCO%206838930

303		https://www.newspapers.com/image/302201500/?match=1&terms=%22Robert%20Forcum%22

304		https://www.eater.com/2016/9/1/12533030/money-laundering-restaurant

305		https://www.occrp.org/en/investigations/holy-rollers-the-religious-leaders-using-churches-to-launder-illicit-cash-across-the-americas

306		https://thebusinessprofessor.com/en_US/criminal-civil-law/loan-back-method-of-money-laundering-definition

307		A quitclaim deed transfers the owner's entire interest in a property but makes no promises at all about the veracity and/or extent of the owner's title.

308		.When I reported this to the Florida State Attorney's office, they did nothing about it. The IRS, however, did come after me, going so far as to seize my back accounts while they investigated.

309		Interview with Mary Smith.

CHAPTER SIXTEEN

EVERY BREATH YOU TAKE

By May 2011, our days in Florida were numbered – we just didn't know it yet. Everything that kept my family there would soon be taken from us, including our safety and security. On May 4, Ed Spooner was nominated by President Obama as the U.S. Marshall for the Northern District of Florida. This same man had been instrumental in covering up Nobles' crimes, particularly the firearms violations and who had tried to frame me to cover up the murder by Nobles witnessed by my sons.

He had effectively bailed Mike Nobles out of jail, signing an appearance bond for him after a second judge released him on his own recognizance. Then his department attorney had conspired to fabricate records in the case as "the police" disposed of Nobles' guns.

Just over a week later, the President appointed George Sheldon the head of the Federal Administration for Children and Families. Under Sheldon's watch, the Florida Department of Children and Families (DCF) had been weaponized to cover up sexual abuse and human trafficking of children, systematically falsifying reports and destroying records while local state and federal authorities hid behind them in an elaborate shell game. Now, just as the so-called child protection investigators were paid off, he was receiving his political payoff.

The next day, May 18, I was summoned to a board room at work in a bizarre charade in front Brad Sheehan, other management, and Air Line Pilots Association representatives. I was told I must sign an employment contract. The contract required that I remain alcohol free, even though I had never had any FAA reportable incident, never failed any test or had ever been the subject of any complaint, other than the one by Nobles. Of course, there would be regular testing, which I had already started, and a requirement that I attend a gazillion meetings run by Birds of a Feather International, an Alcoholics Anonymous-style relapse prevention group, Alcoholics Anonymous meetings, and a for-pay Relapse Prevention group. To call the experience humiliating and uncalled for would be an understatement. I balked at the extra meetings beyond the weekly Relapse Prevention group I was already attending. I was already gone three or four days per week. As the only parent in my children's lives, I was not going to leave them alone to attend a meeting every night for a problem I didn't have and had never been diagnosed with. The AA meeting requirement was removed, and I signed under duress.

* * *

That summer, I made a new friend – or so I thought. It turned out to be another con. My neighbor, George Polansky, suddenly showed an interest in my family after three years or more or less of no contact. He offered to let me and the kids fish off his dock. I had helped him build a seawall. His father had been a Salvation Army minister. He claimed his uncle Johnny was a U.S. Marshall and personal friends with John Walsh, the host of *America's Most Wanted*.

He methodically pried information from me. Eventually, he asked me to give him the burnt dental remains and a computer disk holding a ton of scanned documents. This was allegedly sent to the FBI headquarters in Quantico, Virginia, for examination. Every time I saw him after that, he told me the U.S. Marshals were impressed with my work, and that any day now his uncle Johnny was going to call, or John Walsh was going to call. Any day there was going to be a big bust. He was blowing smoke up my rear end. That day never came. I am sure the evidence, like every other record and evidence I provided to law enforcement agencies, had disappeared. Obviously, someone or some agency put Curious George up to this task.

* * *

I don't remember the exact dates, but I reached out to the FBI one last time. First, I went to the FBI office with my records, the cellphones given to me by Mike Nobles and Jerry Williams, and samples of evidence I retrieved from the trailer. I was stonewalled trying to set up a meeting with Agent Kinard. I called later to try to talk with Tim Kinard again, who had lied to me. Instead, I got a hostile James Stewart, who said "I am not going to discuss Nobles' guns."

Lied to by the Feds, I reached out to the Southern Poverty Law Center. After multiple calls and letters, I finally got a call from Mark Potok, who was quite rude and told me that he had forwarded my complaint to Randy Beach of the ATF. Beach was lying, claiming a "grey area in the law," and hiding behind Joey Forgione and Donna Parish, who repeatedly tried to frame me. We were running around in circles cleaning up after the Nobles. Every time I reached out, just as I had to the National

Center for Missing and Exploited Children, my DCF Inspector General complaint, these complaints were forwarded to the very people engaged in the coverup.

* * *

I also tried to track down Nobles' former accomplices, thinking they would be happy to talk about the snitch who put them in prison. I was wrong. The closest I came was Ernie Yarbrough, Timothy Yarbrough's son and white supremacist, who since has been elected as an Alabama congressman trying to return Alabama to the Dark Ages. He said he would talk to "people," and if those people wanted to talk, he would put us in touch. I changed my phone number after the whole creepy incident.

My kids remained in treatment with Pamela Powers at Lutheran Services. Pam, a military veteran experienced in treating combat veterans with PTSD, had testified on their behalf before the sideshow in former JAG officer Judge Bergosh's court. As a side note, treatment through Lutheran Services had previously been promised at the Santa Rosa Kids House and then blocked by Rick Karshna and the DCF just like it had been offered then blocked at the Emerald Coast Child Advocacy Center. It would be problematic to have an official record of my sons' disclosures and treatment in a facility tied to the government.

As my kids' treatment cost was enormous, even after insurance, I took Pam's advice to apply for victims' compensation. I received a denial stating that, according to law enforcement, no crimes had been committed against my sons. And furthermore, an "ineligible person" had filed. The same game. Nothing happened, and I wasn't the father even though I was the legal father of my sons who had very real PTSD from very real crimes. My kids had been raped by their grandfather and his accomplices. Now they were being raped by the government.

I wasn't surprised, but I was livid. Local law enforcement and state officials had put my sons in harm's way, covered up the crimes that traumatized them, and prevented them from receiving desperately needed treatment. I gathered my kids' records and drove to the Capitol Building in Tallahassee with the hope of meeting Attorney General Pam Bondi. I did not get a meeting with her, but I sat and waited until someone was willing to talk with me. The records were reviewed, and the victim's compensation was approved. Over the next year or so, they paid more than $10,000 in copayments and deductibles for my sons' treatment for trauma caused by crimes covered up by the government.

On July 8, 2011, I received a response to the Florida Department of Law Enforcement from Inspector General Al Dennis – spinning, stonewalling, and denying wrongdoing.

* * *

Now it was August 10. The FAA substance abuse program I had been admitted to through a fake DUI and fake medical history required an annual psychological evaluation. Again, despite qualified people in my own area, an Atlanta doctor was handpicked to continue this fraudulent charade. Dr. Charles Richard Harper, an old Freemason right-wing Navy doc, and friend of FAA Doctor Michael Berry, ordered me to go to one of his pals. Dr. John Doyle is another old ex-military dinosaur and former Air Force flight surgeon who happened to have once lived in Blue Water Bay in Niceville. His home was just off Winged Foot Drive, one of many streets in the area with Masonic names, such as Nimrod Circle. Dr. Doyle evaluated me and determined I did not meet the criteria for alcoholism or abuse, and yet made the bizarre recommendation that I remain in the program. But this was not good enough for Dr. Harper who would proceed to twist Dr. Doyle's arm to get him to amend his report.

* * *

Through therapy and talking to me, my sons had disclosed being severely sexually assaulted by Nobles and unidentified others with a wooden implement. Gabe drew pictures for his therapist – they looked exactly like the "magic wands" made by Nobles' warlock brother, Roger. A ritual right out of Aleister Crowley's *The Equinox*. Therapist Powers told me I should have the kids examined, which I did with their doctor, Dr. Perez. The kids told him what had happened.

Mike Nobles' brother, claimed on social media he learned about "harmony and balance" from his father, Oscar Nobles. Balance between dark and light. Good and evil. God and Lucifer. Agape and Thelema. The number 93. Hocus pocus. You could say Roger is the black sheep of the family as he let out the family secret. Witchcraft. Backwoods Alabama voodoo. Roger Nobles is a former Church of Christ minister, turned Wiccan, turned Shaman, and most recently claims to be a Reiki healer. He was once a member of the Texas Witches. He used to sell magic wands and staffs online. My sons described him as Paw Paw's evil twin. He is also an Air Force veteran. He collects spell books, books on the Kabbalah, and other witchcraft books. His reading list is published online and includes *The Complete Book of Black Magic and Witchcraft*, *To Stir a Magick*

Cauldron, Hereditary Witchcraft, The Gnostic Gospels, Solitary Witch the Ultimate Book of Shadows for the New Generation, The Essential Kabbalah, Italian Witchcraft, Celtic Myth and Magick, and a *Witches' Bible."* Five of these have Pentagrams on the cover.

* * *

On August 12, Dr. Perez made a report to the abuse hotline. Child protection agencies do not investigate such crimes, only law enforcement. No one in law enforcement responded, but DCF investigator Connie Edgar did. I was furious, of course. She had previously initiated a response when the kids were kidnapped in 2008, and then ordered to cease her investigation by superiors before ever contacting me. She had been the assigned investigator in the case of the report made by Dr. Elaine Wood and had promised a finding and a safety plan, only to be overruled when Rick Karshna took over and decided to "do it differently this time." Differently meant falsifying yet another report after contacting and colluding with Jennifer Clark in Okaloosa County at the Emerald Coast Children's Advocacy Center.

It appeared, however, that this time would be different. She interviewed Gabe. Toby was not home. During her interview, Gabe affirmed what had happened to him in detail. I provided her with a pile of records, including the psychological evaluations and diagnosis of PTSD. She said she would come back to interview Toby, but never returned. After days passed, I called her. She acted sheepish and evasive at first. Finally, she admitted her superior, Pete Gallas, had ordered her to cease her investigation. This was the third time she was blocked from investigating.

Just like with Janine Williams at the FDLE, Officer Nelson and Sergeant Geiser at the Niceville Police, James Lorenz at the Walton County Sheriff's Department, and Deputy Kyle in Santa Rosa who had requested an arrest warrant, superiors blocked her. Nobles was Teflon, untouchable. Here is the narrative of her report.:

NARRATIVE:
Sometime between October 2008 and April 2009, grandpa stuck a sharp stick in Gabriel's rectum. Gabriel has been complaining of pain and blood in his bowel movements. His rectum is inflamed and slightly swollen. The stick is about 10-12 inches long and about half an inch around. No other details are known.

IMPLICATIONS FOR CHILD SAFETY:
The father and the oldest child have been located and the home seen. There are no conditions in the home that would pose a threat

of harm to the children. There is no history of violence and there is criminal history that is of concern. The father interacted with the child in an appropriate and caring manner. There are no concerns at this time of drug or alcohol use and the father is not biologically related to the children and there is a friend staying at the home. There is a pattern of reports and the allegations are serious and severe as they are regarding sexual abuse. The child was seen by his PCP due to having an irritated rectum and CPI will staff with the CPT as well due to his disclosure.

Child Vulnerability Implications:
The children are 8 and 10 years of age and Gabriel has been diagnosed with explosive disorder, ADD, possible bi-polar, and PTSD and is taking psychotropic meds. Toby has also been diagnosed with PTSD and both boys are seeing a counselor. Gabriel has been Baker Acted due to violence against others and suicidal thoughts. Toby has not yet been interviewed so his behaviors are not yet known.

Protective Capacities Implications:
There is a prior history although the boys have not been in care. The father interacted appropriately with the oldest child and appears to be protective of the boys. The mother and father do not have a good relationship and the mother has not been around the boys since Christmas. The father appears to comprehend what is going on and has no history of abuse. The father does not have support in the local area and his family is in Georgia. The father has been compliant up to this point.

Overall Safety Assessment:
The children are safe in the care of their father and there appears to be many questions that need answered regarding what has happened to these boys. The children have been consistent in their assertion that something has happened to them as far as abuse. Both have been diagnosed with PTSD as though they have been through a traumatic event. CPI will work with this investigation and attempt to answer some of the questions as well as bring resolution to these allegations. This investigation will is ongoing pending collateral contacts as well as obtaining medical information and interviewing the AP and the other child."

The finding portion on Edgar's report is identical to so many other DCF reports. Blank. No investigation, no collateral witnesses interviewed.

A whitewash. More importantly, no law enforcement investigation again. On August 18, on doctor's orders, Gabe was examined at Sacred Heart Hospital for the unexplained bleeding he thought was from previous sexual abuse. Results were inconclusive. He would later have nose bleeds and even bled from his eye on one occasion at school. The source was never identified. Exposure to toxins at 1118 Rhonda Drive? *Maybe…*

* * *

On August 22, Gabe had his routine appointment with his psychiatrist, Dr. Henry Doenlen. I needed paperwork signed for work so that I could be approved for intermittent FMLA (Family and Medical Leave Act) to care for Gabe. He had suffered multiple breakdowns and hospitalizations, and I was told this would be the best avenue for the future. Dr. Doenlen had never evaluated Gabe himself but relied on previous evaluations and diagnosis. He had to evaluate Gabe personally to sign the paperwork. During this evaluation, Gabe again disclosed horrific mental and sexual abuse. Dr. Doenlen made a report to the abuse hotline. No one responded. Again.

* * *

As I dealt with the aftermath of Nobles' abuse of my kids, and the ongoing coverup in Florida, Dr. Harper in Atlanta, who had sabotaged my career to cover for Nobles, was now covering his ass because of his friend Dr. Doyle's report. At Dr. Harper's request, Dr. Doyle published an amendment to his report on the same day that Dr. Doenlen made a report that received no response. Here is what the amendment stated:

> Case discussed with Dr. Richard Harper, AME. Patient has a diagnosis of alcoholism per the FAA that contributed to his separation from the USAF. The patient is stating that a diagnosis was never made and that it was removed from his contract. He denies treatment for alcoholism in the USAF. When I reviewed the DSM 4 Criteria for alcohol dependence or abuse he denies criteria. I find his denials concerning and support monitoring.

I simply answered his evaluation questions honestly, and he produced another pack of lies. He dropped this amended report in the mail and sent it to me as a warning, signed "Dr. H." Shut up and don't make waves. There was no diagnosis and certainly no diagnosis that led to my separation from the Air Force. The story had gone from alcohol abuse based on a fake DUI, to alcoholism, based on a fake medical history, to an alcoholic in denial. Slander, defamation, smear and control.

* * *

On September 1, a DCF report was closed regarding the complaint by Gabe's psychiatrist. Throughout all of this, neither Gabe's psychiatrist nor his doctor were ever contacted by any official. This totaled at least eighteen reports, thirteen of which were closed with no investigation and five closed with blatantly falsified reports, all by the same three so-called investigators.

None of these reports received any investigation. Jennifer Clark and Heather Pagano from the ECCAC acting under the supervision of Donna Parish (herself a Church of Christ official), and washed-up ex-cop and failed Republican candidate, Rick Karshna, who was colluding with Clark and Pagano to falsify records and internal documents. A law enforcement investigation was supposedly required with every report. It appeared the puppet master behind all of this was Tom Dunn, the Case Advocate and the Emerald Coast Child Advocacy Center.

As a result of the outrageous conduct of Officers Forgione and Kearnes, I requested a meeting with the police chief. On September 9, his secretary sent an email to arrange a meeting on September 15. I responded on September 12 agreeing to the appointment. The day before the meeting, the police chief's secretary, Sheila Bates, emailed me to cancel the meeting. I never got the meeting I requested. I would repeatedly receive the same treatment as I attempted to get meetings with the Okaloosa County Sheriff and with DCF Circuit One Administrator Janice Thomas who both hid behind lying lawyers.

* * *

On September 16, I sent a letter to Sheriff Larry Ashley regarding his agency's refusal to investigate crimes and the outright coverup of crimes. On September 21, I filed a complaint with the Florida DCF Inspector General. On October 18, I had to use my FMLA with a doctor's note from Gabe's psychiatrist due to "severe mental illness," meaning severe PTSD.

On October 19, the DCF Inspector General responded to my complaint which had been investigated by Donna Parish, the primary person responsible for the crimes. In other words, the perpetrator was assigned to investigate herself – just like the Warren Commission. The response contained 146 lies.

Parish denied Clark's efforts to frame me with false reports to law enforcement and through the DCF, which are thoroughly documented. She denied any part in the false restraining order, which Clark instructed Christy to file following Parish's written instructions, again thoroughly documented. She tap danced around Clark's false report claiming there were no disclosures of abuse. And she denied that the Nobles were ever foster parents.

* * *

On November 2, I received more stonewalling from Sheriff Ashley, a letter from attorney Marsha Weaver again refusing to investigate crimes claiming all my allegations had previously been reviewed and closed as "unfounded," even though none of the allegations were ever investigated, and all the efforts to investigate were shut down. There was not a single law enforcement record anywhere regarding the sexual assaults, exploitation and endangerment of my kids reported more than 10 times. Another cowardly official hiding behind a lying lawyer.

I finally filed a lawsuit against the Florida Department of Family and Children naming all the parties involved in the coverup of abuse, including the primary guilty parties: Rick Karshna, Jennifer Clark, and Heather Pagano, as well as their supervisors and the Circuit One Administrator Janice Thomas.

* * *

On December 3, FAA Administrator Randy Babbitt was charged with DUI. He failed a breathalyzer test, proving he was above the legal blood-alcohol limit. Meanwhile, I was in purgatory for a fake DUI and fake medical history manufactured by his top medical officials set in motion by Dr. Harper, a self-described alcoholic doctor with a DUI conviction. Babbitt failed to notify his superiors or the FAA and proceeded to fly a test flight two days later. The charges were dropped on a technicality, and he proclaimed himself innocent. Just like the DUI of Florida Representative Matt Gaetz, the powerful and privileged are rarely held accountable.

* * *

On December 14, the office of State Attorney Bill Eddins responded. I had complained to the state attorney regarding the refusal to prosecute Nobles about the firearms and the corrupt handling of the case. I was told the review would take several weeks.

On January 1, 2012, Gabe was hospitalized at the Peachford Hospital mental health clinic in Atlanta after suffering a breakdown. He hyperventilated and turned blue as he talked about the murders he witnessed in front of hospital staff after learning he would be admitted and separated from me.

Having had the FDLE engage in a shell game, and the Florida Department of Children and Families' outright lies in their response to my complaint, I appealed to Florida Governor Rick Scott. On January 4 and 9, I received letters from Erin Romeiser, office of the Chief Inspector General, forwarding my complaint to the DCF for review, an agency which had already been caught in a web of lies and obstruction and had let the primary perpetrator investigate herself. The shell game continued.

* * *

On January 19, Gabe had a violent outburst at school that ultimately led to his expulsion. A kid tagged him with a ball, and he exploded, attacking the other child, which was caught on camera. Gabe had been a very peaceful nonviolent child before his abduction with no issues other than quirks from his autism. On January 23, I received a letter from a DCF attorney, Katie George, again denying that the Nobles were foster parents. These victims of a monster had been erased just like the foster kids in Walton County possibly tied to the same network.

On January 25, State Attorney Bill Eddins sent me a letter assigning my complaint sent to his office to Tommy Tucker. Tucker provided an almost comical response on February 1, 2012. He wrote that there was insufficient evidence to prosecute Nobles for possession of firearms by a felon or murder. It had to be one of the most documented and witnessed cases of firearms possession by a felon in history, not to mention the associated crimes by DCF investigators and law enforcement, records falsification and evidence destruction. The murder was never investigated.

The eyewitnesses were never interviewed except for a deposition that was set up to frame me. The kids truthfully testified to witnessing murder, testimony that Bill Eddins tried to bury. He claims allegations of sexual abuse were investigated by the appropriate state agency. The DCF does not investigate sexual abuse, but law enforcement is mandated to. DCF personnel who had placed foster children in his home and erased their records, engaged in a flagrant coverup and had no authority to investigate.

The DCF destroyed records, falsified reports, and tried to boomerang reports made by mandatory reporters on me while local, state, and ultimately federal authorities engaged played a shell game to hide behind these lies. Local state and federal officials used the DCF as a dumping ground to establish plausible deniability. Mr. Tucker, however, told me he had been called by Tom Dunn, who claimed there was no evidence of sexual abuse in the Nobles' home. Dunn was everywhere lobbying for Nobles with the State Attorney, interfering in a lynching and murder case in Walton County and blocking sexual abuse investigations. All the while, he misled me into believing he and Forgione were planning to investigate while he was smearing me and blocking investigations.

In response to one last effort to have the DCF Inspector General investigate the crimes by Clark, Parish, Pagano, and Karshna, I received a response from Chris Hirst, Inspector General, on February 28, 2012, refusing to investigate.

* * *

After being essentially excommunicated from Calvary Chapel to punish my kids for being victims, we tried another church: the Church of the Living Water. This is a Pentecostal church attached to Pastor Bobby Harrell's house (probably for tax reasons). We were careful not to talk about what had happened to us. One day some redneck who looked like he crawled out of the movie "Deliverance" walked up to me in front of the church one day and hit my forehead.

He claimed that God told him to cast out my demon of sexual immorality. I'm not sure what that demon was; I wasn't engaged in sex of any kind with anyone. Seemed like projection protecting lowlifes engaged in human trafficking. We then went to Life Church, which was started by Dale Waltman after he left Calvary Chapel. We did so even though he betrayed my kids and committed a felony by not reporting the sexual offenses disclosed to him.

I decided to give him another chance. I even let him baptize Toby. This is when I was assaulted by Larry, friend of ex-Office of Special Investigations Agent Joe Figueroa, who was living in our home still caring for my kids while I was away. I never confided much in Larry, who was pretty crazy and had served jail sentences in two states for violating restraining orders protecting his ex-wife and son.

Joe and Larry came to Life Church to check up and intimidate me. Larry screamed and shoved me, telling me I was endangering my children by talking about Mike Nobles and what they had witnessed. He then slammed me against a wall. I assume OSI Joe must have filled in Larry.

* * *

I didn't document the date, but it was near the time of Gabe's expulsion from school. The boys sat in the car in my sight continuously at a convenience store. I went inside, and Brian Riggs, Michael Nobles' son-in-law and an accessory to several of Nobles' crimes, had followed us into the parking lot. He charged toward my car with my kids inside screaming. The man who covered up sexual abuse, participated in a kidnapping, hid guns in his home and subjected my son to violent beatings with a belt, said he planned to report me to the DCF for briefly leaving my kids, even though they were in my plain sight. The kids were terrified. Toby later said he was afraid Brian would kidnap him again.

Lighthouse Private Christian Academy was our last reason to stay in Florida. I wanted the kids to have stability, stay with the friends they had made and have a loving comfortable environment to learn. When Gabe was expelled, it was the last straw. Being threatened, stalked and framed for years, their mother had vanished for two years, and we had been banned from the church that the kids loved, It was time to go – we were no longer safe in the Florida Panhandle. It felt like the movie *Mississippi Burning*. I was subjected to repeated efforts to frame me, received death threats, and I was stalked and pulled over by cops for no reason.

During my last day in Florida, I saw the same Santa Rosa County deputy everywhere I went, the cop involved in covering up the kidnapping. I cannot say with certainty he was following me, but it sure seemed like it. I just wanted to get across the state line to Georgia where I thought we would be safe. Boy was I wrong. We quickly packed a truck and headed for home, expecting to find peace and start over.

But the devil would go down to Georgia.

CHAPTER 17

THE DEVIL WENT DOWN TO GEORGIA

We rented a mobile home next to my parents' property. Our 14-year-old landlord needed a driver. I had gone from living on the bay to a rented mobile home with a teenage redneck landlord. But I was OK; at least we would have some peace, I thought. I enrolled the boys into Mossy Creek Elementary School near our new home. The principal was Jennifer Green, a member of The Torch, a Church of God in Habersham County

Despite a collection of Bible verses on her office wall and a collection of miniature angels – and violating the separation of church and state with prayer in public school – she would later show a lack of the love of Jesus in her heart. When I enrolled the kids, I shared some of their history and records with her so she would be aware of their disabilities and needs. Instead of accommodating them, she became Gabe's nemesis.

* * *

Shortly after moving to Georgia, I looked up some old cases in Okaloosa County and found a case I had not seen – a divorce filing by my wife. The record showed I had filed a motion to represent myself and had filed a response to the case along with a financial affidavit. This was deeply disturbing because I was completely unaware of the case and had not been served yet. These were fake filings, allegedly from me, and fraud and manipulation of the legal system.

I contested the case and won. Her attorney eventually resigned because her client was not cooperating. This was an indication to me that Christy again was being used as a pawn to get the boys back in her father's hands.

They say that the definition of insanity is trying the same thing over and over and expecting a different outcome. I might qualify as insane for continuing to find a home at evangelical and Pentecostal churches, only to keep getting the same horrific results. The first church we attended was The Torch, a Church of God megachurch in northeast Georgia.

Congressman Doug Collins, another preacher turned politician, has been there for gun safety courses. That is what they worship – guns and

Republican right-wing politics as they tell people from the pulpit who to vote for.

I tried to reach out to Collins for help with my issues involving federal agencies. His staff threw me and my kids out of his office. Fine Christian – a real hero for children. Habersham County Sheriff Joey Terrell, who taught Sunday school there, offered to examine the evidence I had retrieved from the utility trailer – evidence that no one in Florida would examine. I provided him with a thumb drive filled with documents. It was all returned to me unexamined with no explanation.

Next, I went directly to the Georgia Bureau of Investigation. I got the same results. I met with Senior Pastor Franklin and shared some of my material, hoping he could provide guidance. He did not have much to say. Then I met with Mike Thomas. The associate pastor suggested I destroy all my records along with physical evidence and pretend the abuse never happened.

We left the church for a biker church, Church on the Hill. John Lance preaches right-wing political rhetoric on social media. They were nice enough. I shared what my kids had experienced and showed him Gabe's pictures. He immediately recognized it as "Knight Templar" stuff. He said he would make some calls to Florida. Apparently, he did because he would never talk about it again. He offered me a cabin in the woods to hide.

But I am not a coward.

I found a new therapist for the kids in Georgia who referred Gabe for psychological testing on March 1 and 3, 2012. The diagnosis was PTSD, ADHD, and sexual abuse. Soon after, he was tested and diagnosed with autism.

* * *

Three weeks later, I went for an assessment to the Mustard Seed Counseling Services. I had been required to attend weekly "relapse prevention" sessions since 2010, at my expense, because of my fake DUI and fake medical history. I now needed a place to continue my sessions in Georgia. I was evaluated by Kim Blackburn, who determined I did not meet criteria to attend their program. I told them I was required to keep my job, so I was allowed to attend.

After attending their groups for a while, Kim recommended I instead meet with the director of the program, Mike Johns, one on one. I think this happened because he realized alcohol was not the real issue and that counseling would help me through my lengthy bouts of trauma.

Johns, who ran the drug court for the county, was perplexed about how I ended up in this program – especially how I could be in an aftercare program having never been diagnosed or treated. So, on April 9, 2012, he had me sign a release for a records request from Dr. Harper, who had been able to contain his scheme so far through keeping everything in house.

This poking at the hornet's nest may have triggered what happened next. After my old beat-up vehicle died, I had to borrow money to buy an old Jeep from my nephew. I drove it to work just once and it was stolen on April 20, 2012, my birthday but also another event on Hitler's birthday. To this day it has never been found. I believe someone was sending me a message.

This was the beginning of the end of my flying career, and all hell was about to break loose. This was the first of several requests ignored by Dr. Harper who would ultimately repeatedly defy subpoenas for records that belonged to me. That's about when the monitoring program changed. I was required to fly monthly to Atlanta for company meetings in addition to all the other meetings I had to attend. Additionally, instead of a single monthly urinalysis, the random testing was handed over to a private contractor, and I could be tested an unlimited number of times per month. Every morning, I had to call a number to see if I was on the list for the day and if so, scramble to a lab. I couldn't make any plans, even on my days off.

All this was done without my consent. There was no medical review officer (MRO). My personal and private medical information was sent to a private contractor that demanded I urinate in a cup without any releases from me and no legal basis to demand my bodily fluids. Eventually, the company tried to twist my arm to sign a back-dated release. I refused to. The resentment grew. Every one of these meetings, every illegal invasion of my privacy and unreasonable search and seizure of my bodily fluids were extensions of acts of stalking and witness tampering by Mike Nobles – all to cover for him and his foul house. To cover up murder.

Fast forward to June 2012. Gabe's therapist reaffirms his diagnosis of PTSD. In July, life grew especially ugly. I had another exam with Dr. Harper because he dated the medical certificates to expire every six months. This happened despite my special issuance letter, which required only an annual evaluation, and as a reminder, was requested on my behalf by Dr. Harper without my knowledge.

When asked to see my records, Dr. Harper refused. To this day, I remain locked out of my own medical records despite repeated requests and subpoenas. I inquired again about the fake DUI, and he exploded with "what do you want to do? Undo your diagnosis of alcoholism?" Of course, I never had any diagnosis and still haven't. I then asked him why I had to come every six months when only an annual examination was required (and he charged a premium, cash-only rate). He said everyone had to do the same. I was on to him, and he knew it. The next day he called me and told me it was time again to see the "shrink" and instructed me to make another appointment with Dr. Doyle, who had unethically amended his report a year prior at Dr. Harper's request.

I had already been referred to Dr. Michael Vaughn at Peachford Hospital. Dr. Vaughn's lofty credentials included being the Director of Addiction Services at Peachford and the Medical Director of Metro Atlanta Recovery Residence (MARR), which the FAA uses for substance abuse evaluations and treatment. Dr. Harper pitched a tantrum. I was wasting my money, he said, and would not accept an evaluation from Dr. Vaughn.

* * *

That was the last straw. On August 8, I went to the Richard B. Russell Federal Building in Atlanta – ironic as this former U.S. senator was a Freemason and a racist – and filed a federal lawsuit against Drs. Harper, Doyle, Berry, Silberman, and former FAA Administrator Babbit. On August 14, Dr. Vaughn gave me a clean bill of health at my appointment.

Fed up, I also filed a complaint with the Department of Transportation Inspector General. The IG refused to investigate. Over the next three weeks, however, I was subjected to five "random" drug and alcohol tests from my airline in retaliation. I had had one random test in the previous 11 years. On August 22 I applied through an attorney for disability insurance for Gabe. The coverage was denied. I fired the attorney and appealed on my own.

Dr. Berry and his pal Dr. Harper refused to accept Dr. Vaughn's report and tried to force me back to one of their military flight surgeon pals willing to doctor records. I refused. Then Christian Crusader Brad Secker of the Air Line Pilots Association calls to scream at me that I am "in jail" and must serve my sentence.

In jail? For a fake DUI? I hung up on him. He called me over and over in a panic, but I refused to take his calls. I was done. But the war was getting to me. I couldn't sleep anymore. I went back to Dr. Vaughn on August 23 and was diagnosed with general anxiety, which was really the onset of PTSD. I was prescribed medication. I called work and explained why I was out and was placed on medical leave.

On August 24, I sent a thumb drive full of records to David Wiley at the Gainesville FBI office that documented outrageous crimes, including numerous crimes by public officials. I never received a response. Next, I received a letter, dated August 28, from FAA employee Sandy Clymer, the very person who believes she sees angels and planted a fake DUI in my records. She threatened to revoke my pilot's license if I did not return to Dr. Doyle for another examination. I called her bluff. This would have created an immediate option to appeal, and the shitshow behind it could never stand the light of day.

* * *

Based on their records and intake evaluations, Gabe and Toby were accepted into counseling on August 30 at the Children's Center for Hope & Healing where they continued to process and describe the horrific abuse they suffered and the murder they witnessed. As the counselors there observed, kids don't make this stuff up. The next day I filed a motion to dismiss the case against the Florida Department of Families and Children as I more than had my hands full – fighting to save my career.

Sparing you the legal details, I ended up with a case in state court against Drs. Harper and Doyle in Gwinnett County, and an appeal of my medical certification and lawsuit in federal court in Gainesville. Harper and Doyle hired five law firms – I represented myself. On October 23, I sent subpoenas to Dr. Harper via FedEx and the Gwinnett County sheriff. Both files were served on October 24. These were for depositions scheduled for November 12. I rented a room and had a court reporter and videographer. I had to borrow money from my mother to pay for this.

On October 24, attorney Clifford Hardwick, an Army veteran, Freemason, and member of the same lodge as Harper, sent a nasty letter filled with personal attacks to Mike Johns of the Mustard Seed Counseling and denying that Harper had any of the records Mike had requested. Mike had made numerous requests beginning the previous March. This was apparently triggered by the subpoenas as he had ignored repeated previous requests for months.

* * *

I and the boys were approached in a convenience store and invited to a Halloween event at the Harvest Assembly of God church. We agreed. Another setup – I soon found myself in a nightmare. Within a couple of weeks, someone left a $50 bill in my car. Soon after, I was offered a job by Joe Johnson, one of the church leaders working on his house. I needed the money but couldn't help but remember how Jerry Williams at Calvary Chapel in Florida shook my hand with a $100 bill in it to buy gifts and groceries and a cellphone while prying for information and pressuring me to shut up about Nobles.

Ed Ferrell had offered the carrot and stick at the Destin Church of Christ. Both Ed and Jerry were from Birmingham, Alabama. They used the same lines and tactics – get a divorce, move away, find another woman to marry, forget about Nobles. It turns out that Joe was a rabid white supremacist and, like Jerry, an Army veteran. Another "patriot" from Birmingham, Alabama. Over the following months, Joe would use the same tactics and lines. The pastor, Jimmy Sargent, warned me to keep my mouth shut when I showed him the pictures Gabe drew. He was part-time pastor and full-time used car salesman who bragged about ripping off the "unsaved" and railed against other local churches for being too liberal.

The church was racist and particularly homophobic. When I shared some of my story with Sargent he said, "this runs deep" and warned me the sheriff was a Freemason. What I didn't know was that Jimmy Sargent, a right-wing extremist radical, was the chaplain for the Freemason sheriff. The longer we stayed, and the longer I worked for Johnson, the more awkward it became. He would refer to President Obama as "super nigger" and express the desire that someone kill him. After we were left homeless, I looked into public housing, which Joe discouraged because, well, you know, of the people who live there. He threw the N-word around all the time. The church had only white members.

* * *

On November 8, I filed an appeal of my medical certification in federal court in Gainesville. This would become a case that would drag on for 13 months amidst government stonewalling, stalling, and hiding records. On November 12, Harper, without any prior indication otherwise, failed to appear at the deposition in contempt of court. I was stuck with the bill.

Two things happened the next day. Attorney Hardwick sent me a nasty threatening letter, one of many he would send, and Mike Johns performed a thorough evaluation and concluded that I did not meet criteria for treatment or monitoring for any substance abuse and should be released from the program. I am sure Harper put the letter straight into the trash. On November 15, I requested my records from Harper via certified mail. He refused to accept the mail. On the same day, I filed a motion of contempt against Harper.

Judge John Doran refused to enforce his own subpoenas. The same day, I received a letter from my company's HR representative, Kathy Harris: "I'm sorry you are running into problems with resolving your legal issues," she wrote. *Legal issues caused by the company.*

My union, Air Line Pilots Association (ALPA), refused to help me. I finally met with Brad Secker, ALPA attorney, Terry Saturday, and another ALPA representative, Sterling Roach, who just sat there the whole time with a smirk on his face. I brought all my records. They refused to look at them. They all acted like Jimmy Hoffa and tried to twist my arm to go back to Dr. Doyle and beg for mercy – it was only one more year. Only one more year of being punished for standing up for my kids. One more year of humiliation and invasion of privacy and violations of my constitutional rights.

All to serve one purpose: *Covering the tracks of Mike "Mickey" Nobles, his business associates, and whatever was going on with those houses. To cover up murder. I wasn't going to lie for the government. Certainly not to protect Mike Nobles.*

* * *

On November 28, Sandy "She Talks to Angels" Clymer threatened legal enforcement against my pilot's license if I would not surrender my medical certificate, which I wasn't using because I was on medication that restricted my ability to fly. I was waiting for a revocation letter of my medical claim so I could appeal. I was told it was revoked, but I needed a formal letter to appeal through the NTSB within 90 days. This appeal was denied because I didn't have a revocation letter. Just after the 90 days had expired, I received a letter withdrawing my special issuance medical authorization. Games were being played, and I was just a pawn. I filed an amended appeal with the letter.

* * *

On December 7, Gabe was deemed permanently disabled with PTSD by an administrative judge based on my appeal after firing the law firm I had hired. Four days later, he was back in the hospital with suicidal and homicidal thoughts. Right after my son's release, I couldn't find a job, living off odd jobs and food banks and food stamps. FAA Administrator Michael Huerta asked for a 30-day extension on my appeal so his lead attorney could take a vacation. More games and stall tactics.

* * *

On January 16, 2013, I made a complaint to the White House regarding the whole mess, starting in Florida.

On February 12, the FAA administrator filed a brief claiming I was not entitled to an appeal as the previous appeal had been denied. On February 20, I filed a detailed response. No one responded.

On March 5, I received a response to my White House complaint from Calvin A. Shivers, acting section chief of the Violent Criminal Threat Division. FBI Director Christopher Wray handpicked him for this role. His letter claimed there were no violations of federal law to investigate. More spin, stonewalling and denials, as I can provide an extensive list of federal crimes committed, including crimes by federal officials.

* * *

On March 26, Leon Rodriguez, Director US Department of Health and Human Services, Office for Civil Rights, in response to a HIPAA violation complaint against Harper, responded by claiming that Harper, who examined me every six months and kept and transmitted reports and records, was not bound by HIPAA laws. A bizarre circling of the wagons and certainly a lie. Dr. Harper believed he was above any rules or laws. In response to federal complaints, he claimed he was a private doctor with no federal jurisdiction. In response to a state complaint, he claimed he "worked for the FAA" (a lie) and that he wasn't bound by the rules of ethics of the Georgia Composite Board of Medical Examiners.

On April 8, I filed an amended appeal of my medical certification in federal court. The FAA Administrator had 21 days to respond. There was no response.

I had now been out of work since August 2012. All my sick time had been used up. *Some company employees donated sick time (which was only available for one-time use), and that was used up too.* My sons were still in psychiatric care, taking medication, and in therapy when we lost our health insurance. I scrambled to get food stamps and desperately looked for a job. I would eventually learn that Atlantic Southeast Airlines was refusing to verify my employment. I applied for Medicaid insurance for the kids and was approved. I also applied with the Veterans Administration for healthcare for myself and was approved. All of this was despite bizarre claims I had been "court martialed and convicted" and had a "less than honorable discharge," which would preclude me from receiving benefits.

I applied for unemployment benefits. On April 23, my benefits were approved – a paltry $330 a week that was much better than nothing. As soon as Atlantic Southeast Airlines (ASA), which became the now defunct ExpressJet Airlines, was notified, and they lied to the Georgia Department of Labor. On May 3, they claimed I had been suspended because I failed to maintain my medical qualifications. This came despite the fact they provided me with documentation that I was on medical leave.

I was out of work because of criminal fraud that they and their hired doctor had perpetrated. Plus, I was medically unable to fly because of my medications from the anxiety they caused. My unemployment was withdrawn before the first check. I appealed. I went to Georgia Legal Services and asked for legal aid in my appeal. I was promised assistance. It never happened.

First, a hearing was scheduled for May 30 and then delayed to June 24. I had been paying union dues for more than a decade and had lost my license insurance. In response to my inquiry about receiving benefits, I received a letter on May 15 from the Air Line Pilots Association Chief Council, David Semanchik, stating that I could not receive benefits because I needed to be under the care of a doctor. Since I didn't require treatment, I had not seen a doctor.

In other words, I could not work because of a disease the experts said I didn't have and couldn't receive insurance benefits because I wasn't being treated for the disease.

* * *

On June 4, Barbara Diane Pye-Tucker of Georgia Legal Services, which had promised to represent me in my unemployment case, sent me a letter making startling claims. She claimed I took leave from work due to "personal issues" and then was suspended by my employer for losing my medical certification, which she claimed was my fault.

Her source of this information was allegedly from me. Of course, I never said this nor was it true. The ventriloquist effect again. She was circling the wagons for the company.

* * *

Throughout this nightmare, I continued to receive regular harassment from Freemason attorney Clifford Hardwick, earnestly defending his lodge mate. His slanderous allegations included claims that I was charged and convicted of some unidentified alcohol-related offence. Other accusations were that I had been arrested after being found passed out naked in my yard and even more-bizarre claims that I had been "court martialed and convicted" of some unidentified offense.

He played the crazy card claiming I had a "self-admitted psychological history." He suggested I was dangerous. He then sued me for slander for simply spelling out the hard cold facts of what Dr. Harper and his accomplices did.

* * *

On May 24, Deputy Assistant Attorney General Roy L. Austin responded to a lengthy detailed civil rights complaint I had filed accompanied by a disc containing lengthy documentation. Some of the same documents that were sent to Janine Williams at the FDLE and others who had denied receiving them.. He cleverly didn't deny any of my claims, as they were all true. Instead, he claimed they weren't civil rights violations.

I think he needs to go back to law school. My rights to free speech and against illegal search and seizure had been trampled. My right to an attorney and to be released on bond after being placed under false arrest were trampled. My rights to privacy veteran's rights, the Pilot's Bill of Rights, due process – all trampled. My career was stolen through federal crimes.

* * *

There were at least eight plots to frame me on false charges. Caged like an animal. Death threats. Illegal surveillance. Stalked. Effectively blocked from accessing any state or federal agency for recourse as they rapidly aligned under federal pressure to lie. Blocked from the court system as judges were handpicked who engaged in and allowed outrageous conduct by the government. My children were kidnapped, exploited in child pornography, and exposed to gruesome violence that left them disabled with no recourse. The government not only covered up the crimes but attempted to prevent the children from mental health treatment.

* * *

Things soon appeared to escalate. On June 10, the following government officials seemingly blocked my appeal of my medication certifications that had been tampered with through a series of federal crimes:

- U.S. Attorney and the future Acting Deputy Attorney General Sally Quillian Yates.

- Acting Assistant Attorney General and future White House Council Stuart F. Delery.

- Assistant U.S. Attorney Lisa D. Cooper (interestingly, her specialty was white collar crime).

- Federal Aviation Administration Assistant Chief Counsel for Enforcement Peter J. Lynch.

- The U.S. Department of Justice Civil Division Senior Counsel Marcia K. Sowles.

- Dianna Kelleher, Assistant Branch Director.

Their rationale was built upon two big lies: that I did not have a right to appeal for a special issuance medical certificate, and that I had not exhausted other means of appeal. The NTSB, the only other avenue, had already slammed the door. And the special issuance was a fake and a result of a series of interstate federal crimes by a band of old ex-military dinosaurs. I never applied for it, never had any exam, and never filled out any application – all done behind my back.

That fraudulent certificate replaced a valid medical certificate that was never revoked as there was no basis, only "canceled" in a game of smoke and mirrors that included a fake DUI. U.S. Attorney General Eric Holder and all the president's men and women had been backed into a corner over Mike Nobles and a house in Niceville, Florida. They were willing to make me, my children and other children collateral damage and were willing to violate my due process rights.

To add insult to injury, an IRS letter threatening to seize my assets. It was dated the same date of the filing by the lynch mob of attorneys yet mailed days before the date on the letter – predated to coincide with the assault on my constitutional rights by the DOJ, Department of Transportation, and the FAA.

This was the second time the IRS had targeted me during this ordeal. The first time I had to fight it in federal court (and won). In that case, the IRS seized what little money I had in my bank account under the pretense of a student loan I had cosigned with my ex-wife Christy for her massage therapy school. But they never even attempted to collect from her; she lived with a fiancé who was raking in money in the oil fields. I was raising the children she gave birth to with no support from her. It felt obvious to me that this was nothing but federal intimidation.

On top of this army of lawyers, I was ganged up on by five law firms in the Gwinnett County case against Harper. (I dismissed the case against Doyle for simplicity to focus on Harper). Harper and his Freemason pals were cranking up the heat on me.

* * *

White supremacist Joe Johnson, from the Alabama of Harvest Assembly of God, warned me that if I didn't drop the lawsuit, someone might burn down my house. I felt trapped working for him and attending his church, yet I was concerned leaving might draw attention. As this was unfolding, I contacted every press outlet I could, trying to get the story covered. The *Atlanta Journal-Constitution*, Atlanta news stations, the *Gaines-*

ville Times, and my hometown paper in which I had appeared so many times for my awards and honors.

No one would report the story. As the full might of the federal government came down on a hometown boy to cover for a monster, the cover story on the *White County News* was about a new crosswalk in town.

Out of work, and with no income other than odd jobs and no unemployment insurance, we left our rented mobile home and moved into a barely livable guest house of my parents that had been built for my deceased grandmother. As we were moving out, the landlord sent a handyman over to do repairs. He carried a loaded gun and left it lying on the kitchen counter. My son Gabe had a small cheap Chinese four-wheeler I had given him for Christmas in Florida. The handyman wanted to buy it. I told him I would ask Gabe. When I came back it was gone. He had stolen it, practically admitted it, and dared me to call law enforcement.

If this wasn't rock bottom, it was awfully close. I had the church of the Sheriff's Department chaplain offer me a carrot and stick and threaten to burn my house down because I was suing a Freemason John Birch Society nutcase who had sabotaged my career with the help of his pals including a woman who believes she sees angels; she had planted a DUI in my records to cover up a lynching by my white supremacist father-in-law and a cop. Now, some gun toting redneck working for my 14-year-old landlord had stolen my autistic son's four-wheeler as we were being forced out of a mobile home.

* * *

To say we received a chilly reception in my hometown would be an understatement. Gabe's evangelical Christian principal, Jennifer Greene, put a target on his back. She constantly hounded him, accusing him of being a troublemaker and called me and my elderly mother almost daily to complain. She wanted me to put Gabe in a reform school that was practically a prison with a history of students committing suicide. Gabe was a good kid who simply needed the right services. I provided, not once but twice, the documentation of his mental illness, PTSD, as well as his autism.

One day, Greene called my mother. Gabe was gasping in a chokehold by a School Resource Officer. My mother called me. I rushed to the school. I wanted to know why my son was not in special education and why his needs were not being accommodated. I went to the office of the school nurse. His medical records and statement of disability, which had twice been provided to the school, had apparently been thrown in the trash by this fine Christian woman.

* * *

Gabe was deemed disabled by the Social Security Administration, yet his vindictive principal denied him special education services. He was placed into special ed after I threatened to sue the school system. He eventually landed in a special program where he bonded with a Black coach and teacher. *He thrived.*

I desperately needed a job. I even applied for jobs at the local McDonald's and Dairy Queen. Instead of getting a job offer, the Dairy Queen manager called the police on my sons. This restaurant is decked out in Christian décor and plays Christian music continuously. We were eating there one day when Gabe and Toby got into it. One threw a drink at the other, hardly the crime of the century. Next thing we knew, the County Sheriff's department was there harassing two little kids. We were marked.

ExpressJet refused to verify my employment, and I couldn't find a job. I finally found one repairing gambling machines for a ministry connected to the state of GA. The owner had a huge picture of himself and Nathan "the Real Deal" Deal in his office. I worked about an hour and was abruptly escorted out of the building without explanation. Did Georgia now have a bounty on my head? I messed with the wrong good ol boys.

* * *

Speaking of the Sheriff's Department, I went there one day to discuss the events in Florida and my concern of the Nobles snatching the boys. I got no help. The next day, I found a note on my door from Georgia's Child Protection Services demanding I call immediately. They wanted me to submit to a psychological evaluation. I told them no thanks as I had already passed five others. I tried to start a business doing yard work and handyman jobs. I put out a flyer. I got a few jobs – and a lot of strange calls.

I responded to one and went to the spectacular home of a man and his wife overlooking a Chattahoochee River waterfall. He was inquisitive and said he had friends who could help with my business. One of them was Doug Collins, a preacher turned congressman whose staff had already thrown me out of his office.

The man later told me he was a leader of Tea Party Patriots and wanted me to speak at an event. To say I was creeped out was an understatement. Now the Tea Party Patriots were probing me. I had this potential business partner until Georgia Child Protective Services showed up at his house. He got cold feet.

My unemployment hearing was delayed until July 2. I subpoenaed Brad Sheehan, Kathy Harris, Dr. Harper, and a lot of records, including the email from Nobles, correspondence between Harper and the company, and my records from him. My elderly father (now deceased) came to the hearing with me to sit with my kids outside the room as I didn't have a sitter. Mike Johns of Mustard Seed Counseling and Doug Helms, former ASA chief pilot, were standing by to testify on my behalf. Dr. Harper defied the subpoena, and the company defied the subpoenas for records. In total he and my airline defied subpoenas nine times without consequences.

ExpressJet had stated in their filing that they were represented by TALX UCM Services. Instead, they showed up unannounced with the Ford Harrison law firm from Atlanta who denied being served the subpoenas. I was there prepared to make my case with my records, fake DUI, the evaluations (including the one from Dr. Vaughn), and two star witnesses. But it was a waste of time. I was forced to sit there and listen to Ford Harrison attorneys slander me, claim I was never looking for a job and even claim that I did not meet the standards to ever be employed by ExpressJet. I was probably more qualified and experienced than most of their pilots and have always maintained the highest standards and have a record to prove it. Meanwhile, Sheehan and Harris continued to lie for the company, deny any connection to Dr. Harper or responsibility for the evaluations they forced on me by him and others – even though they contracted and paid for them and threatened to fire me if I did not comply.

Sheehan was particularly nasty and dishonest, again he tried to claim I had somehow been less than honest on my job application and, as someone who never served, he slandered my military service. The hearing officer was nasty as well. He interrupted me every time I attempted to make a point. Most importantly, he refused to let me submit any records as evidence and would not let my witnesses testify. He also rubber stamped the company and Harper's defiance of the subpoenas.

After forcing me to sit there through slander and verbal abuse and refusing to let me present a case or witnesses, he ruled in favor of the company. It was unbelievable.

* * *

On the same day as this hearing, July 2, Elma Brooks of the EEOC rubber-stamped HIPAA, Privacy Act, and ADA violations against me, including blocking my disability insurance and unemployment insurance. They said the EEOC had no jurisdiction, which is simply not true.

I appealed my unemployment to the next level – another rubber-stamped decision. I inquired again about getting representation from

Georgia Legal Services for my appeal. This time I got an even nastier letter packed with lies from Barbara Diana Pye-Tucker, the lawyer from Gainesville, Georgia.

> We believe you were responsible for maintaining your license. Because a license is required to do your job, we believe Georgia employment law deems you to be at fault for the suspension or reduction in hours and you cannot receive unemployment benefits. Please note that you also told me that you refused to go to one or more evaluations requested by the FAA last year. Before then you had been under scrutiny by the FAA for some time but were still licensed to work. After that refusal your license was suspended.

I was once again dumbfounded at the dishonesty and lack of integrity of yet another government agency lying and putting words in my mouth. I never told her I refused an evaluation. Drs. Harper and Berry refused to accept my evaluation and the recommendation of two heads of substance abuse programs, Dr. Vaughn and Mike Johns. They also tried to force me to go back to an unethical doctor in their racketeering network who was willing to lie and violate my rights. There were leaders in the parade of old ex-military men, starting with Tom Dunn and Robert Norris, who messed with my life. My license was never suspended and never has been. My ability to use it was being held hostage through criminal fraud regarding my medical certification, for the sole purpose of covering the tracks of a monster, Michael Nobles.

They protected a cold-blooded psychopath who left my sons disabled – just another bureaucrat without a conscience spinning government talking points in an ongoing Orwellian way. But who was behind the curtain. That was the big question. Which three-letter agency was to blame?

* * *

On July 17, LaSharn Hughes, the executive director of Georgia Composite Medical Board, rubberstamped Harper's of HIPAA, Privacy Act and RICO violations, obstruction of justice, hiding records, contempt of court and theft. I also filed complaints against Harper for his fraud with the Doraville Police and Georgia Bureau of Investigation. I was never contacted. For Attorney Clifford Hardwick's misconduct, repeatedly lying to the court, hiding records and defying subpoenas, I filed a bar complaint. It was rejected on August 5 by William P. Smith III, Ethics Council, State Bar of Georgia.

On August 20, Tinorah Frett of the U.S. Department of Labor, in response to a complaint from the Uniformed Services Employment and Re-employment Rights Act (USERRA), spun a web pack of lies protecting the company and Harper and blaming me for the whole ordeal, even arrogantly claiming a "passenger" made the complaint, knowing this to be false, and claiming this charade had nothing to do with my military service.

However, the sole allegation from this charade by Dr. Harper and Atlantic Southeast Airlines were lies about my military service. She claimed it was all about "safety," mimicking ExpressJet management. The company had no relationship with Harper, she said. The company had claimed to me he was the company doctor. They contacted him and forced me to go to him. Dr. Harper "discovered" a history of alcohol abuse and alcoholism, she claimed. But he claimed it was "the FAA" who was responsible yet they had done exactly what he specifically requested based on his lies. Meanwhile, the company disavowed any responsibility.

* * *

I reached a point where I could no longer fight. I had severe PTSD; I couldn't sleep; I ended up in the hospital. I had filed several motions in my federal court case. Dr. Berry, for example, refused to even accept service. I asked that the court order the U.S. Marshalls to serve him.

I filed motions for contempt. I ended up adding the airline and ALPA to the case. They were served and never responded, so I filed motions for a summary judgment as they missed the deadline. I filed motions to compel because the government, airline, and Harper were hiding records, which has continued to this day.

With some sarcasm intended, I filed a writ of *habeas corpus*. Brad Secker had claimed I was in jail and demanded that someone produce the evidence. Where was this DUI? Who diagnosed and treated me? It was all made up.

The case was transferred twice, judge shopping in my opinion, and Judge Richard Story sat on all my motions before dismissing them all in one fell swoop. Most disappointing and somewhat shocking was his denial of my request for a court-appointed attorney. I was stripped of my constitutional rights by multiple federal agencies including the FAA administrator and the U.S. attorney general. The federal government had weaponized the IRS against me and blocked my access to unemployment benefits and other benefits to which I was legally entitled. Story acknowledged the appropriateness at times to appoint an attorney for a plaintiff, but claimed it wasn't necessary in this case.

I couldn't even afford paper or ink for my printer as the government put the squeeze on me and my disabled kids. He demanded I rewrite my complaint, which he would review for "frivolity." There was nothing frivolous that required the army of lawyers to come after me and a slew of government agencies to lie.

I realized that nothing I did would matter. I wasn't going to get a hearing no matter what. I had to let it go for the time being. In similar fashion, the Gwinnett County case against Harper drug on until January 9, 2014, when the judge dismissed my case and ordered me to pay Harper's fees, including those incurred for suing his victim. Judge Doran never held him accountable for hiding records and defying subpoenas. He walked out of the courtroom with his smug attorney as they patted each other on the back. I can envision him and his lawyer hanging out on the golf course or Masonic Lodge with Judge Doran laughing about the whole matter.

I am hesitant to include this, but it is an important part of my story. Some members of my own family started to turn on me. Particularly, one of my sisters, a member of the Torch Church and Free Chapel in Gainesville where Jentzen Franklin, a member of Donald Trump's inner circle, is pastor. My sister and her family lived right behind us. She intensely pressured my parents to put me and my kids on the streets (they didn't), and she and her children treated my sons as subhuman. Her kids would walk by every day and either pretend my sons weren't there or just glare at them. Gabe and Toby didn't understand. They just wanted to be friends and play together. But that wasn't allowed. They will never forget this, and they carry those wounds to this day.

* * *

My escape, my Florida nightmare, had grown worse in my home state and hometown. I was now homeless except for the generosity of my parents. I was a man without a country, as they say – stripped of my rights as a citizen and hung out to dry by my own government.

I now felt like I was living in a banana republic. Stonewalled, lied to, and retaliated against over and over. The message was always the same. Shut up or else! I have been asked why it took me this long to feel this way. The answer isn't so simple but here is my best attempt.

At first, I thought I was dealing with a church cover up. Then it spread to a state agency and law enforcement agencies in three Florida counties. Ultimately it spread to Tallahassee and to the Governor's office. So, Florida was the problem, right? So, we left for our safety. And the cover up followed us to Georgia and ultimately spread from Florida, to Atlanta, Oklahoma City, San Francisco, and to Washington DC, even dirtying the hands of the United States Attorney General and other top DC brass.

But the reality is, I was naïve. I believed in America as portrayed by Hollywood. In Reagan's "shining light on a hill". I grew up watching *Hill Street Blues"* and then *Law and Order* and all its spinoffs. Cops who would stop at nothing to get to the truth and get the bad guys. I liked the movie *The Untouchables.* Dogged G-men, above corruptibility, risking life and limb to enforce the law. Then the press. Reporters risking it all in a relentless pursuit of the truth, wherever it leads. And churches, of course, were inherently good. An America of church picnics, little white houses with picket fences, and flags waving.

As Don Henley would say, "(I've) been poisoned by these fairy tales." I was forced to face the reality of an America where law enforcement agencies conform to money, power, and political pressure, and protect some of the vilest criminals. The incorruptible G-men make deals with devils and will lie to the public and hang victims out to dry. Many churches care more about money, right wing politics, and protecting their reputations than they do about children or saving souls. The press is controlled by money power and politicians and true investigative journalism is dead. And the politicians just want to protect their power and gravy train. An America with an underworld of organized crime, spooks, kooks, secret societies, and wealthy power brokers. With *integrity* on the verge of extinction. It was "The End of the Innocence."

My faith in religion and churches, corporate America, labor unions, politicians, law enforcement and government in general, remain forever shattered. I suffered severe PTSD inflicted largely by my own government yet denied insurance benefits. I lived in fear of having my kids snatched again, being framed again, or murdered by some crazy redneck "patriot."

I know no one would notice or care. It wouldn't even be reported. And if it was, it would be murder called suicide. The crazy alcoholic killed himself, they would say.

It would take me years to recover.

> *Every time we turn our heads the other way when we see the law flouted, when we tolerate what we know to be wrong, when we close our eyes and ears to the corrupt because we are too busy or too frightened, when we fail to speak up and speak out, we strike a blow against freedom and decency and justice.*
> – Robert F. Kennedy

> *Rather Fail with Honor Than Succeed by Fraud*
> –Sophocles

Epilogue

Betwen 2013 and 2016 I did my best to rebuild my life and my sanity. I did what I could to make a living, supplemented with food banks and food stamps, often doing back breaking work that I was too old for. I finally landed a job as a zipline instructor. What seemed like a crazy idea ended up good for my mental health. Being outdoors in nature, working with nice people, and getting a lot of exercise. I still wanted to go back into aviation in some capacity. I applied for a job in Colorado building aviation charts and didn't get the job. I was also turned down for a job fueling planes in Gainesville, Georgia. Finally, I spotted an ad for a copilot in a flight simulator for training that didn't require a medical certificate. I applied for and was contacted by a recruiter who recruited me for a position in the Midwest as a flight simulator instructor. Before I knew it, Toby and I were headed west in an old Chrysler minivan with no heat or air and windows that didn't work. I had $300 in my pocket and my mother's Discover card for hotel rooms. Since then, I have trained thousands of pilots from all over the world. Today, as a senior instructor, I also issue licenses and assess pilots' skills and safety for the company and the FAA. Meanwhile, it appears I will never fly again as that would require me lying for corrupt officials, and ultimately covering the tracks of a monster who victimized my kids, and other kids, neither of which I will ever do. In 2019, I remarried an amazing woman, and in 2021 we had a son, and in 2024 my first daughter.

In 2022, after watching some disturbing documentaries about cover-ups of child abuse, my whole story came flooding back to me. Haunted by the ghosts of the missing foster children from Walton County and the crimes against my sons and their relatives which they witnessed, I started digging out and organizing my records. I made a few calls and records requests which resulted in the return of the creep show. The Okaloosa County Sheriff's Department hacked my google account. Someone from Georgia named Charles Rogers contacted me offering all sorts of information and help. I discovered after he hacked my Facebook account that he was a Freemason and a Shriner. I was accosted at a public event by a total stranger who claimed to be a flight instructor. He grilled me about my qualifications, where I worked, where I lived, etc., and then tried to start a fight. I was harassed by total strangers on Facebook, all who fit the same profile. My efforts to reach out to the press again failed. I had a glimpse of hope when I found a Hollywood producer interested in a documentary. After reviewing the material, he backed out, citing concerns he and his wife had for their safety. Finally, in August 2022, I signed a contract with a ghostwriter to put my story into book form. On September 9, 2022, she emailed me saying that her brakes had failed, and she had been seriously injured in an accident. Shortly after that she vanished, cut off all contact, and kept the funds I had paid her having performed no work.

Undeterred, my wife and I travelled to Omaha in September 2022 to meet with another ghostwriter. He ended up passing the work to a friend and accomplished writer, Travis Heerman, who worked on the project until December 2023. On December 4, 2023, Travis and my publisher interviewed Mary Smith who reiterated the harassment and threats she had received from Nobles, Forgione, the Okaloosa County Sheriff's Department, the Florida Department of Children and Families, and other agencies. She also dropped another bombshell regarding a gay friend of hers who had been lynched and burned which had been covered up by local authorities. She had been forced to move from her home (where dead bodies had been dumped on the curb) and still fears for the safety of her family. Travis was about to start work on this portion of the book, when on December 21, 2023, he was in a fatal motorcycle accident. There were no witnesses or other vehicles involved.

Just hours after I learned of Travis' accident, I received a call from Mary Smith. Her autistic son, who has a heart condition, had just been arrested at the gates of Eglin AFB, possibly the Niceville Police and Okaloosa County Sheriff's Department following through on years of threats to target her children if she didn't shut up.

Department of Children and Families Investigator, Jennifer Clark, was rewarded with a position as Chief Operating Officer for the Emerald Coast Child Advocacy Center while Rick Karshna was promoted to Program Manager.

Joey Forgione is now writing parking tickets for the city of Destin while Josep Kearnes remains at the Niceville Police Department.

Larry Ashley replaced Ed Spooner as Sheriff and retired in 2020.

Ed Spooner was nominated by the President as U.S. Marshal for the Northern District of Florida on May 4, 2011. In May 2021, Spooner was inducted into the Law Enforcement Hall of Fame.

Stephen Hurm, after covering up the most obscene and document-ed case of weapons possession by a felon, was appointed as the Director of the Division of Licensing for the Florida Department of Agriculture where he oversaw screening weapons permits statewide. His wife, daugh-ter of former Florida Governor turned Senator, Bob Graham, following a failed run for Governor of Florida, was appointed as Assistant Secretary of Education by President Joe Biden.

Lashawn Riggans went on to serve as Deputy County Attorney for Leon County, the home of Florida's state capital, and was elected judge in Leon County in November 2024.

George Sheldon was appointed by the President as Acting Assistant Secretary for the federal Administration for Children and Families where he served from 2011 to 2013. He had a failed run for Attorney General of Florida in 2014.

Sally Quillian Yates was named Deputy Attorney General in 2015 and served as Acting Attorney General in January 2017 at the request of Donald Trump who fired her 10 days later for refusing to enforce an illegal order.

Stuart Delery went on to become the White House Counsel under President Biden from July 2022 to September 2023.

Roy L. Austin Jr is now Vice President of Civil Rights, Meta (Facebook).

Calvin A. Shivers was named the assistant director of the Criminal In-vestigation Division at FBI Headquarters in 2020 by Director Christo-pher Wray

Dr. Michael Berry was promoted to Deputy Federal Air Surgeon in March 2014, then to the Federal Air Surgeon in January 2017. Dr Good-man was promoted to his Deputy.

Brad Sheehan was made the Vice President of Safety at Delta Airlines, then promoted to Vice President of Flight Operations. James Brimberry is the Program Manager for Equal Opportunity at Delta Airlines. Kathy Harris is a Vice President at Universal Music Group.

Leslie Michael Osman continues to enrich himself in real estate in Flor-ida. His brother Ty was killed in an alleged fishing accident in July 2020.

Michael Nobles and his son-in-law bought a mini farm in 2023 in Harri-son, Arkansas, arguably the most racist town in America and the home of the Knights of the Ku Klux Klan led by Thomas Robb, another former John Birch Society member who replaced David Duke, who you may remember marched with Nobles' Patriot Network in South Carolina in support of the Confederate flag. He started a family compound with his wife Wanda, his son Billy, and Christy and her new husband. Christy tried to bribe Toby into joining them there in 2024. He declined and still lives with me. 1118 Rhonda remains in his sole ownership, as he removed his wife from the deed in 2015. It apparently can't be sold. The whereabouts of the treasures removed remain a mystery.

Gabe has been working and living on his own for over a year with some help from me with his personal affairs. He is still under the care of a psychiatrist but has been able to come off his medication. He has been deemed permanently disabled with PTSD for a third time.

In July 2024, I made Freedom of Information Act (FOIA) requests to the FAA and Department of Justice. These were regarding the sabotage of my medical certification and the Justice Department blocking my appeal. I requested correspondence with Attorney General Eric Holder or others at the DOJ regarding my appeal, any application I submitted for a special issuance. I also asked for the source of the fake DUI. To date they have not responded to my request. I also reached out to every important character in the story whose contact information I could find to interview. I received only one response, from Stuart Delery, who, upon learning of the nature of my request for an interview, clammed up and was unresponsive.

As of the publishing of this book, my sons have never received justice, Michael Nobles remains free, the foster children from Sharon Lake remain missing, my right to use my pilot's license remains held hostage, and my reputation remains forever smeared.

Despite all the defeats, my sons and I stood our ground in a storm of lies, powerplays, and corruption. Through all the retaliation they received, my kids were brave and consistently told the truth, and that truth was buried. I went head-to-head with some of the most powerful people and organizations in the country, ending up alone and impoverished in the end, and having done nothing wrong. I simply told the truth, stood up for my kids, and asked for justice that was ever elusive. Most importantly though, we stayed together as a family and maintained our integrity. Sometimes that is the best you can do. And in the end that is more valuable than any amount of money and power.

> *I believe that unarmed truth and unconditional love will have the final word in reality. This is why right, temporarily defeated, is stronger than evil triumphant.*
> – Martin Luther King, Jr.

TRUTH AND CONSEQUENCES?

By Dr. Richard B. Spence

I f you've gotten this far, you've read Mark's story and are likely trying to process what you've read. I still am, and I've been involved with it for months. As stories go, it's a tragedy, a triumph, and a mystery. Maybe a whole set of mysteries. If you're looking for a quick synopsis or a top-ten-takeaways, you've come to the wrong place. Instead, what follows is an outline of how *Houses of the Holy* came to be, how I came to be involved with it, and maybe most importantly, how Mark's ordeal compares to and resonates with other research I've done. Correspondences and similarities emerged at every turn, which I found surprising, interesting, and sometimes disturbing. Certainly, Mark's tale is more than a bitter custody battle, a case of in-laws from hell, or an incredible string of bad luck. But how deep and wide does the rabbit hole go? Is there more to the story than the injustices done to Mark Harris and his sons?

But first, let's address the elephant in the room: is Mark Harris a "reliable narrator." After all, there's another side to this story, the side of Mike Nobles and various public officials who have always, and doubtless still do, maintain that Mark is "crazy." More to the point, paranoid. Frankly, if it wasn't for the documentary evidence and expert testimony that Mark has marshalled in his behalf, I might come to the same conclusion.

The basic definition of paranoia is the *unwarranted* belief that one is being persecuted, harassed, or betrayed. You're not crazy if the bastards really are out to get you, though the experience alone might be enough to drive you near or even over the edge. My impression of Mark was of a man who was angry, frustrated, and easily provoked to suspicion. But given what he's been through, I don't think those are irrational responses. All things considered, I think he's held it together remarkably well. It's also worth noting, as this book proves, that he hasn't thrown his hands up in despair. He still maintains what some might argue is a naïve faith that justice will prevail. I hope he's right. But as to Mark's mental state, his capacity as a "reliable narrator," I leave the last words to the bevy of psychiatric professionals who, under oath, weighed in on the matter. While some suggested he was "obsessive-compulsive" and driven to defend his sons and himself, the "the Nth degree," *none* found evidence that he was "not of sound mind." Mark may be a lot of things, but he's not any crazier than the rest of us.

* * *

Now let's come back to the question of how this book came to be and how and why I became involved. According to Mark, he'd been "pounding on the doors of the press, local, national, and international since 2008," but no one was willing to touch the story with the proverbial ten-foot pole. After all, that would mean challenging the opinions of law enforcement, the judiciary and bureaucratic officialdom, based on accusations that seemed, on the surface, well, *paranoid*. But in May 2022, Mark finally found someone who willing look beneath the surface, Kris Millegan, editor of Trine Day Press. In January 2023, a book deal was made. Another question was whether Mark was best suited to tell his story. He had amassed a vast array of information, but he wasn't a writer. Because the story was so personal and painful, it was possible for the anger and frustration could overwhelm the narrative. The writing needed a professional hand.

The first "ghost" to come on board, before the Trine Day deal was made, was Sara Miller. But she bowed out in September 2022, after suffering a serious car accident when her brakes failed. It was just an accident. But considering that Mark's antagonists, who he has portrayed as devious, widely connected, and violent, were very much alive at that time, and may still be, one didn't have to be paranoid to suspect something more sinister. Next came writer Robert Frasse, who also signed a contract. However, before any real work was done, and for uncertain reasons, he also backed out.

Frasse passed the baton to Travis Heermann who came on-board in early 2023. A graduate of the Odyssey Workshop whose mission is to "… help developing writers of fantasy, science fiction, and horror improve their work." Travis was an experienced author and award-winning screenwriter with thirty books under his belt, mostly in the sci-fi and horror genres, plus nine more as a ghostwriter. He was enthusiastic about Mark's project, if daunted by the sheer amount of information that had to be collated and condensed. He persevered and by December 2023 had completed the bulk of the manuscript. But on the 21st of that month, fate, or something, struck again. Another of Travis' passions was riding his motorcycle. That day, on a routine ride, he inexplicably crashed and suffered a traumatic brain injury. Despite the best hopes and medical effort, he passed away in April 2024. The fact that two ghostwriters had left the project through potentially suspicious vehicular mishaps, one of them fatal, most definitely cast a chill over things. While I'm inclined to attribute both incidents to bad luck, I'd be lying if I said there isn't just an inkling of doubt.

Travis's death once again left the book in limbo until a new writer, Patrick Norton, fearlessly signed-on to finish the task. That he did, and here we are.

* * *

Kris Millegan brought me into the project in mid-2023, which requires a little explanation about who I am. Basically, I'm a retired historian who got his PhD at the University of California, Santa Barbara in the early 80s. I started out as a modern Russian historian, but guided by the rule of "one thing leads to another," I gradually branched out into fields such as espionage, secret societies, and occultism. I dislike the term "expert," but I confess to having a possibly unhealthy amount of knowledge about some rather arcane subjects. After teaching for thirty-four years at the University of Idaho, I retired in 2020 only to soon find myself as busy as ever with various personal and contract research projects. But I was exclusively doing what I wanted, and that makes a big difference. Before I retired, I'd started doing work for *The Great Courses* which produces educational series and documentaries. My first was *The Real History of Secret Societies*, followed by *Crimes of the Century* and *Secrets of the Occult*. So, somewhere along the line, I became the Secret Societies, Spies and Occultism Guy. And that, I suppose, is why Kris brought me in.

* * *

Houses of the Holy is full of direct and indirect references to things like the Freemasons, the Knights Templar, the Ku Klux Klan, and something that smells a little like Satanism. These, in turn, all connect to what's broadly termed the Occult. "Occult" means hidden, specifically hidden, from sight. What's ostensibly hidden is a whole other world of knowledge and power which can be accessed through the aid of things like rituals and spirits and utilized in this world. The fundamental mechanism is Magick, so dubbed by English occultist Aleister Crowley who described it as "the art and science of causing change to occur in conformity with will." In other words, bending reality, or more simply, manifesting. Or the ultimate way of cheating. The fundamental instrument of magick is ritual, and the more people participating in the ritual, the more powerful it can be. It's not necessary that you or I believe any of this. But that doesn't stop other people from believing so and acting on that belief. Think of it this way: Do Mark's alleged antagonists seem like people who would shy away from any chance to cheat in life, to enhance their wealth and power, even at the cost of their soul?

The problem is determining whether someone is serious about occultism or just playing with it. People who affect the vampire aesthetic aren't into blood-sucking. But every now and then there are those who want to make things real, usually with negative results. Take, for instance, the weird pictures drawn by Gabe after his first abduction by his grandfather. I don't believe these are random images dreamed up by a small child. They are based on something he saw, but what? Did Grandpa Mike give a wild Halloween party? The drawings are a grab bag of seeming occult imagery, including masked and robed figures, a Maltese cross, altars, skulls, a burning skeleton or body, a dragon, and arguably most significantly, a kind of "bat goat." The last is very reminiscent of Baphomet, or the Sabbatic Goat, a figure frequently associated with witchcraft and Satanism, and rightly or wrongly, with the Knights Templar. And references to the Templars, Baphomet and Freemasonry, occur throughout Mark's narrative.

* * *

Freemasonry is a huge topic, so I can barely scratch the surface here. Suffice it to say, that it isn't a brand name or trademark. No one owns it, or ever has, and a wide variety of beliefs and practices have been carried on under that name. Whatever someone tells you, Freemasons never initiate women, but you can bet some other so-called Freemasons have done this. While some Masonic groups require professed allegiance to Christianity, one only has to believe in a Supreme Being, a "Great Architect of the Universe." That can be Jehovah, Allah, Buddha—or Satan. The boilerplate description of Freemasonry is . .. a system of morality, veiled in allegory and illustrated by symbols." You could say it's a description that describes absolutely nothing. Simply put, Freemasonry can be whatever you want to make it.

Mark ultimately characterized the variety he encountered as "backwoods, neo-Confederate, white supremacist, KKK, Southern Freemason voodoo," and that may be as accurate a description as you can get. While many Freemasons would shudder at the thought, there is a long-standing interconnection between Masonry and the KKK. An illustrative case in point can be found, in of all places, 1920s Oklahoma. At the time, Oklahoma politics was dominated by the Democratic Party which you'd think would have made governing easy. But the Oklahoma Democratic Party was dominated by two not-so-secret secret societies, Freemasonry and the Klan. The former, largely composed of businessmen and professionals, protected the interests of class, while the latter claimed to protect the interests of race, the White one. Membership, to some degree, overlapped. In 1923, Governor John Walton, a Freemason, was impeached after he defied the Klan by imposing martial law in the wake of the Tulsa race riots. But in 1929, pro-KKK Governor, Henry Johnson, who was also Grand Master of the Oklahoma City Lodge, was also impeached. Among other issues, he may have strayed too far into occult practices. His confidential secretary and closest associate, Mrs. Mamie Hammond, also happened to head the women's auxiliary of the Klan. She was also a professed spirit medium who instructed Johnson on how to use seances and spirits to guide his decisions.

* * *

Freemasonry's influence wasn't just limited to politics. The longtime head of the Oklahoma State Highway Commission, Cyrus Avery, was, you guessed it, a Freemason. He's perhaps best known as the "Father of Route 66" and influenced both state and Federal highway policies. Back around 1914, he formed the Albert Pike Highway Association to push for a national highway system. Albert Pike is an interesting namesake. Besides being a prominent American Freemason, he was a Confederate general, an avowed White supremacist, and a reputed founder of the first Ku Klux Klan. And allegedly much more, but we'll come back to him. As for Cyrus Avery, he was unceremoniously booted as highway commissioner by fellow Freemason Johnson, which may also have played a part in Johnson's impeachment. This stuff just doesn't happen in Florida.

What brought these Oklahoma Ku Kluxer Masons to my attention was another peculiar research interest of mine, conspiracy theorist James Shelby Downward who was born and raised there. He's probably best known for his essay on the supposed mystical underpinnings of the JFK assassination, "King-Kill 33." Downard is also someone to which the term "paranoid" is frequently applied, and in this case not without reason. To say that his effusions often strain credulity is an understatement. Downard was probably crazy, whatever that means exactly, but being crazy doesn't necessarily make him wrong. Downard's tie-in to Mark's story is his obsession with "Masonic Sorcery;" rituals, often conducted in public view, organized by professed Freemasons, and aimed at bending reality to their will. In Downard's rather nightmarish vision, this sorcery includes everything from depraved "sex circuses," to presidential assassinations, the creation of the atom bomb, the space program, and the naming of highways. This isn't to argue that Downard is right about any of this, only that he seems to be talking about something eerily similar to what Mark encountered in Florida. It's worth noting that most of Downard's life was spent in the South.

Masonic sorcery, including alleged devil worship, also comes up in the so-called Taxil Hoax of 1890's France. So too does the above-mentioned name of Albert Pike. Leo Taxil was the pen name of French journalist-writer Gabriel Antoine Jogand-Pages who started out writing semi-pornographic stories about the sex lives of popes. But in the late 1880s, he affected a return to the bosom of the Church and over the next several years churned out works such as The Secrets of Freemasonry and The Devil in the 19th Century. Taxil claimed that Freemasonry was run by a secret Satanic order, the Palladists, who revered the Knights Templar and their goat-god idol, Baphomet, who engaged in all manner of reality-bending rituals, including<stess back into the light, one Diana Vaughn. Naturally, critics insisted that Taxil was making the whole thing up and demanded that he publicly reveal the supposed Diana Vaughn. In 1897, he agreed to do so, but instead of putting her on stage, he boldly confessed that the whole tale was indeed a hoax designed to make fools out of those who believed it. You'd think that would have been the end of it, but no. Then and now, some insist that Taxil spun an at least partly true story, then denounced it as a hoax to poison the well and discredit the very idea. Downard would doubtless say they were on to something. But he was crazy. Wasn't he?

* * *

Lastly, let's bring this meandering Afterword back to the Florida Panhandle, the modern day, and a couple of incidents that might suggest Mark's experiences aren't unique. In July 2008, Okaloosa County Sheriff's deputy, Anthony Forgione, was killed while attempting to take into custody an escaped mental patient, Mark Rohlman. After shooting Forgione, Rohlman either took his own life or was gunned down by other deputies, no one seemed quite sure. If the Forgione name looks familiar, it's because Anthony Forgione was the brother of one of Mark Harris's alleged tormentors, Niceville policeman, Joey Forgione. The backstory is more interesting. According to his family, Rohlman had been exhibiting signs of mental instability. He had "come to fear a vast government and law enforcement conspiracy" which had "taken over his brain." Sounds crazy. So, Rohlman was involuntarily committed for a 72-hour observation under Florida's Baker Act. He was "Baker-Acted," which is the same thing Mike Nobles tried to do to Mark. Rohlman apparently didn't agree with this and escaped twice before the final, fatal confrontation. Some interesting coincidences, to say the least.

Then, in January 2016, another Niceville Florida police officer contacted the Okaloosa County Sheriff's Department, the Florida Department of Law Enforcement, and maybe most interesting, the U S Air Force Office of Special Investigations (OSI). He claimed to be working on "a very serious case" that somehow concerned them. The officer was subsequently judged to be experiencing "a mental health issue that was causing him to become delusional." He was Baker-Acted, placed under observation, and put on leave. His name and the nature of what he was investigating was not released. Just another crazy guy, or is there a pattern here? Frankly, I'm not sure. But I wonder.

The conclusion, if one can be found here, is that Mark's story, parts of it at least, isn't unique. It resonates in suggestive and sometimes uncanny ways with the experiences and perceptions of other people in other places at other times. It's not just some weird Florida thing.

PHOTOGRAPHS AND DOCUMENTS

Prepositions and Conjunctions

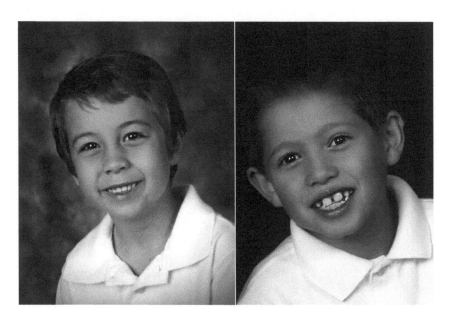

Toby and Gabe Lighthouse Private Christian Academy Photos

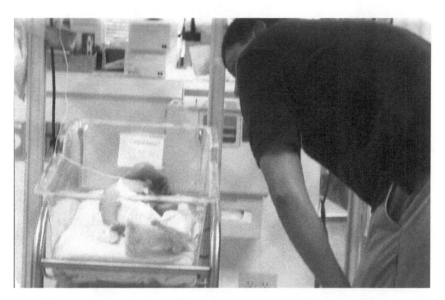

This was the first time I saw Toby in the hospital immediately after his birth.

Gabe and I looking over Hell in Grand Cayman during a cruise. Little did we know the hell to come.

An unsolicited handmade card made by Gabe for me. One of many.

Toby and Gabe on the beach for Toby's 5th birthday. One of their last days of freedom and security. They were kidnapped 6 days later.

The blues brothers.

Gabe and Toby during their soccer days. They both loved to play but never would go back after their trauma.

In Air Force pilot training circa 1992.

Gabe's first year in Lighthouse Private Christian Academy. He still talks about and misses his best friend Devin, who is in the blue shirt.

Toby's first year at Lighthouse Private Christian Academy. His teacher miss Bonnie loved him and tried to protect him only to suffer abuse from DCF investigator Rick Karshna

Toby as a teenager with me at church after moving to the Midwest for my new job

Nobles as a youth chaperone to Honduras in 1996 at the age of 46 from the Niceville newspaper. Christy is partially visible in the picture. His other roles accessing children included school board president of Agape Christian Academy, Niceville Church of Chirst, deacon in charge of "elementary education, Destin Church of Christ, and youth chaparone on another mission trip in 2008 at the Destin Church of Christ at the age of 58.

Pictures of foster children from Christy's scrapbook. This book was shown to Jennifer Clark who, with her supervisor, denied Nobles was ever a foster parent.

DEPARTMENT OF THE AIR FORCE
HEADQUARTERS 16th SPECIAL OPERATIONS WING (AFSOC)

4 Jun 99

MEMORANDUM FOR All Reviewing Authorities

FROM: 16 OSS/DO

SUBJECT: Character Statement—Capt Mark C. Harris

1. I am Lt Col Charles A. Hamilton, currently the Operations Officer for the 16th Operations Support Squadron and I will assume command of the 16th Special Operations Squadron on 23 Jul 99. I have 19 years of active commissioned service. I am the Operations Officer for a squadron of approximately 200 people and have been in this position since 17 Aug 98.

2. I am aware of the basis for the proposed discharge against Capt Mark C. Harris and I am aware the this letter will be used in determining whether the allegations against Capt Harris are true and whether he should be discharged from the Air Force. I have known Capt Harris since he began to work as the Squadron Commander's executive officer in late August of last year. My contacts with Capt Harris have been mostly work related but we have seen each other in social settings occasionally. At work, I consider myself as one of Capt Harris's supervisors although strictly interpreted he works for the commander. At the office, I observe and interact with Capt Harris almost continually as I can see him at his desk when I am at mine and we often work closely together on projects and suspenses for the commander.

3. Mark came to us under somewhat of a cloud as the incident that started this series of events had already occurred. The 9 SOS/CC sent him to us as a temporary measure. When he arrived, we were already in the process of looking for a new executive officer and the commander and I asked Mark if he would take over those duties for what we thought would be a very brief period. We knew Mark was in some sort of trouble but we didn't know the details. Mark readily accepted and started to work as the executive officer immediately. As far as I know Mark had no previous experience in this type of position but his aptitude for writing and editing was immediately apparent. What impressed me far more though was Mark's willingness to work hard and his dedication to doing whatever it took and staying as long as was required to get the work done. At one point in the fall of last year, Col Koenig, the Operations Group Commander, wanted the Group Mission briefing rewritten and assigned that task to our squadron. We gave the assignment to one of our Assistant Operations Officers and Mark, without being asked, volunteered that he was competent in the use of Microsoft Powerpoint and would be willing to help update the briefing. Mark ended up putting in a lot of late, late nights working on the slides and worked through

Any Time ... Any Place

One of numerous character references related to my military board of inquiry. Col Hamilton also courageously testified on my behalf despite unlawful command influence by the Wing Commander and leaders of the 9th Special Operations Squadron in an effort to prevent such testimony. Two pages.

at least one weekend to get the briefing completed on time. The Group Commander and Deputy Group Commander were ecstatic with the results and said it compared well with the wing briefing which they had paid to have professionally done. Mark has taken his duties as executive officer very seriously. Many times when I have told Mark to leave at the end of the day when it was only he and I in the office he would decline and stay until after I had left. He would spend his time profitably by continuing to review and revise performance reports or awards or do other tasks that needed doing.

4. Mark displayed initiative as our executive officer. When our temporary duty lieutenant left to begin pilot training, we needed someone to finish the projects he had started including a reissue of the pagers in the unit. I hadn't asked Mark to take the projects because he was already very busy but he insisted he could do them and he did. When Col Poole, the Deputy Operations Group Commander, wanted to completely review the number of cellular phones required by the squadrons in the group, he asked Mark to accomplish the job based upon his excellent wok with the briefing and other projects. It was a challenging project since it required coordination with all of the units in the group and some of them were sensitive to the possibility of losing some of their cellular phones. Mark once again did a terrific job. Tracking OPR and EPR progress from initiation through completion had historically been done very poorly in our squadron and one of the commander's priorities was to create a system to fix that problem. Mark organized a team to address that issue and led them through several iterations of a new process. The system we have in place now is giving us one of the best on time rates in the group.

5. Mark always displays a very professional appearance and demeanor. His conduct toward both his subordinates and superiors alike is absolutely impeccable and he is very well-liked throughout the unit. His dedication to and capacity for work amaze me, especially when I compare him to myself at a comparable time in my career.

6. I believe this incident in no way reflects the true character and usual behavior of Mark and I am confident nothing like it will occur again. Mark has valuable talents to offer the Air Force, ahs a very impressive work ethic, and genuinely wants to contribute to the Air force, as I've discovered in conversations with him. I very highly and in the strongest terms recommend Capt Mark Harris be retained in the US Air Force.

CHARLES A. HAMILTON, Lt Col, USAF
Operations Officer

HEADQUARTERS 16th SPECIAL OPERATIONS WING (AFSOC)

18 November 1999

Lt Col James D. Smith
Commander
215 Bennett Ave
Hurlburt Field FL, 32544-5800
(850) 884-6164

Dear Employer

I am eager to offer the highest recommendation for Mark Harris, who I have directly supervised for more than a year.

I took command of the 16th Operations Support Squadron in August 1998 shortly after Mark arrived in the squadron. At that time I asked him to temporarily become my executive officer. A commander's executive officer is a personal assistant. He reviews all correspondence, organizes the commander's schedule, and sees that issues and problems are solved at the lowest practical level. This position became permanent as Mark became an integral and invaluable part of my command staff and the organization as a whole.

I have worked closely with Mark on a daily basis. He is highly motivated, self-disciplined, dependable, and loyal. His hard work to support the principles and goals of this organization has been exemplary.

I do not have any direct personal knowledge of Mark's flying skills as he has worked for me in a non-flying capacity. However, he recently obtained his commercial multi-engine rating. I observed him diligently studying in his spare time and know that he successfully completed the course and check-ride in a short period of time.

I would be more than happy to have Mark work for me at any time in the future but unfortunately, he is separating from the Air Force.

I am confident that Mark will be successful in whatever he endeavors, and I highly recommend him for any position for which he is eligible. Please feel free to call me at anytime if you require any additional information.

Sincerely

JAMES D. SMITH

Any Time . . . Any Place

A recommendation letter from my last supervisor in the military whose career was threatened by General Donald Wurster for supporting me and ordered to lie in court.

At The Zoo

5703 Gulf Breeze Pkwy

Gulf Breeze, FL 32563

(850)934-0180

November 1, 2008

To whom it may concern,

Mark Harris, father of Toby and Gabe Harris, has had his children enrolled in our school since August of 2008. Since that time, he has been a Model parent. He has always ensured that the boys' homework is complete. He has been here on time every morning and has ensured their prompt pick up so that they do not have to be placed in after care.

The teachers have described Mr. Harris as a good, loving parent who puts his boys first in his life. He completes his nightly reading log and has proven that his interest lies in their academic and social improvement.

He has had over 7 conferences with teachers and administration. Each time, he has taken the information very seriously and has always worked with the school to make positive efforts towards getting the boys what they need to succeed.

He has exhibited good moral values while having his sons enrolled here. His primary and genuine focus is the well being of Gabe and Toby. We consider him to be an exemplary parent.

Joanna Morris
Principal

A letter written by the principal of Lighthouse Private Christian Academy the day after my kids were kidnapped. She had previously made a report to the Florida DCF who lied to her and never responded.

Dear Sir or Madam;

I would like to take this opportunity to commend Mark Harris. I have worked both as his supervisor and as his Captain in airline operations. The first few years that I knew Mark I was a Chief Pilot in the Atlanta base and had the responsibility of evaluating pilot performance and regulatory compliance. Mark was always at the top of his peer group in both categories. Further, I served the airline as an instructor and check airman wherein I observed and evaluated the professional performance and procedural compliance of pilot skills. While I never gave Mark a line check or instructed him in a training session, I did fly numerous flights with him over our ten years together and find him to be a fine aviator. I assure you he is fully dedicated to regulatory and procedural compliance. If my family was flying and I saw that he was our pilot, I would feel safe with and for my family.

Mark Harris is required to go through classroom training and simulator evaluation twice a year and has done so in a studied and superior manner. I would hold him up as an example of how a pilot should conduct himself at work and in the presence of his family. Mark is both a fine professional aviator and a dedicated family man.

I have had the pleasure of flying the line with Mark many times over the past years. In our time together he'd share things that his children were doing and how he loved being with them. The separation from them, during elements of the divorce, was hard on Mark. His undying love for them and his wish that they maintain a strong parent-child growth together is paramount. He loves his children and would do anything needed to help them prosper and be secure.

If I could stand before you I would implore you to consider his love and heartfelt oneness with his children. He will serve their best interest in all that he does for years to come and will sacrifice as needed to provide opportunities for them.

Your Honor, I am proud of this man and find him a fine professional pilot and a dedicated family man. He will, in my opinion, serve his children well for all the years God will allow him to be here on this earth. I'd gladly hire his adult children knowing the values he has instilled in them. Please feel free to contact me directly if there are any questions where I may be of further assistance.

Sincerely and Respectfully,

Douglas L. Helms

A friend of the court brief written by Atlantic Southeast Airlines Chief Pilot Doug Helms. Doug later was listed as a witness in an unemployment appeal hearing after Brad Sheehan and ASA management lied to the Department of Labor and blocked my unemployment benefits. I was blocked from presenting any witnesses or evidence, by the hearing officer, however.

385

We build strong kids,
strong families, strong communities.

To: Whom It May Concern
From: Bob Grant, Branch Director
Date: October 7, 2008
As To: Personal Recommendation

Mark Harris and his boys, Toby and Gabe, have been members of the Pullum YMCA for almost two years. He and the boys belonged to our Adventure Guide Program for dads and their children. Toby and Gabe also participated in Baseball and Soccer at our Y. Mark also keeps the boys involved in Martial Arts on Saturday mornings

I have personally seen Mark and the boys interact and have observed his positive parenting skills. During Adventure Guide meetings and outings, I have seen the boys happy and carefree. I have never seen the boys unhappy when they are around their dad. When he has to correct them in a positive verbal manner, they readily listen and the misbehavior stops.

I would be glad to answer any further questions concerning Toby, Gabe, or Mark. Please do not hesitate to call me at the YMCA, 936-0049.

A character letter by the YMCA director who coached Toby in Soccer dated just 3 weeks before the Florida Department of Children and Families alleged that I was "erratic and unstable."

Date: 10/02/2008 11:26 AM
From: 7022263 - Charles Tutt
To: 7010139 - Douglas Helms

Cc:

Subject: RE: Mark C. Harris 16534
Attachments:
Message:

Doug, thanks for the info we will take a look at using Mark. How are things with you?

I appreciate everyones hard work and it is showing in our performance numbers

Charlie

Date: 10/02/2008 10:07 AM
From: 7010139 - Douglas Helms
Subject: RE: Mark C. Harris 16534

Hello Sir Charlie and Good Morning,

I'd like to make you aware of a man (F.O.) who flies for us. He is Mark C. Harris #16543. He recently he gained custody of his children and has a nanny who keeps them while he is on overnights. He told me he may apply for a leave so he can work at another job until his kids get settled in at his home. Maybe for a few months or so.

Charlie, this is such a good man and a dedicated ASA employee I thought I'd ask if there is anything you need done at the G.O. for that time frame where he might be of help. He'd get "FO" pay and he has a Masters degree. What a good find for you for a short time assist in one of many areas. I deeply suggest you talk with him before you decide either way. He'll be around for a long time and would be a great help on short term projects.

I know times are tight and people are turned and sent away for the consideration of a shrinking budget. Here is an opportunity to put a person to use who'd earn less but still be dedicated.

Respectfully and sincerely,

Doug Helms.

http://www.ourasa.com/ASA/MyMessages/Message.aspx?MsgID=2285478&Inbox=1&Bo... 10/2/2008

An email that Chief Pilot Doug Helms sent to the airline vice president on my behalf. Two years later the management would aid and abet Mike Nobles and 4 years later set out to destroy me and starve my kids.

From: The Most Excellent Way Ministry

Calvary Chapel Gulf Breeze

To: Whom It May Concern

Subject: Mark Harris

Date: March 15, 2010

It is my pleasure to recommend Mark Harris as a good and faithful man of God. I have known him personally several years and can vouch for his character and integrity. I know Mark as being a true believer in Jesus Christ, a fine man and a wonderful father. I am pleased to endorse him in any and every way.

Sincerely,

Tom Read

Ministry Assistant

Calvary Chapel Gulf Breeze

A nice letter from one of the ministry team at Calvary Chapel. His bible study was canceled a short time later, I suspect in retaliation because of his support for me, and the church leaders later circled the wagons to protect Mike Nobles. Nearly all of the church members at this extreme right cultish church have since turned on me and have spread claims that I am "mentally ill."

Family & Child Development

348 Miracle Strip Parkway, Suite B-3
Fort Walton Beach, FL 32548
Phone: (850) 862-3772
Fax: (850) 863-4574

Don G. Brown, M.Ed., Th.D.
Licensed Marriage & Family Therapist

Pearle Brown, Ed.D.
Licensed Mental Health Counselor
Licensed Marriage & Family Therapist

E. Glya Brown, Ph.D.
Licensed Mental Health Counselor
Licensed Marriage/ Family Therapist

David A. Silvers, M.S., LMHC, NCC
Licensed Mental Health Counselor
National Board Certified Counselor

Radford McGrath, MS
Licensed Mental Health Counselor
National Certified Counselor

Koehan Shuster, MA, LMFT
Licensed Marriage & Family Therapist

Cindy L'Abbe, MSW
Registered Clinical Social Worker, Intern

Claudia Hamilton, MS, LMFT
Licensed Marriage & Family Therapist

11/7/08

To Whom It May Concern:

I have been providing family therapy for Mark Harris and his two sons, Gabe and Toby, since August 19,2008. Mr. Harris originally brought his boys to see me because of recent information the boys had told him about their Aunts, Faith and Emily, and their Grandfather, Mr. Nobles. Gabe and Toby had told their father that their Aunts were fondling with their "winnies" while their Grandfather would peak in, and watch them from the door.

On 9/24/08, Toby and Gabe were brought in for a session by their nanny, Marilyn. They had just spent the weekend before with their mother, Christy. During this session, Toby informed me that his mother had taken them to his Grandfather's house over the weekend. Toby then provided detailed information of abuse that had occurred while he was there. After the session, I immediately made a report with DCF. I then called the father to inform him of the report.

It is my professional opinion that abuse has been occurring within the Grandfather's home. Both boys, Gabe and Toby, have shown signs of sexual abuse. Mr. Harris wants the boys to have a good relationship with their mother, and had been allowing her to see the boys whenever she wanted. However, even though there had been great concern about the Grandfather (her father), she has continued to bring them to his home.

I believe the children were significantly improving in their behavior, and communication skills while in the care of their father, Mark Harris. I believe him to be a very loving and caring father, whose primary interest is only in providing the best home possible for his sons, Gabe and Toby.

Sincerely,

Karleen Shuster, LMFT

Documentation of disclosures of sexual abuse by my sons to their therapist and the fact that she made a report (this was the first of two) to the abuse hotline which was ignored and received no response. This an all reports by mandatory reporters were attributed to me and used to label me crazy and bring false reporting cases against me in what I call "the boomerang." This same day DCF investigator Jennifer Clark attempted to frame me for "false reporting" through three avenues base on a second report made by this therapist which should have resulted in an Amber Alert.

LIGHTHOUSE PRIVATE CHRISTIAN ACADEMY AT "THE ZOO"
www.lighthousepca.com
**5703 Gulf Breeze Parkway
Gulf Breeze, Florida 32563
850-934-0180**

April 19, 2010

To whom it may concern,

Toby Harris was displaying some inappropriate behavior in class on October 13th, 2008. Based on concern from a teacher, I made a call to abuse hotline to make a report concerning Toby Harris. Someone returned the call and told me that the case had already been reported and was in the system. Therefore, I contacted Toby's therapist, Karleen Shuster and told her what they had told me. She said she had just reported the abuse and that is probably why it was already in the system. She informed me that DCF would probably be coming to see me at the school. Over the next two weeks, no one ever came to speak to me at the school and then Toby and Gabe were removed from my school at the end of October. *Rick karshna*

Toby Harris returned to LPCA in February of 2009. After his return, a gentlemen named Rick (from DCF) did stop by my school to speak to Toby's teacher, Ms. Emmons. I was not at the school that day. However, the teacher, Ms. Bonnie Emmons stated that he asked her just a few questions about Toby's behavior. Ms. Emmons said "I am worried about Toby so please check into the Grandfather". But, she said that the gentlemen's response was as if he didn't believe that Toby had been abused.

My notes indicate that when he was in his father's care, his behavior was calm and secure. When he was in his mother's care or away from his father, his behavior was radical and insecure. Mr. Harris, the father, has displayed good parenting skills. Since Toby and Gabe have been in his care and have now both returned to school, their behavior and their academics have improved significantly.

Sincerely,

Joanna Morris
Owner – LPCA

A letter by Lighthouse Private Christian Academy Principal Morris documenting DCF Investigator Rick Karshna's cover up of abuse.

Licensed Psychologist
PY0004162

p: 850.664.7690 f: 850.664.7691
email: doc@mccainphd.gccoxmail.com

February 14, 2011

Patient Name: Harris, Gabriel
Date of Birth: 5/15/01
Patient Name: Harris, Toby
Date of Birth: 10/25/03

To Whom It May Concern:

Please be advised that I performed psychological testing batteries on both Gabe and Toby Harris in June, 2010. The testing in both cases is consistent with a diagnosis of Posttraumatic Stress Disorder as a result of abuse by the maternal grandfather, Michael Nobles. In the opinion of the undersigned, further contact with Mr. Nobles is contraindicated as this would most likely cause further trauma. If you have any comments or questions, please do not hesitate to contact me at the number listed below.

Sincerely,

Marianne L. McCain, Ph.D.
Licensed Psychologist

Dr. Marianne McCain's diagnosis of Gabe and Toby with PTSD due to abuse from Michael Nobles, consistent with a unanimous opinion of a small army of therapists, psychologists, psychiatrists, a medical doctor, and school officials. She also noted in her evaluation that there had been not investigation. To date there has still been no investigation, only spin, denials, and stonewalling.

KELLY BECK, LMHC

68 Beal Pkwy.
Fort Walton Beach, FL 32548
(850) 243-7035
Fax (850) 243-8529

Feb. 19, 2011

Re: Gabriel and Toby Harris

To Whom It May Concern:

This letter is in reference to Gabriel and Toby Harris. They have been participating in individual and family therapy with myself for the past year due to Post Traumatic Stress Disorder (acute) regarding allegations of sexual and emotional abuse by their maternal grandfather, Mr. Nobles. I would like to recommend that there is no contact with their paternal grandfather at this point in time. It would be detrimental to the boys' mental health and will trigger any PTSD symptoms.

In addition, I would like to recommend that a Guardian Ad Litem be appointed to this case to advocate for the children.

I hope you find this information helpful. Please feel free to contact me should you have any questions or concerns.

Sincerely,

Kelly Beck, LMHC

Kelly Beck, LMHC
FL Licensed Mental Health Counselor (MH 5763)

Documentation of treatment for PTSD attributed to abuse from Mike Nobles by therapist Kelly Beck. This is a small sampling of records. The kids required many years of treatment, and the professionals all have been in agreement regarding the source of abuse. Gabe has been deemed permanently disabled from his abuse and still sees a psychiatrist. Note she requested a guardian Ad Litem, something I repeatedly requested from the court which kept attacking my rights as a parent but was repeatedly denied.

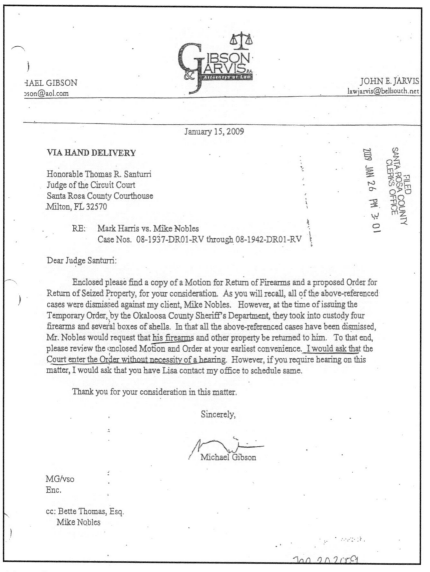

A letter by attorney Michael Gibson which accompanied his motion to have Mike Nobles firearms returned. The motion claimed that Nobles had no criminal history. Gibson knew his client was a felon. He showed consciousness of guilt by asking that the order be entered without a hearing, which was required but never occurred as this all happened behind my back. Note that my own attorney was notified and she concealed it from me.

~~D FOR SANTA ROSA COUNTY, FLORIDA~~
~~AMILY LAW DIVISION~~

...ter of

Mark Harris,
Petitioner,
and

Case No.: 08-1940-DR-01-RV

Mike Nobles,
Respondent.

_____/

ORDER ON MOTION TO WITHDRAW AS COUNSEL OF RECORD

THIS CAUSE having come on to be heard upon the Motion to Withdrawal of

Counsel of Record and the Court having reviewed same, it is

ADJUDGED that:

1. Mr. Harris is not able to meet the financial obligations as agreed in the
   Retainer Contract.

2. At hearing scheduled January 14, 2009 before this court Petitioner was
   present and orally consented to the withdrawal of counsel in all Domestic
   Violence Injunction cases in which he is a party.

3. Motion to Withdraw as Counsel of Record is hereby GRANTED.

4. All future correspondence shall be forwarded to:

   Mark Harris   ∠ Doesn't exist
   3010 East Bay Boulevard
   Gulf Breeze, FL 32563

DONE AND ORDERED in chambers this 2l day of _____Jan_____, 2009.

/S/ Thomas R. Santurri
JUDGE OF THE CIRCUIT COURT

Cc:
Bette M. Thomas, Esq.
Michael Gibson, Esq.

This order by Judge Santurri made an unsolicited change of my address to a non-existing address so that I would not get a copy of the order returning firearms to a felon which he signed the next day, out of court, with no hearing. This was one of several outrageous out of court acts by Santurri. Again, my attorney was provided this and concealed it from me.

Okaloosa County

Law Enforcement Service & Excellence

Date: March 30, 2011

To: Mark Harris

From: Mary Collins

Ref: Michael Nobles

The following items have been provided as per your request.

1. Copies of the Evidence and Chain of Custody cards signed by Mr. Nobles on February 16, 2009.

2. The photo copy of the driver licenses of Michael S. Nobles and William S. Nobles.

3. A copy of the Motion for Return of Firearms

We cannot provide a copy of the FCIC/NCIC check as this is not public record and we can only provide that information to law enforcement personnel. The original Evidence and Chain of Custody cards, photo copy of the driver licenses and our copy of the Motion for Return of Firearms are retained in the Okaloosa County Sheriff's Office Evidence Unit.

Cordially,

Marylou M. Collins

Marylou Collins

Evidence Custodian

Okaloosa County Sheriff's Office

1250 N. Eglin Parkway

Shalimar, Florida 32579

Office: (850) 651-7422

❑ 1250 N. Eglin Parkway, Shalimar, FL 32579-1234 ★ Phone (850) 651-7410 ★ Fax (850) 609-3048
❑ 296 Brackin Street, Crestview, FL 32539-2909 ★ Phone (850) 689-5650 ★ Fax (850) 689-5556
"The Okaloosa County Sheriff's Office provides equal access and equal opportunity in employment and services and does not discriminate"

Note that Michael Nobles provided a court order with his name, provided his driver's license, submitted to a background check, and signed the evidence cards. Nobles, his attorney, and the sheriff's department attorney would all lie about this later and claim the guns were returned to Nobles' son, Billy, who committed a series of documented crimes for his father, including threatening to murder me.

One of the evidence cards signed by Mike Nobles as the Okaloosa County Sheriff's Department, a circuit judge, Mike Nobles' attorney, my attorney, the Florida Department of Children and Families, the Niceville Police Department, and FBI agent Tim Kinard all conspired to lie and cover up the arming of a dangerous felon by the court and law enforcement. Some of his weapons were later disposed of secretly by the police, after he was arrested and the Sheriff's department attorney conspired to fabricate evidence in the case. Destruction of evidence and obstruction of justice.

FIRST APPEARANCE

__ OF ARREST: WARRANT (✓) BOND SET: _1st App_
CAPIAS ( )
BY: _Judge Arinsted_

( ) PROBABLE CAUSE ARREST

NAME: _Nobles, Michael_ _4-10-09_
(LAST) (FIRST) (MIDDLE) (DATE)

CHARGES: 1) _Poss Firearm by Convicted Felon_

3) _____ 4) _____

BACKGROUND SUMMARY

FTA'S: ( ) Yes (✓) No   How Many: _____

PROBATION: ( ) Yes ( ) No ( ) Felony ( ) Misdemeanor   Officer: _____

Phone: _____

LOCAL RESIDENT: (✓) Yes ( ) No   How Long: _Area 25 yrs, present 18 yrs_

EMPLOYMENT: (✓) Yes ( ) No   Employer: _Sandpiper Cove - 3 yrs_

Occupation: _Security Officer_   Income: _____

Recommended Bond: _5,000 C/S_   ) Sign w/

Pretrial Supervision: ( ) Yes (✓) No

Conditions: _____

_____

_____

_____

_____

_____

_____

A paltry $5000 bond set for a dangerous felon caught with an arsenal of guns and ammo. But it would get worse as Nobles would get two first appearances from two judges in the same day and bailed out by the sheriff.

STATE OF FLORIDA
COUNTY OF OKALOOSA

STATE OF FLORIDA
VS.
MICHAEL NOBLES

09CF 7145
001

Know All Men By These Presents: That we, **MICHAEL NOBLES** as principal, and **NA** and **NA** as sureties, are held and firmly bound unto the governor of the STATE OF FLORIDA, and his successors in office, in the sum of **ROR** Dollars for the payment whereof well and truly to be made we bind ourselves, our heirs, executors and administrators, jointly and severally, firmly by presents.
Signed and sealed, this **10TH** day of **APRIL 2009** The condition of this obligation is such that if the said **MICHAEL NOBLES** (Defendant) shall appear at the next term of the **CIRCUIT** Court to be held in **CRESTVIEW** (City) in and for **OKALOOSA** County on the **5TH** day of **MAY 2009** at **1: 30 PM** o'clock (AM) (PM) to answer a Charge of: **POSS OF FIREARM BY CONVICTED FELON 4 CTS** shall appear from day to day and term to term of said Court and not depart the same without leave, and submit to the orders and process of the Court, then this obligation to be void, else to remain in full force and virtue.

_____
(Principal)

_____
(Address)

_____
(Surety)

_____
(Address)

_____
(Surety)

_____
(Address)

TAKEN BEFORE AND APPROVED BY ME THIS

____ day of *April* 20 09

EDWARD M SPOONER, Sheriff, Okaloosa County, Florida

By_____

A second bond set for Nobles by a second judge, William Stone, and signed by the Sherrif and future US Marshall Ed Spooner the same day as the first, releasing Nobles on his own recognizance while he plotted to skip the country and threatened to murder witnesses. Another example of judicial corruption.

WILLIAM "BILL" EDDINS
STATE ATTORNEY
FIRST JUDICIAL CIRCUIT OF FLORIDA

Please reply to Pensacola Office

January 29, 2010

Mark Harris
6010 East Bay Blvd.
Gulf Breeze, FL. 32563

RE: Michael Nobles

Dear Mr. Harris:

I have received your letter together with the enclosures regarding the allegations you
have made against Michael Nobles. I have reviewed your complaint in detail and have
discussed, on more than one occasion, with the Okaloosa County Supervisor, Bill
Bishop. Based upon my review and my discussions with Bill Bishop, there is insufficient
evidence to pursue criminal charges. Therefore, my office will take no further action in
this matter.

Sincerely,

WILLIAM EDDINS

WE/klm

In what had to be one of the most witnessed and documented iron clad cases of possession of firearms by a felon as well as numerous related crimes, State Attorney Bill Eddins
claimed there was insufficient evidence to prosecute the case. Important because the
cases of sexual abuse, kidnapping, and murder were handled in the same manner by the
same people and also important because what those guns were guarding and the fact
that they were there to kill cops.

THE FLORIDA BAR

651 EAST JEFFERSON STREET
TALLAHASSEE, FL 32399-2300

JOHN F. HARKNESS, JR.
EXECUTIVE DIRECTOR

850/561/5600
WWW.FLORIDABAR.ORG

May 25, 2010

Mr. Mark Harris
6010 E Bay Blvd
Gulf Breeze, FL 32563

Re: Michael Gibson; The Florida Bar File No. 2010-00,837 (01A)

Dear Mr. Harris:

All correspondence and documents submitted in this matter have been carefully reviewed. Many of your allegations do not have any evidence to support them. If the Bar seeks to discipline the lawyer, it is required by Supreme Court ruling to show, by "clear and convincing" evidence that there has been a violation of one or more of the Rules Regulating. Your complaint also states that Mr. Gibson provided inaccurate information in his Motion to Return Firearms. Mr. Gibson has explained what happened and what he did to make sure the firearms were not released to his client.

The Florida Bar Board of Governors' standing board policy states that in the absence of specified exceptions, isolated instances of malpractice and/or incompetent representation will not be pursued under the disciplinary system. **This is not to say that the attorney complained of committed malpractice or failed to provide competent representation, but rather that such allegations are the basis of your complaint.**

There is insufficient evidence from the materials provided that Mr. Gibson has violated any of the rules adopted by the Supreme Court of Florida which govern attorney discipline. Accordingly, continued disciplinary proceedings in this matter are inappropriate and our file has been closed. The computer record will be purged and the file destroyed one year from the date of closing.

Sincerely,

Annemarie Craft, Bar Counsel
Attorney Consumer Assistance Program
ACAP Hotline 866-352-0707

cc: Mr. Michael Gibson

This letter shows the Florida Bar Association covering for attorney Michael Gibson, who lied to the court to arm a felon, and then prepared a false affidavit at the request of Sheriff's Department Attorney Steve Hurm to cover it up. Note that the Bar lied claiming that the guns which were in fact released to Nobles were not. This was pattern of government agencies covering the tracks of those who protected Nobles which continued to the United States Attorney General.

WILLIAM "BILL" EDDINS
STATE ATTORNEY

OFFICE OF
STATE ATTORNEY
FIRST JUDICIAL CIRCUIT OF FLORIDA

P.O. Box 12726
Pensacola, FL 32591
Telephone: (850) 595-4200
Website: http://sao1.co.escambia.fl.us

February 1, 2012

Mark Harris
6010 East Bay Blvd.
Gulf Breeze, FL 32563

RE: Michael Nobles

Dear Mr. Harris:

I have reviewed letters, documents, and reports which you have provided regarding Michael Nobles. After reviewing these documents and meeting with you, I have determined that there is insufficient evidence to warrant criminal charges. Any issues regarding the Petition for Injunction must be addressed by the Circuit Court responsible for these matters. Allegations regarding child abuse have previously investigated by the appropriate state agency who have determined that allegations of any criminal violation cannot be established. There is insufficient evidence to prosecute Mr. Nobles for either possession of a firearm by a convicted felon or homicide.

For these reasons, I am closing my investigation and no further action will be taken.

Sincerely,

Tom Tucker
Investigator

An Equal Opportunity / Affirmative Action Employer
Serving Escambia, Okaloosa, Santa Rosa and Walton Counties

The absurd position of the State Attorney was that the Florida Department of Children and Families who placed foster children in the home of a monster and then erased their records was the appropriate agency to investigate child rape and human trafficking. His claims of insufficient evidence in the firearms case reaches the comical level and the homicide was never investigated by any agency.

Florida Department of
Law Enforcement

Gerald M. Bailey
Commissioner

Office of Executive Investigations
Post Office Box 1489
Tallahassee, Florida 32302-1489
(850) 410-8240
www.fdle.state.fl.us

Charlie Crist, Governor
Bill McCollum, Attorney General
Alex Sink, Chief Financial Officer
Charles H. Bronson, Commissioner of Agriculture

July 14, 2009

Mr. Mark Harris
6010 East Bay Boulevard
Gulf Breeze, FL. 32563

RE: FDLE File EI-73-8481/IR8

Dear Mr. Harris:

Your recent letter to the Florida Department of Law Enforcement (FDLE) was forwarded to the Office of Executive Investigations for review. In your letter, you requested an investigation into Michael Nobles regarding allegations of Child Abuse. Your complaint submits that your children were sexually abused and kidnapped twice by Mr. Nobles, who was assisted in the crimes by members of his church. You additionally note that Mr. Nobles is involved in organized crime and has been provided with information by unidentified Okaloosa County Law Enforcement Officers.

Upon review of your letter, it was determined that your complaint is similar to a complaint submitted by you to the Florida Department of Children and Family (DCF). The issues you describe have been previously reviewed by DCF and are more appropriately handled by a department familiar with your situation. To ensure that your concerns are addressed, our office is forwarding your complaint letter to DCF for review and any action deemed appropriate.

Should you have any questions regarding our review, you may contact Inspector Christopher Pate at (850) 410-8240.

Sincerely,

Mark Perez
Chief Inspector
Office of Executive Investigations

MP/cp

CC: Lisa Carden,
       Florida Department of Children and Family

Service • Integrity • Respect • Quality

This letter demonstrates the elaborate shell game as Florida Department of Law Enforcement Chief Inspector Mark Perez forwarded a complaint regarding sexual abuse, kidnapping, organized crime, and case fixing by law enforcement to the Florida Department of Children and Families, an obviously absurd notion and an agency that was systematically falsifying reports. A clever means of plausible deniability

State of Florida
Department of Children and Families

Governor

George H. Sheldon
Secretary

July 20, 2009

Mark Harris
{mailto:mharris7321967@yahoo.com}

Dear Mr. Harris:

Thank you for your letter to the office of Governor Charlie Crist. Your letter was forwarded to the Department of Children and Families. This office has reviewed the information and determined that there is not sufficient means to locate information to enter a report. If you have additional means of locating the victims, please contact the Florida Abuse Hotline at 1 (800) 962-2873 or fax us at 1 (800) 914-0004. This office will re-assess the information to determine if a report can be generated for investigation at that time. You have indicated that you have reported this information in the past to the department. If you have concerns for the manner in which the investigation was handled you may also contact the Client Relations Coordinator at (850) 595-8216.

Sincerely

Walt Cook
Director, Florida Abuse Hotline

1317 Winewood Boulevard, Tallahassee, Florida 32399-0700

Mission: Protect the Vulnerable, Promote Strong and Economically Self-Sufficient Families, and Advance Personal and Family Recovery and Resiliency

RICK SCOTT
GOVERNOR

TALLAHASSEE, FLORIDA 32399-0001
www.flgov.com
850-488-7146
850-487-0801 fax

June 15, 2011

Mr. Mark Harris
6010 E. Bay Blvd.
Gulf Breeze, FL 32563

RE: Chief Inspector General Case # 201106140002

Dear Mr. Harris:

The Office of the Chief Inspector General received your complaint information on June 14, 2011, in which you expressed concerns about criminal and court matters relating to a child protective investigation.

Please be advised that this office does not have jurisdiction over criminal matters, local governments or their employees (such as police officers or Sheriff's Departments), court matters, or state attorneys. Criminal allegations should be reported to a local law enforcement agency, and concerns about the conduct of law enforcement officers can be submitted to the applicable local government or Internal Affairs Division. Regarding legal concerns relating to your court case, you may wish to contact a private attorney who may be able to advise you of other civil remedies that may be available to you. If you cannot afford an attorney, pro bono legal services may be available through Florida Legal Services, Inc. Their website address is www.floridalegal.org and their phone number is (850) 385-7900. Please note that, due to the nature of your concerns, we are referring your complaint to the Inspector General for the Florida Department of Law Enforcement for review of any issues that may fall within his jurisdiction.

Additionally, please be advised that this office does not have jurisdiction over employees of the Department of Children and Families. The Inspector General for the Department of Children and Families is the appropriate authority to review these concerns. Therefore, by copy of this letter, we are forwarding your complaint to the Inspector General for the Department of Children and Families for review and action deemed appropriate.

Thank you for bringing this matter to our attention. In the event that you have any further questions, please contact the Inspector General's office for the Florida Department of Law Enforcement at (850) 410-7000 or Inspector General's office for the Department of Children and Families at (850) 488-1225.

Sincerely,

Erin Romeiser
Investigations Manager
Office of the Chief Inspector General

ER:jh

cc/enc: Al Dennis, Inspector General
cc/enc: Dawn E. Case, Inspector General

Florida Department of
Law Enforcement

Gerald M. Bailey
Commissioner

Office of the Inspector General
Post Office Box 1489
Tallahassee, Florida 32302-1489
(850) 410-7000
www.fdle.state.fl.us

Charlie Crist, Governor
Bill McCollum, Attorney General
Alex Sink, Chief Financial Officer
Charles H. Bronson, Commissioner of Agriculture

July 8, 2011

Mr. Mark Harris
6010 E. Bay Blvd.
Gulf Breeze, FL 32563

Dear Mr. Harris:

The Florida Department of Law Enforcement (FDLE) Office of Inspector General has received your letter, forwarded by the Executive Office of the Governor, which indicates that the FDLE has shown reckless disregard for the law and the safety of your family by refusing to discuss your issues with you, allowing you to be interviewed and denying have received information that was provided by you. Thank you for bringing this matter to my attention.

As the Inspector General for the FDLE, it is my responsibility to ensure accountability, integrity, and efficiency within our agency. After careful review of all documentation provided by you and review of the responses you have received from the FDLE, it is my determination that the FDLE has responded to your matter in accordance with FDLE's policies and procedures and applicable Florida laws. Furthermore, your request to have firearms removed from a convicted felon should be directed to your local law enforcement agency. Complaints against your local law enforcement agency should be directed to that agency's Internal Affairs.

If we can be of any further assistance to you, please contact Inspector Meschelle Pittman or myself at (850) 410-7000.

Sincerely,

Al Dennis
Inspector General

cc: Kurt Posey, FDLE Government Analyst

AD/mp

Service • Integrity • Respect • Quality

Spin and denials from Florida Department of Law Enforcement Al Dennis covering up crimes by public officials including the fabrication of evidence by FDLE attorney Steve Hurm.

State of Florida
Department of Children and Families

Rick Scott
Governor

David E. Wilkins
Secretary

Vicki Abrams
Regional Managing Director
Northwest Region

Date: October 19, 2011

To: Heather Robinson
        Office of Inspector General

From: Lisa Carden
        Client Relations Coordinator, Circuit 1

Subject: Response to Office of Inspector General Correspondence Number
2011090297 Mark Harris, complainant

Based on a complaint filed by Mr. Harris on October 3, 2010 the   Northwest Region
Family Safety Program Office conducted a Quality Assurance Review of all Child Abuse
and Neglect reports received between September 5, 2008 to October 15, 2009.   The
review (see attached report) found no evidence to support any of Mr. Harris's
complaints outlined in his September 21, 2011 correspondence to your office.

On numerous occasions, through out the past year, I have attempted to schedule a
meeting with Mr. Harris on behalf of Janice Thomas. Mr. Harris has yet to follow though
with my request to set a mutually convenient date and time that we can meet to discuss
his issues.

As to his complaint about Child Protective investigator Jennifer Clark: There was no
evidence found to support any of the statements made by Mr. Harris.

Northwest Region, Circuit 1
1160 Governmental Center, Suite 611• Pensacola, Florida 32502-5734

Mission: Protect the Vulnerable, Promote Strong and Economically Self-Sufficient Families, and
Advance Personal and Family Recovery and Resiliency

Letter regarding a response to a Florida DCF Inspector General complaint which contained 146 lies, including denials that Jennifer Clark filed a police report and denials
that Mike and Wanda Nobles were foster parents. Janice Thomas refused my repeated
requests for an appointment and refused to respond to me directly. The crimes of DCF
investigator Jennifer Clark are well documented and she was rewarded. This is one example of numerous letters like this from the DCF denying any wrongdoing by its employees who flagrantly falsified reports and destroyed records.

Department of Children and Families

Governor

David E. Wilkins
Secretary

October 21, 2011

Mark Harris
6010 E. Bay Boulevard
Gulf Breeze, FL 32563

Dear Mr. Harris:

Thank you for contacting the Office of Inspector General on October 21, 2011, concerning the handling of child protective investigations by the Department and its employees.

Your allegations were previously reviewed by Circuit 1 Administration and a full Quality Assurance Review was completed. Please note that a copy of the response completed by Circuit 1 Administration was mailed to you on October 20, 2011. Based on this information, there were no new issues that would warrant involvement by this office at this time.

Sincerely,

Heather Robinson
Operations & Management Consultant Manager
Office of Inspector General

State of Florida
Department of Children and Families

Governor
David E. Wilkins
Secretary

January 23, 2012

Vicki Abrams
NW Regional
Managing Director

Mark Harris
6010 East Bay Boulevard
Gulf Breeze, Florida 32563

Dear Mr. Harris:

This letter is as a follow-up to my prior correspondence dated January 10, 2012 concerning your records request. The Department searched for documents related to your request as detailed below:

1) Records involving statements made by DCF investigators to the Inspector General pertaining to 2008 case;
2) Personnel files for Richard Karshna, Heather Pagano, Jennifer Clark, and Sarah Johnson; and
3) Foster care records for the Nobles home.

There are 28 pages in the file pertaining to statements made to the Inspector General pertaining to the 2008 case involving your family. The personnel office estimates that the number of pages contained in the personnel files for Richard Karshna, Heather Pagano, Jennifer Clark and Sarah Johnson contain 979 pages. And regarding your request for foster care records for the Nobles home, a search of the Department's foster care program records did not reveal any such records.

Enclosed is an invoice for the prepayment of the records you seek. Upon receipt of your personal check, cashiers check or money order in the amount of **$569.05**, we will initiate the reproduction process and mail the redacted records to you. Please be advised that the records will be redacted according to statutory requirements which may affect the actual number of pages produced. Please remit prepayment within thirty days of the date of this letter. If you would like to narrow your request in order to reduce your costs, please advise.

Sincerely,

KATIE GEORGE
Assistant Regional Counsel
Northwest Region

KG/sa
Enclosure:

Circuit One Legal • 160 Governmental Center • Suite 601 • Pensacola, Florida 32502-5734
Telephone: (850) 595-8057 • Facsimile: (850) 595-8232

Mission: Protect the Vulnerable, Promote Strong and Economically Self-Sufficient Families, and
Advance Personal and Family Recovery and Resiliency

One of multiple denials by Florida Officials that Nobles was a foster parent. Also note that the personnel files of the four DCF investigators totaled nearly 1000 pages, much of which I believe were complaints. At least two of these investigators were rewarded and the worst offender, Jennifer Clark became Chief Operating Officer for the Emerald Coast Child Advocacy Center while Rick Karshna was promoted to management as a DCF program manager.

Department of Children and Families

Governor

David E. Wilkins
Secretary

February 28, 2012

Mark Harris
6010 E. Bay Boulevard
Gulf Breeze, FL 32563

Dear Mr. Harris:

On January 5, 2012, the Executive Office of the Governor's Office of the Chief Inspector General forwarded your complaint to the Department of Children and Families Office of Inspector General (OIG) concerning the handling of your prior correspondences relating to child protective investigations and the actions of various Department personnel.

Your concerns have been thoroughly reviewed and previously addressed by Circuit 1 Administration and the OIG. It should be noted that on October 20, 2011, you were provided with a copy of a report completed by Circuit 1 Administration addressing each of your concerns.

Based on the OIG review, there do not appear to be any issues that would warrant further OIG involvement. No further action will be taken by this office at this time.

Sincerely,

Chris Hirst
Inspector General
Office of Inspector General

More spin, lies and denials from the Florida Department of Families and Children Inspector General of an agency under George Sheldon which systematically falsified reports, intimidated witnesses and destroyed incriminating records while the law enforcement agencies with jurisdiction to investigate used them as an alibi of plausible deniability. A formula used over and over by various agencies and the court.

U.S. Department of Justice

Federal Bureau of Investigation

WH #01222013-219

Washington, D. C. 20535-0001

MAR . 5 2013

Mr. Mark Harris
885 Partin Road
Cleveland, GA 30528-9111

Dear Mr. Harris:

I am writing in response to your January 16, 2013, correspondence addressed to President Obama which was forwarded to the Department of Justice and subsequently referred to the FBI. In your correspondence you expressed concern regarding illegal firearm possession and various other violations.

In order for the FBI to initiate an investigation of any complaint we receive, specific facts must be present to indicate that a violation of federal law within our investigative jurisdiction has occurred. Based on the information provided in your correspondence, there is no violation of federal law. Consequently, the FBI has no investigative jurisdiction. If you have any information that an actual crime has been committed, please reach out to the nearest law enforcement agency.

I appreciate your bringing this matter to our attention, and I hope this information will be helpful to you.

Sincerely,

Calvin A. Shivers
Acting Section Chief
Violent Criminal Threat Section

This is a response from the White House claiming no violations of federal law. The federal laws violated included but were not limited to possession of firearms by a felon, a lynching on federal property, federal racketeering violations and falsification of records by FAA officials, and numerous civil rights violations against me and my sons.

DEPARTMENT OF HEALTH & HUMAN SERVICES   Office of the Secretary

_____

Director
Office for Civil Rights
Washington, D.C. 20201

March 26, 201

The Honorable Doug Collins
Member, U.S. House of Representatives
111 Green Street SE
Gainesville, GA 30501
Attn: Lisa Simmons

RECEIVED
APR 0 1 2013
CONGRESSMAN DOUG COLLINS

Transaction Number:

Dear Representative Collins:

Thank you for your inquiry on behalf of your constituent, Mr. Mark Harris, concerning the health
information privacy regulation (Privacy Rule). Your correspondence to the Assistant Secretary for
Legislation, U.S. Department of Health and Human Services, was referred to the Department's Office for
Civil Rights (OCR) for response. Mr. Harris seeks your assistance with a Privacy Rule complaint
involving Dr. Charles Harper, d.b.a. Aeromedical, Inc.

OCR enforces the HIPAA Privacy, Security, and Breach Notification Rules and also enforces Federal civil
rights laws which prohibit discrimination in the delivery of health and human services based on race, color,
national origin, disability, age, and, in certain circumstances, sex and religion. The HIPAA Rules apply to
covered entities, which include only: (a) a health care clearinghouse; (b) a health plan; or
(c) a health care provider that transmits any health information in electronic form in connection with a
transaction for which HHS has adopted standards.

Please be advised that Mr. Harris filed a complaint with OCR's Atlanta Regional Office on September 26,
2012. After investigating the complaint, the Regional Office determined that Aeromedical Inc., does not
meet the definition of a covered entity. Therefore, the requirements of the HIPAA Rules do not apply, and
as such, the Regional Office closed the complaint. Mr. Harris was notified of this decision in a letter dated
March 14, 2013.

We trust that this information is helpful to you. If we can be of further assistance, please do not hesitate to
contact this office.

Sincerely,

Leon Rodriguez

cc: OCR Region IV
        Attn: Ivey Belton

This letter from Leon Rodriguez, the Director of the Department of Health and Human
Services Office of Civil Rights, makes the outlandish and false claim that Dr. Charles
Richard Harper was not bound by HIPAA laws which he flagrantly violated in addition
to criminal fraud, theft, and violations of the Privacy Act. Rodriguez was promoted to
Deputy Assistant Attorney General for Civil Rights at the Department of Justice after
covering up my civil rights violations.

U. S. Department of Justice

Civil Rights Division

Office of the Assistant Attorney General   *Washington, D.C. 20530*

MAY 2 4 2013

RECEIVED
MAY 3 1 2013
CONGRESSMAN DOUG COLLINS

The Honorable Doug Collins
U.S. House of Representatives
111 Green Street S.E.
Gainesville, GA 30501

Dear Congressman Collins:

This responds to your letter to the Assistant Attorney General for the Office of
Legislative Affairs dated April 11, 2013, regarding a complaint by your constituent Mark Harris,
in which Mr. Harris alleges that his civil rights and those of his children were violated by federal
officials from the U.S. Marshals Service, the FBI, the ATF, and FAA, and various Florida state
officials. In particular, Mr. Harris alleges that a number of these officials failed to investigate
or repressed evidence in cases involving Mr. Harris's father-in-law. Among other things,
Mr. Harris alleges that his sons witnessed their grandfather murder a man, but officials retaliated
against Mr. Harris for bringing the murder to the attention of law enforcement, and arrested him
on charges of making a false report.

The Criminal Section of the Civil Rights Division enforces the federal criminal civil
rights statutes pertaining to incidents of official misconduct. These matters generally involve
allegations of excessive physical force by law enforcement officials. We have carefully
reviewed the information Mr. Harris provided and have determined that it does not disclose a
prosecutable violation of federal criminal civil rights statutes. Accordingly, we cannot authorize
a criminal investigation of his complaint.

We hope this information is helpful. Please do not hesitate to contact the Department if
we may be of assistance with this or any other matter.

Sincerely,

Roy L. Austin, Jr.
Deputy Assistant Attorney General

This letter from the Deputy Assistant Attorney General denies the outrageous civil
rights violations against me which included false imprisonment, the theft of my career
through criminal fraud, and dozens of incidents of illegal search and seizure.

```
OFFENSE REPORT                              OKALOOSA CO SHERIFF'S OFFICE
OCSO08OFF014591                             Printed On:  09/21/2010 @ 12:05
Weapon
Location Category              Residence
Location Type                  Offender's residence
Location Description
Location Status
Number of Premises Burglarized       0
Target
Entry Method
Point of Entry (POE)
POE Visible From
Point of Exit
Suspect Actions                - Other
Circumstances
Weather
Lighting Condition
Security Used
Crime Scene? :        No
If NO, Explain :   no scene

Crime Scene Officer:
Physical Evidence Collected:         0
```

```
< NARRATIVE >
DATE      TIME     TYPE         OFFICER REPORTING     CALL #  REP TAKER   EDIT DATE  EDIT TIME
1/2/2009  16:56   INITIAL      BELLAMY, JENNIFER A     094   BELLAJ      1/2/2009   17:05
Status: APPROVED    ROBERT W NORRIS       2/16/2009   08:47
CAD INCIDENT DISPOSITION CODE: [57-0] [  K] [] []
```

Jennifer Clark, DCF CPI contacted this Investigator in regards to false reports of abuse called into DCF.

Detailed supplemental narrative to follow.

```
2/13/2009  17:07   INVESTIGATIVE  BELLAMY, JENNIFER A   094   BELLAJ      2/13/2009   17:08
Status: APPROVED    ROBERT W NORRIS       2/16/2009   08:47
```
This Investigator was contacted by Jennifer Clark, CPI with DCF. She related that suspect Mark Harris was continually making reports to the hotline alleging sexual abuse of his sons and his nieces. J. Clark advised that several of the allegations had already been investigated and found to be unsubstantiated. She also advised that the mother/wife to Mark Harris has separated from him and is currently seeking a divorce. C. Harris feels these reports are being made in retaliation for her leaving and does not feel that her children or sisters have been victims or are at risk of any type of abuse. J. Clark advised that forensic interviews were scheduled of the two female juveniles on 11/10/08 and will soon be scheduled for the two male juveniles. She was requesting this Investigator's assistance in attending the forensic interviews. J. Clark was going to be contacting Santa Rosa County in regards to a complaint of Mark Harris filing false reports.

On 11/10/08 this Investigator attended the Forensic Interviews of ///////////// (the recording is the best record of the interview). Neither child disclosed being a victim of any

```
OCSO08OFF014591          Page 2 of 3        [ BELLAJ        01/02/2009 16:56  ]
```

This is a false police report filed by Florida Department of Children and Families investigator Jennifer Clark at the instructions of her supervisor Donna Parish, who like Mike Nobles, was a Church of Christ leader. Note that this was a response to an abuse hotline call by my sons' therapist, not me, which required an Amber Alert. Clark and Parish exhibited consciousness of guilt by denying filing this report.

OFFENSE REPORT
OCSO08OFF014591

OKALOOSA CO SHERIFF'S OFFICE
Printed On: 09/21/2010 @ 12:05

type of abuse. Both children denied touching either ///////// or observing either being touched as was alleged.

On 11/25/08 Forensic Interviews were conducted with ///////////////; this Investigator was not present. The following are statements are excerpts obtained from the reports prepared by N. Fryback, CPT after completion of the interviews (the reports are the best record):

• ////////reported that//////touched his "privates" on one occasion while they were alone in her bedroom. ///////reported that ////// told him not to tell anyone. //////// denied that anyone witnessed this incident and denied any knowledge of his brother having been touched on his privates. ///////reported that he told his mother and father about the incident after it occurred.

• ////////disclosed having witnessed his aunt, //////, pull down the pants of his brother and touch his "weenie". He reported that he and//////were "peeking" through the doorway and witnessed the incident occur. He reported having told only his grandmother.////// denied that either /////////had ever touched his "weenie".

Due to the inconsistencies of the statements of /////////////there is insufficient evidence that the incident occurred. All reports/allegations made to DCF have been closed with No Indicators.

This case will be closed but will be available to Santa Rosa County should any criminal charges be brought against Mark Harris.

Case Status: Closed.

< END OF NARRATIVE >

Offense Status	No -- Cleared		Reporting Officer	
Closed	# Clearances	0	094 BELLAMY, JENNIFER A	
	Clearance Date		OCSO/INV/CRIMINV/GENERAL INVEST	
Warr./Arr. No.	Clearance Type			
	Except. Clear. Type		*Forward for Approval / Followup To :	
	Age Classification		OCSO/INV/CRIMINV	

Supervisor -APPROVED ROBERT W NORRIS				Case Screening Supv.		Investigator
	Yes	Concur	No			
Date Time	No	PtlF/U	No	Date	Time	094
02/16/2009 08:47	No	InvF/U	No			BELLAMY, JENNIFER A

Report Last Modified 02/16/2009   08:47

OCSO08OFF014591 | Page 3 of 3 | [BELLAJ | 01/02/2009 16:56]

This is the second page of DCF Investigator Jennifer Clark's report showing both children affirmed the allegations in an interview, which Clark buried and lied about in her report. Note that the investigator, Jennifer Bellamy continued to pursue charges in another county after the kids affirmed the allegations in a recorded interview and in a pattern of conduct. Former OSI agent Robert Norris' name appears on the report as in other reports related to Nobles.

OFFENSE REPORT   OKALOOSA CO SHERIFF'S OFFICE
OCSO08OFF011074   Printed On: 11/06/2009 @ 13:13

Status: APPROVED   TOMMY M FREDERICK   9/10/2008   ·11:29
CAD INCIDENT DISPOSITION CODE: [60-1] [B]

Synopsis:

Deputy Sheriff Keith Soares is submitting this report as it relates to a sex offense involving juveniles. This incident occurred in Niceville, Okaloosa county, Florida between March and June 2008.

9/7/2008   20:46   SUPPLEMENT   SOARES, KEITH A   234   REZZARD   9/7/2008   22:30
Status: APPROVED   TOMMY M FREDERICK   9/10/2008   11:29

On September 07, 2008 I responded to 300 Mary Esther Blvd for a report of a sex offense. Upon arrival I made contact with Mark Harris (Mark) who stated his two son's, ▨▨▨▨▨▨▨who is seven years old and ▨▨▨▨▨▨▨▨▨who is four years old, told him on August 8, 2008 that their ▨▨▨▨▨▨▨▨ who is about 12 years old and ▨▨▨▨▨▨▨, who is about 10 years old, committed the offense of sexual battery against them.

Mark stated this offense would have occurred at the residence of their Grandfather, Michael Nobles (Mike) in Niceville and between the dates of March to June of 2008 at least two separate times. Mark could not be more specific about the dates and the amount of times this occurred because he could not get that information from ▨▨▨and ▨▨▨▨

Mark stated specifically, ▨▨▨ told him his ▨▨▨▨▨▨ "played with his weenie" when he was at his Grandparent's house; ▨▨▨ and ▨▨▨ refer to the Grandparents, as Paw Paw and Grammy. ▨▨▨ stated it occurred in ▨▨▨ and ▨▨▨room on the couch; but later said on the bed which Mark believed ▨▨▨was describing a second incident. ▨▨▨told Mark ▨▨▨left the room and right after that, ▨▨▨held ▨▨▨ down, pulled down just the front of his pants and using her fingers pulled his penis and slapped it. ▨▨▨ told Mark he pretended that it tickled and was able to kick her off of him. ▨▨▨told Mark ▨▨▨did not use her mouth for anything when Mark asked him about it. ▨▨▨repeatedly requested Mark to not tell ▨▨▨ Mark stated ▨▨▨ has repeated this incident a total of two times to him and once to a Therapist he is currently seeing, (Katleen ▨▨▨, ▨▨▨). Mark added ▨▨▨ has seen Shuster a total of three times as of September 07, 2008 but only mentioned the specifics about the sexual battery the last time, which was about September 03, 2008.

Mark asked ▨▨▨if he had been touched by anyone which he replied no. ▨▨▨ did tell Mark about the incident where he ▨▨▨not ▨▨▨ hold ▨▨▨down in the bedroom, pull the front of his pants down, and using her fingers pulled ▨▨▨ penis and then slapped it. ▨▨▨told Mark ▨▨▨called ▨▨▨ penis "Daddy." ▨▨▨also mentioned to Mark, during this same incident he observed Paw Paw's eye looking through the cracked door. Mark stated he felt ▨▨▨was discussing an incident which happened to him and not ▨▨▨ because ▨▨▨ repeatedly denies ▨▨▨ being involved. While Mark continued to get further and more information from ▨▨▨ he started crying and told him he didn't want to talk about anymore and that he was afraid of the devil. Mark asked ▨▨▨who told him about the devil, which he replied ▨▨▨ Mark stated Shuster attempted to speak with ▨▨▨ about the

OCSO08OFF011074   Page 5 of 9   [PACKERM   09/07/2008 17:29 |

incident, but [REDACTED] refuses to talk about it with her.

Mark stated he has had suspicions of something possibly going on at Mike's residence while [REDACTED] and [REDACTED] were being watched by him for the last six years but never had any type of direct evidence. Mark provided me a brief history of events which led up to this report by stating about six years ago he was asked to help fix or clean up Mike's work computer because it was running sluggish and he had knowledge to fix it. When Mark looked at the Internet History Files he identified several titles of web pages which included the words "father daughter incest," "pre-teen," "pre-puberty," "underage," "little girls," and many with "daddy" in the titles. Mark did not open any of the web pages but told his wife Christy Harris (Christy) about it and she stated those were probably opened and viewed by her brother, Billy Nobles (Billy), who lived with Mike at the time. Mark stated they did not speak to Billy for a long time and Christy believed Billy was on anti-depressants at or about this time the work computer was viewed. Mark stated about two years ago he saw similar titles in the history of Mike's home computer. Mark did not open any files but based on the date and time, he believed Mike was the only one at home who had access to the computer.

Mark stated on July 18, 2008, when Mike was in Mexico, he was given permission by Mike's wife, Wanda Nobles (Wanda), to enter the residence and use Mike's home computer. Mark saw a picture of [REDACTED], who is six years old and the [REDACTED] of Mike, in a small bikini where she is laying on the ground on her back with her feet on the ground, knees in the air and she is "spread eagle" where the view of the camera is directly facing her crotch. Mark did not see any nude pictures of [REDACTED] but felt this picture was very risqué when encompassed with all the other information and allegations against Mike. Mark also saw a password protected program which had a title of "mother teaches young daughter to give blowjob." Mark used a free trial of an internet service and obtained the following information from Mike's home computer:

Date Read: July 18, 2008, 10:42
Times Read: 5
Times Forwarded: 0
Read Duration: 3 min, 15 sec
Recipient IP: 64.12.117.135
Recipient Language: en-us
Recipient Location: US,,,"America Online"
Recipient Browser: Moozilla

Mark stated he believed this information shows Mike purposely masks the location, city and state of his computer address to avoid being detected by law enforcement. Mark stated Mike has file sharing software, password breaking software, web cam viewing software and what appears to have regular external hard drives or similar devices attached to the home computer; Mark did not locate any external drives and has not viewed any actual child pornography on the computer. Mark stated prior to him viewing the home computer on July 18, 2008, Mike told a family friend and/or co-worker Mark Smith that he takes his internet router to work with him and that he sleeps with it under his pillow at night.

Mark confided all of this information with [REDACTED], who I believe is possibly Mike Smith's spouse, who is an outside source of the family. Mark stated [REDACTED] told him that she spoke with another individual, who she did not name, about the incident and this

OFFENSE REPORT   OKALOOSA CO SHERIFF'S OFFICE
OCSO08OFF011074   Printed On: 11/06/2009 @ 13:13

unknown person said they knew Mike has been molesting his Daughters and Grand
Daughters all these years but could never prove it. With the exception of her name, Mark
wanted to keep ▨▨▨▨ anonymous unless she was absolutely needed later for the
investigation, which he feels she will assist in speaking with investigators.

Mark stated because of these events he has not brought over ▨▨▨ and ▨▨ to
Mike's residence since June 28, 2008 but believes Christy has at least twice. Mark went on to
talk about behavior patterns occurring in all of the family members involved and feels the
patterns of behavior observed help prove the allegations of sexual abuse by Mike, at least
circumstantially.

Mark stated he has waited to report this incident because he is not the Biological
Father of ▨▨ and ▨▨ and was waiting for legal custodial rights to the boys which he
states is in effect as of September 01, 2008. Mark stated he is still legally married to Christy
but they are both currently separated. Mark is afraid of losing ▨▨ and ▨▨ and believes
Mike will try and retaliate by not allowing Mark to see the boys and to try and discredit him
and his testimony anyway possible.

Mark was also very concerned about Christy finding out that he has reported this
incident because she may side with Mike and try to take ▨▨ and ▨▨ away from him.
Mark added Christy has hinted comments about being sexually abused as a child but never
confirms it or identifies a possible suspect.

During the interview with Mark, I learned he had already made a report for the
sexual battery of ▨▨ and ▨▨, through the 800 ABUSE Hotline on Friday through the
internet while he was in Atlanta. Mark stated Department of Children and Families
Investigator Sarah Johnson came to his residence in Santa Rosa County to interview him
about the incident regarding ▨▨ and ▨▨ Mark also discussed with Department of
Children and Families Investigator Johnson the possible child pornography on Mike's home
computer, the possibility of Mike sexually abusing ▨▨▨ and her older Sister, ▨▨ while
they were growing up in the home and the possibility of sexual abuse to ▨▨ Mark stated
Department of Children and Families Investigator Johnson, did not give him any paperwork
or pamphlets, and told him to make another call to the 800 ABUSE Hotline on September 08,
2008, regarding the incident so that Okaloosa County Department of Children and Families
Investigators can pick up the case and interview the kids involved while they were at school.
Mark stated Department of Children and Families Investigator Johnson also told him he
should make a report with Okaloosa County Sheriff's Office regarding the possible child
pornography on Mike's home computer.

I contacted Department of Children and Families Supervisor Donna Parrish, who
advised me to initiate an offense with the Okaloosa County Sheriff's Office and submit a copy
to the 800 ABUSE Hotline under a Law Enforcement Report to ensure there will be a joint
and co-operated effort to investigate the allegations with Okaloosa County Sheriff's Office.

I made contact with the Department of Children and Families by phone through
the 800 ABUSE Hotline and spoke with operator Doug #5644. I provided a Victim's Right
Brochure to Mark along with an offense number. Mark already came in to the interview with
a pre-typed 3-page statement. I had Mark complete an Affidavit of Complaint form

OCSO08OFF011074   Page 7 of 9   [PACKERM   09/07/2008 17:29   ]

417

summarizing his testimony and swore him to the pre-typed statement and Affidavit of Complaint. I will attach his pre-typed statement to the Affidavit of Complaint as a supplement to avoid him re-writing the statement by hand.

Mark stated because he is a pilot, he will be out of town for the next three days but will be available to speak with investigators by cell phone when he is not in the air. Mark stated, he is scheduled to be back home after the three days departure for a total of four days in a row.

Due to the numerous people involved with this incident and listed in this report the following is a list of the family structure:

Mark did not know the address and phone number of Billy, Rewena and ////// but knew they lived in Crestview. Mark also did not know the address where Christy is staying, due to their separation, but knows it is in the Seminole area of Niceville. Mark did not have enough information regarding ////// and ////// other than their names, where they reside and that they are home schooled by Wanda, so they were not entered into the Persons Section of this report after my interview with Mark and will needed to be added later by the follow-up case officer; this also applies to //////

Case Status: Pending

9/11/2008 13:54   SUPPLEMENT   EASTERDAY, PAUL MONTY   038   EASTERM   9/11/2008 13:57
Status: APPROVED   ROBERT W NORRIS   9/11/2008   15:46

On September 11, 2008 I made contact with Niceville Police Department, Inv. Forgeoni, who advised me that he was aware of this case and was already investigating the allegations. I

OFFENSE REPORT
NFD08OFF000868

COPY

NICEVILLE POLICE DEPARTMENT
Printed On: 11/09/2009 @ 10:49

Weapon
Location Category — Residence
Location Type — Offender's residence
Location Description — SINGLE FAMILY
Location Status — Inhabited
Number of Premises Burglarized — 0
Target — - Person
Entry Method — - Unknown
Point of Entry (POE) — - Other
POE Visible From — - Street
Point of Exit — - Other
Suspect Actions — - Knew Victim
Circumstances — Child abuse
Weather — - Unknown
Lighting Condition — Unknown
Security Used — - Other
Crime Scene? : No
If NO, Explain : NO SCENE

Crime Scene Officer:
Physical Evidence Collected: 0

(handwritten right margin: report triggered / FBI visit on this / date at which / Nobles requested / Forgione be...)

< NARRATIVE >

DATE	TIME	TYPE	OFFICER REPORTING	CALL #	REP TAKER	EDIT DATE	EDIT TIME
2/5/2009	07:47	INITIAL	FORGIONE, JOSEPH C	007	JFORGIONE	2/5/2009	08:05

Status: APPROVED   JOSEPH C FORGIONE   2/5/2009   08:05

SUMMARY *(handwritten: 3 Days before being "forwarded" to him by OCSD)* *(Investigator, reporting officer and reviewer. No accountability)*

On 09/08/08 I conducted a Joint Child Abuse Investigation with Department of Children & Families located at 1118 Rhonda Dr. It was reported that 12 year old and 10 year old has sexually abused by Michael Nobles for sometime. Discovery interview were conducted with both.

DISCOVERY

Both and appear to be well taken care of. They seem to be happy in their home life. While speaking with them they both did not disclose any type of sexual or physical abuse. *(handwritten: Only witness interviewed was perpetrator)*

STATEMENT BY MICHAEL

While speaking with Michael he denies any of the allegation. Michael believes the report is false.

At this time there is no evidence supporting any sexual or physical abuse. I request the children to be be placed in play therapy and/or counseling. This case will be closed as

NPD08OFF000868   Page 2 of 3   [JFORGIONE   09/09/2008 10:09]

(handwritten: This was a lie & never happened)

133

This shows how an honest cop's detailed, accurate report was forwarded to Niceville Police Officer Joey Forgione and effectively made to disappear with no investigation. Note that Forgione is the reporting officer, investigator, and supervisor. Because this looked bad it was later altered to show that Joseph Kearns, who had no part in this was the investigator. It was modified on February 5, 2009, in response to my involving the FBI on that date. Again, former OSI Agent Robert Norris' name appears on this report. In identical fashion, the detailed and accurate firearms report, not included here, taken by an honest cop, officer Nelson, was made to go away by the same officers, Kearns and Forgione, who both later conspired to cover up murder by trying to frame me.

```
OFFENSE REPORT                                          WALTON COUNTY SHERIFFS OFFICE
WCSO10OFF000935                                         Printed On:   09/22/2010 @ 13:25

CHARGES/OFFENSES
Statute: 837.05.2                      Counts : 1        UCR: 260A        NCIC :

   Charge :   MAKING FALSE REPORT
   Desc :     FALSE INFO TO LEO RE CAPITAL FELONY
   General Offense Code... (GOC) :   F   Facilitate
   Arrest Charge Level..... (ACL) :  F   Felony
   Arrest Charge Degree... (ACD) :   T   Third Degree
   Arrest Offense Number (AON) :     4803
```

```
Weapon
Location Category                      Non-residence
Location Type                          Other non-residence
Location Description                   Range Rd 210
Location Status                        None
Number of Premises Burglarized         0
Target
Entry Method                           - Unknown
Point of Entry (POE)
POE Visible From
Point of Exit
Suspect Actions
Circumstances                          Unknown
Weather                                - Unknown
Lighting Condition                     Night
Security Used
Crime Scene? :       No
If NO, Explain :     No Crime Scene due to time lapse from time of incident.

Crime Scene Officer:       119         MARTIN, JOSH
Physical Evidence Collected:           0
```

```
< NARRATIVE >
DATE      TIME     TYPE        OFFICER REPORTING      CALL #   REP TAKER    EDIT DATE  EDIT TIME
2/26/2010  13:29   INITIAL     MARTIN, JOSH           119      JMARTIN      4/13/2010  07:48
Status: APPROVED   JAMES R LORENZ       3/1/2010  11:34
```

On 02-24-2010 Sgt. Lorenz received a phone call from an individual who identified himself as Mark Harris. He began telling Sgt. Lorenz about a murder and a possible location of the body. M. Harris said his children had told him about the incident and described to possible whereabouts of the body. M. Harris advised Sgt. Lorenz he would be available on Friday and would show us where his children told him the body was buried.

On 02-26-2010 at approx. 10:00 am Sgt. Lorenz and myself met with M. Harris and several members of Eglin Air Force Base Security Services at the Raceway store on US Hwy 90 in Mossyhead. After a brief discussion we all traveled from the Raceway to Range Rd 210 to the location that M. Harris had described.

Upon arrival at the end of Range Rd 210, Sgt. Lorenz and myself walked out into the woods to attempt to find the tree M. Harris was talking about. The tree was alleged to be burned from the top to the bottom and the grave site was at the bottom of the tree. Sgt. Lorenz and myself first searched the area but was unable to locate any evidence of a possible grave site

```
WCSO10OFF000935          Page 3 of 8          [ JMARTIN        02/26/2010  13:29  ]
```

This falsified statement by Deputy Josh Martin begins with a lie and just keeps getting worse. It claims I called Sgt Lorenze. I did not contact the Walton County Sheriff's Department, Eglin Range Patrol did. I also never reported a grave. We looked for and found the burnt tree which I reported to Eglin Range Patrol as they had requested. Eglin Range Patrol then called Walton County.

OFFENSE REPORT   WALTON COUNTY SHERIFFS OFFICE
WCSO10OFF000935   Printed On: 09/22/2010 @ 13:25

and several trees in the area had been burned during a previous control burn in the area. After the initial search was performed we returned to the roadway where our vehicles were parked.

I then asked M. Harris to sit down inside Sgt. Lorenz's vehicle in order to conduct an interview to gain more information on the alleged incident. Also present for the interview was Inv. Camacho who was a member of the Office of Special Investigations with Security Services. I asked M. Harris if he could tell me what his children had told him about the incident. M. Harris stated his kids had been separated from him between October 31, 2008 and January 26, 2009 at which time they were in the custody of their mother and grandfather. The maternal grandfather was identified as Michael Stephen Nobles of Niceville. His children, ⬛⬛⬛ and ⬛⬛⬛, told him their grandfather had killed a man and buried him in their presence. The children told their father "Papa" had killed a man in his home in Niceville and then buried the body.

The alleged victim was shot in the living room of the grandfather's residence at 1118 Rhonda Dr. in Niceville, FL. The subject was shot in the stomach with what the kids referred to as an "old pistol". The subject sat in the floor groaning and died about two minutes later. The only conversation the children heard was their grandfather say, " Jack Stevens, get against the wall" and the subject only said "stop" just prior to being shot.

The children said the a bag was then placed over the feet and head of the body and tied in the middle. The body was removed from the residence and originally buried in the back yard near a tree. The body was later removed and one of the children described the smell as being that of "10,000 rotten squid" and the fluid that leaked from the bag as being green and purple. After being removed from the original burial site, the body was then transported using a utility trailer pulled by an early 2000 model Ford Explorer green in color. According to the children, the body was then taken to the site described by the children as being on Range Rd. 210 and there burned and buried again. M. Harris stated his children once told him the body was dismembered but have since changed their story and said they got that from a video game their grandfather had gotten for them.

The children also stated their grandfather had replaced the flooring in his house due to blood being on the carpet. I asked M. Harris if the kids had told him what time of the day the alleged incident had occurred and he stated, " The boys said it was in the middle of the night when the body was moved because there was no other vehicles on the road." M. Harris said the boys told him that all of it occurred at night and did not tell him how long after the shooting it was before the body was buried at the residence. The children also stated that nobody else was at the residence but them and the grandfather when it occurred. I asked M. Harris if the kids were able to describe the victim and he said the kids described the victim as an older white man with gray hair that walked hunched over and their grandfather referred to him as Jack Stevens. I asked M. Harris if the kids recognized the man or seen how he had got to the residence. The kids did not recognize the man or know how he got there.

M. Harris stated that he was invited into the residence on Feb. 5. 2009 and while inside noticed the flooring had been replaced. M. Harris stated he also observed tracks in the yard coming from the alleged original burial site in the back yard of the residence.

WCSO10OFF000935   Page 4 of 8   [JMARTIN   02/26/2010 13:29   ]

Most of this statement is in fact accurate although it omits the existence of a very unique tree obviously intentionally burned which perfectly fit the description my son made in advance and that both children identified. The claim that the kids did not know the man is false. They knew his name and had played board games with him.

OFFENSE REPORT
WCSO10OFF000935

WALTON COUNTY SHERIFFS OFFICE
Printed On: 09/22/2010 @ 13:25

due to the Children being involved and he stated, "No, I have not said anything to her because she is Bi-Polar and is not being treated".

I asked M. Harris if M. Nobles still owned the vehicle and trailer that was allegedly used to transport the body. He stated the Explorer had been given to his wife and she had since sold it to somebody else. He stated the trailer belonged to him and he had gotten it back since the incident. M. Harris stated he had purchased some Luminol online and sprayed the trailer to see if he could find anything and a spot on the bottom of the trailer "glowed". He said his kids then told him they thought their grandfather had pressure washed the trailer after the transport of the body. M. Harris stated he had spoken to Lt. Shalee with the Niceville Police Department and took the trailer to them to see if they would test it and was told to go back home so he tested it himself.

During the interview M. Harris made several comments about past and present activity that his father-in-law has been involved in. He stated M. Nobles was a convicted felon and still owns several firearms which he keeps in the home with him. M. Nobles had give one of his daughters a handgun when she moved out and tried to give his wife one when she moved out. M. Harris said he had contacted the Bureau of Alcohol, Tobacco and Firearms (ATF) and spoke to an agent by the name of Gregory Moore in the Nashville, TN office about the firearms. He was then referred to the Pensacola, FL office where he spoke to agent Randal Beech. M. Harris also stated M. Nobles had built a home on property that belongs to C. Walter Ruckel and his kids told him they had seen "machine guns", explosives and safes containing large amounts of money and gold coins. According to M. Harris, the M. Nobles is a member of more than one anti-government organization and was convicted in 1996. The conviction was supposedly for attempting to get people to file false tax returns to attempt to overthrow the government.

M. Harris also stated during the interview that there had been accusations of abuse on the children by the grandfather. He said the grandfather had threatened to kill the children's pets in front of them and crucify the children if they ever talked to anybody about the alleged abuse or murder that they had witnessed.
M. Harris provided some drawings that he first stated the children had drawn describing the incident. Later M. Harris stated he had drawn one of the pictures and one of his children used it to show him how the body was removed from the residence and taken to the original burial site. These drawings have been scanned into case management and entered into evidence.

M. Harris was unable to give a written statement at the scene due to us not having an Affidavit of Complaint with us. He stated he would be able to come to the office on Monday March 1, 2010 and provide us with an Affidavit of Complaint about the incident.

There was no physical evidence found at the scene to support the allegations and no charges have been filed at this time.

SUPPLEMENT   MARTIN, JOSH   119   JMARTIN   4/14/2010   10:40
Status: APPROVED   JAMES R LORENZ   3/2/2010   22:41

On 03-02-2010 at approximately 11:00 am M. Harris came to the Walton County Sheriff's Office in order to give a sworn statement on the alleged incident. He was

WCSO10OFF000935   Page 5 of 8   [JMARTIN   02/26/2010 13:29   ]

Again, most of this part of the complaint is accurate and it is true although I did not draw any pictures of the murder nor claimed I did. Nowhere in the report is the fact that the trailer containing evidence was in their custody. It was never examined, and I had a difficult time getting it returned, after which I discovered it was full of evidence.

accompanied by his youngest son, ▨▨▨▨▨▨, I escorted them to Sgt. Lorenz's office in order and was waiting on Sgt. Lorenz to return.

While waiting I was standing by the door to the office and the minor child was sitting in one of the chairs in front of the desk and M. Harris was standing to the left and in front of his son. I heard M. Harris say to his son, " They need to talk to me about the place ya'll showed me in the woods." The child looked up at his father with a very confused look on his face. M. Harris then stated, " You know, the place you and your brother showed me in the woods". The child looked at his father again and stated, " What woods". This conversation was strictly between M. Harris and his son , ▨▨▨▨ and was not at all part of any interview.

Sgt. Lorenz returned to his office and noticed M. Harris had the child with him. He informed M. Harris that we needed to talk to him by his self and his son could not be present. Sgt. Lorenz asked M. Harris if he thought his son would be willing to wait outside the office door until the interview was complete. M. Harris asked his son if he would wait outside the door but the child did not want to leave the room. Sgt. Lorenz informed M. Harris again that we could not conduct an interview on him with the child present due to the fact the child is a possible witness in the case. It was then determined that M. Harris would call Sgt. Lorenz at a later date to set up an interview.

End of Statement

| 4/12/2010 10:46 | INVESTIGATIVE | LORENZ, JAMES R | C038 | JLORENZ | 4/28/2010 10:12 |
| Status: APPROVED | JAMES R FANNIN | 4/12/2010 11:27 | | | |

On 02/22/10 Inv. Armstrong informed me that she had received a telephone call from Lt. Callahan informing her that Mr. Mark Harris had informed him that his sons had witnessed their grandfather kill a man and bury his body on the military reservation. Lt. Callahan did not have Mr. Harris contact information at this time and would contact this department at a later time with the information.

On 02/24/10 I was contacted by Lt. Callahan, who stated that he was contacted on 02/10/10, by Mark Harris, who stated that his boys had informed him they had witnessed their grandfather, Michael Nobles, kill a man and bury his body on the military reservation approximately twenty years ago. Mr. Harris went on to state that knowing his father-in-law, he believes this could actually happen.

Mr. Harris stated his boys had told him that the location of the incident is in the area east of state Hwy 285 and south of Hwy 90, near some railroad tracks and a concrete bunker.

Mr. Harris requested their help in finding the location his sons had described earlier. Lt. Callahan replied there was a mission in progress in that area and they would have to wait.

On 02/20/10, Mr. Harris called again and was given directions to the area of range road 214 and 210, which is near the area he described.

On 02/22/10, Mr. Harris contacted Lt. Callahan and stated he thought he and his sons had found the area of the crime.

Lt. Callahan supplied me with Mr. Harris's contact information.

The statement at the top of the Page by James Lorenz regarding my son's response was a lie to discredit my kids. I would urge the reader to compare this claim to my sons' testimony. The next statement is a jumbled-up mess that doesn't resemble anything I reported although it does accurately reveal that it was Eglin Range Patrol who called the Walton County Sherrif's Department, not I as previously claimed. What I did report in a sworn and notarized statement and what was recorded at the scene on tape by Eglin AFB OSI were both destroyed.

OFFENSE REPORT
WCSO10OFF000935

WALTON COUNTY SHERIFFS OFFICE
Printed On: 09/22/2010 @ 13:25

On 02/24/10, I contacted Mr. Harris and informed him of the purpose of my telephone call. Mr. Harris stated that his sons, ▨and ▨▨▨ were removed from him approximately four years ago, where they resided with their mother and grandfather Michael Nobles in Niceville Florida.

Mr. Harris stated he had recently regain custody of his sons and they had informed him of an incident where they witness their grandfather, Michael Nobles kill, hang, and burn a body in the Mossy Head Area.

I asked Mr. Harris to give me an approximate time frame of the incident and he replied within the last year. I then asked Mr. Harris what are the ages of his sons and he replied ▨▨ ▨▨ and Gabriel ▨▨.

I told Mr. Harris that Lt. Callahan had informed me this incident occurred approximately twenty years ago. Mr. Harris stated that was not true. Mr. Harris went on to say that there is an on going custody battle between him and his soon to be ex-wife.

I asked Mr. Harris, when could he show me the location of the crime, and he replied Friday, 02/26/10.

I contacted Lt. Callahan by telephone and informed him of the content of Mr. Harris's statement. Lt. Callahan stated that Mr. Harris implied the incident occurred a long time ago. I asked Lt. Callahan if he would complete a voluntary statement for me. Lt. Callahan replied he would and would send the statement to the Walton County Sheriff's Department.

6/24/2010 22:10   INVESTIGATIVE   SCONIERS, JOSHUA M.   C074   JSCONIERS   6/24/2010   22:13
Status: APPROVED   LORENZ, JAMES R   6/25/2010   06:59

On June 24th, 2010 I spoke with Mrs. Sue Thorn of the Stat Attorney's Office in DeFuniak Springs, FL. I had requested that Mrs. Thorn get in contact with Assistant State Attorney Greg Anchors with regards to prosecution in this case. Mrs. Thorn told me that according to Mr. Anchors that this case was going to be Williams ruled being as the same crime has already been charged in Okaloosa County, FL resulting from an arrest of Mark Harris by the Valparaiso Police Department. I was advised that at this point I could go ahead and close out the Walton County investigation. This case will now be closed out. END OF STATEMENT.

< END OF NARRATIVE >

WCSO10OFF000935   Page 7 of 8   [JMARTIN   02/26/2010 13:29   ]

The false claim by Joshua Sconiers regarding me, that there was "an ongoing custody battle between him and his soon to be ex-wife" is particularly revealing. This was neither true nor did I say anything like it, but this was the persistent game, cover Mike Nobles tracks by pretending there was some divorce or custody dispute. Sconiers, whose LinkedIn profile starts with a bible verse, is now a DeFuniak Springs City Councilman.

Polygraph Report

On July 13, 2010 Mark Chapman Harris was administered a polygraph examination. The purpose of the examination was to determine his truthfulness regarding his reporting to the Niceville, Florida Police Department of a murder he alleges was committed by his father in law Michael Nobles.

Pre-test Statement
During the pre-test portion of the examination Mr. Harris made the following statements:

In September, 2009 my two children told me that their grandfather Michael Nobles had murdered a man in their presence in the living room of his home in Niceville, Florida. My oldest son told me this man's name was Jack Stevens. They told me that their grandfather had shot this man and then put a plastic bag over his head and another over his feet and taped it in the middle. The children said he then buried the body in his back yard.

The children then told me that sometime later their grandfather dug the body up which my oldest son described in detail. They said he placed the body on a trailer and took it to the woods and hung it in a tree and burned it. My oldest son who was seven at the time then described in detail the place where the body was burned.

I reported what my children had told me to the Niceville, Florida Police Department in November, 2009. I was arrested in March, 2010 and charged with, "Falsely Reporting Information to Law Enforcement Officers Concerning a Capital Felony".

Polygraph Examination
During the actual polygraph examination Mr. Harris was asked the following listed relevant questions:

1. Are you deliberately lying when you say that your children told you that their grandfather had murdered a man in Niceville, Florida?
2. Have you in anyway encouraged your children to lie about that murder?
3. Are you deliberately lying about this murder just to get your father in law in trouble?

Conclusion
After careful analysis of the polygraph charts it is the opinion of this Polygraph Examiner that Mr. Harris was truthful when answering "No" to the above listed relevant questions.

S. Neil Rucker
Polygraph Examiner

A copy of the polygraph I voluntarily submitted to and passed regarding the murder, along with passing numerous psychological evaluations, excelling in psychological testing, and passing drug and alcohol testing.

All:

Below is a follow-up message I sent to Mark Harris this morning via myMessage (so we have utilized an official Company communication method), with the correct pilot release attached. Additionally, I spoke with Mark Wollman in general terms regarding this matter, although he certainly had all the details – at least from Harris' perspective.

Apparently he and Harris have spoken on more than one occasion regarding these matters. Wollman conveyed to me that he has advised Harris to sign the release and get up here expeditiously to be tested. Wollman advised that the contract allows the Chief Pilot to require such testing if we have reason for doing so.

We are not receiving other documents in a very timely manner – in fact I have not received the documents from the public documents I requested. so I think we are at a point where we need to require the test (especially while ALPA is backing our decision) and get him up here ASAP. I think that such a directive will have to come from Flight Ops., as it is invoking a privilege conveyed under the terms of the CBA (if I understand this correctly). Is this correct?

Wollman advised that we set up the appointment and direct Harris to show up for it. A phone call from a CP telling him we have set up an appointment, etc. might take the "directive" sting out of the conversation. If we know this is the net outcome, then why continue to wait on this other material. This is becoming very untimely.

As a matter of logistical concern, Dr. Harper will be going on vacation for two weeks, beginning the first of March.

Jim

An email from James Brimberry to "All" plotting to force me into a series of illegal evaluations, beginning with Dr. Harper who Brimberry lied and claimed was the company doctor. This shows that Mark Wollman, of the Airline Pilots Association who I had asked for advice after my job was threatened by Niceville Police Officer Forgione was party to this bizarre charade and conspired to set a trap for me instead of helping me.

As we discussed, ASA is not interested in getting involved in your personal matters, nor do we feel that it is our appropriate role. However, given the concerns regarding the specific nature of, and reason for, your discharge from the military (contained on your DD214) and subsequent concerns about how the application was marked; the concerns brought forth by Mr. Nobles; and the knowledge that you already underwent an independent psychiatric evaluation on your own, which cannot be located , cause ASA to believe, in an abundance of caution, an independent evaluation by our doctor is the most prudent and expeditious way to resolve this matter.

I very much appreciate the information you have provided thus far. Even though it is not medical in nature, I would like for our Company doctor to review it, with your permission. I am not qualified to determine if there is information contained in the documents that would help in this process, but he is qualified to make that determination. If you have other information, particularly, the information from the doctor who evaluated you, that would be very helpful as well.

I received a call from ALPA representative Mark Wollman regarding your situation. He suggested that you have given permission for me to discuss the details of our concerns regarding this matter. Please confirm that I have your permission to discuss the matter in detail with him. My number is 404-856-1292.

Regards,

Jim

Jim Brimberry

General Manager, HR

Jim Brimberry
General Manager - Human Resources
Atlantic Southeast Airlines
(404) 856-1292

There was no issue with my military discharge, the company had my DD214, and my application was clearly marked. In fact, I went above and beyond to be honest and had been inappropriately grilled about it during my job interview. The company later back-pedaled and admitted these facts. Note that he calls Dr. Harper "our company doctor." The company later disavowed any relationship with Dr. Harper.

An excerpt of my ASA job application (top) in which I went above and beyond to be honest and an excerpt of my January 2010 FAA Medical Application (bottom) in which nothing related to alcohol was marked yes as there was nothing to report. I was falsely accused of lying in both by officials who in fact were lying.

Summary and Recommendation

Mr. Harris is a 42-year-old commercial airman embroiled in a messy dispute surrounding marital separation and custody issues. He does appear to have a history consistent with alcohol abuse and possibly dependence in the period 1991-98. During that time, he appears to have had multiple blackouts, heavy drinking episodes and all this culminated in an arrest for indecent exposure during an episode of alcohol intoxication. Records from a treating psychologist show treatment occurred at that time, and he was deemed not to have ongoing alcohol or other issue of psychopathology. He had a one-week treatment in 1999 through the Air Force for Alcohol Intoxication.

In December 2009 and February 2010 he was interviewed by a board certified psychiatrist as noted in this report, and no evidence of mental disorder, including active substance use disorder, were found, with diagnosis of Partner Relational problems noted.

The psychological testing and interview by Dr. Hill found no cognitive or emotional difficulties to impair him from flying. My own clinical interview is consistent. As long as he remains abstinent, the airman appears to be fit to fly, based on his representations, my interview, the psychological testing, and other records noted. Given his self-report of two years free of alcohol use, I am not recommending any additional treatment at this time. My understanding is that you, Dr. Harper, will continue to follow this airman.

Sincerely,

Michael A. Haberman, M.D.

Michael A. Haberman, M.D.

This is a summary of Dr. Haberman's report. Dr. Haberman is the right-wing extremist doctor who spread around a racist "diagnosis" of President Obama as a narcissistic sociopath and compared him to Adolf Hitler. Just as his politically motivated "diagnosis" of the president, here he "diagnosed" me with a bizarre and vague "history consistent with alcohol abuse" from over a decade prior which was irrelevant under FAA regulations even if true, and all based on a cut and paste job of records related to one isolated and non-reportable incident over a decade prior which was sealed by a court. In his opening statement he repeated a Goebbels lie, one repeated over and over by government officials at the local state and federal level, that I was embroiled in a messy "custody dispute." There was no custody dispute, both of my sons suffered severe PTSD, had been psychologically tortured, witnessed murder, and one had already been hospitalized for PTSD and remains disabled as a result. The claims that I received treatment by a psychologist for substance abuse disorder and treatment in the military for substance abuse were total fabrications. Absent in this report and a subsequent report are the six days I spent locked in a cage starting the day after this evaluation. And there was certainly no basis for Dr. Harper to "continue to follow" me.

AEROMEDICAL, INC.
C.R. HARPER, M.D.
BOARD CERTIFIED IN AEROSPACE MEDICINE
FELLOW IN THE AMERICAN COLLEGE OF PREVENTIVE MEDICINE
2000 CLEARVIEW AVENUE SUITE 215
PHONE 770-457-3532   FAX 770-457-1200

April 30, 2010   RE: MARK C. HARRIS

CHARLES CHESANOW, M.D.
CHIEF PSYCHIATRIST, F.A.A.

DEAR DR. CHESANOW,

MR. HARRIS , A 42 YEAROLD A.S.A. PILOT WAS EVALUATED BY ME ON 3-4-10 AT THE REQUEST OF THE
AIRLINE DUE TO COMPLAINTS OF HIS FATHER -IN- LAW REGARDING HIS MENTAL STABILITY. BASED ON
MY INTERVIEW WITH HIM, I FELT THAT MR. HARRIS WAS EMOTIONALLY STABLE BUT BECAUSE OF THE
CHRONICITY AND EXTREME COMPLEXITY OF THE COMPLAINTS AND THE ISSUE OF HIS GENERAL
DISCHARGE FROM THE U.S.A.F. THAT A FULL P&P EVAL WOULD HELP CLARIFY THE ISSUE REGARDING
HIS FITNESS TO FLY UNDER PART 67. AN ETG PERFORMED ON THE DATE OF MY EVAL WAS NEGATIVE.

THE EVALUATION DID CLEAR HIM FROM ANY SIGNIFICANT PSYCHIATRIC DISORDER BUT DID REVEAL A
HISTORY OF ALCOHOL ABUSE AND/ OR DEPENDENCE.. HIS HISTORY IS WELL DOCUMENTED IN THE
ENCLOSED RECORDS. HE HAS BEEN ABSTINENT SINCE THE SUMMER OF 2008 AND ATTENDS A WEEKLY
GROUP AT HIS CHURCH, "THE MOST EXCELLENT WAY", WHICH IS ADDICTION BASED.

BASED ON THE EVALUATIONS AND HIS HISTORY, I WOULD RECOMMEND A SPECIAL ISSUANCE, FIRST
CLASS, WITH A STRUCTURED MONITORING PERIOD FOR 3 YEARS WITH :

    1. ANNUAL PSYCHIATRIC EVALUATION, 2. RANDOM ALCOHOL/DRUG SCREENS, 3. WEEKLY
    ATTENDANCE IN A STRUCTURED AFTERCARE GROUP.

SINCERELY,

CR Harper M.D.

C.R. HARPER, M.D. AM.E. 9852

ENCLOSURES

Dr. Harper, a Freemason and John Birch Society right wing extremist, sent this memo to
the FAA on May 4, 2010, the same day FAA employee Sandy Clymer planted a fake DUI
in my records. This was completely behind my back and with no releases ever signed by
me. He alleged a vague "history of alcohol abuse and/or dependence claiming it was
"well documented."The documentation was Dr. Haberman's cut and paste job regarding
an evaluation from over a decade prior which found me free of any alcohol disorder. He
also alleges the "issue" of my military discharge which of course was not an issue and
had always been fully disclosed to my employer and every employer. Dr. Harper was a
self-described alcoholic and did in fact have a real DUI conviction.

```
                           Applicant Notes
                             08-10-2010


    Name:     HARRIS, MARK CHAPMAN              SSN:     999318883
    ApplID:   1999022574                        PI NUM:  2166456



    [RCARTER (AAM-300);  08-04-2010 11:36:53 AM]
    release usual policy.

    [TBROWN (AAM-313);  07-14-2010 1:46:07 PM]
    (1-22-10 pe) recvd file from Dr. Sager in Washington...sending sustain denial
    of 5-4-10 due to hx of alcoholism...for reconsideration a/m should be refered
    by sponsor (Dr. Harper)  to an aftercare group that satisfies HIMS
    requirements...we would reconsider him for a special issuance after he has been
    in aftercare for at least two months...we would like to review  aftercare
    report before making a final recommendation.  File to Dr. to sign denial ltr,
    mail, file.

    [SNORWOOD (AAM-300);  07-14-2010 8:07:33 AM]
    (pe 1/22/10) Washington file to T.Brown.

    [KLINCOLN (AAM-240);  06-24-2010 2:28:23 PM]
    Rec'd fax (2 page board of inquiry findings and recommendations worksheet dtd
    7/1/99) fr 200 sent to him by Dr Harper - copy to DIWS/AAM-331 for file and to
    Dr Sager to include in his review.

    [TBROWN (AAM-313);  05-04-2010 3:48:43 PM]
    (1-22-10 pe) Kathy Lincoln called and said they recvd package from Dr. Harper
    for consideration of special issuance and monitoring program...Kathy said a/m
    is an ASA pilot and was issued a med cert...reports are scanned in and she will
    give file to Dr. Sager for review.  In the meantime since a/m has med cert
    AMCD will send general denial ltr due to hx of alcohol abuse (possible alcohol
    dependence)  and request med cert.  File to Dr. to sign denial ltr, corres, 14
    day pending.

    [SCLYMER (AAM-312);  05-04-2010 9:23:47 AM]
    (pe 1/22/10) Releasing to DUI as requested.

    [GCARICO1 (AAM-330);  08-07-2009 11:27:19 AM]
    (01/28/2009) sending a dupe cert. to a/m per request.

    [DARHARRIS (AAM-300);  08-07-2009 11:20:35 AM]
    1/28/09 pe issued clear.  Ok to send dup medical

    [GCARICO1 (AAM-330);  08-05-2009 2:28:30 PM]
    SENDING TO GEN. REVIEW TO BE CLEARED FOR DUPE CERT.

    [SSCOTT (AAM-330);  03-08-2006 11:35:56 AM]
    PE 01-16-06  A/M is second class and does not need an ECG A/M called and told
    him to disregard.

    [DPRINC (AAM-330);  02-09-2006 8:07:08 AM]
    pe 1/06   sending need ecg ltr
```

Notes since deleted from my FAA medical file to cover their tracks showing Sandy Clymer, a religious fanatic who believes she has seen angels, planting a fake DUI in my records at 9:23 AM, "as requested," documentation that the package was received from Dr. Harper the same day, entered at 3:48 PM, generating a letter denying my medical which had been approved months prior could not be legally denied. Also documented is the receipt of privacy act protected military records over a month later as Dr. Berry rifled through my confidential records looking for dirty laundry to cover his tracks, finding nothing, and resorting to making things up. The FAA continues to hide and refuse to produce records in this matter and is in violation of a FOIA request.

U.S. Department
of Transportation
**Federal Aviation
Administration**

Mike Monroney Aeronautical Center
Civil Aerospace Medical Institute (CAMI)
Aerospace Medical Certification Division

P.O. Box 26080
Oklahoma City, OK 73125-9914

May 05, 2010

CERTIFIED AND REGULAR MAIL

MARK CHAPMAN HARRIS
6010 E BAY BLVD
GULF BREEZE FL 32563-9725

                              Ref: PI# 2166456
                                    MID# 200004583542
                                    App ID# 1999022574
Dear Mr. Harris:

Consideration of your application for airman medical certification and report
of medical examination completed on January 22, 2010, discloses that you do
not meet the medical standards as prescribed in Title 14 of the Code of
Federal Regulations (CFR), Section 67. Specifically under paragraph(s) or
section(s) 67.107(b)(3), 67.207(b)(3), 67.307(b)(3), Medical Standards and
Certification, due to your history of alcohol abuse (possible alcohol
dependence).

Therefore, pursuant to the authority delegated to me by the Administrator of
the Federal Aviation Administration (FAA), your application for issuance of
an airman medical certificate is hereby denied.

This denial does not constitute an action of the Administrator under 49 USC
44703 and is subject to reconsideration by the Federal Air Surgeon (FAS) of
the FAA. A request for such reconsideration may be made pursuant to Title 14
of the CFR, Section 67.409, by submitting a written request in duplicate to
the Federal Air Surgeon, ATTN: Manager, Aerospace Medical Certification
Division, AAM-300, P.O. Box 26080, Oklahoma City, Oklahoma 73125-9914. In
the event no application for reconsideration is made within 30 days of this
action, you will be deemed to have acquiesced in the denial and to have
withdrawn your application for a medical certificate.

You are advised that it is unlawful under Title 14 of the CFR, Section 61.53,
for you to exercise airman privileges unless you hold an appropriate medical
certificate. Further, it is unlawful for the holder of a medical certificate
to exercise such privileges if that holder has a known medical history or
condition, which makes him or her unable to meet the physical requirements
for the certification.

You are requested to forward any previously issued unexpired medical
certificate(s) to this office in the enclosed postage-paid business envelope.

If you do not return your medical certificate(s) within fourteen (14) days,
your file will be sent to our regional office for consideration of legal
enforcement action.

        Page 2 of 2
                                              PI# 2166456
                                              MID# 200004583542
                                              App ID# 1999022574
                                              Mark Chapman Harris

Use of the above reference numbers on future correspondence and/or reports
will aid us in locating your file.

Sincerely,

William Mills, MD for

Warren S. Silberman, D.O., M.P.H.
Manager, Aerospace Medical Certification Division
Civil Aerospace Medical Institute

A letter from Dr. William Mills dated the day after the receipt of Dr. Harper's package and the entry of a fake DUI in my records. This letter "canceled" my medical certificate in an illegitimate smoke and mirrors manner that prevented an appeal`. Note that it alleges my application from the previous January was being denied, falsely claiming it disclosed a history of alcohol abuse (see the previous excerpt of my application) which disclosed nothing as there was nothing to disclose. When these officials were caught planting a fake DUI in my records the allegation changed to alcoholism with a fake medical history to support.

FAX 5369

AEROMEDICAL INC.
C.R. HARPER, M.D.
Board Certified in Aerospace Medicine
Fellow in the American College of Preventive Medicine
2600 Clearview Ave S-215 ♦ Doraville, GA 30047
Phone 770-457-8532 Fax 770-457-1200

5399

6·2·10

Re: MARK C. HARRIS

Dr. Chesanow,

Enclosed is basic information requested by Dr. Berry regarding his general discharge from the USAF 10 years ago. It was directly related to his drinking alcohol to excess.

Dr. Sager said he felt Mr. Harris would be OK with the outlined monitoring program. I would appreciate expediting his approval.

Thanks,

Dr. Harper

A memo by Dr. Harper documenting that Dr. Berry requested and illegally obtained my confidential military records which contained nothing relevant to my medical fitness other than an evaluation in the military which cleared me of any alcohol use disorder, which was almost comically called "week-long outpatient treatment" by Berry's accomplices. I never signed any releases, and this information was spread from coast to coast. Berry threatened to obtain it illegally from a general officer friend of his if I didn't produce it and said I would never fly again if I didn't.

U.S. Department
of Transportation
**Federal Aviation
Administration**

Mike Monroney Aeronautical Center
Civil Aerospace Medical Institute (CAMI)
Aerospace Medical Certification Division

P.O. Box 26080
Oklahoma City, OK 73125-9914

July 14, 2010

CERTIFIED AND REGULAR MAIL

MARK CHAPMAN HARRIS
6010 E BAY BLVD
GULF BREEZE FL 32563-9725

Ref: PI# 2166456
MID# 200004583542
App ID# 1999022574

Dear Mr. Harris:

Your file has been reviewed by our Chief Psychiatrist in the Federal Air Surgeon's office.

In view of your request reconsideration, we have again reviewed your complete file and regret that we have no alternative except to sustain our previous denial dated May 4, 2010 due to your history of alcoholism.

For reconsideration, your medical sponsor (Dr. C.R. Harper) should refer you to an aftercare group that satisfies our HIMS requirements and we would be glad to consider you for a special issuance after you have been in aftercare for at least two months. We would like to review these aftercare reports before making a final recommendation.

Use of the above reference numbers on future correspondence and/or reports will aid us in locating your file.

Sincerely,

Stephen H. Goodman, M.D.
Senior Regional Flight Surgeon
Western Pacific Regional Medical Office

Enclosure: Envelope

cc: Reddoch E Williams M.D.
    C.R. Harper, M.D.

TAB

A letter from Dr. Goodman, the Senior Regional Flight Surgeon for the FAA's Western Pacific Regional Office (where I have never lived nor worked) denying an appeal I never made to ensure I didn't attempt to appeal a scheme of fraud that had all occurred behind my back. Goodman was later promoted to Berry's deputy in Washington. This denial of a fake appeal changed the initial allegation of alcohol abuse, justified with a fake DUI, to alcoholism, supported by a fake medical history. This began with a fake passenger complaint which actually came from Nobles after which I was sent to what turned out to be the fake company doctor, Dr. Harper.

John E. Doyle, III, M.D.
5448 Yorktowne Drive
Atlanta, Georgia 30349
678-251-3247 / Fax 770-994-0106

PATIENT NAME: HARRIS, MARK
MEDICAL RECORD #:   8933
DATE OF SERVICE: 08/10/2011
DATE OF ADDENDUM: 08/22/2011

FAA EVALUATION ADDENDUM

Case discussed with Dr. Richard Harper, AME. Patient has a diagnosis of alcoholism per the FAA that contributed to his separation from the USAF.

The patient is stating that such a diagnosis was never made and that it was removed from his contract. He denies treatment for alcoholism in the USAF. When I reviewed DSM 4 Criteria for Alcohol Dependence or Abuse with him, he denies criteria.

I find his denials concerning and support monitoring.

John E. Doyle, III, M.D.   8-22-11
                                            DATE

This is Dr. Doyle's amendment to his report (after he found me free of diagnostic criteria for alcoholism or abuse and unethically recommended that I stay in the program anyway). This was solicited by Dr. Harper, who was not happy with the evaluation, which was consistent with all others. Dr. Doyle, another old military doctor, unethically changed his report at the request of Dr. Harper and his lobbying. To date, no one who has evaluated me has made such a diagnosis and FAA doctors do not diagnose people and are required to rely on treatment records. In this case they don't exist. It was my going outside this network for an ethical and unbiased evaluation a year later that caused the whole matter to blow up, as Dr. Berry refused to accept that evaluation and attempted to force me to go back to Dr. Doyle, while simultaneously Dr. Harper refused me access to my records and refused to tell me the source of the DUI.

For more information: housesoftheholy.net

MILITARY MADNESS

I t was July 1998, I was 31 years-old, a USAF Special Operations pilot, and you might say living the dream at Eglin AFB in the Florida Panhandle. I lived with my grandparents in Destin. A resort beach town, my friends and fellow airmen played hard and partied hard in our free time. On duty, we worked hard.

On the eve of July 18, a long-awaited military leave was due to begin the very next day. There had been an allegation of sexual assault by an instructor pilot, a captain I had known for years. This and other incidents had been brushed under the rug. On the eve of a squadron commander change of command, an emergency commander's call was announced where squadron Operations Officer, Lt Hank Col Sanders, announced he would "rip the lips off" the next person to screw up. It would be me.

The next day, the sun rose, expectations were high all around, and my friends and I spent the day on my boat. A 25-foot Sea Ray Cabin Cruiser, I planned to spend my entire vacation aboard her enjoying being on the water, spending time with my buddies. The high-energy day on the boat passed without incident, but we ended up overheating the engine. It had seized up, and we wound up being towed in. My vacation plans were all but ruined. The next day, vacation plans shot, one of my cohorts and I, feeling very let down, spent the day and into the evening at AJ's on the water. We shot the breeze, rehashed recent events, and drank way too many Mai Tais.

What followed could provide a premise for a keystone cop movie, but it was more akin to a "Good cop, Bad cop" scene in a B movie.

* * *

Following a day and evening of commiseration drinking, I was plastered. Back home, as the night wore on, in a random act of drunkenness I wandered out into my yard buck naked. Probably to smoke a cigarette. I heard a woman yell at me, then her husband appeared and startled me, and I went back inside. The next thing I knew, the next thing I remember, I was inside my house in bed. Two Okaloosa County Deputies were shining flashlights in my face. A neighbor, whose place was quite a way down the street, had apparently reported that her daughters and some other kids saw me out there. I never saw them. Had I known, I would have been mortified as you can imagine, but I was oblivious and went to bed to sleep it off.

Before I knew what hit me, they dragged me out of my house and arrested me on charges of Lewd and Lascivious Acts in the Presence of a Child. I tried to think, tried to grasp what they were talking about. I hadn't seen any children. No children were present or near my home.

No warrant, these guys broke into my home, conducted an illegal search, seizure, and hauled me away. A shock to this guy who had always believed the cops are on our side, and you're innocent until proven guilty. Not according to these two, or at least to one of the two.

Reports were filed. The whole thing was bizarre and getting more and more so as the evening wore on. One of the two police officers had put words in the neighbors' mouths, and there began the first step in the destruction of the rest of my career, *and the rest of my life.*

* * *

Let's review. Drunk and naked, I popped out of my house and into my yard to smoke. Heard a woman yell and ran back inside. I was drunk at my own home at the wrong place at the wrong time. Some kids out walking got a glimpse of me from nearly a football field distance away. The mother of one of the kids, high and intoxicated herself, got bent out of shape and called the police. That is in short, all that happened. But the story would grow and grow and grow.

What happened next? Judge William Stone, who I would encounter again years later, issued a bizarre and somewhat unconstitutional order. He banned me from the entire "Destin Florida Area." My parents drove down and rescued my dog. For several months, I had to live with a friend in Fort Walton.

* * *

Ten days later, 28 July 1998, a rising star of special operations, the Operations Group Commander for the 16th Special Operations Wing, issued an order detailing me to the 16th Operations Support Squadron at Hurlburt Field. That same day, my access to classified information was administratively suspended. I floundered for a week or so trying to find something productive to do. Then the Commander, Lt. Col. James Smith, called me into his office and asked if I would be his Executive Officer. I had no idea what that entailed, but I agreed and dove right in. A high-profile position, I excelled and ended up tasked with several special projects. Elevating me to this position enraged Col. Hoffman, who tried to block this move was overruled by his superiors.

* * *

Almost two months later, on September 8, 1998, the Assistant District Attorney brought charges based on the "bad cop's" report from that night. But the "witnesses" and the "good cop" contradicted his report in the long run. His statement repeated his fabricated claim that he had entered my home out of "fear for the safety of the occupants," and false claims that children were in front of my home.

As a result of the nature of the charges, I was ordered to attend counseling. I went to Dr. Fred DeShon, PhD, who would counsel my kids years later. I saw him on a weekly basis. He performed a thorough evaluation, including psychological testing, found me free of any issues, and deemed the matter an isolated incidence from alcohol intoxication. He even used hypnosis during which I had no recollection of seeing or hearing children that night. The same conclusion as the USAF Alcohol and Drug Awareness and Treatment ADAPT found later. The evaluation was "Alcohol Intoxication," and I was cleared to fly. Also, because of the referral, I was required to attend a two-day class, something routine. Over a decade later, this would be called "weeklong outpatient treatment" by a corrupt doctor running a con game to justify claims that I had had some sort of diagnosis and treatment in the military.

* * *

It gets worse. On Oct 22, 1998, prior to any trial or resolution of the civil case, a Special Information File was initiated, and my security clearance was pulled as well as my authority to bear arms. This was highly unusual and punitive given the case was still open.

A navigator in the squadron who knew me was concerned about the situation. Dismayed at the actions of a Col. Hoffman and the squadron leadership, he asked for a meeting with Col. Hoffman. He told Col. Sanders that I was a good pilot who deserved another chance. Lt. Col. Sanders told him that if he wanted to talk to Col. Hoffman about it, he "better wear a flak jacket." He then said that Hoffman would not support me because I had filed an Inspector General (IG) complaint against him. I had not, but a friend had called the IG on my behalf regarding the punitive actions that had been taken. The IG did nothing but report it back to Col. Hoffman.

* * *

On January 7, 1999, I entered a plea of no contest to a minor misdemeanor with adjudication withheld (no conviction) and the record to be sealed. This was after the witnesses testified and refuted the false and salacious claims by the Okaloosa County Sheriff's department. Ready to take responsibility, I expected a letter of reprimand, or letter of counseling, which would have been appropriate for the case. Instead, 15 April 1999, Col. Hoffman initiated action to permanently disqualify me from aviation service. In other words, I would have been stripped of my wings and aeronautical rating. And he did this retroactively. Suddenly my flight pay was stopped. But thankfully, the Colonel ultimately failed in his attempt to ban me from my beloved aviation career, and my rating was retained.

* * *

Then, on 20 April 1999, a USAF Special Operations Commander signed a "Show Cause Notification," requiring me to show cause for retention, and that if I did not apply for discharge, a Board of Inquiry (BOI) would convene. I would be represented by military attorneys at the Area Defense Council. I was pressured by the command to accept discharge under Honorable (General) conditions. But I wanted my day in court, and on April 26 I responded demanding a Board of Inquiry. Curiously, the charges regurgitated the already discredited police report. Discredited by the witnesses themselves.

Fast forward, by this time it had been nearly a year since I had been assigned to the 16th SOS working as an Executive Officer directly under the supervision of Lt. Col. James Smith. I was due a performance report, but Col. Hoffman would not relinquish that duty to Col. Smith, my direct supervisor. If this stream of events was not so heartbreaking, it would be the basis for a *Hogan's Heroes* episode, a sitcom. So, he ordered a captain in his squadron, who had not supervised me, to write the report. Nevertheless, Lt. Col. Smith wrote a glowing Letter of Evaluation (LOE) for me to be converted to an Officer Performance Report, but it was sabotaged. That captain sent me this email describing what happened on May 11:

> Mark,
> Got your LOE that Col Smith wrote. I took that and plugged it into OPR form. Needless to say, Hoffman changed shit, and I met with him and told him I wouldn't feel comfortable signing something I did not write. He talked to legal guys about what can be put in an OPR and a bunch of other shit. I have also told him repeatedly

that I don't know how I could be your rater when you were here 1 month out of the 12. I guess he wants his finger on it. Anyhow, I have the LOE and will keep it in my possession. I will also keep a copy of the final OPR. Let me know any thoughts"

On May 31, I was sent a copy of the Referral Officer Performance Report and given a deadline to respond. It contained slanderous and false information put in the report by Hoffman over objections by the captain forced to write it who made a memorandum of record to protect himself.

"Officer was performing well as an aircraft commander, then administratively removed from flying pending the outcome of a criminal trial by local authorities. Officer pleaded no Contest to the offense of Indecent Exposure and was convicted; discharge initiated.... Officer is unqualified and has no access to classified and undergoing administrative discharge proceedings."

So, on June 7, my attorney asked for an extension in responding to the referral OPR as he was out of town. The request was denied with the following handwritten note from our Col. Hoffman.

"I expect to receive Capt. Harris' response by 1630, 15 June 1999. Capt. Harris has had 11 days to respond and now he has another 4."

I appealed the report and won. It was therefore removed from my records, as it was deemed to have inappropriate and false information in it. One of numerous small battles I won along the way. It seemed to me, and to others, that Hoffman was out to get me. Of note, this unfortunate situation occurred merely two days after Lt. Col. Sanders' threat was issued. Colonel Hoffman had taken command just hours before my arrest, and this was a colossal embarrassment in the minds of Sanders and Hoffman. They were bound and determined, you might say, to make me pay in the eyes of everyone. And further enraged by having their efforts blocked by superiors and the IG call.

* * *

As the BOI (Board of Inquiry) neared, lacking any real case, the JAG office was desperately digging for dirt. They called friends and family, even a girl I had briefly dated that summer, trying to uncover any dirt, but they found none. How had they uncovered all these phone numbers?

On the Friday before the BOI hearing, several disturbing events/developments occurred. Lt. Colonel Smith called me to his office. He was distraught. As a huge supporter of mine who had put me in a prominent role and fought to keep me there, he had been called to the Wing Commander's office where he was ordered, yes ordered, to lie under oath at the BOI and say he supported my discharge. Col. Wurster, who had tried to talk Col Hoffman out of pursuing my discharge, had ordered a Code Red (like in *A Few Good Men*) you might say. Colonel Wurster was said to be a do-the-right-thing kind of guy. In this case, "doing the right thing" meant unlawful command influence to satisfy petty desires for revenge by a rogue squadron commander and his bible thumping, loose cannon, sidekick, Hank Sanders. But Col. Smith would end up being quite creative in expressing what he really felt while complying with this unlawful order.

* * *

Meanwhile, as the testimony before the Board would reveal, other witnesses were being threatened with retaliation if they testified on my behalf. Their careers hung in the balance. (Think *Hogan's Heroes*, picture Colonel Klink leveling a report against Hogan to the Commandant, securing his own hide.) Funny in the TV show, but not in real life, not to me and my military colleagues. Several officers and one first sergeant approached me, told me that they couldn't testify for me out of fear for their careers and retaliation.

The Group Commander, Col. Lyle Koenig, had promised to support me in opposing my discharge. He suddenly reversed himself, lying to my face saying he had supported my discharge all along. General Koenig was later quietly allowed to retire with a demotion after allegations of sexual misconduct and his role in the atrocities at Abu Ghraib prison.

The same day as Col. Koenig's backstab, the Friday before the Board, the JAG, Major Plummer (now a General and the top JAG in the Air Force) produced new "depositions" (which were not actual depositions) as evidence. These documents – signed by the same witnesses who had already been deposed and renounced the false claims – regurgitated the Okaloosa report and added even wilder exaggerations. To prevent me from facing my accusers who had tried to correct the false report, they claimed that the witnesses were out of town and unavailable to testify, which I would learn later was a lie. The fix was in.

* * *

When the Military BOI convened, their [Hoffman and Sanders'] intent to make me a scapegoat seemed to direct the outcome. The wagons were circled. The BOI convened on Monday, June 29, 1999. A BOI is structured like a trial with a judge who is called the "*Legal Advisor.*" There were 28 exhibits by the Government, most irrelevant to this inquiry. The Defense had 49 exhibits, including 20 glowing character statements, mostly from officers who had worked with me, including a Colonel, and numerous records showing my exemplary record and achievements. On the other hand, there were negative false claims put forth that had already been refuted by previous testimonies by these same people.

* * *

When it was time for opening statements at the BOI, my attorneys agreed to my request to make it myself, which I was completely entitled to do. Consider that I had been subjected to a smear and defamation campaign for a year, it was time to speak up for myself, and I did so as follows:

"Colonel Coleman and members of the board, good afternoon. I am Captain Mark Harris. I am currently the executive officer for the commander of the 16 Operations Support Squadron at Hurlburt, and in the board, you're going to hear a lot about me."

Major Bruce: "Ma'am, we need to ask for an out of board session."

The courtroom was cleared.

* * *

This Major Bruce threw what most of us would refer to as a tantrum. He claimed I didn't have the right to make an opening statement. I clearly did. How dare I defend myself and tell the truth about that night. In the end, the *Legal Advisor* [judge] ruled in my favor, but with a warning that exposed the bias she would show throughout. She was undoubtedly furious that she hadn't been told about my request in advance.

"We could've avoided all of this on the record, but you didn't do that. Okay. I understand that you wanted a tactical advantage. I guess you won this time, but you won't the next."

A chilling warning by a biased judge. And she kept her promise. That was our last win. A three-ring circus ensued.

* * *

The board members were brought back, and I was allowed to complete my statement in which I briefly explained what really happened that night, not only my claim, but supported by the depositions of witnesses. I was simply drunk and naked in my own yard at the wrong time. I never saw any children, nor did they come anywhere near my home that had now turned into a house of cards.

When Col. Hoffman testified that he wanted me out of his squadron because of the charges (but before he knew any of the facts), he admitted to going after my security clearance. He, like Lt. Col. Sanders, said I was an "average pilot." This was refuted by my witnesses and my records. When men like this set out to destroy you, they pull out all the stops. He admitted that he tried to block me from being the executive officer for the 16th OSS, and that he had complained to his superiors, Col. Koenig and Col. Wurster about me being elevated to this role.

Major Bruce: "Did you give him a letter of reprimand, UIF, for his criminal behavior downtown?"

"No, I did not."

"Why is that?"

"Based on talking with legal counsel at the time, *my goal was to do what was necessary to get him out of the Air Force*"

* * *

And there it was. Prior to knowing any facts, and admittedly having never read the witnesses' testimonies, Col. Hoffman acknowledged he was willing to do whatever it took to get me out of the Air Force. Including perjury, obstruction of justice, and unlawful command influence.

Two officers testified to threats they had received regarding their testimony. One had been threatened with physical violence if he testified regarding an incident in which two officers exposed themselves, urinating on a bar in Germany. Something that showed a gross double standard. Col. Hoffman, when questioned about this incident, denied any knowledge of it. He then back peddled and claimed that he had investigated, and it wasn't true. It was true. But the board would hear none of this as the room was cleared again, as had been during any testimony that exposed unlawful command influence and a double standard.

* * *

Then the Cross Examination by Sumner. Neighbors testified on my behalf, underlining how the whole situation had been out of hand; friends and colleagues reiterated the same, that this was all out of hand. Colonel Hoffman, most notably, admitted he had prevented Col. Smith, my then immediate superior, from submitting a positive performance review on my behalf.

The Government then rested their case, having produced not a single witness to any misconduct on my part. A three-ring circus of malicious and vicious liars out for blood. Meanwhile, the board was never allowed to hear the most important testimony, and I was not allowed to face my accusers, the neighbors, to challenge them with their ever-changing stories.

There would be another out of board hearing where my attorneys pointed out again that I had never been adjudicated guilty of anything. And that I had never admitted to nor pled no contest to lewd and lascivious conduct in front of anyone. The court *Legal Advisor* again engaged in her half-baked reasoning. She was nasty and arrogant. She repeatedly made the false claim that I pled guilty to an offence and was convicted. Neither had occurred.

"The rulings of the legal adviser are final! That's my ruling. You've made your record. I've provided you with the written opinion. That's my ruling. Rulings of the legal advisor are final!"

* * *

In the end, and I'll spare you the details of further courtroom drama (fun and games you might say). I was left a stunned victim of unlawful command influence, obstruction of justice, and denied my constitutional right to due process. As were my attorneys and many others. After hearing Major Plummer lie, spin, and try to outright destroy me, the board found the heart of the allegations to be unfounded. But they voted to discharge me anyway. However, *my service was honorable, and so was my discharge.*

It was a sad day. At the end, the room had fallen quiet; some didn't know what to say. Some expressed their condolences. One airman cried all day. Meanwhile the fallout continued. A major who had written me a letter of support had his promotion sabotaged by our Col. Hoffman. He was subsequently forced to retire. The captain who bravely testified to the double standard had his instructor training slot pulled. The JAG, Captain Plummer, gloated about it to one of my squadron mates.

* * *

I continued to work hard as Col. Smith's executive officer. One day he told me I needed to start focusing on myself and quit working so hard. It would be difficult to let go. I worked on an additional rating at the Aero Club to prepare for a civilian flying job. I obtained an FAA medical exam where I disclosed all of this and correctly informed that there was really nothing reportable to the FAA. I then flew cargo for a year at Flight Express, and then for the Atlantic Southeast Airlines.

In a few short years, I would come to realize that my Military BOI was but a dress rehearsal for some of life's most destructive and damning realities. This BOI would come to haunt me in so many ways for the rest of my life.

In the main part of *House of the Holy*, you are reading a long sorrowful series of events by a long list of corrupt so-called professionals. And you will hear Mike Nobles and those covering his tracks drag up this dead horse over and over in a smear and distortion campaign, and that is why I am addressing it here to give you, my readers, a brief and abbreviated story of what happened, what led to this BOI following me, damning me, wherever I went, and whenever Nobles needed ammunition against me to deflect from his crimes and misdemeanors.

I accepted, and still accept, responsibility for my behavior that night. I apologized to the neighbors and was prepared to accept a reprimand for what occurred. We make mistakes, we move on, having learned from these very human blunders. But in my case, I received a career death sentence, and these blunders have been distorted and, as I've said, haunted me ever since.

LIST OF CORPORATIONS

The following corporations were all created by Leslie Michael Osman, with various permutations of board members.

- Androgynous (Michael Nobles, Jerry McCormick, Allen Amavanto)
- Androgyny (Leslie Michael Osman, Craig Osman, Phyllis Osman, Miguel Font)
- Androgyny Management (Leslie Michael Osman, Craig Osman, Ty Osman, Miguel Font)
- Androgynal (Michael Nobles, Leslie Michael Osman, Craig Osman, Ty Osman)
- Androgyn (Leslie Michael Osman, Craig Osman, Miguel Font, Phyllis Osman)
- Alchemy (Leslie Michael Osman, Miguel Recalde)
- Augury (Leslie Michael Osman, Phyllis Osman)
- Empyrean Development (Craig Osman, Ty Osman, Leslie Michael Osman)
- Eruditional (Alchemy LLC, Leslie Michael Osman, Phyllis Osman)
- Luminous Builders (Leslie Michael Osman)
- Lumination Homes (Leslie Michael Osman)
- Panoply (Leslie Michael Osman, Michael McCormick)
- Pellucid (Leslie Michael Osman)
- Prescience (Michael Nobles, Craig Osman)
- Primus Apartments (Leslie Michael Osman)
- Recondite (Leslie Michael Osman)
- Solomon Builders (Ty Osman, registered by him in Tennessee)
- Southern Star (Leslie Micheal Osman)
- Tabula Rasa (Craig Osman, Ty Osman, Leslie Michael Osman)

* * *

Examining this list raises questions, draws connections, and paints a picture.

First, let us address the names of the corporations. Every single one is steeped in occult and Masonic symbolism.

All the references to *androgyny* point to the entity called Baphomet, a winged, goat-headed deity or idol that has both male and female attributes. The Knights Templar were labeled heretics in 1309 in part because they were said to worship a deity with this name. The goat-headed image we associate with this name, however, appeared nowhere before the 19th Century. It was created in 1861 by occultist Eliphas Levi in his book *Transcendental Magic: Its Doctrine and Ritual.*[1] There are few symbols more widely used in occult circles than the androgynous, hermaphroditic Baphomet.

Alchemy in this context refers to Freemasonry, where it is a metaphor for the journey of the Freemason as he (or she, in the case of Cagliostro's Rite) ascends through higher and higher degrees of knowledge, transmuting to perfection through lost, ancient knowledge.

The word *augury* means prophetic divination of the future by observing nature, objects, or situations, such as a casting of bones, Nordic runes, or examining the entrails of a sacrifice.

Empyrean refers to the sky or heaven, in particular the highest level of heaven. In Christian religions, the Empyrean is the dwelling place of God and all the souls that have been saved, the source of all Light.

Eruditional is the quality of having or showing great knowledge or learning.

Luminous and *Lumination* are obviously references to light and may go as far as refer to the "luminiferous aether"[2] described in the writings[3] of Albert Pike, Freemason and possibly the founder of the Ku Klux Klan.[4]

Panoply likely refers to the historical meaning of the word, a complete set of a knight's arms and armor, a reference to Knights Templar and their arms.

Pellucid means "translucently clear," which might be innocuous enough except that it also connotes the transmission of light, and is a word used prominently in Albert Pike's writings.

---

1. Bauer, Pat. "Baphomet." Encyclopedia Britannica, 4 Jul. 2023, https://www.britannica.com/topic/Baphomet. Accessed 29 October 2023.
2. Before the discovery of the photon, physicists posited that light was transmitted through space via the luminiferous (light-bearing) aether.
3. Pike, Albert. Morals and Dogma of the Ancient and Accepted Scottish Rite of Freemasonry.
4. https://www.wondriumdaily.com/the-three-generations-of-ku-klux-klan/

Prescience means a foreknowledge of events or divine omniscience. It feels like some sort of in-joke among these people.

The word *primus* normally refers to a presiding bishop (from the Latin, "Pri" meaning "first"); however, in this instance it is being used in the context of a Latin ordinal number, meaning "First" and refers to the "First" Worshipful Master of a Freemasons lodge.

The meaning of *recondite* is dealing with very profound, difficult, or abstruse subject matter, or beyond ordinary knowledge or understanding. Such as esoteric Freemasonry and/or occultism intended for only a select few.

Solomon Builders in Tennessee was founded by Ty Osman, Leslie Michael Osman's brother. The name might be a reference to the Temple of Solomon, where the Ark of the Covenant was kept and augury practiced by the high priests.

Southern Star is the name of numerous Masonic lodges.

Tabula Rasa means "blank slate," but is referred to in Masonic rites when a member is initiated. "When the profane candidate leaves the Chamber of Reflection, he is born anew and prepared to receive instruction as a tabula rasa, or blank slate.[5]"

* * *

The names here illustrate the connections of family, religion, and business. Nearly all of these individuals are fervent evangelicals, or at least pretend to it.

Ty Osman was a leader in Lipscomb University and various Church of Christ congregations and a major player in the construction industry.

Michael McCormick is the son of Jerry McCormick, Mike Nobles' long-time business partner.

Argentinian by birth, Miguel Recalde runs a construction business that seems to migrate around Florida. He was convicted of cocaine trafficking in 1985.[6] Is he a reformed drug-dealer?

All of this makes me wonder about the relationship between Mike Nobles and Leslie Michael Osman. Nobles often crowed about his high-powered lawyer, but who was working for whom?

---

5. https://www.knightstemplar.org/KnightTemplar/articles/fourmasonicelements.pdf
6. https://law.justia.com/cases/federal/appellate-courts/F2/761/1448/277248/

MIKE NOBLES' FINANCIAL DEALINGS

I didn't realize until well after the fact that most of the real estate dealings in which Christy and I had taken part were varying degrees of scam and tax evasion.

EXAMPLE 1.

Wanda Nobles' parents passed away, and Mike convinced me to buy his in-laws' house, renovate, and flip it, as we'd done several times already with other properties.

Soon after, a buyer comes along and makes a lucrative offer to buy the house. So we sold the house, and Nobles pocketed 80% of the profit, Christy and I the rest. But the heirs of the house were Wanda Nobles and her brother.

The house was sold to me at a *deflated* price, screwing his brother-in-law out of a substantial inheritance, then sold again at an *inflated* price, thanks to the white-hot real estate market, a transaction that allowed Nobles to keep a big stack of cash. During that period, a dirt clod beside the road in Florida was worth a gold mine.

Then he "borrowed" an equal sum from one of his shell corporations, so that he could explain to the IRS where the big stack of cash came from. I was a pawn in this particular scheme to defraud his brother-in-law out of his rightful inheritance.

This is called a *loan-back scheme.*[1]

EXAMPLE 2.

A few years before Christy and I broke up, Nobles informed us that he had quit-claimed[2] a share of a condominium to us, without explanation. We never received a key, never spent a night there, never had any use or access to this condominium, the building of which he owned with several other leaders of the Niceville Church of Christ. A couple of years

---

1. https://en.wiktionary.org/wiki/loan-back
2. A quitclaim deed transfers the owner's entire interest in a property but makes no promises at all about the veracity and/or extent of the owner's title.

later, he asked us to sign a quitclaim deed returning the property to him. So we signed it back over to him, despite serious misgivings on my part that we were being used for something shady.

Years later, during a period of serious investigations into Mike Nobles' business dealings, researching the records I discovered that he hadn't quitclaimed the property to Christy and me at all. Don Sublett, who was an elder in both the Niceville and Destin churches, had "sold" the property to me for $30,000 – on paper. I never gave him a cent nor had any knowledge of this transaction.

At the same time, Mike Nobles was being sued for $30,000. So, in effect, he had "bought" some property from one of his cronies among the church leaders to hide $30,000 from his creditors, and used Christy and I as middlemen to hide it.

This was a clear case of fraud.[3]

He was adamant that only my name appear on all the documents of these transactions, which led to me being the only party with any tax liability. He kept assuring me that his lawyer (Leslie Michael Osman) was "running everything through these shell corporations, so I don't have to pay taxes on it."

ENDLESS FINANCIAL SCAMS

I eventually became aware that I had not only been used as a pawn in Mike Nobles' numerous scams, he had orchestrated several other grifts both grand and petty in which he involved his son Billy, and his attorney Leslie Michael Osman, who facilitated much of it.

Multiple pyramid schemes, embezzlement, profiteering, scamming the foster care system.

After Hurricane Ivan passed and the disasters settled, Mike and his son Billy bought a truckload of generators with the intent to price-gouge anyone who needed one when the next storm hit.

On one occasion, Billy faked a robbery at one of his father's Subway restaurants. They kept the money and filed a fraudulent insurance claim.

Later, when these restaurants went out of business and were sold, Billy stole thousands of dollars in free sandwich coupons and was handing them out as gifts.

The failure of the Subway restaurants, according to accusations from Nobles' business partner, Jerry McCormick, was due to Nobles embez-

---

3. When I reported this to the Florida State Attorney's office, they did nothing about it. The IRS, however, did come after me, going so far as to seize my back accounts while they investigated.

zling from those companies, or else those particular money-laundering operations were no longer necessary.

When the Niceville Church of Christ was overseeing the local Food Bank, the church lost its contract with its food provider because Nobles was embezzling.

Possibly the most sinister of his financial scams involved foster children. He would collect foster care support checks from other foster parents in the church – including Mary Smith, who told me about this – and pay them an extra $100 for their trouble. These checks were sent to Hialeah, Florida, where Leslie Michael Osman was based, so he was likely involved, so we can be assured this was not for altruistic purposes, most likely some sort of tax scam.

THE HOUSES OF THE HOLY

ONE: 1118 RHONDA DRIVE, NICEVILLE FLORIDA

Built by prominent panhandle builder and Knight Templar Freemason Constance Wayne Jones. Appears to be the first house in the development yet numbered for the year the Knights Templar were founded. Built on property owned by billionaire developer and right-wing extremist Charles Walter Ruckel II (John Birch Society and Freedom First Society leader) and his son, a prominent member of Pat Robertson's Christian Coalition, Stephen Ruckel. Built under a permit obtained by neo confederate Patriot Network organizer and Church of Christ leader, Michael Nobles yet ownership changed hands the day of his federal conviction in 1986. At the time, Nobles was in business with other connected Church of Christ leaders in corporations with occult, Knight Templar names. The first owner occupant was active-duty Air Force then purchased by Nobles who had originally built the home. This was the home of Nobles' now erased foster children. The home had a security and surveillance system odd for a small plain home, and guns positioned all over the house by Nobles, a felon. Sold in a fraudulent scheme which was never recorded to Carolyn Palmer then taken back by Nobles. Nobles attempted to sell the home to his occultist brother Roger when he fled to South America in 2009, but the deal fell through. Nobles has since removed his wife from the deed yet owns the property, despite the fact that he resides in Arkansas. The site where my sons witnessed murder, and a series of underground structures containing weapons, cash, torture devices, and a Knight Templar temple of sorts, as well as a drug lab.

TWO: 2 WEST KATHY LANE, FREEPORT FLORIDA

This house is located on Lake Sharon in a neighborhood that one resident described as taken over by "fundamentalists and survivalists." The same neighborhood where Nobles business partner and fellow Church of Christ leader Jerry McCormick lived. The house was built for a NACA (the predecessor of NASA) researcher Charles Kelly, who was married to a former Pentagon secretary. Multiple  neighbors reported that there were "very withdrawn" foster children living in the home in the past with foster parents, one who was a "Frenchman" and his wife a Panama City stripper. The house was frequented with friendly visits from the Walton Count Sheriff's Department. I have identified that Frenchman as Michel Raphael Barthelemy. Barthelemy installed a short-wave radio antenna, an expensive swimming pool, and according to neighbors, was throwing money around including buying expensive sports cars. The family including the foster children disappeared in the middle of the night, leaving their belongings as well as computer and camera equipment being used for child pornography. It was all made to go away, and the children are now missing. Barthelemy was in business with a high-ranking Pentagon official, RobRoy McGregor, who appears to have been a follower of Aleister Crowley. Another business partner in these corporations was Church of Christ pastor Bob Lewis, who was tied to prominent Church of Christ minister John Mark Hicks. Meanwhile Hicks was active in the same church in Tennessee as Nobles business partner Ty Osman, another prominent Church of Christ leader and businessman in corporations with Knight Templar names.

THREE: 9 GALE COURT, FREEPORT FLORIDA

This house is a few houses down from 2 West Kathy Lane in Freeport Florida. The number was oddly changed from 8 Gale Court to 9 Gale Court. The property itself was originally owned by an Army major and sold to Jerry McCormick, a Church of Christ Elder, Nobles business partner, and brother-in-law to Church of Christ elder and connect-  ed attorney Leslie Michael Osman. Osman was tied to the mob, corrupt politicians and builders in Hialeah Florida and formed corporations for Nobles, McCormick, and Osman's brothers with Knight Templar occult names. McCormick sold the home to a fellow Church of Christ member who let is sit vacant for years. It was then sold to McCormick's friend and neighbor Charles Merkle. Merkle is a right-wing Vietnam veteran turned military contractor who is tied to former Governor Rick Scott, former right wing Freemason congressman Jeff Miller, and Iran Contra figure Richard Secord. Neighbors reported and I confirmed there were large suspicious fires on the property, as if someone was destroying evidence, while the property was vacant. When I asked Merkle about the history of the home and the fires he became very paranoid and hostile and threatened to have me arrested. As of my last knowledge, the property remains vacant.

FOUR: 65 HAMPTON CIRCLE, NICEVILLE FLORIDA

This home was built by an Alabama builder for an Air Force Officer. It was later sold to Joe Palmer, the pastor of the Niceville Church of Christ, where Nobles and McCor-mic served as elders. The house had an odd "dead space" in it, an area with no doors nor apparent access, and a security system. When Palmer's wife divorced him for mental physical and sexual abuse of her and her children, Nobles and his wife purchased the home in what appears to be an inside fraudulent scheme. This scheme involved buying the home at a grossly deflated price, and selling 1118 Rhonda drive to Carolyn, with no intention of letting her keep it, and never recording the sale. Just a year after the sale, Nobles listed the home for sale but did not want pictures taken inside the home. He then sold the home for $121,000 more than he purchased it for in an inside, sight unseen sale to a prominent and connected builder who appears to have connections to the Nobles. The realtor was cheated out of her commission. The appearance is that the house was special and needed to be kept in friendly hands and Palmer's ex wife was cheated out of her assets and left homeless after Nobles took back 1118 Rhonda Drive.

For more information: housesoftheholy.net

Index

Symbols

2 West Kathy Lane 89, 97, 451
65 Hampton Circle 453
9 Gale Court 87, 88, 452
1118 Rhonda Drive 15, 21, 42, 90, 93, 96, 116, 142, 168, 176, 242, 260, 302, 303, 332, 360, 451, 453

A

Abernathy, Ralph 210, 211
Accardo, Anthony 292
Adams, Tom 306
A Few Good Men 8, 440
Agape Christian Academy 46-48
Agape Lodge 47
Air Line Pilots Association (ALPA) 195, 196, 343, 353
Albert, Joseph 304
Allen, James 24, 91
Alma 4
Amavanto, Allen 94, 445
Anubis 114, 119, 126, 132, 197
Ashley, Shrff 56, 74, 193, 200, 240, 333, 334, 358
ATF 117, 156, 165, 166, 169, 249, 250, 327
Atlanta Journal-Constitution 348
Atlantic Southeast Airlines (ASA) 13, 63, 245, 345, 350
Austin, Roy L. 346, 359

B

Babbitt, Randy 334
Barker, Craig 104
Barthelemy, Michel Raphael 89, 90, 97, 188
Bates, Sheila 333
Beach, Randy 166, 169, 327
Beck, Kelly 212, 235, 250, 262
Benitez, Ramon 307, 308

Bergosh, Gary 103, 247, 253, 257, 260, 274, 275, 328
Berry, Charles 211, 244
Berry, Michael 196, 202, 205, 206, 207, 208, 209, 210, 211, 212, 244, 329, 341, 352, 353, 359
Biden, Joe 359
Birmingham Post-Herald 277, 285
Blackburn, Kim 339
Blackwater 188, 296
Blavatsky, Helena 91
Boggy Bayou Church of Christ 80
Bolden, Abraham 91
Bondi, Pam 328
Boston Church of Christ 73
Brimberry, James 186, 187, 195, 197, 359
Bringsman, Doug 68, 69
Brooks, Elma 351
Brown, Tammy 241
Brunson, Salty 94
Bush, George 82, 161, 177, 247, 253
Bush, George W. 49, 62
Bush v. Gore 62
Bynum, Brad 70, 72, 73, 81, 104, 108, 172, 200
Byrd, Robert 116

C

Caifano, Marshal "Shoes" 292
Califano, Mark 313
Callahan 188
Calvary Chapel 52, 80, 81, 82, 160, 165, 202, 203, 239, 247, 336, 342
Calvary Chapel Gulf Breeze 52
Calvary Christian Academy 75, 107
Capital Times 136
Capone, Al 92, 94
Cardoen, Carlos 293, 294, 318
Cardoso, Silvio 291, 292, 295-298, 306, 307, 310, 312, 313
Carinci, Tito 291, 292
Carter, Tommy 70, 91
Casey, William 277, 293
Cash, Fred and Virgil 304
Castro, Fidel 60

457

74, 75, 76, 77, 80, 82, 83, 84, 85,
86, 87, 88, 90, 91, 93, 98, 100,
101, 103, 104, 105, 116, 135, 137,
143, 144, 146, 147, 150, 151, 154,
157, 159, 161, 163, 166, 167, 168,
169, 172, 175, 176, 178, 179, 184,
189, 192, 193, 200, 201, 204, 212,
233, 234, 239, 241, 242, 243, 247,
270, 272, 274, 277, 283, 284, 285,
286, 289, 290, 293, 295, 309, 312,
313, 314, 326, 327, 329, 336, 340,
344, 348, 444, 447, 449
Nobles, Oscar 272, 329
Nobles, Roger 21, 49, 157, 329
Nobles, Shelly 16, 25, 69, 74, 99, 110,
142, 150, 155, 160
Nobles, Wanda 16, 29, 36, 42, 51, 52,
80, 93, 98, 99, 146, 157, 163, 167,
173, 179, 313, 314, 359, 448
Norquist, Grover 94
Norris, Robert 56, 156, 192, 352
Nunez, Paulino 291

O

Obama, Barack 197, 310, 326, 343
Okaloosa County Sheriff's Department
55, 62, 73, 77, 140, 146, 147, 152,
154, 189, 192, 239, 248, 268, 293,
357, 358
Oliver, James Rex 95
Olson, Jeanna 59, 60
Ordo Templi Orientis 47
Osman, Craig 104, 165, 169, 298, 299,
302, 311, 445
Osman, Leslie Michael 27, 86, 87, 91,
93, 94, 115, 159, 174, 182, 193,
242, 290, 291, 294, 295, 297-299,
302, 304-314, 359, 445, 447, 449,
450
Osman, Ty 91, 298, 299, 302, 359, 445,
447
OSS 293, 442

P

Pagano, Heather 136-139, 143, 145,
150, 152, 158, 172, 178, 187, 192,

200, 253, 333, 334, 336
Palmer, Carolyn 41, 42, 43, 48, 52, 142,
144, 145, 157
Palmer, Joe 20, 41, 42, 43, 48, 52, 81,
90, 100
Parish, Donna 75, 77, 79, 80, 84, 94,
136, 151, 176, 257, 327, 333, 336
Parsons, Jack 47
Paterno, Joseph 295
Patriot Front 286
Patriot Network 27, 63, 93, 99, 156,
277, 278, 282, 284-290, 298-301,
304, 312, 319
Pattison Professional Counseling 25
Paw Paw 1, 54, 59, 111-116, 148, 154,
155, 159, 160, 164, 173, 329
Peaden, Durell 240
Perrine, John 94
Pike, Albert 116, 446
Plew, James E. 92, 94
Polansky, George 327
Posse Comitatus 27, 93, 99, 278, 281,
282, 285, 286, 288
Potok, Mark 327
*Powerhouse Principles: The Ultimate
Blueprint for Real Estate Success
in an Ever-Changing Market.*
310
Powers, Pamela 251, 253, 257, 258, 272,
328
Prado, Ricky 296
Prestridge, Joe 160
Prince, Erik 296
PTSD 33, 46, 86, 111, 160, 212, 250,
263, 272, 275, 328, 330, 331, 333,
339, 340, 341, 344, 349, 353, 355,
360
Pye-Tucker, Barbara Diane 346, 351

R

Read, Greg 308
Read, Tom 203, 308
Reagan, Ronald 91, 94, 277, 286, 293,
295, 296, 302
Regent University 49, 93
Resident Evil 112